PORTABLE
DARKNESS

PORTABLE DARKNESS

AN
ALEISTER CROWLEY READER

Edited with commentary by Scott Michaelsen

With forewords by Robert Anton Wilson and Genesis P-Orridge

HARMONY BOOKS
New York

Grateful acknowledgment is hereby given to Ordo Templi Orientis for permission to reprint the following material:

"Hieroglyphics: Life and Language Necessarily Symbolic," "Woolly Pomposities of the Pious Teacher," and "Do Angels Ever Cut Themselves Shaving?" from *Magick Without Tears* by Aleister Crowley, copyright 1954 by Karl J. Germer for Ordo Templi Orientis. All rights reserved. Used by permission of Ordo Templi Orientis.

"The Juggler" from *The Book of Thoth* by Aleister Crowley, copyright 1944 by Ordo Templi Orientis. All rights reserved. Used by permission of Ordo Templi Orientis.

"De Arte Magica" by Aleister Crowley, copyright © 1988 by Ordo Templi Orientis. All rights reserved. Used by permission of Ordo Templi Orientis.

Published by Harmony Books, a division of Crown Publishers, Inc., 201 East 50th Street, New York, New York 10022

HARMONY and colophon are trademarks of Crown Publishers, Inc.
Manufactured in the United States of America
Library of Congress Cataloging-in-Publication Data
Crowley, Aleister, 1875–1947.
  Portable darkness

  Bibliography: p.
  1. Magic. I. Michaelsen, Scott.   II. Title.
BF1611.C7532   1989   133   88-35789

ISBN 0-517-57128-5
10 9 8 7 6 5 4 3 2 1

First Edition

To my dad and mom,
Howard and Caroline Michaelsen

ACKNOWLEDGMENTS

I would like to thank, first, my three editors at Harmony Books: Esther Mitgang, who initiated the project and trusted my abilities and intentions; and Liz Sonneborn and Margaret Garigan, both of whom exercised a great deal of care and consideration in bringing the manuscript to press.

Thanks also to Genesis P-Orridge and Robert Anton Wilson for their generous words, and to my good friend Peter Sotos, with whom I held many wonderful clarifying conversations on the contents of the book.

Finally, all my love to my wife, final arbiter, and editor, Smith Dudley.

CONTENTS

FOREWORD

Everyone knows the sinister story of how Aleister Crowley and his son, MacAleister, went one dark night into a hotel room in Paris and howled within a magic triangle the nameless names that invoked the Devil. The results, we are told, were eldritch and abominable, as the late great H. P. Lovecraft would say. MacAleister was found *dead* . . . of a heart attack . . . in the dawn's ghastly light, and Aleister himself was off his skull and had to spend six months in a French mental hospital before he partially recovered. But he was a broken man from that time, a pale shadow of his former self, a walking zombie.

This is an entirely typical Crowley story—the kind of horror movie stuff that sensational tabloids have been printing about the Great Beast now for decades. I have seen the story in print dozens of times, in books as well as in schlock papers and magazines. Also typical of the Crowley legend is that, to anybody of ordinary skepticism and common sense, this yarn is hardly credible, for a variety of reasons:

1. It was first published in a novel—a work of *fiction*—by Dennis Wheatley, a writer of sensational thrillers.
2. Crowley's life has been extensively researched by six biographers, four hostile and two friendly, and none have found any record of this invocation or of his spending six months in a French nuthouse.
3. There is no indication that Crowley's son, MacAleister, died of a heart attack.
4. There is no record that Crowley's son, MacAleister, took any interest in his father's Magick—or ever did anything in his whole life, except appear in this wild yarn.
5. Crowley never even had a son named MacAleister.

If I had enough space I could regale you with a hundred similar Crowley stories that have made him the most infamous sorcerer of the twentieth century—all of which are also total works of fiction. P. R. Stephenson in 1931 said Crowley had been the victim of "a campaign of vilification without parallel in the history of English literature." The

xiii

vilification has not ceased in the forty-two years since Aleister was cremated and his ashes scattered over the state of New Jersey.

Even Uncle Al's funeral was an occasion for renewed slander. One continually reads that his last rites consisted of a Black Mass and a reading of a poem on Pan that he had written. The poem part is accurate. The mass was a Gnostic Catholic mass, and had no more in common with a real Black Mass than a dancing hippopotamus has in common with a three-car highway collision.

What did Crowley do to inspire so much hostility? Well, he had a sense of humor similar to that of the Monty Python group many decades before such surrealist satire became fashionable. He obviously was a sincere mystic of some sort but also violently and blatantly opposed organized Christianity (some fundamentalists, and some who do not admit to being fundamentalists, can only understand nonorthodox mystics as agents of the Devil). Uncle Al also had a burning hatred for all forms of hypocrisy and (seemingly) a real dread that his "followers" would try to turn him into a plaster saint after his death. For those reasons, and because he liked to annoy the puritans, he took great pains to see that none of his vices and human foibles were concealed from anyone. When he and his first wife, Rose, divorced (because he would not tolerate her alcoholism any longer), he arranged with her that she would sue him for adultery—not merely a gallant gesture, but a way of ensuring that at least one of his "sins" would be on the legal records forever so that his disciples could never deny it. His one major fear in old age was that "Crowleyanity" would some day supplant Christianity: He protested so violently against that possibility that none of his admirers call themselves Crowleyans (they use the word *Thelemites*—a word from his *Liber AL,* coined from the Greek, that carries connotations of both Magick and Will.) They also never refer to him as Lord or Master or Saviour or Prophet or anything of that sort. Generally, they call him Uncle Al, as I do.

Perhaps the quickest introduction to the real Aleister Crowley is a bit of his verse:

> By all sorts of monkey tricks
> They make my name mean 666;
> Well, I will deserve it if I can:
> It is the number of a Man.

Fully trained in Western Gnostic mysticism, in Sufism, and in such oriental systems as Buddhism, Taoism, and Tantric Hinduism, Crowley knew more about altered states of consciousness than any European of his time. But he was also trained in organic chemistry and had a skeptical streak that prevented his embracing any metaphysical theory literally (although he could use a dozen metaphysical systems metaphorically). Another bit of his verse makes this clear:

> We place no reliance
> On Virgin or Pigeon:
> Our method is Science,
> Our aim is Religion.

Despite his official role as the Beast 666, Uncle Al could even appreciate the inner meaning of mystical Christianity. I learned this directly by performing his Lesser Ritual of the Hexagram (a combination of Christian and Egyptian invocations, and one of the most powerful consciousness-altering techniques I know), which gave me an entirely new and fresh insight into the central Christian symbolism of Crucifixion and Resurrection. Yet to understand the original inner truth of Christianity—its gnosis—was not, in Crowley's mind, any justification for tolerating the vulgar "Christianity" of the churches—which was denounced as "Crosstianity," a cult of masochism, by Bernard Shaw and similarly scorned by every intelligent philosopher for the last three centuries.

So, to the extent that an adept of the gnosis seemed like the Antichrist to fools, Crowley was amused to play the role and pull their legs endlessly. After all, A. C., his chosen initials, are the initials of Antichrist, and Edward Alexander Crowley (his real name) can be equated to 666, with a little cheating. "It is the number of a Man," and he set out to be a Man to the fullest possible extent. I am reminded of the Buddha, who was once asked, "Are you a god?" "No," he replied. "Well, are you a saint?" "No." "Well, what are you?" "I am awake."

Crowley was never a god or a saint (and never let anyone think for a moment that he might be either), but he was *awake*—to a terrifying extent. Whenever I think of the sheer information content of a typical page of Crowley—defining information in the strict mathematical sense as dense unpredictability—I remember Carl Jung's initial response to *Finnegans Wake*. "This is either mental illness," Jung said, "or a degree of mental health inconceivable to most people." You have not fathomed all that is going on in a Crowley poem or in a single prose sentence by him until you have a similar reaction. The great Zen koan Crowley has buried in all his writings, for those who can see deeply into them, is precisely that: Which is it—lunacy or the highest sanity possible to a human being?

Scott Michaelsen answers that question, in his own way, in the marvelous commentaries he has interspersed in this anthology. I will give you a parable and a hint. I once knew a real live Zen master from Japan. As I got to know him, it gradually appeared to me that he had not one personality, but three. When "on the job" as Zen master (*Roshi*) he was absolutely a master, in the sense the most superstitious and naïve will give to that term. When off duty, he was simply a kindly old Japanese gentleman, a bit eccentric but perfectly courteous at all times. When wandering in the woods alone—where I sometimes encountered him—he was the brightest and most curious monkey I ever saw. Later, I got to know him better and discovered that he had not three personalities, but about three dozen. At least!

Aleister Crowley, as I have learned to know him through his writings, through six biographies, and through conversations with some who knew him, was arrogant, acrimonious, agnostic, atheistic, admirable, baffling, bawdy, bisexual, bombastic, benign, clownish, cosmopolitan, chauvinistic, churlish, confusing, cuckoo, cacodoxical, commonsensical, cynical, demoniac, delightful, duplicitous, earthy, esthetic, egotistical, funny, forgiving, forbearing, gross, God-intoxicated, humble, hardworking, honest, intellectual, intolerant, juvenile, kindly, lovable, loathsome, long-suffering, monstrous, mystical, nihilistic, orgulous, poetic, pantheistic, petulant, quarrelsome, queer, rascally, romantic, scholarly, skeptical, tender, tolerant, underhanded, vile, vindictive, whimsical, xenophobic, yeomanly, and uncommonly zealous.

Uncle Al was also one of the great mountain climbers of all time, and wrote about thirty volumes of widely varied poetry (mystical, erotic, romantic, and sometimes hilarious). His capacity for hard work and dedication are awesomely documented in Israel Regardie's *The Eye in the Triangle,* but he called himself "the laziest man in the world." He wrote detective stories and pornography as sidelines and served British intelligence in World War II. He was a great chess player.

A single ego is an absurdly narrow vantage point from which to view the world, he once explained. Who has ears, let him hear.

Actually, you already know Aleister Crowley, for he is part of you. You are as multiselved, polysexual, and chaotic as he was for eight hours out of every twenty-four—one third of your whole life. Unfortunately, you have probably not learned to take that side of your Self seriously, as Crowley did.

As one Zen master said, "There is nothing special about illumination. You do it every night in your sleep. Zen is just a trick for doing it while awake." This anthology of Crowley gives you a few hundred other tricks for doing it while awake. It is worth your attention if you have any ambition to become more than just another robot in the great machine of modern society. Blake described that machine as a Dark Satanic Mill. Philip K. Dick decided it was the Empire's Black Iron Prison. Gurdjieff called it sleepwalking. Alan Watts described it as a cultural madness in which we eat the menu and ignore the meal. Other mystics have called it maya, delusion, literalism, or a kind of hypnosis in which you stare at a map until it becomes the territory and you spend aeons wandering in the map's valleys and hills without ever finding your way back to the non-map world again.

Crowley once said that the giant Death Machine could equally well be named the Abyss or Hell or consciousness, and that it was governed by the Lord of Hallucinations, whose battle cry and mantra is "Truth! Truth! Truth!"

If you want to escape from Truth (and Falsity)—or from Good (and Evil), or from any of the other traps created by the Lord of Hallucinations—turn the page and start reading.

I must warn you, however, that the Attorney General has determined that these pages may be hazardous to your Dogma.

Robert Anton Wilson

FOREWORD
or
THE DELIRIUM OF WISDOM

In *Portable Darkness* Scott Michaelsen has produced a unique insight into, and reappraisal of, a man much maligned by populist prejudice. It has always been far too convenient to clumsily blend various threads of Crowley's immense body of work into an inevitably inconsistent whole, too easy to confuse elements of his colorful, kaleidoscopic, and not always appealing life with his sincere and self-sacrificing grappling with the most complex human and philosophical concepts. Now at last we have an accurate and precise dictionary and commentary that concisely decodes essays and ideas previously considered too obscure to be rewarding to any but the most scholastic readers.

With this very contemporary position in the selection and analysis of Crowley's work, we are quite surprisingly confronted with evidence of a mind attempting to describe the deepest equations of conceptual paradox: the nature of Life, of Language, of meaning, and of human aspiration and potential.

At the end of the day this is what we are trying to do: *Understand*. And they are the brightest, most extremely searching intellects that develop and posit new, stimulating models for us to superimpose over our individual experiences of the oddity of being alive. We have no choice in this matter—we are trapped here briefly, change nothing measured against infinity, at best stretch just slightly nearer to the sky. The most productive thinkers risk all to grasp the deepest and most hidden revelations. Yet if they even suspect they have glimpsed a usable fraction of essential patterns, they are left crippled in the expression of it. Primarily knowledge is passed on through the most flawed and mystical medium of all: Language. Language, like most socialized forms of behavior, is inherited. It must by definition contain within it, coded and drenched in aeons of subjectivity, an infinity of confusion and insight.

So a great thinker such as Crowley, who deserves his place next to Nietzsche, Wittgenstein, and the great structuralists, has to discover by action, then preserve and express through writing, the most intangible and uncomfortable suggestions about humanity. Yet writing, the tool to be used, is riddled with secret strengths and weaknesses. It is the most exciting and corrupt medium.

The most valuable compilations single-mindedly focus our attention upon the central themes of an author and, by their scrutiny, shock our comprehension with an entirely unexpected disclosure that permanently educates us about both the subject and ourselves. Suddenly old contradictions, mysteries, apparent flippancies shed their innate ambiguity, and we see a contemptuous yet compassionate mind at work. Crowley performs an age-old and utterly essential role for society. He synthesizes all threads of knowledge, arcane and contemporary, Eastern and Western, into a functional whole. This very functionality has often been seen as precluding mysticism, yet it seems quite clear that its documentation is intended to engender the flowering of more mystics.

In the West, mysticism has generally been viewed with suspicion. The language necessary to encode its knowledge superficially invites contemptuous dismissal. When aphorisms and conundrums originate in the East we seem to accept them more readily. One wonders, though, if this is not primarily due to a love of exotic quaintness and not a small degree of smug superiority. In the West we tend to believe in a simplistic duality: Love and Hate, Right and Wrong, Good and Evil. If we probe a little more, we see less clear dualities—such as certain motives for Crime and Art, Ritual and Belief—and it seems useful to suggest that mysticism is the precise point of interchangeability between any two concepts.

Taking these thoughts to the expertly chosen Crowley essays and excerpts within these portals, the intense concern with language and multiple aspects of metaphor and code deliberately embedded in every letter at last become far more obvious to the reader. From his lifetime study of Qabalah, gematria, numerology, astrology, myth, glyph, and linguistics, Crowley accepts the inevitability of apparent contradiction and confusion. He then imbibes the heady liquor of wisdom and humor to map out "facts." Previous critiques tend either to religiously and blindly embrace what they feel is superior, unquestionable truth, its very opacity revered as holy; or otherwise generally to reject it as willful obscurity disguising a vacuum of nonsense.

What this book makes clear is that, for Crowley, the language in which every idea is couched is equally as potent as the idea itself. Language and ideas are indivisible powers. He assigns values, symbologies, historical belief systems, and interactions to each letter, even to individual positions and placings when he feels it appropriate. Given the immensity of the territory he is trying to map objectively, this methodical correspondence of word, letter, code, order, pattern, symbol, contradiction, and implication is remarkably thorough and complete. It is a system developed painstakingly over his lifetime to be as Truth-Full and accurate as possibility and impossibility alone could allow, and is quite singularly unique and rich *beyond* words. This exploding thirst for comprehension in Crowley's being, a lust for result and reason that creates a delirium of wisdom quite spectacular in its description, validates for him any means of search and synthesis.

Crowley and Michaelsen go further. Crowley was aware through his methodical exploration of Magick and Yoga that there is another, physical synthesis of data possible. In mystery traditions as far apart as Egypt, Mali, and Tibet, *Breath* itself is synonymous with *Word* and is the integrating link between identity and expression. Breath is the ebb and flow of life itself, the "mysticism" of mortality, the very source of communication. Breath gives body to all language and thus gives language to evolution. It is the anima of the intellect. It represents both the bars of the cage from which a mortal Crowley communicates and his means of liberation from restriction. The actions and impulses of his quest are constructed whilst knowingly constricted and designed. The beast walks into the cage so that without fear for ourselves we can stare right into his eyes and see a glittering light and the power and majesty of his physique.

Only the truly wise and clear may pull off this trick. To choose to be chained to life when sorrowfully aware of its emptiness is the path of a master. Reconciliation and reassessment on an infinity of internal and external levels of being are all that lend implicit value to existing, to time. Wry humor may soften the blow, but in the end the goalless objective, the process in all its complexity, is all we need.

Magick deals with the infinitely small point between sleep and wakefulness, dream and reality, the conscious and the unconscious mind. It dwells in a realm of transitional states amplified to a visible scale. The writer on or from Magick describes, as best he can, a conceptual specter, an intangible fission, a linguistic contradiction. Yet this same moment made crystalline is capable of generating an evolutionary map of comprehension and behavior modification quite omnipotent in its implications. For those who approach Crowley with a sincere but scant background of knowledge, this book will display lucidly and neutrally the immense accuracy and clarity of his writings. It is the most helpful and fluent way in to a massive storehouse of wit and wisdom of any commentary currently available. For those already sated in Crowley's writings, it gives a thoroughly clear, concise formula for understanding without need of any act of faith or fervor. Even the most convoluted and esoteric doctrines, no matter how obscure, are laid out for ease of confident and practical reentry into a system seemingly riddled with impregnable codes. The result is a flowering of visible skill and wisdom that demands, as all such collections must, a positive and real measurement of a philosophical writer previously dismissed all too often by a sensationalist coloring of his work based on the unorthodoxy of his dedicated life.

The rest, as they say, has been said.

Genesis P-Orridge

PREFACE

A Chinese poet reproaches Laotze for saying that those who know Tao speak not thereof, seeing that he proved his own ignorance by writing his five thousand characters about it. But Laotze could not have done otherwise, no more than could his critic . . .

The Magical Record of the Beast

If any sinologists object to anything in this translation, let him go absorb his Yang in his own Yin, as the Americans say; and give me credit for an original Masterpiece. Whatever Lao Tze said or meant, this is what I say and mean.

Aleister Crowley, frontispiece to his translation of the Tao Teh King

What he poured in at the mouth o' the mill as a 33rd Sonata (fancy now!) Comes from the hopper as bran-new Sludge.

The character Bowley in "Ali Sloper," Konx Om Pax

The title of this selection from the work of Aleister Crowley, this century's most renowned occultist, might give one pause. The word *portable* usually signifies someone's idea of a one-volume treatment of essential works. It signals an intention to "cover the ground" and reveal a personal vision logically and clearly in as few a number of works and pages as possible. But what then can be made of *darkness.* Does this portend either something sinister (as in Black Magic) or the absence of Light? What place do either logic or clarity have in the Darkness?

Actually the title *Portable Darkness* was chosen by the publisher; I have grown to live with and love it. It seems to me no more or less profane than many of Crowley's own titles, such as *The Book of Lies, The Diary of a Drug Fiend,* or "Of the Secret Marriages of Gods with Men." I find it no more pretentious than calling an autobiography an "autohagiography" (the autobiography of a saint) and then titling it *The Confessions,* after Augustine, or referring to a portion of one's writings as "The Holy Books" as Crowley did.

I have since tried to chart the implications of a *Portable Darkness* for meaning (and for holiness). For Crowley, both Darkness and Light are conditions from which one must be delivered by the practices of Magick: ". . . The light wherein I write is not the light of reason; it is not the darkness of unreason; it is the L. V. X. [or Light in Extension] of that which, first mastering and then transcending the reason, illuminates all the darkness caused by the interference of the opposite waves of thought; not by destroying their balance, and thereby showing a false and partial light, but by overleaping their limitations. . . ."[1] Darkness, then, needs to be portable—ready to jump into the state of L. V. X., collapsible into that Extension which produces both Darkness and Light, logic and the lack of logic, clarity and the lack of clarity.

Light and Darkness are effects of this Light in Extension. They are linked together and inseparable. "Consider darkness! Can we philosophically or actually regard as different the darkness produced by interference of light and that existing in the absence of light?"[2] Light, Darkness, the Light of Darkness, the Darkness of Light. These conditions shift into one another, play at Light and shadow. Light is essential to the condition called Dark, and vice versa. This Book does not paint Crowley as a Black Master. He appears only as Black as Light. I will do my best (through sleight of hand if necessary) to make his Darkness Portable, to shine on him the same hand-held Black Light he reflects.

Portable Darkness is a broad anthology of Aleister Crowley's work, the first made available to the general reading public. (Past anthological volumes, published by occult presses, have been limited to certain types of work, or to early pieces that appeared in Crowley's periodical *The Equinox*.) Given the sheer volume of writings available to me, I have had to make many difficult choices in editing this book. I should say at the outset that I make no claim to completeness, thoroughness, or even the authority of this anthology. My decisions on what to include reflect a pointed interpretation of his thought, at times straining to find the particular strain I have in mind. Certain concepts that I believe are fundamental to an understanding of Crowley are repeated, with only shades of difference, in a number of works here, and are then seemingly contradicted in others (more "interference of the opposite waves of thought"). Other concepts, just as essential, barely make an appearance or seem to be in code.

The first three sections cover three main lines of Writing and

---

1. "Dedication and Counter-Dedication," *Konx Om Pax*, (reprinted Yogi Publication Society, no place of origin/pub. date), p. viii.
2. "Berashith: an Essay in Ontology," *Collected Works of Aleister Crowley, Volume II* (reprinted Yogi Publication Society, no place of origin/pub. date), p. 235.

experiment—Magick, Yoga and Sex. These include works from "Berashith" (his first important magical essay, written in 1902) to *The Book of Thoth* (1944). The fourth section of this anthology is devoted to his most studied text, *The Book of the Law* (transmitted to him in 1904). The fifth includes selections from my personal favorite of Crowley's works, *The Book of Lies* (1913). I begin each section with an introductory essay.

Though I have quoted from them to a limited degree in my introductory essays, I have avoided excerpts from Crowley's autohagiography and journals. The journals can be extremely arcane, while Crowley's life is already well documented. *Portable Darkness* is not intended to be a history, and I am convinced that the last thing the world needs is another biography of Aleister Crowley. Crowley himself told the world that "there is no such thing as history," and "[I have] never been able to bring myself to face the average memoir."[3] If you're drawn in that direction, I suggest that you go right to the conflicting sources, many of which are included in the bibliography.

I have also avoided the fictions, including novels, short stories, and non-Magick poetry. Crowley's major novels, *Diary of a Drug Fiend* and *Moonchild,* are easy to obtain, and a volume of selected poetry has recently appeared in England.

This volume also does not outline a practical magical program, and includes scant ritual material. I am not now, nor have I ever been, a member of Crowley's magical organizations, the A ∴ A ∴ and the O.T.O., nor a member of any splinter groups formed in his wake. I practice neither Magick nor Yoga. This is a secular reading of Aleister Crowley, a game of hide and seek, a surprising reading taking place in the Dark. It is a reading that intentionally tries not to shed New Light (with its attendant rationalism) on him. Throughout, I merely take Aleister Crowley at his Word, and, like him, do not concern myself with remaining doctrinaire.

Crowley's critics charge that no greater fraud ever lived, and that his work is nothing but a hodge-podge stolen from other sources, poorly rewritten, confused and inconclusive. R. G. Torrens says in *The Golden Dawn—Its Inner Teachings* that Crowley's borrowed insights are "not as pure as the original" and that his writing is "so full of claptrap and leg-pulling that it is difficult to obtain a clear picture of the essentials" (though he later admits to finding "many pearls of wisdom" within the

3. *The Confessions of Aleister Crowley* (New York: Hill and Wang, 1970), p. 114.

corpus).[4] Crowley's literary executor John Symonds has gone so far as to attempt to discredit him by suggesting possible sources for the one work with Crowley's name on its cover that Crowley claimed was written by his angel, *The Book of the Law*.

Through hard work one can try to ascribe each of Crowley's ideas to someone else—whether in literature, philosophy or the history of myth and magic. I myself have found that Crowley's ideas about Magick and its relationship to Language can be traced in part through Eliphas Levi's *Dogme et rituel de la haute magie* (translated as *Transcendental Magic*) and through Egyptian texts concerning Thoth, the god of writing (such as the *Papyrus of Ani*). Like each of these, Crowley's understanding of the Thoth legend leads him to question the very possibility of Origins, Author, Law, Truth.) But when Crowley "stole"— when he "forged ahead"—he often did it grandly, in broad daylight. Forgery might be said to be a masterful display of Portability, displacing words of Dark and Light to a new Writing site.

I would go so far as to say that neither Crowley nor his Magick can be convincingly attributed or localized. Not to Levi, and not to the work of Crowley's sometime magical mentor, S. L. MacGregor Mathers. Not to Egyptian writings, not to the texts of Jewish Qabalism, not to Buddhist and Hindu yogic and tantric manuscripts. Not to the philosophy of Hume, not to Bishop Berkeley, not to Nietzsche. With some nomadic spirit, I make in my introductory essays little or no reference to possible sources for Crowley's ideas or to the history of magic.[5] And I borrow this technique from the master and continuously steal Crowley into my essays (including unattributed ideas and felicitous phrases), often perhaps in ways in which he might not have sensed. My essays are, in any sense, collaborations with his voice in which I subject him to a kind of call and Portable response.

The reader who wishes to seek out more of Crowley's work will find that locating many texts involves a long, relaxed search, though surprisingly a number of major U.S. libraries hold respectable Crowley collections. Some of the Crowley pieces in *Portable Darkness* have never been easy to find in this country as they are published only by

4. R. G. Torrens, *The Golden Dawn—Its Inner Teachings* (London: Neville Spearman, 1969), p. 24 and p. 85.
5. The reader may be surprised to find that the second section of the bibliography includes reference to books that might be described as "formative" to Crowley's development. I might say in defense that part of my purpose is to openly acknowledge, here and now, any additional thievery of which I might be accused.

private presses in very small quantities and available only through specialty bookdealers. Some are today either almost impossible to find or, as rare books, are prohibitively expensive. In all of my citations and in the selective bibliography I have tried to make it as easy as possible for the reader to find full-length texts. Cited reprintings are in almost every case the latest and the most readily available editions or are, at least, very well-known editions. Because so many of Crowley's works are in the public domain, some texts have been printed a number of times by several enterprising publishers, and will no doubt continue to be irregularly available in this fashion.

Having said all this I suspect I have revealed too much, said too much of what *Portable Darkness* is not, could not be, and have forgotten the Darkness Bright. It is now the time of night for you to retire to a room with a reading Light, and for me to pick up this baggage to which I do not belong and Write. As an Aquarius, I am prepared to compose with the double wavy line—my sign—affirming both the creative act and its impossibility—the Silence of composition. "There is an end of the speech; let the Silence of darkness be broken; let it return into the silence of light."[6]

Scott Michaelsen

---

6. "Liber Israfel," reprinted in *Gems from the Equinox* (St. Paul: Llewellyn Publications, 1974), p. 310.

PART I

Qabalah and Magick

this, though, Crowley does not mean to say exactly that all the world is illusion. "Things" may or may not "exist" independent of Language; we only "know" that apprehending and naming them is the "thing" that gives them their "thingness." In *The Book of Lies*, Crowley refers to the "First Triad" of Kether, Chokmah, and Binah as "I Am," "I utter the Word," and "I hear the Word,"[10] a way of saying how the sending and the receiving of the code of signals are bound together with "subject."

For now it is enough to acknowledge our experience of the World in a Word, as an effect born (even the effect of being born) from the infinitely closed (the boundless code, the infinitely great and small) Zero (and all numbers correspond to letters) of Writing and Language, without the power or force of the voice of God to command it. For Qabalists, God does not Speak and create. He does not make the world or save the world through his Word, his Logos (Christ). Rather the Word that is God's infinite name in Hebrew ("YHVH," or "Yahweh," which can never be translated fully but only approached: "I am He who is") serves itself as the formula for creation—the awakening of the New Aeon and the destruction of the old, both at once, setting the boundaries of the universe. The four letters of this "Tetragrammaton" each have a particular position on the Tree. They sit already within a system of thought, not outside it; God, like Angels, is an effect of Language. Just another Zero, not a One. And each of the other Sephira traditionally represents one of the other many names of God.

The origin then of Language—this creation—leaves no trace.[11] Language remains for Crowley an "arrangement," a "chance" operation, and Language is "quite ready-made."[12] A stain on the silence without beginning, a "birth mystery" always already made. "I saw Simplicity and the Universe as a Tree; this being spherical, the branches everywhere and the root nowhere."[13] According to Crowley, the three "Letter Fathers" of the Arabic alphabet, for example, are irretrievably lost. These are represented on the Tree by three non-existent paths stretching from the first three Sephiroth toward a point known as Daath, or Knowledge, that lies between them (yet on a

---

10. *The Books of Lies* (reprinted New York: Samuel Weiser, 1978), p. 10.
11. When in Qabalistic literature the Sephiroth are described as a series of mirrors reflecting down the light of the divine, Kether—which supposedly holds the original lamp or light—shines it into a mirror in order to send it down the Tree. Mirror to mirror to mirror, the problem of origins seems lost in a hall of mirror images.
12. *Magick Without Tears*, p. 12.
13. *The Magical Record of the Beast 666: The Journals of Aleister Crowley* (Quebec: Next Step Publications, 1972), p. 104

different plane, sometimes shown on the Tree and sometimes not). If one could reach Daath, crossing these paths, one might rediscover the origins of Language, but this Knowledge is always just beyond our grasp. (Crowley, by the way, calls "Black Brothers" those occultists who mistakenly try to dwell in Daath.) A search for beginnings will not bear fruit, as Crowley often says. "Not only must we get rid of all subjects, but of all predicates."[14] The formulation of the idea of "beginning," like God (and even Zero), must take place within Language, already part of the Tree, because Language and the origin of consciousness Write together.

The Crowleyan formula of creation—"$0 = 2$"—reflects the "big bang" Magick of Language.[15] "The Father of thought—the Word—is called Chaos—the dyad."[16] All properties and ideas (Words) appear as twos: heaven and not-heaven (earth), head and not-head (heart). "All our contradictories are coordinate curves; they are on opposite sides of the axis, but otherwise are precisely similar."[17] The Tree of Life diagrams the spillage of Zeroes into Twos. For example, the fourth Sephira, Chesed (Mercy) balances its opposite, the fifth, Geburah (Strength). The sixth, meanwhile, Tipereth, on the so-called "Middle Pillar" of the Tree, separates, conjoins, and combines (but doesn't create) the pair. It's Binary, with Tipereth between. All things are divisible "into A, not-A, and the dividing line."[18] "Beyond" it is nothing but the Trinity, the Zero. If one thinks about creation as a piece of string extended infinitely in both directions, then only double "Tom Fool" knots, which pull apart, can be tied. "Always either Naught or Two!"[19] Such are the playful "pranks of [Language's] childhood,"[20] the illusion of hierarchies, of "categories" and "conditions."

The Sephiroth and connecting paths do not directly relate to the world, but are a "convenient" quasi-structure,[21] a kind of mimicking of Language, an "Alphabet of Magick."[22] Through this the world can be

14. "Berashith: An Essay in Ontology," p. 237.
15. *Magick Without Tears*, pp. 52–63.
16. *Magick* (reprinted New York: Samuel Weiser, 1974), pp. 143–144.
17. "Dedication and Counter-Dedication," *Konx Om Pax* (reprinted Yogi Publication Society, no place of origin/pub. date), p. viii.
18. "The Excluded Middle; or The Sceptic Refuted," *Collected Works of Aleister Crowley, Volume II*, p. 266.
19. *Magick Without Tears*, p. 41.
20. *The Book of Thoth* (reprinted New York: U.S. Game Systems, Inc., 1979), p. 128.
21. *Magick*, p. 147.
22. *Magick Without Tears*, p. 48.

ordered, without end. Crowley recommends to all students that they begin Magical training first by starting a diary (beginning to write), and second, by constructing a Qabalah—which are, in the end, the same. Crowley's book *777* attempts one such sorting, with tables that classify *every* idea within the economy of the Tree. Planets, Gods, conditions—each have a position within Qabalah. Thinking of any thing, every thing, in terms of its relationship to the Tree establishes connections and aids the magical memory, building vocabulary. But there is more, always more. "The habit of throwing your thoughts about, manipulating them, giving them a wash and brush-up, packing them away into their proper places in your 'Crystal Cabinet,' gives you immensely increased power over them."[23] That is, "things" lose their power over you when they are seen as effects of the structurings of Language, part of its infinitely collapsing and expanding system. "The fact that you are constantly asking yourself, 'Now in which drawer of which cabinet does this thought go?' automatically induces you to regard the system as the important factor in the operation, if only because it is common to every one of them."[24]

But determining the proper place within the cabinet threatens to tip it over, spill the contents. The traditions of the Qabalah include word manipulations to determine the relationships among ideas. These manipulations shift and multiply meaning to the point where particular meanings seem irretrievable, where words now cast about in multiple directions, appearing in multiple file folders. Just as Zero can be described as a letter(s), Hebrew letters are each assigned a number equivalent, and by addition new correspondences between words emerge. This practice is called "Gematria."[25] Crowley's *Sepher Sephiroth* lists words that add the same, and are therefore "related" to each other, such as "unity," "love," and "emptiness," which all add to 13. Other techniques that Crowley discusses (endorsing some and not others) include finding the "Least Number" of a Word by adding digits together (the 1 and 3, for example, to get 4) and checking this new number's correspondence to the Tarot, permuting by means of a simple child's code of transposed letters, analyzing the shape of letters, and even searching for acrostics within a prose text. Crowley restores these constantly generating words in the "precious jewel" of

23. *Magick Without Tears*, p. 106.
24. *Magick Without Tears*, p. 107.
25. This and the following are discussed in some detail in "Gematria," reprinted in *777 and Other Qabalistic Writings* (York Beach, Maine: Samuel Weiser, 1977), p. 1.

the Qabalah, and as slots bulge the crystal reflects its light back out. An "amazing fertility of thought" is generated by this "scheme."[26] Correspondences become commonplace as connections generate. "It is easy for the Partisan to find his favorite meaning in any Word."[27] Language shines in the carvings, split in all directions.

This arbitrary and seemingly uncontainable system of correspondences, like Language, also closes arbitrarily (Language with 26 letters, no more, and the Tree with its 22 and 10) but it combines, extends, ever opens and flowers within. "Each Sephira is supposed to contain a Tree of Life of its own. Thus we obtain four hundred Sephiroth instead of the original ten, and the paths being capable of similar multiplications, or rather of subdivision, the number is still further extended. Of course this process might be indefinitely continued without destroying the original system."[28] The seeker of the holy confronts this container full of holes and cracks from his paradoxical position within a Qabalah of Language. "He must work backwards, putting the whole of his mental and moral outfit into these pigeon-holes. You would not expect to be able to buy a filing cabinet with the names of all your past, present and future correspondents ready indexed: your cabinet has a system of letters and numbers meaningless in themselves, but ready to take on a meaning to you, as you fill up the files."[29] Some unknown finite number extended in an unknown number of categories.

The implications of such a "Qabalah of Language" are enormous for the practical magician and traditional Golden Dawn occultist. In the system of the Golden Dawn, for example, the Tree maps the aspiring magician's work: one step at a time, he can climb the Tree from matter to God, performing magic ritual and ceremony—meeting a variety of beings and forces on a number of spiritual planes along the way. He climbs in order, ultimately, to apprehend God and the Truth of the universe. The "grades" or levels of attainment in the Golden Dawn system of magic symbolize this climb: each applies to a different position on the Tree. The successful magician will cross over the "Abyss" that stands between the bottom seven Sephiroth and the top three (the Trinity) on the way to attaining mastery. "He has 'cancelled

26. "Man," *Little Essays Toward Truth* (Malton, Canada: Dove Press, approximately 1970), p. 2.
27. "Qabalistic Dogma," *Collected Works of Aleister Crowley, Volume I* (reprinted Yogi Publication society, no place of origin/pub. date), p. 266.
28. *Magick*, pp. 145–146.
29. *Magick*, p. 146.

out' the complexities of the mathematical expression called existence, and the answer is zero."[30] One day he will walk with God, bring God into himself, or perhaps become God. "As above, so below," the often-quoted Emerald Tablet attributed to Hermes declares; God inheres in man, man inheres in God. And Crowley often appears to be in complete agreement with such a program.

But when he attends to the Word, he finds that God and each of his aspirations concerning God is bound to Writing. Crowley is bound to Write: Writing inaugurates the (lack of) beginnings of Magick (as we have noted), Writing is Magick's province (as has been noted in examining the Qabalah), and Writing is Magick's path. "I have omitted to say that the whole subject of Magick is an example of Mythopoeia in that particular form called Disease of Language. Thoth, [Egyptian] God of Magick, was merely a man who invented writing, as his monuments declare clearly enough."[31] (Hermes is the Greek name for Thoth, and therefore the so-called doctrine of signatures—"As above, so below"— could also be re-inscribed under the rubric Writing.) Magick is a branch on the Tree of Life, of Language, branching off from Crowley's Qabalism of non-origin, de-materialization, and dis-containment. Magick Writes, and Words are not only the condition of the problem (for example, Speech formulates the Gods, which *is* the Disease of Language) but also the solution for the magician (exploring the Speech of consciousness is the only way back, the only way to "cure" this creative, definitive illness). "You must construct your own system [of Qabalah] so that it is a living weapon in your hand."[32] A world rooted in the Language is on dangerous ground, capable of blowing away with the next breeze; the "water" in the vessel can be used both to "drive great Engines" and "breaketh the Mountains in Pieces."[33]

For Crowley the climbing of the Tree cannot be simply practical, cannot be rationalized as a single, slow climb to attempt to "undo the Wrong of the Beginning."[34] Rather a Qabalah of Language demands that the highest Sephira, Kether, must be marked as just one more step for the mage. Language involves an endless chain of correspondence, and in the same way Magick is not a goal-directed activity but rather

30. "An Essay Upon Number," reprinted in *777 and Other Qabalistic Writings*, p. 39.
31. *Magick*, p. 197.
32. *Magick Without Tears*, p. 14.
33. *Liber Aleph vel CXI: The Book of Wisdom or Folly* (reprinted Seattle: Aeon Press, 1985), p. 89.
34. "Liber Cordis Cincti Serpente," reprinted in *The Holy Books of Thelema*, p. 75.

a ceaseless practice that puts into question any stop along the way, even the "top."

"And the End is sure. For the End is the Path."[35] A Qabalah of Language is not a climbing but a spiralling circle through Kether and back down to the 10th Sephiroth—Malkuth—and around again, and again. "This chain reaches from Eternity to Eternity . . . ever in circles."[36] Crowley doesn't choose the course of either the Ipsissimus (the magician who has reached Kether and sacrificed belief in everything) or the Gross Materialist. "Alas! but either way is the Last Step; lucky are most of us if only we can formulate some circle—any circle!"[37] Each side of the circle is irrevocably, inevitably, part of the circle. The Zero spills to Two, the Two is reformed into a rather dubious One (analogous, as Crowley notes, to the transitory Buddhist trance where all becomes one), and the One returns to the Zero. "What comes to Naught? . . . For when Naught becomes Absolute Naught, it becomes again the Many. And this Many and this Naught are identical."[38] A ceaseless shuttling back and forth, of spilling and refilling the vessels.

Returning to Thoth, Crowley says that this man who invented writing (and who invented the Tarot, another name for *The Book of Thoth*, another Alphabet for Magick) "represents Wisdom and the Word. He bears in his right hand the Style, in his left the Papyrus. He is the messenger of the gods; he transmits their will by hieroglyphs intelligible to the initiate, and records their acts."[39] Intelligent Writing is sensible to those who can read it. But Writing opens the path for a second reading of Thoth: "The use of speech, or writing, meant the introduction of ambiguity at the best, and falsehood at the worst; they [the Egyptians] therefore represented Thoth as followed by an ape, the cynocephalus, whose business was to distort the Word of the god; to mock, to simulate and to deceive. In philosophical language one may say: Manifestation implies delusion."[40] The Ape shuffles in his partner's wake. The two of them stick to each other like a classic comedy duo—the meaningful and the mockery tied together in a "Tom Fool" knot. Thoth and his Ape—both Writing—symbolize the duplicity of

---

35. *Eight Lectures on Yoga* (Phoenix: Falcon Press, 1985), p. 80.
36. "Liber A'ash vel Capricorni Pneumatica," reprinted in *Gems From the Eqinox*, p. 600.
37. "Dedication and Counter-Dedication," p. x.
38. *The Book of Lies*, p. 176.
39. *The Book of Thoth*, pp. 71–72.
40. *The Book of Thoth*, p. 72.

Magick/Writing. "If there is a possibility of assigning a double meaning to the question you can bank on their finding it, and deceiving you."[41] The Ape is deceptive, the necessary response and the other side to the Wisdom of the Word. The Ape is the ambiguity and indecisiveness of Language—acknowledged. Thoth Writes for origin, manifestation, containment, intelligence, the straight goal, God. The Ape shuffles the deck and turns up the doubles: non-origin, de-materialization, dis-containment, unlogic, the meandering path, Writing.

Once one has begun to Write a Qabalah and to keep a magical journal, the aspirant to Magick embarks on a number of preliminary steps designed to help open he or she to the space of Writing: its space and matter, written by Thoth, accompanied by a spaced-out Ape. Crowley's instruction "Liber III vel Jugorum," for example, recommends breaking "the Yoke [language] upon the neck of the Oxen [man]"[42] by avoiding the use of common words, avoiding the use of letters of the alphabet, and avoiding the use of pronouns and adjectives of the first person. "Liber Thisarb" (the reverse of "Berashith") poses this test: thinking and writing backwards (with both hands). And even then words exert their hold. "The brain will be found to struggle constantly to right itself, soon accustoming itself to accept 'esroh' as merely another glyph for 'horse'. This tendency must be constantly combatted."[43] In case we forget, "When I say 'I see a horse,' the truth is that 'I record in those terms my private hieroglyphic interpretation of the unknown and unknowable phenomenon.' "[44]

So far, constructing a Qabalah from nothing, meditating on Language, Magick's tasks make sense. But it becomes less comprehensible in the face of the other, delirious works of the magician: the Invocations and Spells, the use of Temples and Weapons, the Ceremonies and Dramatic Rituals. Far from what one might expect, Crowley does not shy away from any of this. Gods and spirits spoke through Crowley to deliver holy messages (*The Book of the Law*). He contacted the 30 spirits of the aethyrs according to the techniques of Golden Dawn Enochian magic (documented in *The Vision and the Voice*). He engaged in extended interchange with the wizard Abuldiz, who helped him assemble his magical masterworks. And he certainly authored many statements along the following lines: "My observation of the

---

41. *Magick Without Tears*, p. 368.
42. "Liber III vel Jugorum," reprinted in *Gems from the Equinox*, p. 207.
43. "Liber Thisharb: Viae Memoriae," reprinted in *Gems from the Equinox*, p. 252.
44. *Magick Without Tears*, p. 104.

Universe convinces me that there are beings of intelligence and power of a far higher quality than anything we can conceive of as human . . . and that the one and only chance for mankind to advance as a whole is for individuals to make contact with such Beings."[45] How can this be rectified with the view that "the very existence of language presupposes impotence to communicate directly"?[46]

Rather than disposing of the traditional arts and devices of the magician or occultist, rather than decrying that "God is dead" and being done with it (since that would be simply exchanging God for No God, and the concept "No God" can, as we have seen, be as quickly appropriated within language as "God"), Crowley's Magick reinvents and reinvests in the old ways by Writing through them with the Ape of Thoth.

First, the Magick Language and Weaponry. According to Crowley, Words for magic, such as "Gramarye," and for Magical Ritual, such as "Grimoire," are other names for "Grammars,"[47] and to cast a "Spell" means, literally, "Spelling."[48] Language leaves its marks not just in invocations, but in every part of the magical repertoire. Part II of *Book 4* summarizes the necessary weapons and armaments—The Wand, the Cup, the Dagger, the Disk, The Book, the Bell, and the Robes—as well as their uses, but Crowley waits until Part III to deliver the twist: "The Wand is then nothing but the pen; the Cup, the Inkpot; the Dagger, the knife for sharpening the pen; and the Disk (Pentacle) is either the papyrus roll itself; or the weight which kept it in position, or the sandbox for soaking up the ink."[49]

Magic is Writing, corrupted. Magic (without a "k") veils Writing, rasps with the Disease of Language; Language hides itself in its vestments. Grammar and spelling—Written from thin air—turn themselves into God Words (just as Writing turns itself into Thoth's "monuments"). This amounts to metamorphosing the arts of letter Writing into methods of sending commands by air mail to the angels, transforming Speech into invocations, covering the skeptical Ape with a sheet—now a bonafide ghost. For Crowley, the accoutrements used by the magician are only as good as their ability to engage in the double-sided play of Thoth and his Ape—keeping origins, manifestation and containment at bay, keep-

45. *Magick Without Tears*, p. 217.
46. *Magick*, p. 189.
47. *Magick*, p. 197.
48. A second definition of the Word "Grimoire" is unintelligible gibberish, or nonsense.
49. *Magick*, p. 197.

ing Magick in play. In preparing rituals of Magick, Crowley advocates throwing out the overused, determined symbolism of the occultist in favor of anything less serious in order to "revivify the dead letter",[50] the deadness and the "thingness" that letters and Words threaten. One might be tempted to read the phone book rather than the Tarot, or replace crusty rituals with common rhymes: " 'Jack and Jill went up the hill,' 'From Greenland's icy mountains,' and such, with which it is impossible for the normal mind to associate a feeling of reverence."[51]

When it comes to the magician's arena, the hard and secure temple should be returned into himself. "Let him seek ever to bring inward the symbols, so that even in his well-ordered shrine the whole ceremony revolve inwardly in his heart, that is to say in the temple of his body, of which the outer temple is but an image."[52] Let him bring Magick back to a site that Writes (a site perhaps impossible to cite). Words have special "power" when brought to and through the body. Crowley Writes through himself with the names of God, vibrating God-Names within the body. The vibration of the Word within the body recognizes the effects of Writing, and it all sounds like Language, spilling and spelling, transforming his perception of Knowledge. "It is *because* the names are senseless that they are effective."[53] A Crowleyan "Word of power"—a Word such as "YHVH"—can "transform the planet," transform his sense of the planet. "By this Word he createth Man anew, in an Essential Form of life, so that he is changed in his inmost Knowledge of himself."[54] Words scramble and scribble the world, from the inside out, from the body-mind to the world. Physical Words, for Crowley, shake to earthquake, collapsing man and his cosmos. Collapsing the categories of Man and God, into Writing, which announces while it erases. "We are only able to give a very thin outline of magical theory—faint pencilling by weak and wavering fingers—for this subject may almost be said to be co-extensive with one's whole knowledge."[55]

Within the "temple," the Ceremony and Ritual of Magick respond as well to the challenge of the Ape. Thoth's Ape imitates, "apes," playing at representation. Thoth may hold the stylus, but the monkey dresses

50. "An Account of the A ∴ A ∴," reprinted in *Gems from the Equinox*, p. 37.
51. "Epilogue and Dedication of Volumes I., II., III.: Eleusus," *Collected Works of Aleister Crowley, Volume III* (reprinted Yogi Publication of Society, no place of origin/pub. date), p. 244.
52. "Liber Astarte vel Berylli," reprinted in *Gems from the Equinox*, p. 187.
53. "Epilogue and Dedication of Volumes I., II, III.: Eleusis," p. 223.
54. *Liber Aleph vel CXI: The Book of Wisdom or Folly*, p. 38.
55. *Magick*, p. 149.

better, holds the key to style. Crowley prefers the poetry of sound to didactic prose, drama to realism; in the same way, Ritual for him is a use of Language that undermines didacticism and realism. "The first operation in any actual ceremony is bathing and robing, with appropriate words."[56] Ritual *performs* Words in costume, mocking their solemnity through dramatic solemnity, taking it to excessive limits. "This is the only point to bear in mind, that every act must be a ritual, an act of worship, a sacrament . . . but let it not be self-indulgence; make your self-indulgence your religion."[57] During ceremony, the magician's Will "now . . . is naked and brilliant, now clothed in rich Robes of Symbol and Hieroglyph . . . ready to acquaint thee with thy true Nature, if thou attend unto its Word, its Gesture, or its Show of Imagery".[58] The fact of the matter is show, pageant, pomp. Word not as fact but glamorous images—the spectacle of Language. Crowley says that the "art and craft" of the Magus, the highest grade for any magician still in this world, is "glamour." Magick flaunts its charms, wears crimson robes and hats, speaks in the musical voice.

Crowley Writes of three methods for contacting the gods: "The *Third Method is the Dramatic*, perhaps the most attractive of all; certainly it is so to the artist's temperament, for it appeals to his imagination. . . ."[59] The Ritual needs to be careful constructed—attentive to Language, to high Drama; the climax should always be, in one way or another, a "surprise."[60] Crowley once suggested that the problems faced by the Catholic Church were the result of a loss of "sacrament," "solemnity," "art." In Catholicism, like magic without the "k," nothing is risked. What might revive the Church would be a "special and Secret Mass . . . a Mass of the Mystery of the Incarnation."[61] Such a mass would bring the Word back into play and would—through the doubling of pomp and artifice—bring Thoth back to his Ape.

This is just what Magick promises, offering to its "in-itiates" a "sublime symbolism, artistically arranged,"[62] which can preach, "Live thou in Comedy or Tragedy eternally . . . and perform accordingly the

---

56. *Magick*, p. 226.
57. "The Law of Liberty," reprinted in *The Equinox, Volume III, Number 10* (New York: Thelema Publications, 1986), p. 48.
58. *Liber Aleph vel CXI: The Book of Wisdom or Folly*, p. 5.
59. *Magick*, p. 152.
60. *Magick*, p. 283.
61. "Energized Enthusiasm," reprinted in *Gems from the Equinox*, p. 628.
62. *The Confessions of Aleister Crowley* (New York: Hill and Wang, 1969), p. 704.

false miracles or the true."[63] Ritual should indeed position the whole world on the edge of a circling, spiralling vortex of belief and disbelief—creating, preserving and destroying at the same moment, with the same breath, in the same Word. "The ultimate hieroglyphic must be an infinite."[64]

Which returns (but never finally) to the infinite task and path of the magician. Crowley has told himself at times that to destroy all of Writing's works and return to the Silence constitutes the Great Work. "Let the darkness cover up the writing! Let the scribe depart among his ways."[65] And yet at the same time, when he reaches the top he will slide back to the bottom. "This full stop may never be written . . ."[66] When he finds his Silence, he will of course find the Word. "The only correct and adequate mode of Attainment of Understanding is to shut off and to inhibit the rational mind altogether, thus leaving a *Tabula rasa* upon which the entirely alien faculty—*de novo* and *sui generis*—can write its first word."[67] Crowley can't hold a position at the top of the Tree, can't keep to the Silence, must Write his first Word after the last Word, with disruption. "But now concerning Silence, o my Son, I will have a further word with thee."[68]

At the bottom of the Tree, the water which burst from the vessels has spilled and formed a pond. The ground is hard and the pond has frozen. More ice begging to be broken. We Write, we skate. "We cut a figure on the ice; it is effaced in a morning by the tracks of other skaters; nor did that figure do more than scratch the surface of the ice."[69] We roll, we track in figure eights. In the wake of our paths, in circles and figures of infinity. It figures. "It is no doubt more difficult to learn 'Paradise Lost' by heart than 'We are Seven'; but when you have done it, you are no better at figure-skating."[70] The ground is hard and the Words have frozen. More Words begging to be spoken.

63. "De Thaumaturgia," reprinted in *The Equinox, Volume III, Number 10*, p. 143.
64. *Magick*, p. 99.
65. "Liber Cordis Cincti Serpente," p. 64.
66. *Magick*, p. 110.
67. "Understanding," *Little Essays Toward Truth*, p. 56.
68. *Liber Aleph vel CXI: The Book of Wisdom or Folly*, p. 91.
69. *Magick*, p. 102.
70. "Epilogue and Dedication of Volumes I., II., III.: Eleusis," p. 228.

Berashith: An Essay in Ontology

This first section of Crowley's first magical essay, "Berashith," purports to explain Qabalistic creation. Its mathematical analysis of the original "Nothingness"—of Zero raised to infinity—places any conception of "creation" on dangerous ground.

Taking the ordinary hypothesis of the universe, that of its infinity, or at any rate that of the infinity of God, or of the infinity of some substance or idea actually existing, we first come to the question of the possibility of the co-existence of God and man.

The Christians, in the category of the existent, enumerate among other things, whose consideration we may discard for the purposes of this argument, God, an infinite being; man; Satan and his angels; man certainly, Satan presumably, finite beings. These are not aspects of one being, but separate and even antagonistic existences. All are equally real: we cannot accept mystics of the type of Caird as being orthodox exponents of the religion of Christ.

The Hindus enumerate Brahm, infinite in all dimensions and directions—indistinguishable from the Pleroma of the Gnostics— and Maya, illusion. This is in a sense the antithesis of noumenon and phenomenon, noumenon being negated of all predicates until it becomes almost extinguished in the Nichts under the title of the Alles. (Cf. Max Muller on the metaphysical Nirvana, in his Dhammapada, Introductory Essay.) The Buddhists express no opinion.

Let us consider the force-quality in the existences conceived of by these two religions respectively, remembering that the God of the Christian is infinite, and yet discussing the alternative if we could suppose him to be a finite God. In any equilibrated system of forces, we may sum and represent them as a triangle or series of triangles which again resolve into one. In any moving system, if the resultant

18

motion be applied in a contrary direction, the equilibrium can also thus be represented. And if any one of the original forces in such a system may be considered, that one is equal to the resultant of the remainder. Let x, the purpose of the universe be the resultant of the forces G, S, and M (God, Satan, and Man). Then M is also the resultant of G, S, and $-x$. So that we can regard either of our forces as the supreme, and there is no reason for worshipping one rather than another. All are finite. This argument the Christians clearly see: hence the development of God from the petty joss of Genesis to the intangible, but self-contradictory spectre of to-day. But if G be infinite, the other forces can have no possible effect on it. As Whewell says, in the strange accident by which he anticipates the metre of *In Memoriam:* "No force on earth, however great, can stretch a cord, however fine, into a horizontal line that shall be absolutely straight."

The definition of God as infinite therefore denies man implicitly; while if he be finite, there is an end of the usual Christian reasons for worship, though I daresay I could myself discover some reasonably good ones. [I hardly expect to be asked, somehow.]

The resulting equilibrium of God and man, destructive of worship, is of course absurd. We must reject it, unless we want to fall into Positivism, Materialsm, or something of the sort. But if, then, we call God infinite, how are we to regard man, and Satan? (the latter, at the very least, surely no integral part of him). The fallacy lies not in my demonstration (which is also that of orthodoxy) that a finite God is absurd, but in the assumption that man has any real force.

In our mechanical system (as I have hinted above), if one of the forces be infinite, the others, however great, are both relatively and absolutely nothing.

In any category, infinity excludes finity, unless that finity be an identical part of that infinity.

In the category of existing things, space being infinite, for on that hypothesis we are still working, either matter fills or does not fill it. If the former, matter is infinitely great; if the latter, infinitely small. Whether the matter-universe be $10^{10,000}$ light-years in diameter or half a mile makes no difference; it is infinitely small—in effect, Nothing. The unmathematical illusion that it does exist is what the Hindus call Maya.

If, on the other hand, the matter-universe is infinite, Brahm and

God are crowded out, and the possibility of religion is equally excluded.

We may now shift our objective. The Hindus cannot account intelligibly, though they try hard, for Maya, the cause of all suffering. Their position is radically weak, but at least we may say for them that they have tried to square their religion with their common sense. The Christians, on the other hand, though they saw whither the Manichean heresy must lead, and crushed it, have not officially admitted the precisely similar conclusion with regard to man, and denied the existence of the human soul as distinct from the divine soul.

Trismegistus, Iamblicus, Porphyry, Boehme, and the mystics generally have of course substantially done so, though occasionally with rather inexplicable reservations, similar to those made in some cases by the Vedantists themselves.

Man then being disproved, God the Person disappears for ever, and become Atman, Pleroma, Ain Soph, what name you will, infinite in all directions and in all categories—to deny one is to destroy the entire argument and throw us back on to our old Dvaitistic bases.

I entirely sympathise with my unhappy friend Rev. Mansel, B.D., in his piteous and pitiful plaints against the logical results of the Advaitist School. But on his basal hypothesis of an infinite God, infinite space, time, and so on, no other conclusion is possible. Dean Mansel is found in the impossible position of one who will neither give up his premises nor dispute the validity of his logical processes, but who shrinks in horror from the inevitable conclusion; he supposes there must be something wrong somewhere, and concludes that the sole use of reason is to discover its own inferiority to faith. As Deussen well points out, faith in the Christian sense merely amounts to being convinced on insufficient grounds.[1] This is surely the last refuge of incompetence.

But though, always on the original hypothesis of the infinity of space, &c., the Advaitist position of the Vedantists and the great Germans is unassailable, yet on practical grounds the Dvaitists have all the advantage. Fichte and the others exhaust themselves trying to turn the simple and obvious position that: "If the Ego alone

---

1. Or as the Sunday-school boy said: "Faith is the power of believing what we know to be untrue." I quote Deussen with the more pleasure, because it is about the only sentence in all his writings with which I am in accord.

exists, where is any place, not only for morals and religion, which we can very well do without, but for the most essential and continuous acts of life? Why should an infinite Ego fill a non-existent body with imaginary food cooked in thought only over an illusionary fire by a cook who is not there? Why should infinite power use such finite means, and very often fail even then?"

What is the sum total of the Vedantist position? " 'I' am an illusion, externally. In reality, the true 'I' am the Infinite, and if the illusionary 'I' could only realise Who 'I' really am, how very happy we should all be!" And here we have Karma, rebirth, all the mighty laws of nature operating nowhere in nothing!

There is no room for worship or for morality in the Advaitist system. All the specious pleas of the Bhagavad-Gita, and the ethical works of Western Advaitist philosophers, are more or less consciously confusion of thought. But no subtlety can turn the practical argument; the grinning mouths of the Dvaitist guns keep the fort of Ethics, and warn metaphysics to keep off the rather green grass of religion.

That its apologists should have devoted so much time, thought, scholarship, and ingenuity to this question is the best proof of the fatuity of the Advaita position.

There is then a flaw somewhere. I boldly take up the glove against all previous wisdom, revert to the most elementary ideas of cannibal savages, challenge all the most vital premises and axiomata that have passed current coin with philosophy for centuries, and present my theory.

I clearly foresee the one difficulty, and will discuss it in advance. If my conclusions on this point are not accepted, we may at once get back to our previous irritable agnosticism, and look for our Messiah elsewhere. But if we can see together on this one point, I think things will go fairly smoothly afterwards.

Consider[2] Darkness! Can we philosophically or actually regard as different the darkness produced by interference of light and that existing in the mere absence of light?

Is Unity really identical with .9 recurring?

Do we not mean different things when we speak respectively of 2 sine 60^0 and of $\sqrt{3}$?

---

2. Ratiocination may perhaps not take us far. But a continuous and attentive study of these quaint points of distinction may give us an intuition, or direct mind-apperception of what we want, one way or the other.

Charcoal and diamond are obviously different in the categories of colour, crystallisation, hardness, and so on; but are they not really so even in that of existence?

The third example is to my mind the best. 2 sine 60^0 and $\sqrt{3}$ are unreal and therefore never conceivable, at least to the present constitution of our human intelligences. Worked out, neither has meaning; unworked, both have meaning, and that a different meaning in one case and the other.

We have thus two terms, both unreal, both inconceivable, yet both representing intelligible and diverse ideas to our minds (and this is the point!) though identical in reality and convertible by a process of reason which simulates or replaces that apprehension which we can never (one may suppose) attain to.

Let us apply this idea to the Beginning of all things, about which the Christians lie frankly, the Hindus prevaricate, and the Buddhists are discreetly silent, while not contradicting even the gross and ridiculous accounts of the more fantastic Hindu visionaries.

The Qabalists explain the "First Cause"[3] by the phrase: "From 0 to 1, as the circle opening out into the line." The Christian dogma is really identical, for both conceive of a previous and eternally existing God, though the Qabalists hedge by describing this latent Deity as "Not." Later commentators, notably the illustrious Mac-Gregor-Mathers, have explained this Not as "negatively existing." Profound as is my respect for the intellectual and spiritual attainments of him whom I am proud to have been permitted to call my master, I am bound to express my view that when the Qabalists said Not, they meant Not, and nothing else. In fact, I really claim to have re-discovered the long-lost and central Arcanum of those divine philosophers.

I have no serious objection to a finite god, or gods, distinct from men and things. In fact, personally, I believe in them all, and admit them to possess inconceivable though not infinite power.

The Buddhists admit the existence of Maha-Brahma, but his power and knowledge are limited; and his agelong day must end. I have evidence everywhere, even in our garbled and mutilated version of the Hebrew Scriptures, that Jehovah's power was limited in all sorts of ways. At the Fall, for instance, Tetragrammaton Elohim has to summon his angels hastily to guard the Tree of Life,

3. An expression they carefully avoid using.

lest he should be proved a liar. For had it occurred to Adam to eat of that Tree before their transgression was discovered, or had the Serpent been aware of its properties, Adam would indeed have lived and not died. So that a mere accident saved the remnants of the already besmirched reputation of the Hebrew tribal Fetich.

When Buddha was asked how things came to be, he took refuge in silence, which his disciples very conveniently interpreted as meaning that the question tended not to edification.

I take it that the Buddha (ignorant, doubtless, of algebra) had sufficiently studied philosophy and possessed enough worldly wisdom to be well aware that any system he might promulgate would be instantly attacked and annihilated by the acumen of his numerous and versatile opponents.

Such teaching as he gave on the point may be summed up as follows. "Whence whither, why, we know not; but we do know that we are here, that we dislike being here, that there is a way out of the whole loathsome affair—let us make haste and take it!"

I am not so retiring in disposition; I persist in my inquiries, and at last the appalling question is answered, and the past ceases to intrude its problems upon my mind.

Here you are! Three shies a penny! Change all bad arguments.

I ASSERT THE ABSOLUTENESS OF THE QABALISTIC ZERO.

When we say that the Cosmos sprang from 0, what kind of 0 do we mean? By 0 in the ordinary sense of the term we mean "absence of extension in any of the categories."

When I say "No cat has two tails," I do not mean, as the old fallacy runs, that "Absence-of-cat possesses two tails"; but that "In the category of two-tailed things, there is no extension of cat."

Nothingness is that about which no positive proposition is valid. We cannot truly affirm: "Nothingness is green or heavy, or sweet."

Let us call time, space, being, heaviness, hunger, the categories.[4] If a man be heavy and hungry, he is extended in all these, besides, of course, many more. But let us suppose that these five are all. Call the man X; his formula is then $X^{t+s+b+h+n}$. If he now eat, he will cease to be extended in hunger; if he be cut off from time and gravitation as well, he will now be represented by the formula X^{s+b}.

---

4. I cannot here discuss the propriety of representing the categories as dimensions. It will be obvious to any student of the integral calculus, or to any one who appreciates the geometrical significance of the term X^4.

Should he cease to occupy space and to exist, his formula would then be X^0. This expression is equal to 1; whatever X may represent, if it be raised to the power of 0 (this meaning mathematically "if it be extended in no dimension or category"), the result is Unity, and the unknown factor X is eliminated.

This is the Advaitist idea of the future of man; his personality, bereft of all its qualities, disappears and is lost, while in its place arises the impersonal Unity, The Pleroma, Parabrahma, or the Allah of the Unity-adoring followers of Mohammed. (To the Musulman fakir, Allah is by no means a personal God.)

Unity is thus unaffected, whether or no it be extended in any of the categories. But we have already agreed to look to 0 for the Uncaused.

Now if there was in truth 0 "before the beginning of years," THAT 0 WAS EXTENDED IN NONE OF THE CATEGORIES, FOR THERE COULD HAVE BEEN NO CATEGORIES IN WHICH IT COULD EXTEND! If our 0 was the ordinary 0 of mathematics, there was not truly absolute 0, for 0 is, as I have shown, dependent on the idea of categories. If these existed, then the whole question is merely thrown back; we must reach a state in which the 0 is absolute. Not only must we get rid of all subjects, but of all predicates. By 0 (in mathematics) we really mean 0^n, where n is the final term of a natural scale of dimensions, categories, or predicates. Our Cosmic Egg, then, from which the present universe arose was Nothingness, extended in no categories, or, graphically, 0^0. This expression is in its present form meaningless. Let us discover its value by a simple mathematical process!

$$0^0 = 0^{1\,-\,1} = \frac{0^1}{0^1} \text{ [Multiply by } 1 = \frac{n}{n} \text{]}$$

$$\text{Then } \frac{0^1}{n} \times \frac{n}{0^s} = 0 \times \infty.$$

Now the multiplying of the infinitely great by the infinitely small results in SOME UNKNOWN FINITE NUMBER EXTENDED IN AN UNKNOWN NUMBER OF CATEGORIES. It happened, when this our Great Inversion took place, from the essence of all nothingness to finity extended in innumerable categories, that an incalculably vast system was produced. Merely by chance, chance in the truest sense of the term, we are found with gods, men, stars, planets, devils, colours, forces, and all the materials of the Cosmos: and with time, space, and causality, the conditons limiting and involving them all.[5]

Remember that it is not true to say that our 0^0 existed; nor that it did not exist. The idea of existence was just as much unformulated as that of toasted cheese.

But 0^0 is a finite expression, or has a finite phase, and our universe is a finite universe; its categories are themselves finite, and the expression "infinite space" is a contradiction in terms. The idea of an absolute and of an infinite[6] God is relegated to the limbo of all similar idle and pernicious perversions of truth. Infinity remains, but only as a mathematical conception as impossible in nature as the square root of -1. Against all this mathematical, or semi-mathematical, reasoning, it may doubtless be objected that our whole system of numbers, and of manipulating them, is merely a series of conventions. . . .

5. Compare and contrast this doctrine with that of Herbert Spencer ("First Principles," Part 1.), and see my "Science and Buddhism" for a full discussion of the difference involved.
6. If by "infinitely great" we only mean "indefinitely great," as a mathematician would perhaps tell us, we of course begin at the very point I am aiming at, viz., *Ecrasez l'Infini*.

The Magical Theory of the Universe

This is Chapter 0 of *Magick in Theory and Practice*. At every step of the way—often in its elegant footnotes—it turns around on itself and points out its own conceptual limits, embroidering the study of Magick with(in) the visible borderlines of sense, point-of-view, and symbols.

There are three main theories of the Universe: Dualism, Monism and Nihilism. It is impossible to enter into a discussion of their relative merits in a popular manual of this sort. They may be studied in Erdmann's "History of Philosophy" and similar treatises.

All are reconciled and unified in the theory which we shall now set forth. The basis of this Harmony is given in Crowley's "Berashith"—to which reference should be made.

Infinite space is called the goddess NUIT, while the infinitely small and atomic yet omnipresent point is called HADIT.[1] **These are unmanifest. One conjunction of these infinites is called RA-HOOR-KHUIT,**[2] **a Unity which includes and heads all things.**[3] (There is also a particular Nature of Him, in certain

---

1. I present this theory in a very simple form. I cannot even explain (for instance) that an idea may not refer to Being at all, but to Going. The Book of the Law demands special study and initiated apprehension.
2. More correctly, HERU-RA-HA, to include HOOR-PAAR-KRAAT.
3. The basis of this theology is given in Liber CCXX, AL vel Legis which forms Part IV of this Book 4. Hence I can only outline the matter in a very crude way; it would require a separate treatise to discuss even the true meaning of the terms employed, and to show how The Book of the Law anticipates the recent discoveries of Frege, Cantor, Poincaré, Russell, Whitehead, Einstein and others.

conditions, such as have obtained since the Spring of 1904, e.v.) This profoundly mystical conception is based upon actual spiritual experience, but the trained reason[4] can reach a reflexion of this idea by the method of logical contradiction which ends in reason transcending itself. The reader should consult "The Soldier and the Hunchback" in The Equinox I, I, and "Konx Om Pax".

Unity transcends *consciousness*. It is above all division. The Father of thought—the Word—is called Chaos—the dyad. The number Three, the Mother, is called Babalon. In connection with this the reader should study "The Temple of Solomon the King" in Equinox I, V, and Liber 418.

This first triad is essentially unity, in a manner transcending reason. The comprehension of this Trinity is a matter of spiritual experience. **All true gods are attributed to this Trinity.**[5]

An immeasurable abyss divides it from all manifestations of Reason or the lower qualities of man. In the ultimate analysis of Reason, we find all reason identifed with this abyss. Yet this abyss is the crown of the mind. Purely intellectual faculties all obtain here. This abyss has no number, for in it all is confusion.

Below this abyss we find the moral qualities of Man, of which there are six. The highest is symbolised by the number Four. Its nature is fatherly[6]; Mercy and Authority are the attributes of its dignity.

The number Five is balanced against it. The attributes of Five are Energy and Justice. Four and Five are again combined and harmonized in the number Six, whose nature is beauty and harmony, mortality and immortality.

In the number Seven the feminine nature is again predominant, but it is the masculine type of female, the Amazon, who is balanced in the number Eight by the feminine type of male.

In the number Nine we reach the last of the purely mental qualities. It identifies change with stability.

---

4. All advance in understanding demands the aquisition of a new point-of-view. Modern conceptions of Mathematics, Chemistry, and Physics are sheer paradox to the "plain man" who thinks of Matter as something that one can knock up against.
5. Considerations of the Christian Trinity are of a nature suited only to Initiates of the IX° of O.T.O., as they enclose the final secret of all practical Magick.
6. Each conception is, however, balanced in itself. Four is also Daleth, the letter of Venus; so that the mother-idea is included. Again, the Sephira of 4 is Chesed, referred to Water. 4 is ruled by Jupiter, Lord of the Lightning (Fire) yet ruler of Air. Each Sephira is complete in its way.

Pendant to this sixfold system is the number Ten[7] which includes the whole of Matter as we know it by the senses.

It is impossible here to explain thoroughly the complete conception; for it cannot be too clearly understood that this is a *classification* of the Universe, that there is nothing which is not comprehended therein.

The Article on the Qabalah in Vol. I, No. V of the Equinox is the best which has been written on the subject. It should be deeply studied, in connection with the Qabalistic Diagrams in Nos. II and III: "The Temple of Solomon the King".

Such is a crude and elementary sketch of this system.

The formula of Tetragrammaton is the most important for the practical magician. Here Yod = 2, Hé = 3, Vau = 4 to 9, Hé final = 10.

The Number Two represents Yod, the Divine or Archetypal World, and the Number One is only attained by the destruction of the God and the Magician in Samadhi. The world of Angels is under the numbers Four to Nine, and that of spirits under the number Ten.[8] All these numbers are of course parts of the magician himself

---

7. The balance of the Sephiroth:

Kether	(1)	"Kether is in Malkuth, and Malkuth is in Kether, but another manner."
Chokmah	(2)	is Yod of Tetragrammaton, and therefore also Unity.
Binah	(3)	is Hé of Tetragrammaton, and therefore "The Emperor."
Chesed	(4)	is Daleth, Venus the female.
Geburah	(5)	is the Sephira of Mars, the Male.
Tiphereth	(6)	is the Hexagram, harmonizing, and mediating between Kether and Malkuth. Also it reflects Kether. "That which is above, is like that which is below, and that which is below, is like that which is above."
Netzach	(7)	and Hod (8) balanced as in text.
Jesod	(9)	see text.
Malkuth	(10)	contains all the numbers.

8. It is not possible to give a full account of the twenty-two "paths" in this condensed sketch. They should be studied in view of all their attributes in 777, but more especially that in which they are attributed to the planets, elements and signs, as also to the Tarot Trumps, while their position on the Tree itself and their position as links between the particular Sephiroth which they join is the final key to their understanding. It will be noticed that each chapter of this book is attributed to one of them. This was not intentional. The book was originally but a collection of haphazard dialogues between Fra. P. and Soror A.; but on arranging the MSS, they fell naturally and of necessity into this division. Conversely, my knowledge of the Schema pointed out to me numerous gaps in my original exposition; thanks to this, I have been able to make it a complete and systematic treatise. That is, when my laziness had been jogged by the criticisms and suggestions of various colleagues to whom I had submitted the early drafts.

considered as the microcosm. **The microcosm is an exact image of the Macrocosm; the Great Work is the raising of the whole man in perfect balance to the power of Infinity.**

The reader will remark that all criticism directed against the Magical Hierarchy is futile. One cannot call it incorrect—the only line to take might be that it was inconvenient. In the same way one cannot say that the Roman alphabet is better or worse than the Greek, since all required sounds can be more or less satisfactorily represented by either; yet both these alphabets were found so little satisfactory when it came to an attempt to phonetic printing of Oriental languages, that the alphabet had to be expanded by the use of italics and other diacritical marks. In the same way our magical alphabet of the Sephiroth and the Paths (thirty-two letters as it were) has been expanded into the four worlds corresponding to the four letters of the name יהו׳; and each Sephira is supposed to contain a Tree of Life of its own. Thus we obtain four hundred Sephiroth instead of the original ten, and the Paths being capable of similar multiplications, or rather of subdivision, the number is still further extended. Of course this process might be indefinitely continued without destroying the original system.

The Apologia for this System is that our purest conceptions are symbolized in Mathematics. "God is the Great Arithmetician." "God is the Grand Geometer." It is best therefore to prepare to apprehend Him by formulating our minds according to these measures.[9]

To return, each letter of this alphabet may have its special magical sigil. The student must not expect to be given a cut-and-dried definition of what exactly is meant by any of all this. On the contrary, he must work backwards, putting the whole of his mental and moral outfit into these pigeon-holes. You would not expect to be able to buy a filing cabinet with the names of all your past, present and future correspondents ready indexed: your cabinet has a system of letters and numbers meaningless in themselves, but ready to take on a meaning to you, as you fill up the files. As your business increased, each letter and number would receive fresh accessions of meaning for you; and by adopting this orderly arrange-

---

9. By "God" I here mean the Ideal Identity of a man's inmost nature. "Something ourselves (I erase Arnold's imbecile and guilty 'not') that makes for righteousness"; righteousness being rightly defined as internal coherence. (Internal Coherence implies that which is written *Detegitur Yod*.)

ment you would be able to have a much more comprehensive grasp of your affairs than would otherwise be the case. **By the use of this system the magician is able ultimately to unify the whole of his knowledge—to transmute, even on the Intellectual Plane, the Many into the One.**

The reader can now understand that the sketch given above of the magical Hierarchy is hardly even an outline of the real theory of the Universe. This theory may indeed be studied in the article already referred to in No. V of the Equinox, and, more deeply, in the Book of the Law and the Commentaries thereon: but the true understanding depends entirely upon the work of the Magician himself. Without magical experience it will be meaningless.

In this there is nothing peculiar. It is so with all scientific knowledge. A blind man might cram up astronomy for the purpose of passing examinations, but his knowledge would be almost entirely unrelated to his experience, and it would certainly not give him sight. A similar phenomenon is observed when a gentleman who has taken an "honours degree" in modern languages at Cambridge arrives in Paris, and is unable to order his dinner. To exclaim against the Master Therion is to act like a person who, observing this should attack both the professors of French and the inhabitants of Paris, and perhaps go on to deny the existence of France.

Let us say, once again, that the magical language is nothing but a convenient system of classification to enable the magician to docket his experiences as he obtains them.

Yet this is true also, that, once the language is mastered, one can divine the unknown by study of the known, just as one's knowledge of Latin and Greek enables one to understand some unfamiliar English word derived from those sources. Also, there is the similar case of the Periodic Law in Chemistry, which enables Science to prophesy, and so in the end to discover, the existence of certain previously unsuspected elements in nature. All discussions upon philosophy are necessarily sterile, since truth is beyond language. They are, however, useful if carried far enough—if carried to the point when it becomes apparent that all arguments are arguments in a circle.[10] But discussions of the details of purely imaginary

10. See "The Soldier and the Hunchback," The Equinox I, I. The apparatus of human reason is simply one particular system of coordinating impressions; its structure is determined by the course of the evolution of the species. It is no more absolute than the evolution of the species. It is no more absolute than the mechanism of our muscles is a complete type wherewith all other systems of transmitting Force must conform.

qualities are frivolous and may be deadly. For the great danger of this magical theory is that the student may mistake the alphabet for the things which the words represent.

An excellent man of great intelligence, a learned Qabalist, once amazed the Master Therion by stating that the Tree of Life was the framework of the Universe. It was as if some one had seriously maintained that a cat was a creature constructed by placing the letters C. A. T. in that order. It is no wonder that Magick has excited the ridicule of the unintelligent, since even its educated students can be guilty of so gross a violation of the first principles of common sense.[11]

A synopsis of the grades of the A ∴ A ∴ as illustrative of the Magical Hierarchy in Man is given in Appendix 2 "One Star in Sight." This should be read before proceeding with the chapter. The subject is very difficult. To deal with it in full is entirely beyond the limits of this small treatise.

FURTHER CONCERNING THE MAGICAL UNIVERSE

All these letters of the magical alphabet—referred to above—are like so many names on a map. Man himself is a complete microcosm. Few other beings have this balanced perfection. Of course every sun, every planet, may have beings similarly constituted.[12] But when we

11. Long since writing the above, an even grosser imbecility has been perpetrated. One who ought to have known better tried to improve the Tree of Life by Turning the Serpent of Wisdom upside down! Yet he could not even make his scheme symmetrical: his little remaining good sense revolted at the supreme atrocities. Yet he succeeded in reducing the whole Magical Alphabet to nonsense, and shewing that he had never understood its real meaning.

The absurdity of any such disturbance of the arrangement of the Paths is evident to any sober student from such examples as the following. Binah, the Supernal Understanding, is connected with Tiphereth, the Human Consciousness, by Zain, Gemini, the Oracles of the Gods, or the Intuition. That is, the attribution represents a psychological fact: to replace it by The Devil is either humour or plain idiocy. Again, the card "Fortitude," Leo, balances Majesty and Mercy with Strength and Severity: what sense is there in putting "Death," the Scorpion, in its stead? There are twenty other mistakes in the new wonderful illuminated-from-on-high attribution; the student can therefore be sure of twenty more laughs if he cares to study it.

12. Equally, of course, we have no means of knowing what we really are. We are limited to symbols. And it is certain that all our sense-perceptions give only partial aspects of their objects. Sight, for instance, tells us very little about solidity, weight, composition, electrical character, thermal conductivity, etc., etc. It says nothing at all about the very existence of such vitally important ideas as Heat, Hardness, and so on. The impression which the mind combines from the senses can never claim to be accurate or complete. We have indeed learnt that nothing is in itself what it seems to be to us.

speak of dealing with the planets in Magick, the reference is usually not to the actual planets, but to parts of the earth which are of the nature attributed to these planets. Thus, when we say that Nakhiel is the "Intelligence" of the Sun, we do not mean that he lives in the Sun, but only that he has a certain rank and character; and although we can invoke him, we do not necessarily mean that he exists in the same sense of the word in which our butcher exists.

When we "conjure Nakhiel to visible appearance," it may be that our process resembles creation—or, rather imagination—more nearly than it does calling-forth. The aura of a man is called the "magical mirror of the universe"; and, so far as any one can tell, nothing exists outside of this mirror. It is at least convenient to represent the whole as if it were subjective. It leads to less confusion. And, as a man is a perfect microcosm,[13] it is perfectly easy to re-model one's conception at any moment.

Now there is a traditional correspondence, which modern experiment has shown to be fairly reliable. There is a certain natural connexion between certain letters, words, numbers, gestures, shapes, perfumes and so on, so that any idea or (as we might call it) "spirit", may be composed or called forth by the use of those things which are harmonious with it, and express particular parts of its nature. These correspondences have been elaborately mapped in the Book 777 in a very convenient and compendious form. It will be necessary for the student to make a careful study of this book in connexion with some actual rituals of Magick, for example, that of the evocation of Taphtatharath printed in Equinox I, III, pages 170–190, where he will see exactly why these things are to be used. **Of course, as the student advances in knowledge by experience he will find a progressive subtlety in**

---

13. He is this only by definition. The universe may contain an infinite variety of worlds inaccessible to human apprehension. Yet, for this very reason, they do not exist for the purposes of the argument. Man has, however, some instruments of knowledge; we may, therefore, define the Macrocosm as the totality of things possible to his perception. As evolution develops those instruments, the Macrocosm and the Microcosm extend; but they always maintain their mutual relation. Neither can possess any meaning except in terms of the other. Our "discoveries" are exactly as much of ourselves as they are of Nature. America and Electricity did, in a sense, exist before we were aware of them; but they are even now no more than incomplete ideas, expressed in symbolic terms of a series of relations between two sets of inscrutable phenomena.

the magical universe corresponding to his own; for let it be said yet again! not only is his aura a magical mirror of the universe, but the universe is a magical mirror of his aura.

In this chapter we are only able to give a very thin outline of magical theory—faint pencilling by weak and wavering fingers—for this subject may almost be said to be co-extensive with one's whole knowledge.

The knowledge of exoteric science is comically limited by the fact that we have no access, except in the most indirect way, to any other celestial body than our own. In the last few years, the semi-educated have got an idea that they know a great deal about the universe, and the principal ground for their fine opinion of themselves is usually the telephone or the airship. It is pitiful to read the bombastic twaddle about progress, which journalists and others, who wish to prevent men from thinking, put out for consumption. **We know infinitesimally little of the material universe. Our detailed knowledge is so contemptibly minute, that it is hardly worth reference, save that our shame may spur us to increased endeavour. Such knowledge[14] as we have got is of a very general and abstruse, or a philosophical and almost magical character. This consists principally of the conceptions of pure mathematics. It is, therefore, almost legitimate to say that pure mathematics is our link with the rest of the universe and with "God."**

Now the conceptions of Magick are themselves profoundly mathematical. The whole basis of our theory is the Qabalah, which corresponds to mathematics and geometry. The method of operation in Magick is based on this, in very much the same way as the laws of mechanics are based on mathematics. So far, therefore as we can be said to possess a magical theory of the universe, it must be a matter solely of fundamental law, with a few simple and comprehensive propositions stated in very general terms.

I might expend a life-time in exploring the details of one plane, just as an explorer might give his life to one corner of Africa, or a chemist to one subgroup of compounds. Each such detailed piece of work may be very valuable, but it does not as a rule throw light on

---

14. Knowledge is, moreover, an impossible conception. All propositions come ulti-mately back to "A is A."

the main principles of the universe. Its truth is the truth of one angle. It might even lead to error, if some inferior person were to generalize from too few facts.

Imagine an inhabitant of Mars who wished to philosophise about the earth, and had nothing to go by but the diary of some man at the North Pole! But the work of every explorer, on whatever branch of the Tree of Life the caterpillar he is after may happen to be crawling, is immensely helped by a grasp of general principles. Every magician, therefore, should study the Holy Qabalah. Once he has mastered the main principles, he will find his work grow easy.

Solvitur ambulando: **which does not mean: "Call the Ambulance!"**

What is Qabalah?

A brief appendix to the volume of Qabalistic correspondences, *777,* "What is Qabalah?" alternately refers to the non-entity of Qabalah as language, terminology, system, and instrument. It may be flexible and impermanent, but Qabalah sets unavoidable conditions for the magical mind, as language does. Magick Writes always already within Qabalah.

Qabalah is—

(*a*) A language fitted to describe certain classes of phenomena, and to express certain classes of ideas which escape regular phraseology. You might as well object to the technical terminology of chemistry.

(*b*) An unsectarian and elastic terminology by means of which it is possible to equate the mental processes of people apparently diverse owing to the constraint imposed upon them by the peculiarities of their literary expression. You might as well object to a lexicon, or a treatise on comparative religion.

(*c*) A system of symbolism which enables thinkers to formulate their ideas with complete precision, and to find simple expression for complex thoughts, especially such as include previously disconnected orders of conception. You might as well object to algebraic symbols.

(*d*) An instrument for interpreting symbols whose meaning has become obscure, forgotten or misunderstood by establishing a necessary connection between the essence of forms, sounds, simple ideas (such as number) and their spiritual, moral, or intellectual equivalents. You might as well object to interpreting ancient art by consideration of beauty as determined by physiological facts.

(*e*) A system of classification of omniform ideas so as to enable the mind to increase its vocabulary of thoughts and facts through organizing and correlating them. You might as well object to the mnemonic value of Arabic modifications of roots.

(*f*) An instrument for proceeding from the known to the unknown on similar principles to those of mathematics. You might as well object to the use of $\sqrt{-1}$, x^4, etc.

(*g*) A system of criteria by which the truth of correspondences may be tested with a view to criticizing new discoveries in the light of their coherence with the whole body of truth. You might as well object to judging character and status by educational and social convention.

Hieroglyphics: Life and Language Necessarily Symbolic

This piece is one of a number of letters Crowley wrote to a student during his later years that were compiled in the excellent *Magick Without Tears*. This letter makes its case in a manner that leaves few doubts as to the "existence" of the Qabalah.

Cara Soror,

Do what thou wilt shall be the whole of the Law.

Very natural, the irritation in your last! You write:

But why? Why all this elaborate symbolism? Why not say straight out what you mean? Surely the subject is difficult enough in any case—must you put on a mask to make it clear? I know you well enough by now to be sure that you will not fob me off with any Holy-Willie nonsense about the Ineffable, about human language being inadequate to reveal such Mysteries, about the necessity of constructing a new language to explain a new system of thought; of course I know that this had to be done in the case of chemistry, of higher mathematics, indeed of almost all technical subjects; but I feel that you have some other, deeper explanation in reserve. After all, most of what I am seeking to learn from you has been familiar to many of the great minds of humanity for many centuries. Indeed, the Qabalah is a special language, and that is old enough; there is not much new material to fit into that structure. But why did they, in the first place, resort to this symbolic jargon?

You put it very well, and when I think it over, I feel far from sure that the explanation which I am about to inflict upon you will satisfy you, or even whether it will hold water! In the last resort, I shall

37

have to maintain that we are justified by experience, by the empirical success in communicating thought which has attended, and continues to attend, our endeavors.

But to give a complete answer, I shall have to go back to the beginning, and restate the original problem; and I beg that you will not suppose that I am evading the question, or adopting the Irish method of answering it by another, though I know it may sound as if I were.

Let me set out by restating our original problem; what we want is Truth; we want an even closer approach to Reality; and we want to discover and discuss the proper means of achieving this object.

Very good; let us start by the simplest of all possible enquiries— and the most difficult—"What is anything?" "What do we know?" and other questions that spring naturally from these.

> I see a tree.
> I hear it—rustling or creaking in the wind.
> I touch it—hard.
> I smell it—acrid.
> I taste it—bitter.

Now all the information given by these five senses has to be put together, although no two agree in any sort of way. The logic by which we build up our complex idea of a tree has more holes than a sponge.

But this is to jump far ahead: we must first analyze the single, simple impression. "I see a tree." This phenomenon is what is called a "point-event." It is the coming together of the two, the seer and the seen. It is single and simple; yet we cannot conceive of either of them as anything but complex. And the Point-Event tells us nothing whatever about either; both, as Herbert Spencer and God-knows-how-many others have shown, unknowable; it stands by itself, alone and aloof. It has happened; it is undeniably Reality. Yet we cannot confirm it; for it can never happen again precisely the same. What is even more bewildering is that since it takes time for the eye to convey an impression to the consciousness (it may alter in 1,000 ways in the process!) all that really exists is a memory of the Point-Event, not the Point-Event itself. What then *is* this Reality of which we are so sure? Obviously, it has not got a name, since it never happened before, or can happen again! To discuss it at all we must *invent* a name, and this name (like all names) cannot possibly be anything more than a symbol.

Even so, as so often pointed out, all we do is to "record the behaviour of our instruments." Nor are we much better off when we've done it; for our symbol, referring as it does to a phenomenon unique in itself, and not to be apprehended by another, can mean nothing to one's neighbours. What happens, of course, is that similar, though not identical, Point-Events happen to many of us, and so we are able to construct a symbolic language. My memory of the mysterious Reality resembles yours sufficiently to induce us to agree that both belong to the same class.

But let me furthermore ask you to reflect on the formation of language itself. Except in the case of onomatopoeic words and a few others, there is no logical connection between a thing and the sound of our name for it. "Bow-wow" is a more rational name than dog, which is a mere convention agreed on by the English, while other nations prefer *chien, hund, cane, kalb, kutta,* and so on. All symbols, you see, my dear child, and it's no good your kicking!

But it doesn't stop there. When we try to convey thought by writing, we are bound to sit down solidly, and construct a holy Qabalah out of nothing. Why would a curve open to the right, sound like the ocean, open at the top, like you? And all these arbitrary symbolic letters are combined by just as symbolic and arbitrary devices to take on conventional meanings, these words again combined into phrases by no less high-handed a procedure.

And then folk wonder how it is that there should be error and misunderstanding in the transmission of thought from one person to another! Rather regard it as a miraculous intervention of Providence when even one of even the simplest ideas "gets across." Now then, this being so, it is evidently good sense to construct one's own alphabet, with one's own very precise definitions, in order to handle an abstruse and technical subject like Magick. The "ordinary" words such as God, self, soul, spirit and the rest have been used so many thousand times in so many thousand ways, usually by writers who knew not, or cared not for the necessity of definition that to use them to-day in any scientific essay is almost ludicrous.

That is all, just now, sister; no more of your cavilling, please; sit down quietly with your 777, and get it by heart!

Love is the law, love under will.

Fraternally,

666

Woolly Pomposities of the Pious "Teacher"

Another letter to Cara Soror, "Woolly Pomposities" spells out the value of studies in Qabalistic correspondence. The Qabalah keeps the magician on his toes, alert to the easy formulations of Language.

Cara Soror,

Do what thou wilt shall be the whole of the Law.

I do not think that it was any new kind of electricity. I think it was the passage itself that has given me neuralgia. It disgusts me beyond words.

To put the matter in a nutshell, tersely, concisely, succinctly, the world is being corrupted by all this—

Asthmatic Thinking	Torpid Thinking	Nauseous Thinking
Bovine T.	Uncertain T.	Old-maidish T.
Chawbacon T.	Venomous T.	Purgative T.
Diffuse T.	Whelp T.	Querulous T.
Excretory T.	Yahoo T.	Rat-riddled T.
Fog-bound T.	Zig-zag T.	Superficial T.
Gossiping T.	Ambivalent T.	Tinsel T.
Higgledy-piggledy T.	Broken T.	Unbalanced T.
Ill-mannered T.	Corked T.	Viscous T.
Jibbing T.	Disjointed T.	Windy T.
Kneeling T.	Eight-anna T.	Yapping T.
Leaden T.	Flibberty-gibbet T.	Zymotic T.
Moulting T.	Glum T.	Addled T.
Neurotic T.	High-falutin' T.	Blear-eyed T.
Orphan T.	Invertebrate T.	Capsized T.
Peccable T.	Jazzy T.	Down-at-heel T.

Queasy T.
Rococo T.
Slavish T.
Hypocritical T.
Ignorant T.
Jerry-built T.
Knock-kneed T.
Lazy T.
Messy T.
Nasty T.
Oleaginous T.
Purulent T.
Slattern T.
Unkempt T.
Over-civilized T.
Gluey T.
Crippled T.
Foggy T.
Wordy T.
Opportunish T.
Muddy T.
Unclean T.
Flabby T.
Unsorted T.
Prim T.
Theatrical T.
Vaporous T.
Myopic T.
Flimsy T.
Unfinished T.
Mongrel T.
Irrelevant T.
Hidebound T.
Snobbish T.

Knavish T.
Leucorrhoeic T.
Motheaten T.
Unsystematic T.
Void T.
Waggly T.
Atrophied T.
Bloated T.
Cancerous T.
Dull T.
Eurasian T.
Futile T.
Immature T.
Beige T.
Emaciated T.
Dislocated T.
Slushy T.
Teaparty T.
Negroid T.
Babbling T.
Onanistic T.
Hybrid T.
Nebulous T.
Hurried T.
Empty T.
Vain T.
Loose T.
Bloodless T.
Ersatz T.
Pontifical T.
Unripe T.
Glossy T.
Officious T.
Misleading T.

Evasive T.
Formless T.
Guilty T.
Lachrymose T.
Maudlin T.
Neighing T.
Odious T.
Pedestrian T.
Quavering T.
Ragbag T.
Sappy T.
Tuberculous T.
Veneered T.
Woolly T.
Flat T.
Emetic T.
Insanitary T.
Gloomy T.
Jaundiced T.
Pedantic T.
Flatulent T.
Sluttish T.
Stale T.
Mangy T.
Portentous T.
Loose T.
Wooden T.
Soapy T.
Gabbling T.
Wishful T.
Frock-coated T.
Fashionable T.
Unmanly T.
Slippery T. . . . .

. . . as we find in Brunton, Besant, Clymer, Max Heindel, Ouspensky, and in the catchpenny frauds of the secret-peddlers, the U.B., the O.H.M., the A.M.O.R.C., and all the other gangs of self-styled Rosicrucians; they should be hissed off the stage.

Now that we are agreed upon the conditions to be satisfied if we are to allow that a given proposition contains a Thought at all, it is proper to turn our attention to the relative value of different kinds of thought. This question is of the very first importance: the whole theory of Education depends upon a correct standard. There are facts and facts: one would not necessarily be much the wiser if one got the *Encyclopaedia Britannica* by heart, or the Tables of Logarithms. The one aim of Mathematics, in fact—Whitehead points this out in his little Shilling Arithmetic—is to make one fact do the work of thousands.

What we are looking for is a working Hierarchy of Facts.

That takes us back at once to our original "addition and subtraction" remark in my letter on Mind. Classification, the first step, proceeds by putting similar things together, and dissimilar things apart.

One asset in the Audit of a fact is the amount of knowledge which it covers. $(2 + 5)^2 = 49$; $(3 + 4)^2 = 49$; $(6 + 2)^2 = 64$; $(7 + 1)^2 = 64$; $(9 + 4)^2 = 169$ are isolated facts, no more; worse, the coincidences of 49 and 64 might start the wildest phantasies in your head— "something mysterious about this." But if you write: the sum of the squares of any two numbers is the sum of the square of each plus twice their multiple—$(a + b)^2 = a^2 + 2ab + b^2$—you have got a fact which covers every possible case, and exhibits one aspect of the nature of numbers themselves. The importance of a word increases as its rank, from the particular and concrete to the general and abstract. (It is curious that the highest values of all, the "Laws of Nature," are never exactly 'true' for any two persons, for one person can never observe the *identical* phenomena sensible to another, since two people cannot be in exactly the same place at exactly the same time: yet it is just these facts that are equally true for all men.)

Observe, I pray, the paramount importance of memory. From one point of view (bless your heart!) you are nothing at all but a bundle of memories. When you say "this is happening *now*," you are a falsifier of God's sacred truth! When I say "I see a horse," the truth is that "I record in those terms my private hieroglyphic interpretation of the unknown and unknowable phenomenon (or 'point-event') which has more or less recently taken place at the other end of my system of receiving impressions."

Well, then! You realize, of course, how many millions of billions of memories there must be to compose any average well-trained mind. Those strings of adjectives all sprang spontaneously; I did not look them up in books of reference; so imagine the extent of my full vocabulary! And words are but the half-baked bricks with which one constructs.

See to it, then, that you accept no worthless material; that you select, and select again, always in proper order and proportion; organize, structuralize your thought, always with the one aim in view of accomplishing the Great Work.

Well, now, before going further into this, I must behave like an utter cad, and disgrace my family tree, and blot my 'scutcheon and my copybook by confusing you about "realism." Excuse: not my muddle; it was made centuries ago by a gang of cursed monks, headed by one Duns Scotus—so-called because he was Irish—or if not by somebody else equally objectionable. They held to the Platonic dogma of archetypes. They maintained that there was an original (divine) idea such as "greenness" or a "pig,"and that a green pig, as observed in nature, was just one example of these two ideal essences. They were opposed by the "nominalists," who said, to the contrary, that "greenness" or "a pig" were nothing in themselves; they were mere names (nominalism from Lat. *nomen,* a name) invented for convenience of grouping. This doctrine is plain commonsense, and I shall waste no time in demolishing the realists.

All *a priori* thinking, the worst kind of thinking, goes with "realism" in this sense.

And now you look shocked and surprised! And no wonder! What (you exclaim) is the whole Qabalistic doctrine but the very apotheosis of this "realism"? (It was also called "idealism," apparently to cheer and comfort the student on his rough and rugged road!) Is not Atziluth the "archetypal world"? Is not . . .

Oh, all right, all *right!* Keep your blouse on! I didn't go for to do it. You're quite right: the Tree of Life *is* like that, in appearance. But that is the wrong way to look at it. We get our number two, for example, as "that which is common to a bird's legs, a man's ears, twins, the cube root of eight, the greater luminaries, the spikes of a pitchfork," etc., but having got it, we must not go on to argue that the number two being possessed of this and that property, therefore there *must* be two of something or other which for one reason or another we cannot count on our fingers.

The trouble is that sometimes we *can* do so; we are very often obliged to do so, and it comes out correct. But we must not trust any such theorem; it is little more than a hint to help us in our guesses. Example: an angel appears and tells us that his name is MALIEL

(MLIAL) which adds to 111, the third of the numbers of the Sun. Do we conclude that his nature is solar? In this case, yes, perhaps, because, (on the theory) he took that name for the very reason that it chimed with his nature. But a man may reside at 81 Silver Street without being a lunatic, or be born at five o'clock on the 5th of May, 1905, and make a very poor soldier.

I think you already understand the main point: you must structuralise your thinking. You must learn how to differentiate and how to integrate your thoughts. Nothing exists in isolation; it is always conditioned by its relations with other things; indeed, in one sense, a thing is no more than the sum of these relations. (For the only "reality," in the long run, is, as we have seen, a Point of View.)

Now, this task of organising the mind, of erecting a coherent and intelligible structure, is enormously facilitated by the Qabalah.

When, in one of those curious fits of indisposition of which you periodically complain, and of which the cause appears to you so obscure, you see pink leopards on the staircase, "Ah! the colour of the King Scale of Tiphareth—Oh! the form of Leo, probably in the Queen Scale" and thereby increase your vocabulary by these two items. Then, perhaps, someone suggests that indiscretion in the worship of Dionysus is responsible for the observed phenomena—well, there's Tiphareth again at once; the Priest, moreover, wears a leopard-skin, and the spots suggest the Sun. Also, Sol is Lord of Leo: so there you are! pink leopards are exactly what you have a right to expect!

Until you have practiced this method, all day and every day, for quite a long while, you cannot tell how amazingly your mnemonic power increases by virtue thereof. But be careful always to range the new ideas as they come along in their right order of importance.

It is not unlike the system of keys used in big establishments, such as hotels. First, a set of keys, each of which opens one door, and one door only. Then, a set which opens all the doors on one floor only. And so on, until the one responsible who has one unique key which opens every lock in the building.

There is another point about this whole System of the Qabalah. It does more than merely increase the mnemonic faculty by 10,000 percent or so; the habit of throwing your thoughts about, manipulating them, giving them a wash and brush-up, packing them away into their proper places in your "Crystal Cabinet," gives you immensely increased power over them.

In particular, it helps you to rid them of the emotional dirt which normally clogs them;[1] you become perfectly indifferent to any implication but their value in respect of the whole system; and this is of incalculable help in the acquisition of new ideas. It is the difference between a man trying to pick a smut out of his wife's eye with clumsy greasy fingers coarsened by digging drains, and an oculist furnished with a speculum and all the instruments exactly suited to the task.

Yet another point. Besides getting rid of the emotions and sensations which cloud the thought, the fact that you are constantly asking yourself "Now, in which drawer of which cabinet does this thought go?" automatically induces you to regard the system as the important factor in the operation, if only because it is common to every one of them.

So not only have you freed Sanna (perception) from the taint of Vedana (sensation) but raised it (or demolished it, if you prefer to look at it in that light!) to be merely a member of the Sankhara (tendency) class, thus boosting you vigorously to the fourth stage, the last before the last! of the practice of Mahasatipathana.

Just one more word about the element of Vedana. The Intellect is a purely mechanical contrivance, as accurate and as careless of what it turns out as a Cash Register. It receives impressions, calculates, states the result: that is A double L, ALL!

Try never to qualify a thought in any way, to see it as it is in itself in relation to those other elements which are necessary to make it what it is.

Above all, do not "mix the planes." A dagger may be sharp or blunt, straight or crooked; it is not "wicked-looking," or even "trusty," except in so far as the quality of its steel makes it so. A cliff is not "frowning" or "menacing." A snow-covered glacier is not "treacherous": to say so means only that Alpine Clubmen and other persons ignorant of mountain craft are unable to detect the position of covered crevasses.

All such points you must decide for yourself; the important thing is that you should *challenge* any such ideas.

Above all, do not avoid, or slur, unwelcome trains of thought or distressing problems. Don't say "he passed on" when you mean "he died," and don't call a spade a bloody shovel!

---

1. I hope there is no need to repeat that whether any given thought is pleasant, or undesirable, or otherwise soiled by Vedana, is *totally* irrelevant.

I shall break off this brief note at this point, so that you may have time to tell me if what I have so far said covers the whole ground of your enquiry.

Love is the law, love under will.
Fraternally,
666

Of Silence and Secrecy: and of the Barbarous Names of Evocation

Magicians use Words to invoke the gods, and in this essay, drawn from *Magick in Theory and Practice,* Crowley explains how this practice can have no theory, can not even claim cause and effect. (Notes: the "Goetia" Crowley refers to is an ancient Grimoire of such invocations. Frater Perdurabo is one of Crowley's many magical names, discussed in great detail in my essay "Magick and Lies" in the section *The Book of Lies.*)

It is found by experience (confirming the statement of Zoroaster) that the most potent conjurations are those in an ancient and perhaps forgotten language, or even those couched in a corrupt and possibly always meaningless jargon. Of these there are several main types. The "preliminary invocation" in the "Goetia" consists principally of corruptions of Greek and Egyptian names. For example, we find "Osorronnophris" for "Asor Un-Nefer". The conjurations given by Dr. Dee (vide Equinox I, VIII) are in a language called Angelic, or Enochian. Its source has hitherto baffled research, but it is a language and not a jargon, for it possesses a structure of its own, and there are traces of grammar and syntax.

However this may be, it *works*. Even the beginner finds that "things happen" when he uses it: and this is an advantage—or disadvantage!—shared by no other type of language. The rest need skill. This needs Prudence!

The Egyptian Invocations are much purer, but their meaning has not been sufficiently studied by persons magically competent. We possess a number of Invocations in Greek of every degree of excellence; in Latin but few, and those of inferior quality. It will be noticed that in every case the conjurations are very sonorous, and there is a certain magical voice in which they should be recited. This special voice was a natural gift of the Master Therion; but it can be easily taught—to the right people.

Various considerations impelled Him to attempt conjurations in the English language. There already existed one example, the charm of the witches in Macbeth; although this was perhaps not meant seriously, its effect is indubitable.[1]

He has found iambic tetrameters enriched with many rimes both internal and external very useful. "The Wizard Way" (Equinox I, I) gives a good idea of the sort of thing. So does the Evocation of Bartzabel in Equinox I, IX. There are many extant invocations throughout his works, in many kinds of metre, of many kinds of being, and for many kinds of purposes.

Other methods of incantation are on record as efficacious. For instance Frater I. A., when a child, was told that he could invoke the devil by repeating the "Lord's Prayer" backwards. He went into the garden and did so. The Devil appeared, and almost scared him out of his life.

It is therefore not quite certain in what the efficacy of conjurations really lies. The peculiar mental excitement required may even be aroused by the perception of the absurdity of the process, and the persistence in it, as when once FRATER PERDURABO (at the end of His magical resources) recited "From Greenland's Icy Mountains", and obtained His result.

It may be conceded in any case that **the long strings of formidable words which roar and moan through so many conjurations have a real effect in exalting the consciousness of the magician to the proper pitch**—that they should do so is no more extraordinary than music of any kind should do so.

Magicians have not confined themselves to the use of the human voice. The Pan-pipe with its seven stops, corresponding to the seven planets, the bull-roarer, the tom-tom, and even the violin, have all been used, as well as many others, of which the most important is the bell[2], though this is used not so much for actual conjuration as to mark stages in the ceremony. Of all these the tom-tom will be found to be the most generally useful.

---

1. A true poet cannot help revealing himself and the truth of things in his art, whether he be aware of what he is writing, or no.
2. See Book 4, Part II. It should be said that in experience no bell save His own Tibetan bell of Electrum Magicum has ever sounded satisfactory to the Master Therion. Most bells jar and repel.

While on the subject of barbarous names of evocation we should not omit the utterance of certain supreme words which enshrine (α) the complete formula of the God invoked, or (β) the whole ceremony.

Examples of the former kind are Tetragrammaton, **I.A.O.**, and Abrahadabra.

An example of the latter kind is the great word StiBeTTChePh-MeFSHiSS, which is a line drawn on the Tree of Life (Coptic attributions) in a certain manner.[3]

With all such words it is of the utmost importance that they should never be spoken until the supreme moment, and even then they should burst from the magician almost despite himself—so great should be his reluctance[4] to utter them. In fact, they should be the utterance of the God in him at the first onset of the divine possession. So uttered, they cannot fail of effect, for they have become the effect.

Every wise magician will have constructed (according to the principles of the Holy Qabalah) many such words, and he should have quintessentialised them all in one Word, which last Word, once he has formed it, he should never utter consciously even in thought, until perhaps with it he gives up the ghost. **Such a Word should in fact be so potent that man cannot hear it and live.**

Such a word was indeed the lost Tetragrammaton[5]. It is said that at the utterance of this name the Universe crashes into dissolution. **Let the Magician earnestly seek this Lost Word, for its pronunciation is synonymous with the accomplishment of the Great Work.[6]**

In this matter of the efficacy of words there are again two formulæ exactly opposite in nature. A word may become potent and terrible by virtue of constant repetition. It is in this way that most religions gain strength. **At first the statement "So and so is God"**

---

3. It represents the descent of a certain Influence. See the Evocation of Taphtatharath, Equinox I, III. The attributions are given in 777. This Word expresses the current Kether—Beth—Binah—Cheth—Geburch—Mem—Hod—Shin—Malkuth, the the descent from 1 to 10 via the Pillar of Severity.
4. This reluctance is Freudian, due to the power of these words to awaken the suppressed subconscious libido.
5. The Master Therion has received this Word; it is communicated by Him to the proper postulants, at the proper time and place, in the proper circumstances.
6. Each man has a different Great Work, just as no two points on the circumference of a circle are connected with the centre by the same radius. The Word will be correspondingly unique.

excites no interest. Continue, and you meet scorn and scepticism: possibly persecution. Continue, and the controversy has so far died out that no one troubles to contradict your assertion.

No superstition is so dangerous and so lively as an exploded superstition. The newspapers of to-day (written and edited almost exclusively by men without a spark of either religion or morality) dare not hint that any one disbelieves in the ostensibly prevailing cult; they deplore Atheism—all but universal in practice and implicit in the theory of practically all intelligent people—as if it were the eccentricity of a few negligible or objectionable persons. This is the ordinary story of advertisement; the sham has exactly the same chance as the real. Persistence is the only quality required for success.

The opposite formula is that of secrecy. An idea is perpetuated because it must never be mentioned. A Freemason never forgets the secret words entrusted to him, though these words mean absolutely nothing to him, in the vast majority of cases; the only reason for this is that he has been forbidden to mention them, although they have been published again and again, and are as accessible to the profane as to the initiate.

In such a work of practical Magick as the preaching of a new Law, these methods may be advantageously combined; on the one hand infinite frankness and readiness to communicate all secrets; on the other the sublime and terrible knowledge that all real secrets are incommunicable.[7]

It is, according to tradition, a certain advantage in conjurations to employ more than one language. In all probability the reason of this is that any change spurs the flagging attention. A man engaged in intense mental labour will frequently stop and walk up and down the room—one may suppose for this cause—but it is a sign of weakness that this should be necessary. For the beginner in Magick, however, it is permissible[8] to employ any device to secure the result.

---

7. If this were not the case, individuality would not be inviolable. No man can communicate even the simplest thought to any other man in any full and accurate sense. For that thought is sown in a different soil, and cannot produce an identical effect. I cannot put a spot of red upon two pictures without altering each in diverse ways. It might have little effect on a sunset by Turner, but much on a nocturne by Whistler. The identity of the two spots as spots would thus be fallacious.

8. This is not to say that it is advisable. O how shameful is human weakness! But it does encourage one—it is useless to deny it—to be knocked down by a Demon of whose existence one was not really quite sure.

Conjurations should be recited, not read;[9] and the entire ceremony should be so perfectly performed that one is hardly conscious of any effort of memory. **The ceremony should be constructed with such logical fatality that a mistake is impossible.**[10] The conscious ego of the Magician is to be destroyed to be absorbed in that of the God whom he invokes, and the process should not interfere with the automaton who is performing the ceremony.

But this ego of which it is here spoken is the true ultimate ego. The automaton should possess will, energy, intelligence, reason, and resource. This automaton should be the perfect man far more than any other man can be. It is only the divine self within the man, a self as far above the possession of will or any other qualities whatsoever as the heavens are high above the earth, that should reabsorb itself into that illimitable radiance of which it is a spark.[11]

The great difficulty for the single Magician is so to perfect himself that these multifarious duties of the Ritual are adequately performed. At first he will find that the exaltation destroys memory and paralyses muscle. This is an essential difficulty of the magical process, and can only be overcome by practice and experience.[12]

In order to aid concentration, and to increase the supply of Energy, it has been customary for the Magician to employ assistants or colleagues. It is doubtful whether the obvious advantages of this plan compensate the difficulty of procuring suitable persons[13], and the chance of a conflict of will or a misunderstanding in the circle itself. On one occasion FRATER PERDURABO was disobeyed by an assistant; and had it not been for His promptitude in using the physical compulsion of the sword, it is probable that the circle would

9. Even this is for the weaker brethren. The really great Magus speaks and acts impromptu and extempore.

10. First-rate poetry is easily memorized because the ideas and the musical values correspond to man's mental and sensory structure.

11. This is said of the partial or lesser Works of Magick. This is an elementary treatise; one cannot discuss higher Works as for example those of "The Hermit of Aesopus Island".

12. See "The Book of Lies"; there are several chapters on this subject. But Right Exaltation should produce spontaneously the proper mental and physical reactions. As soon as the development is secured, there will be automatic reflex "justesse", exactly as in normal affairs mind and body respond with free unconscious rightness to the Will.

13. The organic development of Magick in the world due to the creative Will of the Master Therion makes it with every year that passes easier to find scientifically trained co-workers.

have been broken. As it was, the affair fortunately terminated in nothing more serious than the destruction of the culprit.

However, there is no doubt that an assemblage of persons who really are in harmony can much more easily produce an effect than a magician working by himself. The psychology of "Revival meetings" will be familiar to almost every one, and though such meetings[14] are the foulest and most degraded rituals of black magic, the laws of Magick are not thereby suspended. **The laws of Magick are the laws of Nature.**

A singular and world-famous example of this is of sufficiently recent date to be fresh in the memory of many people now living. At a nigger camp meeting in the "United" States of America, devotees were worked up to such a pitch of excitement that the whole assembly developed a furious form of hysteria. The comparatively intelligible cries of "Glory" and "Hallelujah" no longer expressed the situation. Somebody screamed out "Ta-ra-ra-boom-de-ay!", and this was taken up by the whole meeting and yelled continuously, until reaction set in. The affair got into the papers, and some particularly bright disciple of John Stuart Mill, logician and economist, thought that these words, having set one set of fools crazy, might do the same to all the other fools in the world. He accordingly wrote a song, and produced the desired result. This is the most notorious example in recent times of the power exerted by a barbarous name of evocation.

A few words may be useful to reconcile the general notion of Causality with that of Magick. How can we be sure that a person waving a stick and howling thereby produces thunderstorms? In no other way than that familiar to Science; we note that whenever we put a lighted match to dry gunpowder, an unintelligibly arbitrary phenomenon, that of sound, is observed; and so forth.

We need not dwell upon this point; but it seems worth while to answer one of the objections to the possibility of Magick, choosing one which is at first sight of an obviously "fatal" character. It is convenient to quote verbatim from the Diary[15] of a distinguised Magician and philosopher.

---

14. See for an account of properly-conducted congregational ceremonial, Equinox I, IX. "Energized Enthusiasm", and Equinox III. I. Liber XV. Ecclesiae Gnosticae Catholicae Canon Missae. The "Revival meetings" here in question were deliberate exploitations of religious hysteria.

15. In a later entry we read that the diarist has found a similar train of argument in "Space, Time, and Gravitation", page 51. He was much encouraged by the confirmation of his thesis in so independent a system of thought.

"I have noticed that the effect of a Magical Work has followed it so closely that it must have been started before the time of the Work. E. g. I work to night to make X in Paris write to me. I get the letter the next morning, so that it must have been written before the Work. Does this deny that the Work caused the effect?

"If I strike a billiard-ball, and it moves, both my will and its motion are due to causes long antecedent to the act. I may consider both my Work and its reaction as twin effects of the eternal Universe. The moved arm and ball are parts of a state of the Cosmos which resulted necessarily from its momentarily previous state, and so, back for ever.

"Thus, my Magical Work is only one of the cause-effects necessarily concomitant with the cause-effects which set the ball in motion. I may therefore regard the act of striking as a cause-effect of my original Will to move the ball, though necessarily previous to its motion. But the case of magical Work is not quite analogous. For my nature is such that I am compelled to perform Magick in order to make my will to prevail; so that the cause of my doing the Work is also the cause of the ball's motion, and there is no reason why one should precede the other. (Cf. *Lewis Carroll,* where the Red Queen screams before she pricks her finger.)

"Let me illustrate the theory by an actual example.

"I write from Italy to a man in France and another in Australia on the same day, telling them to join me. Both arrive ten days later; the first in answer to my letter, which he received, the second on "his own initiative", as it would seem. But I summoned him because I wanted him; and I wanted him because he was my representative; and his intelligence made him resolve to join me because it judged rightly that the situation (so far as he knew it) was such as to make me desire his presence.

"The same cause, therefore, which made me write to him made him come to me; and though it would be improper to say that the writing of the letter was the direct cause of his arrival, it is evident that if I had not written I should have been different from what I actually am, and therefore my relations with him would have been otherwise than they are. In this sense, therefore, the letter and the journey are causally connected.

"One cannot go farther, and say that in this case I ought to write the letter even if he had arrived before I did so; for it is part of the whole set of circumstances that I do not use a crowbar on an open door.

"The conclusion is that one should do one's Will 'without lust of result'. If one is working in accordance with the laws of one's own nature, one is doing 'right'; and no such Work can be criticised as 'useless', even in cases of the character here discussed. So long as one's Will prevails, there is no cause for complaint.

"To abandon one's Magick would shew lack of self-confidence in one's powers, and doubt as to one's inmost faith in Self and in Nature.[16] Of course one changes one's methods as experience indicates; but there is no need to change them on any such ground as the above.

"Further, the argument here set forth disposes of the need to explain the *modus operandi* of Magick. A successful operation does not involve any theory soever, not even that of the existence of causality itself. The whole set of phenomena may be conceived as single.

"For instance, if I see a star (as it was years ago) I need not assume causal relations as existing between it, the earth, and myself. The connexion exists; I can predicate nothing beyond that. I cannot postulate purpose, or even determine the manner in which the event comes to be. Similarly, when I do Magick, it is in vain to inquire why I so act, or why the desired result does or does not follow. Nor can I know how the previous and subsequent conditions are connected. At most I can describe the consciousness which I interpret as a picture of the facts, and make empirical generalizations of the superficial aspects of the case.

"Thus, I have my own personal impressions of the act of telephoning; but I cannot be aware of what consciousness, electricity, mechanics, sound, etc., actually are in themselves. And although I can appeal to experience to lay down 'laws' as to what conditions accompany the act, I can never be sure that they have always been, or ever will again be, identical. (In fact, it is certain that an event can never occur twice in precisely the same circumstances.)[17]

"Further, my 'laws' must always take nearly all the more important elements of knowledge for granted. I cannot say—finally—how an electric current is generated. I cannot be sure that some totally

---

16. i.e. on the ground that one cannot understand how Magick can produce the desired effects. For if one possesses the inclination to do Magick, it is evidence of a tendency in one's Nature. Nobody understands fully how the mind moves the muscles; but we know that lack of confidence on this point means paralysis. "If the Sun and Moon should doubt, They'd immediately go out", as Blake said. Also, as I said myself. "Who hath the How is careless of the Why".
17. If it did so, how could we call it duplex?

unsuspected force is not at work in some entirely arbitrary way. For example, it was formerly supposed that Hydrogen and Chlorine would unite when an electric spark was passed through the mixture; now we 'know' that the presence of a minute quantity of aqueous vapour (or some tertium quid) is essential to the reaction. We formulated before the days of Ross the 'laws' of malarial fever, without reference to the mosquito; we might discover one day that the germ is only active when certain events are transpiring in some nebula[18], or when so apparently inert a substance as Argon is present in the air in certain proportions.

"We may therefore admit quite cheerfully that Magick is as mysterious as mathematics, as empirical as poetry, as uncertain as golf, and as dependent on the personal equation as Love.

"That is no reason why we should not study, practice and enjoy it; for it is a Science in exactly the same sense as biology; it is no less an Art than Sculpture; and it is a Sport as much as Mountaineering.

"Indeed, there seems to be no undue presumption in urging that no Science possesses equal possibilities of deep and important Knowledge;[19] that no Art offers such opportunities to the ambition of the Soul to express its Truth, in Ecstasy, through Beauty; and that no Sport rivals its fascinations of danger and delight, so excites,

18. The history of the Earth is included in the period of some such relation; so that we cannot possibly be sure that we may deny: "Malarial fever is a function of the present precession of the Equinoxes".

19. Magick is less liable to lead to error than any other Science, because its terms are interchangeable, by definition, so that it is based on relativity from the start. We run no risk of asserting absolute propositions. Furthermore we make our measurements in terms of the object measured, thus avoiding the absurdity of defining metaphysical ideas by mutable standards, (Cf. Eddington "Space, Time, and Gravitation". Prologue.) of being forced to attribute the qualities of human consciousness to inanimate things (Poincaré, "La mesure du temps"), and of asserting that we know anything of the universe in itself, though the nature of our senses and our minds necessarily determines our observations, so that the limit of our knowledge is subjective, just as a thermometer can record nothing but its own reaction to one particular type of Energy. Magick recognizes frankly (1) that truth is relative, subjective, and apparent; (2) that Truth implies Omniscience, which is unattainable by mind, being transfinite; just as if one tried to make an exact map of England in England, that map must contain a map of the map, and so on, ad infinitum; (3) that logical contradiction is inherent in reason, (Russell, "Introduction to Mathematical Philosophy", p. 136; Crowley, "Eleusis", and elsewhere); (4) that a Continuum requires a Continuum to be commensurable with it: (5) that Empiricism is ineluctable, and therefore that adjustment is the only possible method of action; and (6) that error may be avoided by opposing no resistance to change, and registering observed phenomena in their own language.

exercises, and tests its devotees to the uttermost, or so rewards them by well-being, pride, and the passionate pleasures of personal triumph.

"Magick takes every thought and act for its apparatus; it has the Universe for its Library and its Laboratory; all Nature is its Subject; and its Game, free from close seasons and protective restrictions, always abounds in infinite variety, being all that exists.[20]

20. The elasticity of Magick makes it equal to all possible kinds of environment, and therefore biologically perfect. "Do what thou wilt" implies self-adjustment, so that failure cannot occur. One's true Will is necessarily fitted to the whole Universe with the utmost exactitude, because each term in the equation $a + b + c = 0$ must be equal and opposite to the sum of all the other terms. No individual can ever be aught than himself, or do aught else than his Will, which is his necessary relation with his environment, dynamically considered. All error is no more than an illusion proper to him to dissipate the mirage, and it is a general law that the method of accomplishing this operation is to realize, and to acquiesce in, the order of the Universe, and to refrain from attempting the impossible task of overcoming the inertia of the forces which oppose, and therefore are identical with, one's self. Error in thought is therefore failure to understand, and in action to perform, one's own true Will.

Do Angels Ever Cut Themselves Shaving?

A letter from *Magick Without Tears,* this brief piece demonstrates an even more duplicitous perspective on the problem of communicating with beings on other planes. In Magick, belief and disbelief commingle at every step. (Note: Therion—Master Therion, or "The Great Beast"— is yet another of Crowley's adopted names).

Cara Soror,

Do what thou wilt shall be the whole of the Law.

A very witty way to put it! "Do angels ever cut themselves shaving?" *Rem au tetigisti,* again. (English: you big tease?)

What sort of existence, what type or degree of reality, do we attribute to them? (By angel, of course, you mean any celestial—or infernal—being such as are listed in the Hierarchy, from Metatron and Ratziel to Lilith and Nahema.) We read of them, for the most part, as if they were persons—although of another order of being; as individual, almost, as ourselves. The principal difference is that they are not, as we are, microcosmic. The Angels of Jupiter contain all the Jupiter there is, within these limits, that their rank is not as high as their Archangel, nor as low as their Intelligence or their spirit. But their Jupiter is pure Jupiter; no other planet enters into their composition.

We see and hear them, usually (in my own experience) as the result of specific invocation. Less frequently we know them through the sense of touch as well; sometimes their presence is associated with a particular perfume. (This, by the way, is very striking, since it has to overcome that of the incense.) I must very strongly insist, at this point, on the difference between "gods" and "angels." Gods are macrocosmic, as we microcosmic: an incarnated (materialised)

57

God is just as much a person, an individual animal, as we are; as such, he appeals to all our senses *exactly* as if he were "material."

But everything sensible is matter in some state or other; how then are we to regard an Angel, complete with robes, weapons, and other impedimenta? (I have never known a god thus encumbered, when he has been "materialised" at all. Of course, the mere *apparition* of a God is subject to laws similar to those governing the visions of angels.)

For one thing, all the laws that we find in operation on various parts of the "Astral plane" are valid. Two things can occupy the same place at the same time. They are "swift without feet, and flying without wings." They change size, shape, appearance, appurtenances of all sorts, at will. Anything that is required for the purpose of the vision is there at will. They bring their own background with them. They are able to transfer a portion of their energy to the seer by spontaneous action without appreciable means.

But here is where your question arises—what is their "life" like? In the visions, they never do anything but "go through the motions" appropriate to their nature and to the character of the vision.

Are we to conclude that the whole set of impressions is no more than symbolic? Is it all a part of oneself, like a daydream, but a daydream intensified and made "real" because its crucial incidents turn out to be true, as must always occur during the testing of the genuineness of the vision?

It seems to me much simpler to say that these Angles are "real" individuals, although living in a world of whose laws we have no conception; and that, in order to communicate with us, they make use of the symbolic forms appropriate; employ, in short, the language of the Astral Plane.

After all, it's only fair; for that is precisely what we do to them when we invoke them.

Ha! Ha! Ha! I suppose you think you've caught me out in an evasion there! Not so, dear child, not so: this state of affairs is nothing strange.

Ask yourself: "What do I know of Therion's mode of life? Whenever I see him, he's always on his best behaviour. I've hardly ever seen him eat; perhaps he does so only when I am there, so as not to embarrass me by a display of his holiness. His universe touches mine at only a very few points. The mere fact of his being a man, and I a woman, makes sympathetic understanding over a vast range of experience almost impossible, certainly imperfect. Then all his reading and his travels touch mine at very few points. And his ignorance of music makes it an almost grotesque extension of magnanimity for me to admit his claim to belong to the human species . . . U.S.W." Then: "How do we manage to communicate at all? There is bound to be an impassable gulf between us at the best, when one considers that his connotation of the commonest words like 'mountain', 'girl', 'school', 'Hindu', 'oasis', is so vastly different from mine. But to do it *at all*! What actually have we done?"

Think it out!

We have made a set of queerly-shapen marks on a sheet of paper, given them names, attached a particular sound to each, made up (God knows how and why!) combinations of these, given names and sounds to them too, and attached a meaning—hardly ever the same for you as for me—to them, made combinations of these too according to a set of quite arbitrary rules, agreed—so far as agreement is possible, or even thinkable—to label a thought with some such arrangement: and there we are! You have in this fantastically artificial way succeeded in conveying your thought to my mind.

Now, turn back to *Magick*; read there how we work to establish intelligible intercourse between ourselves and the "angels."

If you can find any difference between that method and this, it is more than I can.

Finally, please remember as a general rule that *all* magical experience is perfectly paralleled by the simplest and commonest phenomena of our daily life!

People who tell you that it is "all quite different beyond the Veil" or what not, are blithering incompetents totally ignorant of the nature of things.

On the contrary, I will tell you more about "communication."

There is a method of using Ethyl Oxide which enables one (a) to analyse one's thoughts with a most exquisite subtlety and accuracy, (b) to find out—in the French phrase—"what is at the bottom of the bottle." By this they mean the *final* result of any project or investigation; and this, surprisingly often, is not at all what it is possible to discover by any ordinary means.

For instance, one might ask oneself "Do I believe in God?" and, after a vast number of affirmative answers of constantly increasing depth and subtlety, discover with a shock that "at the bottom of the bottle" one believed nothing of the sort! Or vice versa.

On one occasion the following experiment was carried out. A certain Adept was to make use of the Sacred Vapour, and when the time seemed ripe, to answer such questions as should be put to him by his Scribe. Presently, after about an hour's silence, the Scribe asked: "Is communication possible?"

By this he meant merely to enquire whether it would now be in order for him to begin to ask his prepared list of questions.

But the Adept thought that this *was* Question No. 1: meaning "Is there any valid means of making contact between two minds?"

He remained intensely silent—intensely, as opposed to his previous rather fidgety abstention from talking—for a very long time, and then broke slowly into a long seductive ripple of hushed laughter, suggestive of the possession of some ineffably delicious secret, of a moonlight revel of Pan with his retinue of Satyrs, nymphs and fauns.

I shall say no more, save to express the hope that you have understood this story, and the Truth and Beauty of this answer.

Love is the law, love under will.

Fraternally yours,

666

The Juggler

This brief excerpt from *The Book of Thoth* examines the Tarot card known as "The Juggler," which represents both Thoth and Mercury (a Roman version of Thoth).

This card is referred to the letter Beth, which means a house, and is attributed to the planet Mercury. The ideas connected with this symbol are so complex and so multifarious that it seems better to attach to this general description certain documents which bear upon different aspects of this card. The whole will then form an adequate basis for the full interpretation of the card through study, meditation, and use.

The French title of this card in the mediæval pack is "Le Bâteleur", the Bearer of the Bâton.[1] Mercury is pre-eminently the bearer of the Wand: Energy sent forth. This card therefore represents the Wisdom, the Will, the Word, the Logos by whom the worlds were created. (See the Gospel according to St. John, chapter I.) It represents the Will. In brief, he is the Son, the manifestation in act of the idea of the Father. He is the male correlative of the High Priestess. Let there be no confusion here on account of the fundamental doctrine of the Sun and Moon as the Second Harmonics to the Lingam and the Yoni; for, as will be seen in the citation from *The Paris Working,* the creative Mercury is of the nature of the Sun. But Mercury is the Path leading from Kether to Binah, the Understanding; and thus He is the messenger of the gods, represents precisely that Lingam, the Word of creation whose speech is silence.

Mercury, however, represents action in all forms and phases. He

---

1. Variant: *LE PAGAD*. Origin unknown. Suggestions:
    (1) PChD, terror (esp. Panic fear) a title of Geburah. Also a thigh: i.e. membrum virile. By Arabic analogy, PAChD, causer of terror: Value 93!!
    (2) Pagoda, a phallic memorial: Similar, and equally apt.

is the fluidic basis of all transmission of activity; and, on the dynamic theory of the Universe, he is himself the substance thereof. He is, in the language of modern physics, that electric charge which is the first manifestation of the ring of ten indefinable ideas, as previously explained. He is thus continuous creation.

Logically also, being the Word, he is the law of reason or of necessity or chance, which is the secret meaning of the Word, which is the essence of the Word, and the condition of its utterance. This being so, and especially because he is duality, he represents both truth and falsehood, wisdom and folly. Being the unexpected, he unsettles any established idea, and therefore appears tricky. He has no conscience, being creative. If he cannot attain his ends by fair means, he does it by foul. The legends of the youthful Mercury are therefore legends of cunning. He cannot be understood, because he is the Unconscious Will. His position on the Tree of Life shows the third Sephira, Binah, Understanding, as not yet formulated; still less the false Sephira, Da'ath, knowledge.

From the above it will appear that this card is the second emanation from the Crown, and therefore, in a sense, the adult form of the first emanation, the Fool, whose letter is Aleph, the Unity. These ideas are so subtle and so tenuous, on these exalted planes of thought, that definition is impossible. It is not even desirable, because it is the nature of these ideas to flow one into the other. One cannot do more than say that any given hieroglyph represents a slight insistence upon some particular form of a pantomorphous idea. In this card, the emphasis is upon the creative and dualistic character of the path of Beth.

In the traditional card the disguise is that of a Juggler.

This representation of the Juggler is one of the crudest and least satisfactory in the mediæval pack. He is usually represented with a headdress shaped like the sign of infinity in mathematics (this is shown in detail in the card called the Two of Disks). He bears a wand with a knob at each end, which was probably connected with the dual polarity of electricity; but it is also the hollow wand of Prometheus that brings down fire from Heaven. On a table or altar, behind which he is standing, are the three other elemental weapons.

"With the Wand createth He.
With the Cup preserveth He.

With the Dagger destroyeth He.
With the Coin redeemeth He.

Liber Magi vv. 7–10."

The present card has been designed principally upon the Graeco-Egyptian tradition; for the understanding of this idea was certainly further advanced when these philosophies modified each other, than elsewhere at any time.

The Hindu conception of Mercury, Hanuman, the monkey god, is abominably degraded. None of the higher aspects of the symbol are found in his cult. The aim of his adepts seems principally to have been the production of a temporary incarnation of the god by sending the women of the tribe every year into the jungle. Nor do we find any legend of any depth or spirituality. Hanuman is certainly little more than the Ape of Thoth.

The principal characteristic of Tahuti or Thoth, the Egyptian Mercury, is, firstly, that he has the head of the ibis. The ibis is the symbol of concentration, because it was supposed that this bird stood continuously upon one leg, motionless. This is quite evidently a symbol of the meditative spirit. There may also have been some reference to the central mystery of the Aeon of Osiris, the secret guarded so carefully from the profane, that the intervention of the male was necessary to the production of children. In this form of Thoth, he is seen bearing the phoenix wand, symbolising resurrection through the generative process. In his left hand is the Ankh, which represents a sandal-strap; that is to say, the means of progress through the worlds, which is the distinguishing mark of godhead. But, by its shape, this Ankh (*crux ansata*) is actually another form of the Rose and Cross, and this fact is perhaps not quite such an accident as modern Egyptologists, preoccupied with their attempted refutation of the Phallic school of Archæology, would have us suppose.

The other form of Thoth represents him primarily as Wisdom and the Word. He bears in his right hand the Style, in his left the Papyrus. He is the messenger of the gods; he transmits their will by hieroglyphs intelligible to the initiate, and records their acts; but it was seen from very early times that the use of speech, or writing, meant the introduction of ambiguity at the best, and falsehood at the worst; they therefore represented Thoth as followed by an ape, the cynocephalus, whose business was to distort the Word of the god;

to mock, to simulate and to deceive. In philosophical language one may say: Manifestation implies illusion. This doctrine is found in Hindu philosophy, where the aspect of Tahuti of which we are speaking is called Mayan. This doctrine is also found in the central and typical image of the Mahayan school of Buddhism (really identical with the doctrine of Shiva and Shakti). A vision of this image will be found in the document entitled "The Lord of Illusion".

The present card endeavours to represent all the above conceptions. Yet no true image is possible at all; for, firstly, all images are necessarily false as such; and, secondly, the motion being perpetual, and its rate that of the limit, c, the rate of Light, any stasis contradicts the idea of the card: this picture is, therefore, hardly more than mnemonic jottings.

Liber Israfel

From *The Equinox,* "Liber Israfel" invokes Thoth (Tahuti), who is often portrayed as having the head of an Ibis.

---

0. The Temple being in darkness, and the Speaker ascended into his place, let him begin by a ritual of the Enterer, as followeth.

1. Procul, O procul este profani.

2. Bahlasti! Ompehda!

3. In the name of the Mighty and Terrible One, I proclaim that I have banished the Shells unto their habitations.

4. I invoke Tahuti, the Lord of Wisdom and of Utterance, the God that cometh forth from the Veil.

5. O Thou! Majesty of Godhead! Wisdom-crowned Tahuti! Lord of the Gates of the Universe! Thee, Thee, I invoke.

O Thou of the Ibis Head! Thee, Thee I invoke.

Thou who wieldest the Wand of Double Power! Thee, Thee I invoke!

Thou who bearest in Thy left hand the Rose and Cross of Light and Life: Thee, Thee, I invoke.

Thou, whose head is as an emerald, and Thy nemmes as the night-sky blue! Thee, Thee I invoke.

Thou, whose skin is of flaming orange as though it burned in a furnace! Thee, Thee I invoke.

6. Behold! I am Yesterday, To-Day, and Brother of To-Morrow! I am born again and again.

Mine is the Unseen Force, whereof the Gods are sprung! Which is as Life unto the Dwellers in the Watch-Towers of the Universe.

I am the Charioteer of the East, Lord of the Past and of the Future.

I see by mine own inward light: Lord of Resurrection; Who cometh forth from the Dusk, and my birth is from the House of Death.

7. O ye two divine Hawks upon your Pinnacles!

Who keep watch over the Universe!

Ye who company the Bier to the House of Rest!

Who pilot the Ship of Ra advancing onwards to the heights of heaven!

Lord of the Shrine which standeth in the Centre of the Earth!

8. Behold, He is in me, and I in Him!

Mine is the Radiance, wherein Ptah floateth over the firmament!

I travel upon high!

I tread upon the firmament of Nu!

I raise a flashing flame, with the lightning of Mine Eye!

Ever rushing on, in the splendour of the daily glorified Ra: giving my life to the Dwellers of Earth.

9. If I say "Come up upon the mountains!" the Celestial Waters shall flow at my Word.

For I am Ra incarnate!

Khephra created in the Flesh!

I am the Eidolon of my father Tmu, Lord of the City of the Sun!

10. The God who commands is in my mouth!

The God of Wisdom is in my Heart!

My tongue is the Sanctuary of Truth!

And a God sitteth upon my lips.

11. My Word is accomplished every day!

And the desire of my heart realises itself, as that of Ptah when He createth his works!

I am Eternal; therefore all things are as my designs; therefore do all things obey my Word.

12. Therefore do Thou come forth unto me from Thine abode in the Silence: Unutterable Wisdom! All-Light! All-Power!

Thoth! Hermes! Mercury! Odin!

By whatever name I call Thee, Thou art still nameless to Eternity: Come Thou forth, I say, and aid and guard me in this work of Art.

13. Thou, Star of the East, that didst conduct the Magi!

Thou art The Same all-present in Heaven and in Hell!

Thou that vibratest between the Light and the Darkness!

Rising, descending! Changing ever, yet ever The Same!

The Sun is Thy Father!

Thy Mother the Moon!

The Wind hath borne Thee in its bosom; and Earth hath ever nourished the changeless Godhead of Thy Youth!

14. Come Thou forth, I say, come Thou forth!
And make all Spirits subject unto Me:
So that every Spirit of the Firmament
And of the Ether,
Upon the Earth,
And under the Earth,
On dry land
And in the Water,
Of whirling Air
And of rushing Fire,
And every Spell and Scourge of God the Vast One, may be obedient unto Me!

15. I invoke the Priestess of the Silver Star, Asi the Curved One, by the ritual of Silence.

16. I make open the gate of Bliss; I descend from the Palace of the Stars; I greet you, I embrace you, O children of earth, that are gathered together in the Hall of Darkness.

17. (A pause.)

18. The Speech in the Silence.

The Words against the Son of Night.

The Voice of Tahuti in the Universe in the Presence of the Eternal.

The Formulas of Knowledge.

The Wisdom of Breath.

The Root of Vibration.

The Shaking of the Invisible.

The Rolling Asunder of the Darkness.

The Becoming Visible of Matter.

The Piercing of the Scales of the Crocodile.

The Breaking Forth of the Light!

19. (Follows the Lection.)

20. There is an end of the speech; let the Silence of darkness be broken; let it return into the silence of light.

21. The speaker silently departs; the listeners disperse unto their homes; yea, they disperse unto their homes.

The Principles of Ritual

*From Magick in Theory and Practice, "The Principles of Ritual"
describes the three theories of invocation, and sides with the "aesthet-
ics" of "drama."*

There is a single main definition of the object of all magical
Ritual. It is the uniting of the Microcosm with the Macro-
cosm. The Supreme and Complete Ritual is therefore the
Invocation of the Holy Guardian Angel;[1] or, in the language of
Mysticism, Union with God.[2]

All other magical Rituals are particular cases of this general
principle, and the only excuse for doing them is that it sometimes
occurs that one particular portion of the microcosm is so weak that
its imperfection of impurity would vitiate the Macrocosm of which it
is the image, Eidolon, or Reflexion. For example, God is above sex;
and therefore neither man nor woman as such can be said fully to
understand, much less to represent, God. It is therefore incumbent
on the male magician to cultivate those female virtues in which he
is deficient, and this task he must of course accomplish without in
any way impairing his virility. It will then be lawful for a magician
to invoke Isis, and identify himself with her; if he fail to do this, his
apprehension of the Universe when he attains Samadhi will lack the
conception of maternity. The result will be a metaphysical and—by
corollary—ethical limitation in the Religion which he founds. Ju-
daism and Islam are striking examples of this failure.

To take another example, the ascetic life which devotion to
magick so often involves argues a poverty of nature, a narrowness,

---

1. See the "Book of the Sacred Magic of Abramelin the Mage"; and Liber 418, 8th
Aethyr, Liber Samekh.
2. The difference between these operations is more of theoretical than of practical
importance.

a lack of generosity. Nature is infinitely prodigal—not one in a million seeds ever comes to fruition. Whoso fails to recognise this, let him invoke Jupiter.[3]

The danger of ceremonial magick—the subtlest and deepest danger—is this: that the magician will naturally tend to invoke that partial being which most strongly appeals to him, so that his natural excess in that direction will be still further exaggerated. **Let him, before beginning his Work, endeavour to map out his own being, and arrange his invocations in such a way as to redress the balance.**[4] This, of course, should have been done in a preliminary fashion during the preparation of the weapons and furniture of the Temple.

To consider in a more particular manner this question of the Nature of Ritual, we may suppose that he finds himself lacking in that perception of the value of Life and Death, alike of individuals and of races, which is characteristic of Nature. He has perhaps a tendency to perceive the 'first noble truth' uttered by Buddha, that Everything is sorrow. Nature, it seems, is a tragedy. He has perhaps even experienced the great trance called Sorrow. He should then consider whether there is not some Deity who expresses this Cycle, and yet whose nature is joy. He will find what he requires in Dionysus.

There are three main methods of invoking any Deity.

The **First Method** consists of devotion to that Deity, and, being mainly mystical in character, need not be dealt with in this place, especially as a perfect instruction exists in Liber 175.

The **Second Method** is the straightforward ceremonial invocation. It is the method which was usually employed in the Middle Ages. Its advantage is its directness, its disadvantage its crudity. The "Goetia" gives clear instruction in this method, and so do many other Rituals, white and black. We shall presently devote some space to a clear exposition of this Art.

In the case of Bacchus, however, we may roughly outline the procedure. We find that the symbolism of Tiphareth expresses the nature of Bacchus. It is then necessary to construct a Ritual of

3. There are much deeper considerations in which it appears that "Everything that is, is right". They are set forth elsewhere; we can only summarise them here by saying that the survival of the fittest is their upshot.
4. The ideal method of doing this is given in Liber 913 (Equinox VII). See also Liber CXI Aleph.

Tiphareth. Let us open the Book 777; we shall find in line 6 of each column the various parts of our required apparatus. Having ordered everything duly, we shall exalt the mind by repeated prayers or conjurations to the highest conception of the God, until, in one sense or another of the word, He appears to us and floods our consciousness with the light of His divinity.

The *Third Method is the Dramatic,* perhaps the most attractive of all; certainly it is so to the artist's temperament, for it appeals to his imagination through his aesthetic sense.

Its disadvantage lies principally in the difficulty of its per-formance by a single person. But it has the sanction of the highest antiquity, and is probably the most useful for the foundation of a religion. It is the method of Catholic Christianity, and consists in the dramatization of the legend of the God. The Bacchae of Eurip-ides is a magnificent example of such a Ritual; so also, though in a less degree, is the Mass. We may also mention many of the degrees in Freemasonry, particularly the Third. The 5° = 6° Ritual pub-lished in N° III of the Equinox is another example.

In the case of Bacchus, one commemorates firstly his birth of a mortal mother who has yielded her treasure-house to the Father of All, of the jealousy and rage excited by this incarnation, and of the heavenly protection afforded to the infant. Next should be commem-orated the journeying westward upon an ass. Now comes the great scene of the drama: the gentle, exquisite youth with his following (chiefly composed of women) seems to threaten the established order of things, and that Established Order takes steps to put an end to the upstart. We find Dionysus confronting the angry King, not with defiance, but with meekness; yet with a subtle confidence, an underlying laughter. His forehead is wreathed with vine tendrils. He is an effeminate figure with those broad leaves clustered upon his brow? But those leaves hide horns. King Pentheus, representa-tive of respectability,[5] is destroyed by his pride. He goes out into the mountains to attack the women who have followed Bacchus, the youth whom he has mocked, scourged, and put in chains, yet who has only smiled; and by those women, in their divine madness, he is torn to pieces.

It has already seemed impertinent to say so much when Walter Pater has told the story with such sympathy and insight. We will

5. There is a much deeper interpretation in which Pentheus is himself "The Dying God". See my "Good Hunting!" and Dr. J. G. Frazer's "Golden Bough".

not further transgress by dwelling upon the identity of this legend with the course of Nature, its madness, its prodigality, its intoxication, its joy, and above all its sublime persistence through the cycles of Life and Death. The pagan reader must labour to understand this in Pater's "Greek Studies", and the Christian reader will recognise it, incident for incident, in the story of Christ. This legend is but the dramatization of Spring.

The magician who wishes to invoke Bacchus by this method must therefore arrange a ceremony in which he takes the part of Bacchus, undergoes all His trials, and emerges triumphant from beyond death. He must, however, be warned against mistaking the symbolism. In this case, for example, the doctrine of individual immortality has been dragged in, to the destruction of truth. It is not that utterly worthless part of man, his individual consciousness as John Smith, which defies death—that consciousness which dies and is reborn in every thought. That which persists (if anything persist) is his real John Smithiness, a quality of which he was probably never conscious in his life.[6.]

Even that does not persist unchanged. It is always growing. The Cross is a barren stick, and the petals of the Rose fall and decay; but in the union of the Cross and the Rose is a constant succession of new lives.[7] Without this union, and without this death of the individual, the cycle would be broken.

A chapter will be consecrated to removing the practical difficulties of this method of Invocation. It will doubtless have been noted by the acumen of the reader that in the great essentials these three methods are one. In each case the magician identifies himself with the Deity invoked. To *invoke* is to *call in,* just as to *evoke* is to *call forth*. This is the essential difference between the two branches of Magick. In invocation, the macrocosm floods the consciousness. In evocation, the magician, having become the macrocosm, creates a microcosm. You *in*voke a God into the Circle. You *e*voke a Spirit into the Triangle. In the first method identity with the God is attained by love and surrender, by giving up or suppressing all irrelevant (and illusionary) parts of yourself. It is the weeding of a garden.

In the second method identity is attained by paying special

6. See "The Book of Lies," Liber 333, for several sermons to this effect. Caps. A, Δ, H, IE, IF, IH, KA, KH, in particular. The reincarnation of the Khu or magical Self is another matter entirely, too abstruse to discuss in this elementary manual.
7. See "The Book of Lies", Liber 333, for several sermons to this effect. The whole theory of Death must be sought in Liber CXI Aleph.

attention to the desired part of yourself: positive, as the first method is negative. It is the potting-out and watering of a particular flower in the garden, and the exposure of it to the sun.

In the third, identity is attained by sympathy. It is very difficult for the ordinary man to lose himself completely in the subject of a play or of a novel; but for those who can do so, this method is unquestionably the best.

Observe: each element in this cycle is of equal value. It is wrong to say triumphantly "Mors janua vitæ", unless you add, with equal triumph, "Vita janua mortis". To one who understands this chain of the Aeons from the point of view alike of the sorrowing Isis and of the triumphant Osiris, not forgetting their link in the destroyer Apophis, there remains no secret veiled in Nature. He cries that name of God which throughout History has been echoed by one religion to another, the infinite swelling paean I.A.O.![8]

---

8. This name, I.A.O. is qabalistically identical with that of THE BEAST and with His number 666, so that he who invokes the former invokes also the latter. Also with AIWAZ and the Number 93.

Liber B vel Magi

The title of this essay can be translated as "The Book of the Magus," the text for the magician who has done everything but give up life itself (and become the "Ipsissimus" referred to in the text). The Magus uses the illusion of the Word to create the illusion of the World. Because he is both Silence and Speech, Truth and Falsehood (see also *The Book of Lies* and my essay "Magick and Lies" in Part V), the "Book" cannot be closed, and can only be sealed in "CHAOS."

---

00. One is the Magus: twain His forces: four His weapons. These are the Seven Spirits of Unrighteousness; seven vultures of evil. Thus is the art and craft of the Magus but glamour. How shall He destroy Himself?

0. Yet the Magus hath power upon the Mother both directly and through Love. And the Magus is Love, and bindeth together That and This in His Conjuration.

1. In the beginning doth the Magus speak Truth, and send forth Illusion and Falsehood to enslave the soul. Yet therein is the Mystery of Redemption.

2. By His Wisdom made He the Worlds; the Word that is God is none other than He.

3. How then shall He end His speech with Silence? For He is Speech.

4. He is the First and the Last. How shall He cease to number Himself?

5. By a Magus is this writing made known through the mind of a Magister. The one uttereth clearly, and the other understandeth; yet the Word is falsehood, and the Understanding darkness. And this saying as Of All Truth.

6. Nevertheless it is written; for there be times of darkness, and this as a lamp therein.

73

7. With the Wand createth He.

8. With the Cup preserveth He.

9. With the Dagger destroyeth He.

10. With the Coin redeemeth He.

11. His weapons fulfil the wheel; and on What Axle that turneth is not known unto Him.

12. From all these actions must He cease before the curse of His Grade is uplifted from Him. Before He attain to That which existeth without Form.

13. And if at this time He be manifested upon earth as a Man, and therefore is this present writing, let this be His method, that the curse of His grade, and the burden of His attainment, be uplifted from Him.

14. Let Him beware of abstinence from action. For the curse of His grade is that He must speak Truth, that the Falsehood thereof may enslave the souls of men. Let Him then utter that without Fear, that the Law may be fulfilled. And according to His Original Nature will that law be shapen, so that one may declare gentleness and quietness, being an Hindu; and another fierceness and servility, being a Jew; and yet another ardour and manliness, being an Arab. Yet this matter toucheth the mystery of Incarnation, and is not here to be declared.

15. Now the grade of a Magister teacheth the Mystery of Sorrow, and the grade of a Magus the Mystery of Change, and the grade of Ipsissimus the Mystery of Selflessness, which is called also the Mystery of Pan.

16. Let the Magus then contemplate each in turn, raising it to the ultimate power of Infinity. Wherein Sorrow is Joy, and Change is Stability, and Selflessness is Self. For the interplay of the parts hath no action upon the whole. And this contemplation shall be performed not by simple meditation—how much less then by reason? but by the method which shall have been given unto Him in His initiation to the Grade.

17. Following which method, it shall be easy for Him to combine that trinity from its elements, and further to combine Sat-Chit-Ananda, and Light, Love, Life, three by three into nine that are one, in which meditation success shall be That which was first adumbrated to Him in the grade of Practicus (which reflecteth Mercury into the lowest world) in *Liber XXVII*, "Here is Nothing under its three Forms."

18. And this is the Opening of the Grade of Ipsissimus, and by the Buddhists it is called the trance Nerodha-Samapatti.

19. And woe, woe, woe, yea woe, and again woe, woe, woe unto seven times be His that preacheth not His law to men!

20. And woe also be unto Him that refuseth the curse of the grade of a Magus, and the burden of the Attainment thereof.

21. And in the word CHAOS let the Book be sealed; yea, let the Book be sealed.

PART II

Yoga and Magick

MAGICK AND TRANSCENDENCE

It is at least theoretically possible to exalt the whole of your own consciousness until it becomes . . . free to move on that exalted plane . . . You should note, by the way, that in this case the postulation of another being is not necessary. There is no way of refuting the solipsism if you feel like that. Personally I cannot accede to its axiom. The evidence for an external universe appears to me perfectly adequate. Still there is no extra charge for thinking on those lines if you so wish.

Magick Without Tears

First Point. The student should first discover for himself the apparent position in his brain where thoughts arise, if there be such a point.

"Liber Turris vel Domus Dei"

Then you shall have to be nailed on a red board with four arms, with a great gold circle in the middle, and that hurts you dreadfully. Then they make you swear the most solemn things that you ever heard of, how you would be faithful to the Fairy Prince, and live for nothing but to know him better and better. So the nails stop hurting, because, of course, I saw that I was really being married, and that this was part of it, and I was as glad as glad . . .

The narrator of "The Wake World," Konx Om Pax

(2) This disgusting worm is great Tao. I humbly beg of your sublime radiance to trample his slave.
(3) Regret great toe unintelligible.
(4) Great Tao—T.A.O.—Tao.
(5) What is the great Tao?
(6) The result of subtracting the universe from itself.

"Thien Tao," Konx Om Pax

We know only one thing only. Absolute existence, absolute motion, absolute direction, absolute simultaneity, absolute truth, all such ideas; they have not, and never can have, any real meaning.

"Liber V vel Reguli"

Buddhism, Mysticism in general, and the specific Buddhist discipline of Yoga complement Magick. Aleister Crowley practiced Yoga and

Magick in equal measure, and together. They follow related paths, though they are often described as different by Crowley. The boundaries of this difference need to be explored, in search of their Transcendence, in the same way that Yoga (and Magick) desire to Transcend all difference. Measured against Crowley's original promise, "We shall bring you to Absolute Truth, Absolute Light, Absolute Bliss."[1]

If Magick means forming the circle—turning the corner on the illusion of creation by confronting the objective world and reuniting its oppositions—then Buddhism forms a half circle and slithers back on itself. It leaves nothing behind, denying the real, denying that anything was created to start. The world is sorrow, this sorrow is wondrous illusion, and this illusion masks unsettled, beatific change. Crowley notes that the formula for Magick reads $1 + [-1] = 0$, a physical clash, while the formula for the religious mystic registers $1 - 1 = 0$, a dissolving of what never existed.[2] In this sense, the path of the mystic is a more convenient one than that of the magician, who grates against the presence of other beings. "The process of dissolution is obviously easier than the shock of worlds which the magician contemplates. 'Sit down, and feel yourself as dust in the presence of God; nay, as less than dust, as nothing', is the all-sufficient simplicity of his method."[3]

Crowley views Buddhism as the necessary response to the relativist impasse of Ontology and Science. Magick openly defies and mocks Science—it is a blatant critique of rationalism and logic. Buddhism, he believes, conforms with everything we scientifically know of the universe, and is "scientifically complete."[4] It dissolves into Science and dissolves Science, Transcending its limitations.

But "Yoga means Union,"[5] and general union unites Buddhism and Magick, collapsing the categories which even Crowley posits into a mutually dissolving relationship resembling "the co-operation of lovers."[6] Even though Crowley felt that "the curve of Magick follows a more pleasant track than that of Yoga,"[7] he sought to demonstrate, by theory and practice, that "the way is open for a reconciliation between these lower elements of thought by virtue of their tendency to flower

1. "Liber Porta Lucis," reprinted in *Gems from the Equinox* (St. Paul: Llewellyn Publications, 1974), p. 654.
2. "The Dangers of Mysticism," reprinted in *Gems from the Equinox*, p. 864.
3. Ibid.
4. *Eight Lectures on Yoga* (reprinted Phoenix: Falcon Press, 1985), p. 72.
5. *Eight Lectures on Yoga*, p. 8.
6. *Eight Lectures on Yoga*, p. 74.
7. *Magick Without Tears* (St. Paul: Llewellyn Publications, 1973), p. 506.

into these higher states beyond thought, in which the two have become one. And that, of course, is Magick; and that, of course is Yoga."[8] Yoga, Crowley felt, enhanced the magical Will, while Magick, in turn, developed the discipline demanded of the yogi while counteracting possible pride. (How can one fall into narcissistic reverie when all around you are spirits, demons, gods?)

Beyond this reciprocal relationship, their similarities are many. For example, in Qabalistic practice, the way of the Middle Pillar of the Tree of Life is the way that balances and combines the three pairs hanging out from the tree: Wisdom and Intelligence, Mercy and Strength, Victory and Splendour. We've seen how Crowley's Qabalah affirms the double gesture of creation and destruction. Just as the way of the Middle Pillar feeds on these extremes and cannot chart its "mild" course independent of these pairs, the Buddha's Middle Path (the Noble Eightfold Path) cannot rely on either the senses or asceticism, but must operate in the space between. Second, the magician's crossing of the abyss that separates the top three Sephiroth from the bottom seven (and the alchemist's conversion of base material into gold) resembles in conception the yogi's transcending of self, "feeling yourself as dust".

Crowley's Buddhism—his Yoga—flaunts the abyss, the between, the paradoxical interchange, but always under the veil of the relative "simplicity" of Transcendence.[9] Asked to state the practice of Yoga in as few words as possible, Crowley said, "Sit still. Stop thinking. Shut up. Get out!"[10] His preliminary steps of Yoga are easily demonstrated, divided into two classes (a division he must eventually overcome). Yama and Niyama are "strategic" reflections on vice and virtue, determining best how to answer *The Book of the Law*'s permissive injunctive, "Do what thou wilt shall be the whole of the law." The more "tactical," physical mechanisms are Asana and Pranayama, posture control/breath control, and Pratyhara and Dharana, inhibition of thought/concentration of thought.[11] Crowley's recommended techniques for deploying these

8. *Eight Lectures on Yoga*, p. 71.
9. *Magick* (reprinted New York: Samuel Weiser, 1974), p. 45.
10. *Eight Lectures on Yoga*, p. 32.
11. These steps are explained in depth in Crowley's two chief Yoga texts: *Book 4*, "Part I" (also included in the volume *Magick*), and *Eight Lectures on Yoga*, written many years apart with some disparity in their formulations. Additionally, "Liber E vel Exercitiorum" gives step-by-step procedures for breath, posture and thought control, and "Liber RV vel Spiritus" particularly concerns breath control. These last named texts and others concerning Yoga are reprinted in *Gems from the Equinox*.

steps are legendary and forthrightly induce great physical and mental pain. Some steps are to be practiced until the aspirant's body is covered with sweat and he cries out in agony. Yama and Niyama involves thinking of yourself as a rotting corpse (Crowley notes that the Buddha taught this as well). The inability to control the mind is self-punishable by a razor slash on the wrists and forearms.

John Symonds, literary executor to Aleister Crowley and author of two books about him, suggests that the most important part of Crowley's life work was bringing Eastern religious practice to the West in such a tangible and pragmatic form. What Symonds misses is past this point—where Crowleyan Buddhism and Yoga take on Magick's matters. This Yoga is never as simple as it threatens to become, when it threatens to be.

Demonstration of this is found in the next two stages in Yoga, Dyhana and Samadhi. Crowley describes them as the transcending of the Self—"the annihilation of the Ego"[12]—through the union of the subject and the object (the seer and seen) and all conditions governing them. Razor cuts, rotting bodies, images of death and decay all serve as ways to distance oneself from Self. "Look at the passages in the Holy Books which speak of the action of the spirit under the figure of a deadly poison. For to each individual thing attainment means first and foremost the destruction of the individuality."[13] In the trance state of Dyhana the subject and object become one, while in later Samadhi one feels these same "things rushed together."[14]

When this happens, no Speech is possible. "Be done with speech, O God!"[15] "So that my mind and my body were healed of their disease, self-knowledge."[16] Crowley has come back from this other side, from the place of no place without Self and subject, but he cannot accurately describe it to us. "It is indescribable even by the masters of language."[17] The experience, he says, is beyond speech. "Even when one has become accustomed to Dyhana by constant repetition, no words seem adequate."[18] Out of this inability, he resorts to linking Yoga to other "experiences," for example, to the tingle of an unknown

---

12. *Magick*, p. 30.
13. *Magick*, p. 79.
14. *Magick*, p. 36.
15. "Liber Liberi vel Lapidis Lazuli," reprinted in *The Holy Books of Thelema* (York Beach, Maine: Samuel Weiser, 1983), p. 21.
16. "Liber Liberi vel Lapidis Lazuli," p. 22.
17. *Magick*, p. 29.
18. Ibid.

book's "internal sensation," its "meaning unexpressed in any form."[19] Again, not surprisingly, the words of this particular book would only confuse the issue. "An end to the letters of the words! An end to the sevenfold speech."[20]

But here he has already introduced the first of many metaphors about Yoga. That of which Crowley cannot speak must, it seems, continue to be said. "Let it be clearly understood that something unexpected is about to be described."[21] As with Magick, Crowley has greater faith in the ability of "the aesthetic method" than in pure description. Some of the Holy Books, for example, poetically describe Transcendence. He also specifically compares Dhyanic and Samadhic trances to the experience of dreams (and he suggests meditating on dreams), intoxication (the person who returns from Dyhana to speak of it appears intoxicated to the rest of the world), and madness. "Only madness, divine madness, offers an issue."[22] At the moment the yogi transcends, "then will all phenomena which present themselves to him appear meaningless and disconnected, and his own Ego will break up into a series of impressions having no relation one with the other, or with any other thing. Let this state then become so acute that it is in truth Insanity. . . ."[23] so that "Attainment *is* insanity."[24] Madness and dreams: (in) exactly those states which have no place in the union, in the thinking of union—which cannot be "experienced" so much as lived. To describe the Transcendence of the Ego as a kind of insanity is to attempt to lock up that which, because it is mad, cannot be held in check.

Crowley aligns Yoga with the project of Science—its "method and research"[25]—in particular the philosophy-sciences of his day, not only ontologies, but the practical sciences as well. "In all Trances of importance . . . the Postulant should have acquired the greatest possible knowledge and Understanding of the Universe properly so called. His rational mind should have been trained thoroughly in

19. *Magick*, p. 37.
20. "Liber Liberi vel Lapidis Lazuli," p. 33.
21. *Magick*, p. 29.
22. *The Book of Thoth (Egyptian Tarot)* (reprinted New York: U. S. Game Systems, Inc., 1979), p. 57.
23. "Liber Os Abysmi vel Daath," reprinted in *Gems from the Equinox*, p. 244.
24. *The Magical Record of the Beast 666: The Journals of Aleister Crowley* (Quebec: Next Step Publications, 1972), p. 86
25. "Science and Buddhism," *Collected Works of Aleister Crowley, Volume II* (reprinted Yogi Publication Society, no place of origin/pub. date), p. 258.

intellectual apprehension: that is, he should be familiar with all Science."[26] Beyond that, Yoga "speaks" in the language of Science. Crowley speaks of Yoga scientifically. "For in the uniting of elements of opposite polarities is there a glory of heat, of light, and of electricity."[27] Heat, light, electricity, and gas. "Body and mind, in the widest sense, are the obstacles in the Path of the Wise: the paradox, tragic enough as it seems, is that they are also the means of progress. How to get rid of them, to pass beyond or to transcend them, is the problem, and this is as strictly practical and scientific as that of eliminating impurities from a gas, or of adroitly using mechanical laws."[28] Fuels, vehicles of Energy, Energy to Transcend. "If only that furnace be of transcendent heat."[29]

Crowley cannot speak of the loss, the union, the Transcendence, which is why he resorts to these metaphors—and he must. Since Science and Philosophy are branches of Knowledge that incessantly think, that can never turn off the mental tap, they might at first seem to ground these electrical discharges too greatly. (For example, at one point Crowley discusses the possibility that the "spasm" of Dhyana and Samadhi is nothing but the bursting of a small, over-excited blood vessel in the brain.) But even the metaphors of Science are as lost as loss, as union, as Transcendence, because we are lost to Science. "[We are] in much the same position as the electricians of a generation ago in respect of their science. We are assured of the immensity of the force at our disposal; we perceive the extent of the empire which it offers us, but we do not thoroughly understand even our successes and are uncertain how to proceed in order to generate the energy most efficiently or to apply it most accurately to our purposes."[30] In other words, if Science is as (un)scientific as Yoga, as Crowley presumes, there should be a problem: how can Science hope to explain the unexplainable, Yoga? "I have my own personal impressions of the act of telephoning; but I cannot be aware of what consciousness, electricity, mechanics, sound, etc., actually are in themselves. And although I can appeal to experience to lay down 'laws' as to what conditions

26. "Wonder," *Little Essays Toward Truth* (Malton, Canada: Dove Press, approximately 1970), p. 19.
27. "De Lege Lebellum," reprinted in *Gems from the Equinox*, p. 119.
28. "Trance," *Little Essays Toward Truth*, p. 41.
29. "Liber Porta Lucis," p. 655.
30. *The Confessions of Aleister Crowley* (New York: Hill and Wang, 1970), pp. 703–704.

accompany the act, I can never be sure that they have always been, or ever will again be, identical."[31]

As is typical with Crowley, that which seems grounded always rests on a trap door, preventing replication of Science's and Yoga's little experiments. Rational Science, to which he often appeals, is a perceptual "illusion," like information gleaned by looking through a telescope, yet it is "correct" for all that.[32] In fact, the Science to which Crowley appeals in his essay "Science and Buddhism" appears to be about the limits of perception—of Veils, of Illusions, of "the Mystery of the Laws."[33] He puts faith in a fourth dimension that might lead the way to these "furrin parts," yet which also might remain incomprehensible and inconceivable.[34] Always hidden is the total understanding that would be Transcendence itself. "The truth of the matter appears to be that as reason is incompetent to solve the problems of philosophy and religion, *a fortiori* science is incompetent."[35] Yet Science works for Crowley as metaphor; he utilizes this paradox of the rational illusion—the invalid metaphor of Science—to leap over the physical world into Yoga.

Until now Crowley has spoken nothing but gibberish when it comes to Yoga and Trances. All of his attempted explanations of Transcendence result in metaphors set loose like helium balloons. He needs to speak a word heavier than Science, a word of which he barely or rarely speaks in the presence of Yoga: Death. A meta-metaphor to avoid at all costs, a place where Science comes up short, gets planted in the ground six feet deep. Perfect ontological knowledge might only be found, if at all, at the very threshold of Death. Crowley compares the catastrophic Samadhi to "the first death among the people that one loves."[36] And as far as Yoga goes, the ultimate loss of Self (the ultimate Union of Subject and Object) must be one's own Death. "Death is the crown of all."[37] Death is a sovereign threshold of consciousness which, once crossed, cannot be recrossed. The Self will not return to write Essays about the experience.

31. *Magick*, p. 204.
32. "Knowledge," *Little Essays Toward Truth*, p. 53.
33. *Liber Aleph vel CXI: The Book of Wisdom and Folly* (reprinted Seattle: Aeon Press, 1985), p. 78.
34. *Magick Without Tears*, p. 240.
35. "Epilogue and Dedication of Volumes I., II., III.: Eleusis," *Collected Works of Aleister Crowley, Volume III*, p. 228.
36. *Magick*, p. 32.
37. *Liber AL: The Book of the Law* (reprinted Berkeley: O.T.O., 1982), Section II, Verse 72.

Yoga plays at Death, feigns the End in its Samadhic spasm of metaphor. And so the loss of Self is described by Crowley violently. "He [the magical yogi] must develop in himself a Will of Destruction, even a Will of Annihilation."[38] In the words of Crowleyan Science, it is a "Storm,"[39] a "Catastrophe,"[40] an "Explosion,"[41] a "Combustion."[42] The violence of Science, the Scientific bombing.

Within the Samadhic sensation are two further gradations of Trance, according to Crowley. First is Atmadarshana, which involves forms, ideas, conceptions "destroyed"[43], and for which he can find no simile (though with "destruction" he already has, and will again with "the universal blaze is darkness"[44]). Second is Shivadarshana, the "destruction" and "annihilation" of Atmadarshana[45] (which again Crowley describes through a host of analogies).

Even after the bombing, Crowley continues to speak, because there is still so much left to destroy, so many metaphors left to approach Death, because he is not yet Dead. Dhyanic Transcendence (the very idea of it) must be followed by its destruction in Samadhi, then the Samadhic idea's destruction in Atmadarshana, and Atmadarshana's destruction in Shivadarshana. When will this chain reaction end? "The adept was rapt away in bliss, and the beyond of bliss, and exceeded the excess of excess."[46] And even so, given that he is on the verge of Death and that he can't telephone or send electrical signals from the grave, "we have tried to say as little as possible rather than as much as possible."[47]

In this excessive destruction, simultaneous with the Transcendence of time and space, simultaneous with the yogi's "Death," Crowley states that something "critical" appears, something Speakable, something that obviously does not Transcend because he continues to speak so much about so little. That therefore reduces the spasm to a quasi-spasm. "All Trances of Samadhic intensity are in a sense timeless; but it may be said that most of them are marked by well-defined issues of a critical character. That is, the entry to each is

38. "Liber Turris vel Domus Dei," reprinted in *Gems from the Equinox*, p. 228.
39. *Magick*, p. 37.
40. "Dedication and Counter-Dedication," *Konx Om Pax* (reprinted Yogi Publication society, no place of origin/pub. date), p. x.
41. "Energized Enthusiasm," reprinted in *Gems from the Equinox*, p. 639.
42. "Liber Samekh Theurgia Goetia Summa Congressus Cun Daemone," reprinted in *Gems from the Equinox*, p. 347.
43. *Magick*, p. 39.
44. *Magick*, p. 40.
45. *Magick*, p. 39.
46. "Liber Cordis Cincti Serpente," reprinted in *The Holy Books of Thelema*, p. 62.
47. *Magick*, p. 40.

quasispasmodic."[48] Yoga is the Knowing of (the Impossibility of) Spasm, of Transcendence, of the Critical Thinking of Death in Life. Crowley notes in his *Confessions* that in order to achieve Samadhi one has to understand what one is getting. "In this view Dhyana would be rather like an explosion of gunpowder carelessly mixed; most of it goes off with a bang, but there is some debris of the original components."[49] And one can speak of Samadhi only from the speech of memory, and it can be explained only "so far as I can see"[50]; its results are "refracted through diverse media."[51]

At this point where Speech intersects Yoga, in the Writing of the Medium—as it has been Written all along in grave and scientific reporting of technique and results, in Crowley's Writings, another explosion takes place. An explosion when "the Absolute can only express itself through the Relative."[52] That brings then both Speech and Yoga to the brink that Breaks. And Breaks, according to Crowley, are interruptions in the meditation, classified as (a) immediate physical sensations, (b) events prior to meditation, that now break into the yogi's thought, (c) "day-dreams," (d) the thought, "How well I am doing it!,"(e) auditory "atmospherics," described as "odd sentences or fragments of sentences" in the air, and (f) *the desired result itself.*"[53] Transcendence breaks when one thinks about the nearness of Transcendence. Transcendence breaks when one perceives the word and the sentence. Finally, Transcendence breaks when one Transcends, since as soon as the yogi who is in Life Transcends, he knows it (he knows he is not Dead). Or he knows it as soon as he returns to Life (which he must), and so he has not Transcended, because he felt it was only always (painfully) near (or separate) and because this sensation can only be formulated within Self-Language. "Burn up thyself within thy Self."[54] At the risk of pounding a Word to Nothing, in Crowley's broken Yoga, to Transcend is not to Transcend, but to perhaps conduct an "interrogation"[55] in broken English concerning this Transcendence which can never be Transcendence. It can only be the Words of Transcendence in need of Transcendence by more Words of Transcendence. Always within, incomplete.

48. "Beatitude," *Little Essays Toward Truth*, p. 24.
49. *Eight Lectures on Yoga*, pp. 47–48.
50. *Magick*, p. 37
51. *Magick*, p. 36.
52. *The Magical Record of the Beast 666: The Journals of Aleister Crowley*, p. 86.
53. *Magick*, p. 27.
54. *Liber Aleph vel CXI: The Book of Wisdom or Folly*, p. 50.
55. *Magick*, p. 32

And where the impossibility of the Speech meets the inevitability of Speech, always already, where the Speech of Transcendence meets the impossibility of its Speech ("Our very speech almost compels us to think of the Universe in this way"[56]), Yoga starts to look like a piece of Swiss cheese, as Crowley actually suggests[57]. It is like holes held together by electrical current in the air. In *The Book of Lies*, Crowley admits that at the end of Samadhi he finds himself no closer to knowing what has been "chewed up" in the blitzkrieg. "The one of which I am most certain . . . [is that gourmet food] destroys the digestion."[58] And after swallowing one more metaphor, a digestion digression, it would still be further to say "whether this is the ultimate attainment," or even "what it confers."[59] As Crowley reported his visions in the desert, "This lands us in the quagmire of zigzagginess."[60]

Using a metaphor that Crowley was extremely fond of, that of the SunSponge (which, by the way, came to him in a dream), the Universe resembles an infinite space twinkling with innumerable bright spots—thoughts and ideas, subjects and objects. The stars begin to fill this space; an infinite series of stars spread across the sky. But even when the infinite space is completely ablaze with light, when stars crowd the sky, the distinction between them remains somehow intact. "I am unable to say at what period it may be called complete."[61] Even the Transcendence of separateness leaves gaps. The impossible union of space and star explodes the explosion/union of the World and the Self, and Language escapes through the twists and tunnels.

"The aspirant . . . may leap forth upon It [the Universe] with the massed violence of his Self, and destroying both these, become that Unity whose name is No Thing."[62] After the explosion of his Universe, his name, his Self, there is always another name. Even Nothing is named—outside pure Transcendence. What's left? To marshall "all the force won by its old woe and stress in now annihilating Nothingness"?[63] "I fully understand how necessary is the final renunciation of Buddha;

56. *The Confessions of Aleister Crowley*, p. 256.
57. *Eight Lectures on Yoga*, p. 9.
58. *The Book of Lies* (reprinted New York: Samuel Weiser, 1978), p. 104.
59. *Magick*, p. 40.
60. *The Vision and the Voice* (reprinted Dallas: Sangreal Foundation, Inc., 1972), p. 82.
61. Eight Lectures on Yoga, p. 56.
62. "De Lege Lebellum," p. 120.
63. *The Book of Lies*, p. 174.

though renunciation is an absurd term, in the case. The problem is, however, whether this renunciation is possible, whether there is or can be, any kind of Nothing which does not contain the necessity of creation within itself."[64] And "though ye treasure in your heart the sacred word that is the last lever of the key to the little door beyond the abyss, yet ye gloss and comment thereupon; for the light itself is but illusion."[65] Beyond the abyss is another word, another "gloss" on experience.

This is Crowleyan Schizophrenia—"a lovely word"[66]—where he falls into a Trance as he inhales and out while he exhales, where he can lose sense of his right hand while he writes with his left. Where with one side of his brain Crowley calls Yoga the partner of Magick, and with the other admits that "Buddhism had got on my nerves."[67] His "I" has become transitory, a face that he wears when he wishes, and meditates away. And the furnace that burns is also a "furnace of ecstasy"[68], where in "one" can achieve the Transcendence of consciousness, and the consciousness of Transcendence. "We are to unite . . . and then annihilate both the party of the first part aforesaid and the party of the second part aforesaid. This evidently results in further parties—one might almost say cocktail parties—constantly increasing until we reach infinity. . . ."[69]

Yoga pushes the button, sets off the infinity of (non)explosive mushrooms (as metaphor) as a sign that "I am tearing at nothing. I will not heed. For even this dust must be consumed with fire."[70] And Crowley finds that "the Word is broken up. There is Knowledge. Knowledge is Relation. These fragments are Creation. The broken manifests Light."[71] The broken is Light, the Breaks are Transcendence. Crowley rashly thinks of not thinking, though "there is . . . no true antithesis between the conditions of Trance and those of ratiocination and perception."[72] This mushrooming too seems Magick, but also, "it is Nirvana, only dynamic instead of static—and this comes to the same

64. *The Magical Record of the Beast 666: The Journals of Aleister Crowley*, p. 132.
65. *The Vision and the Voice*, p. 47.
66. *Eight Lectures on Yoga*, p. 12.
67. *The Confessions of Aleister Crowley*, p. 256.
68. *Eight Lectures on Yoga*, pp. 12–13.
69. *Eight Lectures on Yoga*, p. 31.
70. *The Vision and the Voice*, p. 233.
71. *The Book of Lies*, p. 10.
72. "Trance," p. 42.

thing in the end."[73] In the end: Death in Life, Life in Death. "As it is written 'Kill thyself' and again 'Die daily'."[74]

At the limit of Transcendence—when "to pass beyond" in life turns into another set of Words with which to chart the boundaries of desire— Death becomes the border of Universe and Self, and the infinite party and play of the Language of Death becomes the source of perpetual chaotic motion. "How then shall He end His Speech with Silence? For He is Speech. He is the First and the Last. How shall He cease to number Himself?"[75] Samadhi, that which rushes together and explodes in Death, is also the "Pylon of the Temple"[76], that which stabilizes in Life.

With the acknowledgement of such metaphors, "his experiences will no more be regarded as catastrophic."[77] Instead of the catastrophe of death, there is the catastrophe of metaphor and interpretation. "The divine consciousness is such that I could write endless books upon the meaning of any single word. . . . In the beginning it is nice to find the difficult word explained by three or four easy ones; but as soon as the analysis goes deeper, one is up against *obscurum per obscurius* . . . ('to explain the obscure by the more obscure', a phrase which the alchemists used about themselves) . . . every time. All one's progressions add alike to infinity."[78] "What then am I? I am a transient Effect of infinite Causes, a Child of Changes. . . . Contemplate the play of Illusion by thine Instrument of Mind and Sense, leaving it without Care to continue its own Path of Change."[79]

"Let the Invisible inform all the devouring Light of its disruptive vigour!"[80] "So that the stable was shaken and the unstable became still."[81] "The One Thought vanished; all my mind was torn to rags:— nay! nay! my head was mashed into wood pulp, and thereon the Daily Newspaper was printed."[82]

73. "Liber II," reprinted in *The Equinox, Volume III, Number 10* (New York: Thelema Publications, 1986), p. 10.
74. "De Lege Lebellum," p. 128.
75. "Liber B vel Magi," reprinted in *Gems from the Equinox*, p. 647.
76. *Liber Aleph vel CXI: The Book of Wisdom or Folly*, p. 77.
77. "Liber Samekh Theurgia Goetia Summa Congressus Cum Daemone," p. 335.
78. *The Magical Record of the Beast 666: The Journals of Aleister Crowley*, p. 106.
79. *Liber Aleph vel CXI: The Book of Wisdom or Folly*, pp. 93–94.
80. "Liber Liberi vel Lapidis Lazuli," p. 31.
81. "Liber Cordis Cincti Serpente," p. 79.
82. *The Book of Lies*, p. 120.

Yoga for Yahoos. First Lecture:
First Principles

Taken from a series of *Eight Lectures on Yoga* given in London in 1939, "First Principles" begins by simplifying the goal ("Yoga means union") and ends by saying that this "absolute," on the far side of annihilation, will undergo continuous modification, and that the problems will be "of attention, of investigation, of reflexion."

Do what thou wilt shall be the whole of the Law.

It is my will to explain the subject of Yoga in clear language, without resort to jargon or the enunciation of fantastic hypotheses, in order that this great science may be thoroughly understood as of universal importance.

For, like all great things, it is simple; but, like all great things, it is masked by confused thinking; and, only too often, brought into contempt by the machinations of knavery.

(1) There is more nonsense talked and written about Yoga than anything else in the world. Most of this nonsense, which is fostered by charlatans, is based upon the idea that there is something mysterious and Oriental about it. There isn't. Do not look to me for obelisks and odalisques, Rahat Loucoum, bul-buls, or any other tinsel imagery of the Yoga-mongers. I am neat but not gaudy. There is nothing mysterious or Oriental about anything, as everybody knows who spent a little time intelligently in the continents of Asia and Africa. I propose to invoke the most remote and elusive of all Gods to throw clear light upon the subject—the light of common sense.

(2) All phenomena of which we are aware take place in our own minds, and therefore the only thing we have to look at is the mind; which is a more constant quantity over all the species of humanity than is generally supposed. What appear to be radical differences,

91

irreconcilable by argument, are usually found to be due to the obstinacy of habit produced by generations of systematic sectarian training.

(3) We must then begin the study of Yoga by looking at the meaning of the word. It means Union, from the same Sanskrit root as the Greek word Zeugma, the Latin word Jugum, and the English word yoke. (✔ Yeug—to join.)

When a dancing girl is dedicated to the service of a temple there is a Yoga of her relations to celebrate. Yoga, in short, may be translated "tea fight," which doubtless accounts for the fact that all the students of Yoga in England do nothing but gossip over endless libations of Lyons' 1s. 2d.

(4) Yoga means Union.

In what sense are we to consider this? How is the word Yoga to imply a system of religious training or a description of religious experience?

You may note incidentally that the word Religion is really identifiable with Yoga. It means a binding together.

(5) Yoga means Union.

What are the elements which are united or to be united when this word is used in its common sense of a practice widely spread in Hindustan whose object is the emancipation of the individual who studies and practises it from the less pleasing features of his life on this planet?

I say Hindustan, but I really mean anywhere on the earth; for research has shown that similar methods producing similar results are to be found in every country. The details vary, but the general structure is the same. Because all bodies, and so all minds, have identical Forms.

(6) Yoga means Union.

In the mind of a pious person, the inferiority complex which accounts for his piety compels him to interpret this emancipation as union with the gaseous vertebrate whom he has invented and called God. On the cloudy vapour of his fears his imagination has thrown a vast distorted shadow of himself, and he is duly terrified; and the more he cringes before it, the more the spectre seems to stoop to crush him. People with these ideas will never get to anywhere but Lunatic Asylums and Churches.

It is because of this overwhelming miasma of fear that the whole subject of Yoga has become obscure. A perfectly simple problem has been complicated by the most abject ethical and superstitious nonsense. Yet all the time the truth is patent in the word itself.

(7) Yoga means Union.

We may now consider what Yoga really is. Let us go for a moment into the nature of consciousness with the tail of an eye on such sciences as mathematics, biology, and chemistry.

In mathematics the expression a plus b plus c is a triviality. Write a plus b plus c equals 0, and you obtain an equation from which the most glorious truths may be developed.

In biology the cell divides endlessly, but never becomes anything different; but if we unite cells of opposite qualities, male and female, we lay the foundations of a structure whose summit is unattainably fixed in the heavens of imagination.

Similar facts occur in chemistry. The atom by itself has few constant qualities, none of them particularly significant; but as soon as an element combines with the object of its hunger we get not only the ecstatic production of light, heat, and so forth, but a more complex structure having few or none of the qualities of its elements, but capable of further combination into complexities of astonishing sublimity. All these combinations, these unions, are Yoga.

(8) Yoga means Union.

How are we to apply this word to the phenomena of mind?

What is the first characteristic of everything in thought? How did it come to be a thought at all? Only by making a distinction between it and the rest of the world.

The first proposition, the type of all propositions, is: S is P. There must be two things—different things—whose relation forms knowledge.

Yoga is first of all the union of the subject and object of consciousness: of the seer with the thing seen.

(9) Now, there is nothing strange or wonderful about all this. The study of the principles of Yoga is very useful to the average man, if only to make him think about the nature of the world as he supposes that he knows it.

Let us consider a piece of cheese. We say that this has certain qualities, shape, structure, colour, solidity, weight, taste, smell, consistency and the rest; but investigation has shown that this is all illusory. Where are these qualities? Not in the cheese, for different observers give quite different accounts of it. Not in ourselves, for we do not perceive them in the absence of the cheese. All "material things," all impressions, are phantoms.

In reality the cheese is nothing but a series of electric charges. Even the most fundamental quality of all, mass, has been found not to exist. The same is true of the matter in our brains which is partly responsible for these perceptions. What then are these qualities of which we are all so sure? They would not exist without our brains; they would not exist without the cheese. They are the results of the union, that is of the Yoga, of the seer and the seen, of subject and object in consciousness as the philosophical phrase goes. They have no material existence; they are only names given to the ecstatic results of this particular form of Yoga.

(10) I think that nothing can be more helpful to the student of Yoga than to get the above proposition firmly established in his subconscious mind. About nine-tenths of the trouble in understanding the subject is all this ballyhoo about Yoga being mysterious and Oriental. The principles of Yoga, and the spiritual results of Yoga, are demonstrated in every conscious and unconscious happening. This is that which is written in *The Book of the Law*—Love is the law, love under will—for Love is the instinct to unite, and the act of uniting. But this cannot be done indiscriminately, it must be done "under will," that is, in accordance with the nature of the particular units concerned. Hydrogen has no love for Hydrogen; it is not the nature, or the "true Will" of Hydrogen to seek to unite with a molecule of its own kind. Add Hydrogen to Hydrogen: nothing happens to its quality: it is only its quantity that changes. It rather seeks to enlarge its experience of its possibilities by union with atoms of opposite character, such as Oxygen; with this it combines (with an explosion of light, heat, and sound) to form water. The result is entirely different from either of the component elements, and has another kind of "true Will," such as to unite (with similar disengagement of light and heat) with Potassium, while the resulting "caustic Potash" has in its turn a totally new series of qualities, with still another "true Will" of its own; that is, to unite explosively with acids. And so on.

(11) It may seem to some of you that these explanations have rather knocked the bottom out of Yoga; that I have reduced it to the category of common things. That was my object. There is no sense in being frightened of Yoga, awed by Yoga, muddled and mystified by Yoga, or enthusiastic over Yoga. If we are to make any progress

in its study, we need clear heads and the impersonal scientific attitude. It is especially important not to bedevil ourselves with Oriental jargon. We may have to use a few Sanskrit words; but that is only because they have no English equivalents; and any attempt to translate them burdens us with the connotations of the existing English words which we employ. However, these words are very few; and, if the definitions which I propose to give you are carefully studied, they should present no difficulty.

(12) Having now understood that Yoga is the essence of all phenomena whatsoever, we may ask what is the special meaning of the word in respect of our proposed investigation, since the process and the results are familiar to every one of us; so familiar indeed that there is actually nothing else at all of which we have any knowledge. It *is* knowledge.

What is it we are going to study, and why should we study it?

(13) The answer is very simple.

All this Yoga that we know and practice, this Yoga that produced these ecstatic results that we call phenomena, includes among its spiritual emanations a good deal of unpleasantness. The more we study this universe produced by our Yoga, the more we collect and synthesize our experience, the nearer we get to a perception of what Buddha declared to be characteristic of all component things: Sorrow, Change, and Absence of any permanent principle. We constantly approach his enunciation of the first two "Noble Truths," as he called them. "Everything is Sorrow"; and "The cause of Sorrow is Desire." By the word 'Desire' he meant exactly what is meant by 'Love' in *The Book of the Law* which I quoted a few moments ago. 'Desire' is the need of every unit to extend its experience by combining with its opposite.

(14) It is easy enough to construct the whole series of arguments which lead up to the first "Noble Truth."

Every operation of Love is the satisfaction of a bitter hunger, but the appetite only grows fiercer by satisfaction; so that we can say with the Preacher: "He that increaseth knowledge increaseth Sorrow." The root of all this sorrow is in the sense of insufficiency; the need to unite, to lose oneself in the beloved object, is the manifest proof of this fact, and it is clear also that the satisfaction produces only a temporary relief, because the process expands indefinitely. The thirst increases with drinking. The only complete satisfaction conceivable would be the Yoga of the atom with the entire universe. This fact is easily perceived, and has been constantly expressed in the mystical philosophies of the West; the only goal is "Union with God." Of course, we only use the word 'God' because we have been brought up in superstition, and the higher philosophers both in the East and in the West have preferred to speak of union with the All or with the Absolute. More superstitions!

(15) Very well, then, there is no difficulty at all; since every thought in our being, every cell in our bodies, every electron and proton of our atoms, is nothing but Yoga and the result of Yoga. All we have to do to obtain emancipation, satisfaction, everything we want is to perform this universal and inevitable operation upon the Absolute itself. Some of the more sophisticated members of my audience may possibly be thinking that there is a catch in it somewhere. They are perfectly right.

(16) The snag is simply this. Every element of which we are composed is indeed constantly occupied in the satisfaction of its particular needs by its own particular Yoga; but for that very reason it is completely obsessed by its own function, which it must naturally consider as the Be-All and End-all of its existence. For instance, if you take a glass tube open at both ends and put it over a bee on the window-pane it will continue beating against the window to the point of exhaustion and death, instead of escaping through the tube. We must not confuse the necessary automatic functioning of any of our elements with the true Will which is the proper orbit of any star. A human being only acts as a unit at all because of countless generations of training. Evolutionary processes have set up a higher order of Yogic action by which we have managed to subordinate what we consider particular interests to what we consider the general welfare. We are communities; and our well-being depends upon the wisdom of our Councils, and the discipline with which their decisions are enforced. The more complicated we are, the higher we are in the scale of evolution, the more complex and difficult is the task of legislation and of maintaining order.

(17) In highly civilised communities like our own (*loud laughter*), the individual is constantly being attacked by conflicting interests and necessities; his individuality is constantly being assailed by the impact of other people; and in a very large number of cases he is unable to stand up to the strain. "Schizophrenia," which is a lovely word, and may or may not be found in your dictionary, is an

exceedingly common complaint. It means the splitting up of the mind. In extreme cases we get the phenomena of multiple personality, Jekyll and Hyde, only more so. At the best, when a man says "I" he refers only to a transitory phenomenon. His "I" changes as he utters the word. But—philosophy apart—it is rarer and rarer to find a man with a mind of his own and a will of his own, even in this modified sense.

(18) I want you therefore to see the nature of the obstacles to union with the Absolute. For one thing, the Yoga which we constantly practice has not invariable results; there is a question of attention, of investigation, of reflexion. I propose to deal in a future instruction with the modifications of our perception thus caused, for they are of great importance to our science of Yoga. For example, the classical case of the two men lost in a thick wood at night. One says to the other: "That dog barking is not a grasshopper; it is the creaking of a cart." Or again, "He thought he saw a banker's clerk descending from a 'bus. He looked again, and saw it was a hippopotamus."

Everyone who has done any scientific investigation knows painfully how every observation must be corrected again and again. The need of Yoga is so bitter that it blinds us. We are constantly tempted to see and hear what we want to see and hear.

(19) It is therefore incumbent upon us, if we wish to make the universal and final Yoga with the Absolute, to master every element of our being, to protect it against all civil and external war, to intensify every faculty to the utmost, to train ourselves in knowledge and power to the utmost; so that at the proper moment we may be in perfect condition to fling ourselves up into the furnace of ecstasy which flames from the abyss of annihilation.

Love is the law, love under will.

Dhyana

This and the following piece, "Samadhi," are both from *Book 4*. As is typically the case with Crowley, his skepticism toward his own formulations of Dhyana lies just below the surface of this carefully worded text: "Dhyana may be false; but, if so, so is everything else."

This word has two quite distinct and mutually exclusive meanings. The first refers to the result itself. Dhyana is the same word as the Pali "Jhana." The Buddha counted eight Jhanas, which are evidently different degrees and kinds of trance. The Hindu also speaks of Dhyana as a lesser form of Samadhi. Others, however, treat it as if it were merely an intensification of Dharana. Patanjali says: "Dharana is holding the mind on to some particular object. An unbroken flow of knowledge in that subject is Dhyana. When that, giving up all forms, reflects only the meaning, it is Samadhi." He combines these three into Samyama.

We shall treat of Dhyana as a result rather than a method. Up to this point ancient authorities have been fairly reliable guides, except with regard to their crabbed ethics; but when they get on the subject of results of meditation, they completely lose their heads.

They exhaust the possibilities of poetry to declare what is demonstrably untrue. For example, we find in the Shiva Sanhita that "he who daily contemplates on this lotus of the heart is eagerly desired by the daughters of Gods, has clairaudience, clairvoyance, and can walk in the air." Another person "can make gold, discover medicine for disease, and see hidden treasures." All this is filth. What is the curse upon religion that its tenets must always be associated with every kind of extravagance and falsehood?

There is one exception; it is the A∴A∴, whose members are extremely careful to make no statement at all that cannot be verified in the usual manner; or where this is not easy, at least avoid

98

anything like a dogmatic statement. In Their second book of practical instruction, Liber O, occur these words:

"By doing certain things certain results will follow. Students are most earnestly warned against attributing objective reality or philosophical validity to any of them."

Those golden words!

In discussing Dhyana, then, let it be clearly understood that something unexpected is about to be described.

We shall consider its nature and estimate its value in a perfectly unbiassed way, without allowing ourselves the usual rhapsodies, or deducing any theory of the universe. One extra fact may destroy some existing theory; that is common enough. But no single fact is sufficient to construct one.

It will have been understood that Dharana, Dhyana, and Samadhi form a continuous process, and exactly when the climax comes does not matter. It is of this climax that we must speak, for this is a matter of *experience* and a very striking one.

In the course of our concentration **we noticed that the contents of the mind at any moment consisted of two things, and no more**: the Object, variable, and the Subject, invariable, or apparently so. **By success in Dharana the object has been made as invariable as the subject.**

Now the result of this is that the two become one. This phenomenon usually comes as a tremendous shock. It is indescribable even by the masters of language; and it is therefore not surprising that semi-educated stutterers wallow in oceans of gush.

All the poetic faculties and all the emotional faculties are thrown into a sort of ecstasy by an occurrence which overthrows the mind, and makes the rest of life seem absolutely worthless in comparison.

Good literature is principally a matter of clear observation and good judgment expressed in the simplest way. For this reason none of the great events of history (such as earthquakes and battles) have been well described by eye-witnesses, unless those eye-witnesses were out of danger. **But even when one has become accustomed to Dhyana by constant repetition, no words seem adequate.**

One of the simplest forms of Dhyana may be called "the Sun." The sun is seen (as it were) by itself, not by an observer; and although the physical eye cannot behold the sun, one is compelled to make the statement that this "Sun" is far more brilliant than the sun of nature. The whole thing takes place on a higher level.

Also the conditions of thought, time, and space are abolished. It is impossible to explain what this really means: only experience can furnish you with apprehension.

(This, too, has its analogies in ordinary life; the conceptions of higher mathematics cannot be grasped by the beginner, cannot be explained to the layman.)

A further development is the appearance of the Form which has been universally described as human; although the persons describing it proceed to add a great number of details which are not human at all. This particular appearance is usually assumed to be "God."

But, whatever it may be, **the result on the mind of the student is tremendous**; all his thoughts are pushed to their greatest development. He sincerely believes that they have the divine sanction; perhaps he even supposes that they emanate from this "God." **He goes back into the world armed with this intense conviction and authority.** He proclaims his ideas without the restraint which is imposed upon most persons by doubt, modesty, and diffidence;[1] while further there is, one may suppose, a real clarification.

In any case, the mass of mankind is always ready to be swayed by anything thus authoritative and distinct. History is full of stories of officers who have walked unarmed up to a mutinous regiment, and disarmed them by the mere force of confidence. The power of the orator over the mob is well known. It is, probably, for this reason that the prophet has been able to constrain mankind to obey his law. It never occurs to him that any one can do otherwise. In practical life one can walk past any guardian, such as a sentry or ticket-collector, if one can really act so that the man is somehow persuaded that you have a right to pass unchallenged.

This power, by the way, is what has been described by magicians as the power of invisibility. Somebody or other has an excellent story of four quite reliable men who were on the look-out for a murderer, and had instructions to let no one pass, and who all swore subsequently in presence of the dead body that no one had passed. None of them had seen the postman.

The thieves who stole the "Gioconda" from the Louvre were probably disguised as workmen, and stole the picture under the very eye of the guardian; very likely got him to help them.

---

1. This lack of restraint is not to be confused with that observed in intoxication and madness. Yet there is a very striking similarity, though only a superficial one.

It is only necessary to believe that a thing must be to bring it about. This belief must not be an emotional or an intellectual one. It resides in a deeper portion of the mind, yet a portion not so deep but that most men, probably all successful men, will understand these words, having experience of their own with which they can compare it.

The most important factor in Dhyana is, however, the annihilation of the Ego. Our conception of the universe must be completely overturned if we are to admit this as valid; and it is time that we considered what is really happening.

It will be conceded that we have given a very rational explanation of the greatness of great men. They had an experience so overwhelming, so out of proportion to the rest of things, that they were freed from all the petty hindrances which prevent the normal man from carrying out his projects.

Worrying about clothes, food, money, what people may think, how and why, and above all the fear of consequences, clog nearly every one. Nothing is easier, theoretically, than for an anarchist to kill a king. He has only to buy a rifle, make himself a first-class shot, and shoot the king from a quarter of a mile away. And yet, although there are plenty of anarchists, outrages are very few. At the same time, the police would probably be the first to admit that if any man were really tired of life, in his deepest being, a state very different from that in which a man goes about saying he is tired of life, he could manage somehow or other to kill someone first.

Now the man who has experienced any of the more intense forms of Dhyana is thus liberated. The Universe is thus destroyed for him, and he for it. His will can therefore go on its way unhampered. One may imagine that in the case of Mohammed he had cherished for years a tremendous ambition, and never done anything because those qualities which were subsequently manifested as statesmanship warned him that he was impotent. His vision in the cave gave him that confidence which was required, the faith that moves mountains. There are a lot of solid-seeming things in this world which a child could push over; but not one has the courage to push.

Let us accept provisionally this explanation of greatness, and pass it by. Ambition has led us to this point; but we are now interested in the work for its own sake.

A most astounding phenomenon has happened to us; we have had an experience which makes Love, fame, rank, ambition, wealth, look like thirty cents; and we begin to wonder passionately, "What is truth?" The Universe has tumbled about our ears like a house of cards, and we have tumbled too. Yet this ruin is like the opening of the Gates of Heaven. Here is a tremendous problem, and there is something within us which ravins for its solution.

Let us see what explanations we can find.

The first suggestion which would enter a well-balanced mind, versed in the study of nature, is that we have experienced a mental catastrophe. Just as a blow on the head will make a man "see stars," so one might suppose that the terrific mental strain of Dharana has somehow over-excited the brain, and caused a spasm, or possibly even the breaking of a vessel. There seems no reason to reject this explanation altogether, though it would be quite absurd to suppose that to accept it would be to condemn the practice. Spasm is a normal function of at least one of the organs of the body. That the brain is not damaged by the practice is proved by the fact that many people who claim to have had this experience repeatedly continue to exercise the ordinary avocations of life without diminished activity.

We may dismiss, then, the physiological question. It throws no light on the main problem, which is the value of the testimony of the experience.

Now this is a very difficult question, and raises the much larger question as to the value of any testimony. Every possible thought has been doubted at some time or another, except the thought which can only be expressed by a note of interrogation, since to doubt that thought asserts it. (For a full discussion see "The Soldier and the Hunchback," "Equinox," I.) But apart from this deep-seated philosophic doubt there is the practical doubt of every day. The popular phrase, "to doubt the evidence of one's senses," shows us that that evidence is normally accepted; but a man of science does nothing of the sort. He is so well aware that his senses constantly deceive him, that he invents elaborate instruments to correct them. And he is further aware that the Universe which he can directly perceive through sense, is the minutest fraction of the Universe which he knows indirectly.

For example, four-fifths of the air is composed of nitrogen. If anyone were to bring a bottle of nitrogen into this room it would be exceedingly difficult to say what it was; nearly all the tests that one could apply to it would be negative. His senses tell him little or nothing.

Argon was only discovered at all by comparing the weight of chemically pure nitrogen with that of the nitrogen of the air. This had often been done, but no one had sufficiently fine instruments even to perceive the discrepancy. To take another example, a famous man of science asserted not so long ago that science could never discover the chemical composition of the fixed stars. Yet this has been done, and with certainty.

If you were to ask your man of science for his "theory of the real," he would tell you that the "ether," which cannot be perceived in any way by any of the senses, or detected by any instruments, and which possesses qualities which are, to use ordinary language, impossible, is very much more real than the chair he is sitting on. The chair is only one fact; and its existence is testified by one very fallible person. The ether is the necessary deduction from millions of facts, which have been verified again and again and checked by every possible test of truth. There is therefore no *à priori* reason for rejecting anything on the ground that it is not directly perceived by the senses.

To turn to another point. One of our tests of truth is the vividness of the impression. An isolated event in the past of no great importance may be forgotten; and if it be in some way recalled, one may find one's self asking: "Did I dream it? or did it really happen?" What can never be forgotten is the *catastrophic*. The first death among the people that one loves (for example) would never be forgotten; for the first time one would *realize* what one had previously merely *known*. Such an experience sometimes drives people insane. Men of science have been known to commit suicide when their pet theory has been shattered. This problem has been discussed freely in "Science and Buddhism," "Time," "The Camel," and other papers. This much only need we say in this place, that **Dhyana has to be classed as the most vivid and catastrophic of all experiences**. This will be confirmed by anyone who has been there.

It is, then, difficult to overrate the value that such an experience has for the individual, especially as it is his entire conception of things, including his most deep-seated conception, the standard to which he has always referred everything, his own self, that is overthrown; and when we try to explain it away as hallucination, temporary suspension of the faculties or something similar, we find ourselves unable to do so. You cannot argue with a flash of lightning that has knocked you down.

Any mere theory is easy to upset. One can find flaws in the reasoning process, one can assume that the premisses are in some way false; but in this case, if one attacks the evidence for Dhyana, the mind is staggered by the fact that all other experience, attacked on the same lines, will fall much more easily.

In whatever way we examine it the result will always be the same. **Dhyana may be false; but, if so, so is everything else.**

Now the mind refuses to rest in a belief of the unreality of its own experiences. It may not be what it seems; but it must be something, and if (on the whole) ordinary life is something, how much more must that be by whose light ordinary life seems nothing!

The ordinary man sees the falsity and disconnectedness and purposelessness of dreams; he ascribes them (rightly) to a disordered mind. The philosopher looks upon waking life with similar contempt; and the person who has experienced Dhyana takes the same view, but not by mere pale intellectual conviction. Reasons, however cogent, never convince utterly; but this man in Dhyana has the same commonplace certainty that a man has on waking from a nightmare. "I wasn't falling down a thousand flights of stairs, it was only a bad dream."

Similarly comes the reflection of the man who has had experience of Dhyana: "I am not that wretched insect, that imperceptible parasite on earth; it was only a bad dream." And as you could not convince the normal man that his nightmare was more real than his awakening, so you cannot convince the other that his Dhyana was hallucination, even though he is only too well aware that he has fallen from that state into "normal" life.

It is probably rare for a single experience to upset thus radically the whole conception of the Universe, just as sometimes, in the first moments of waking, there remains a half-doubt as to whether dream or waking is real. But as one gains further experience, when Dhyana is no longer a shock, when the student has had plenty of time to make himself at home in the new world, this conviction will become absolute.[2]

Another rationalist consideration is this. The student has not been trying to excite the mind but to calm it, not to produce any one

2. It should be remembered that at present there are no data for determining the duration of Dhyana. One can only say that, since it certainly occurred between such and such hours, it must have lasted less than that time. Thus we see, from Frater P.'s record, that it can certainly occur in less than an hour and five minutes.

thought but to exclude all thoughts; for there is no connection between the object of meditation and the Dhyana. Why must we suppose a breaking down of the whole process, especially as the mind bears no subsequent traces of any interference, such as pain or fatigue? Surely this once, if never again, the Hindu image expresses the simplest theory!

That image is that of a lake into which five glaciers move. These glaciers are the senses. While ice (the impressions) is breaking off constantly into the lake, the waters are troubled. If the glaciers are stopped the surface becomes calm; and then, and only then, can it reflect unbroken the disk of the sun. This sun is the "soul" or "God."

We should, however, avoid these terms for the present, on account of their implications. Let us rather speak of this sun as "some unknown thing whose presence has been masked by all things known, and by the knower."

It is probable, too, that our memory of Dhyana is not the phenomenon itself, but of the image left thereby on the mind. But this is true of all phenomena, as Berkeley and Kant have proved beyond all question. This matter, then, need not concern us.

We may, however, provisionally accept the view that **Dhyana is real; more real and thus of more importance to ourselves than all other experience**. This state has been described not only by the Hindus and Buddhists, but by Mohammedans and Christians. In Christian writings, however, the deeply-seated dogmatic bias has rendered their documents worthless to the average man. They ignore the essential conditions of Dhyana, and insist on the inessential, to a much greater extent than the best Indian writers. But to any one with experience and some knowledge of comparative religion the identity is certain. We may now proceed to Samadhi.

Samadhi

This piece explores and then undermines the line between Dhyana and Samadhi. After groping beyond both toward Transcendence, Crowley finds the Impossibility of describing "ultimate attainment."

More rubbish has been written about Samadhi than enough; we must endeavour to avoid adding to the heap. Even Patanjali, who is extraordinarily clear and practical in most things, begins to rave when he talks about it. Even if what he said were true he should not have mentioned it; because it does not sound true, and we should make no statement that is *à priori* improbable without being prepared to back it up with the fullest proofs. But it is more than likely that his commentators have misunderstood him.

The most reasonable statement, of any acknowledged authority, is that of Yajna Valkya, who says: "By Pranayama impurities of the body are thrown out; by Dharana the impurities of the mind; by Pratyahara the impurities of attachment; and by Samadhi is taken off everything that hides the lordship of the soul." There is a modest statement in good literary form. If we can only do as well as that!

In the first place, what is the meaning of the term? Etymologically, *Sam* is the Greek συν-, the English prefix "syn-" meaning "together with." *Adhi* means "Lord," and a reasonable translation of the whole word would be "Union with God," the exact term used by Christian mystics to describe their attainment.

Now there is great confusion, because the Buddhists use the word Samadhi to mean something entirely different, the mere faculty of attention. Thus, with them, to think of a cat is to "make Samadhi" on that cat. They use the word Jhana to describe mystic states. This is excessively misleading, for as we saw in the last section, Dhyana

106

is a preliminary to Samadhi, and of course Jhana is merely the wretched plebeian Pali corruption of it.[1]

There are many kinds of Samadhi[2]. *Some authors consider Atma-darshana, the Universe as a single phenomenon without conditions, to be the first real Samadhi.* If we accept this, we must relegate many less exalted states to the class of Dhyana. Patanjali enumerates a number of these states: to perform these on different things gives different magical powers; or so he says. These need not be debated here. Any one who wants magic powers can get them in dozens of different ways.

Power grows faster than desire. The boy who wants money to buy lead soldiers sets to work to obtain it, and by the time he has got it wants something else instead—in all probability something just beyond his means.

Such is the splendid history of all spiritual advance! One never stops to take the reward.

We shall therefore not trouble at all about what any Samadhi may or may not bring as far as its results in our lives are concerned. We began this book, it will be remembered, with considerations of death. Death has now lost all meaning. The idea of death depends on those of the ego, and of time; these ideas have been destroyed; and so "Death is swallowed up in victory." We shall now only be interested in what Samadhi is in itself, and in the conditions which cause it.

Let us try a final definition. Dhyana resembles Samadhi in many respects. There is a union of the ego and the non-ego, and a loss of the senses of time and space and causality. Duality in any form is abolished. The idea of time involves that of two consecutive things, that of space two non-coincident things, that of causality two connected things.

These Dhyanic conditions contradict those of normal thought; but in Samadhi they are very much more marked than in Dhyana. And while **in the latter it seems like a simple union of two things, in the former it appears as if all things rushed together and**

1. The vulgarism and provincialism of the Buddhist canon is infinitely repulsive to all nice minds; and the attempt to use the terms of an ego-centric philosophy to explain the details of a psychological whose principal doctrine is the denial of the ego, was the work of a mischievous idiot. Let us unhesitatingly reject these abominations, these nastinesses of the beggars dressed in rags that they have snatched from corpses, and follow the etymological signification of the word as given above!
2. Apparently. That is, the obvious results are different. Possibly the cause is only one, refracted through diverse media.

united. One might say that in Dhyana there was still this quality latent, that the One existing was opposed to the Many non-existing; in Samadhi the Many and the One are united in a union of Existence with non-Existence. This definition is not made from reflection, but from memory.

Further, it is easy to master the "trick" or "knack" of Dhyana. After a while one can get into that state without preliminary practice; and, looking at it from this point, one seems able to reconcile the two meanings of the word which we debated in the last section. From below Dhyana seems like a trance, an experience so tremendous that one cannot think of anything bigger, while from above it seems merely a state of mind as natural as any other. Frater P., before he had Samadhi, wrote of Dhyana: "Perhaps as a result of the intense control a nervous storm breaks: this we call Dhyana. Samadhi is but an expansion of this, so far as I can see."

Five years later he would not take this view. He would say perhaps that Dhyana was "a flowing of the mind in one unbroken current from the ego to the non-ego without consciousness of either, accompanied by a crescent wonder and bliss." He can understand how that is the natural result of Dhyana, but he cannot call Dhyana in the same way the precursor of Samadhi. Perhaps he does not really know the conditions which induce Samadhi. He can produce Dhyana at will in the course of a few minutes' work; and it often happens with apparent spontaneity: with Samadhi this is unfortunately not the case. He probably can get it at will, but could not say exactly how, or tell how long it might take him; and he could not be *sure* of getting it at all.

One feels *sure* that one can walk a mile along a level road. One knows the conditions, and it would have to be a very extraordinary set of circumstances that would stop one. But though it would be equally fair to say: "I have climbed the Matterhorn and I know I can climb it again," yet there are all sorts of more or less probable circumstances any of which would prevent success.

Now we do know this, that **if thought is kept single and steady, Dhyana results**. We do not know whether an intensification of this is sufficient to cause Samadhi, or whether some other circumstances are required. One is science, the other empiricism.

One author says (unless memory deceives) that twelve seconds' steadiness is Dharana, a hundred and forty-four Dhyana, and seventeen hundred and twenty-eight Samadhi. And Vivekananda, commenting on Patanjali, makes Dhyana a mere prolongation of

Dharana; but says further: "Suppose I were meditating on a book, and I gradually succeeded in concentrating the mind on it, and perceiving only the internal sensation, the meaning unexpressed in any form, that state of Dhyana is called Samadhi."

Other authors are inclined to suggest that Samadhi results from meditating on subjects that are in themselves worthy. For example, Vivekananda says: "Think of any holy subject:" and explains this as follows: "This does not mean any wicked subject."(!)

Frater P. would not like to say definitely whether he ever got Dhyana from common objects. He gave up the practice after a few months, and meditated on the Cakkras, etc. Also his Dhyana became so common that he gave up recording it. But if he wished to do it this minute he would choose something to excite his "godly fear," or "holy awe," or "wonderment."[3] There is no apparent reason why Dhyana should not occur when thinking of any common object of the sea-shore, such as a blue pig; but Frater P.'s constant reference to this as the usual object of his meditation need not be taken *au pied de la lettre*. His records of meditation contain no reference to this remarkable animal.

It will be a good thing when organized research has determined the conditions of Samadhi; but in the meantime there seems no particular objection to our following tradition, and using the same objects of meditation as our predecessors, with the single exception which we shall note in due course.

The first class of objects for serious meditation (as opposed to preliminary practice, in which one should keep to simple recognizable objects, whose definiteness is easy to maintain) is *various parts of the body*. The Hindus have an elaborate system of anatomy and physiology which has apparently no reference to the facts of the dissecting-room. Prominent in this class are the seven Cakkras, which will be described in Part II. There are also various "nerves", equally mythical.

The second class is *objects of devotion*, such as the idea or form of the Deity, or the heart or body of your Teacher, or of some man whom you respect profoundly. This practice is not to be commended, because it implies a bias of the mind.

---

3. It is rather a breach of the scepticism which is the basis of our system to admit that anything can be in any way better than another. Do it thus: "A. is a thing that B. thinks 'holy.' It is natural therefore for B. to meditate on it." Get rid of the ego, observe all your actions as if they were another's, and you will avoid ninety-nine percent of the troubles that await you.

You can also meditate on *your dreams*. This sounds superstitious; but the idea is that you have already a tendency, independent of your conscious will, to think of those things, which will consequently be easier to think of than others. That this is the explanation is evident from the nature of the preceding and subsequent classes.

You can also meditate on *anything that especially appeals to you*.

But in all this one feels inclined to suggest that **it will be better and more convincing if the meditation is directed to an object which in itself is apparently unimportant**. One does not want the mind to be excited in any way, even by adoration. See the three meditative methods in Liber HHH (Equinox VI).[4] At the same time, one would not like to deny positively that it is very much *easier* to take some idea towards which the mind would naturally flow.

The Hindus assert that the nature of the object determines the Samadhi; that is, the nature of those lower Samadhis which confer so-called "magic powers." For example, there are the Yogapravritti. Meditating on the tip of the nose, one obtains what may be called the "ideal smell"; that is, a smell which is not any particular smell, but is the archetypal smell, of which all actual smells are modifications. It is "the smell which is *not* a smell." This is the only reasonable description; for the experience being contrary to reason, it is only reasonable that the words describing it should be contrary to reason too.[5]

Similarly, concentration on the tip of the tongue gives the "ideal taste"; on the dorsum of the tongue, "ideal contact." "Every atom of the body comes into contact with every atom in the Universe all at once," is the description Bhikku Ananda Metteya gives of it. The root of the tongue gives the "ideal sound"; and the pharnyx the "ideal sight."[6]

---

4. These are the complements of the three methods of Enthusiasm (A ∴ A ∴ instruction not yet issued up to March 1912).

5. Hence the Athanasian Creed. Compare the precise parallel in the Zohar: "The Head which is above all heads; the Head which is *not* a Head."

6. Similarly Patanjali tells us that by making Samyama on the strength of an elephant or a tiger, the student acquires that strength. Conquer "the nerve Udana," and you can walk on the water; "Samana," and you begin to flash with light; the "elements" fire, air, earth, and water, and you can do whatever in natural life they prevent you from doing. For instance, by conquering earth, one could take a short cut to Australia; or by conquering water, one can live at the bottom of the Ganges. They say there is a holy man at Benares who does this, coming up only once a year to comfort and instruct his disciples. But nobody need believe this unless he wants to; and you are even advised to conquer that desire should it arise. It will be interesting when science really determines the variables and constants of these equations.

The Samadhi *par excellence*, however, is Atmadarshana, which for some, and those not the least instructed, is the first real Samadhi; for **even the visions of "God" and of the "Self" are tainted by form. In Atmadarshana the All is manifested as the One: it is the Universe freed from its conditions. Not only are all forms and ideas destroyed, but also those conceptions which are implicit in our ideas of those ideas.**[7] Each part of the Universe has become the whole, and phenomena and noumena are no longer opposed.

But it is quite impossible to describe this state of mind. One can only specify some of the characteristics, and that in language which forms no image in mind. It is impossible for anyone who experiences it to bring back any adequate memory, nor can we conceive a state transcending this.

There is, however, a very much higher state called **Shivadarshana**, of which it is only necessary to say that **it is the destruction of the previous state, its annihilation**; and to understand this blotting-out, one must not imagine "Nothingness" (the only name for it) as negative, but as positive.

The normal mind is a candle in a darkened room. Throw open the shutters, and the sunlight makes the flame invisible. That is a fair image of Dhyana.[8]

But the mind refuses to find a simile for Atmadarshana. It seems merely ineffective to say that the rushing together of all the host of heaven would similarly blot out the sunlight. But if we do say so, and wish to form a further image of Shivadarshana, we must imagine ourselves as suddenly recognizing that this universal blaze is darkness; not a light extremely dim compared with some other light, but darkness itself. It is not the change from the minute to the vast, or even from the finite to the infinite. It is the recognition that the positive is merely the negative. The ultimate truth is perceived not only as false, but as the logical contradictory of truth. It is quite useless to elaborate this theme, which has baffled all other minds hitherto. We have tried to say as little as possible rather than as much as possible.[9]

---

7. This is so complete that not only "Black is White," but "The Whiteness of Black is the *essential* of its Blackness." "Naught = One = Infinity"; but this is only true *because* of this threefold arrangement, a trinity or "triangle of contradictories."
8. Here the dictation was interrupted by very prolonged thought due to the difficulty of making the image clear. Virakam.
9. Yet all this has come of our desire to be as modest as Yajna Valkya!

Still further from our present purpose would it be to criticise the innumerable discussions which have taken place as to whether this is the ultimate attainment, or what it confers. It is enough if we say that even the first and most transitory Dhyana repays a thousand-fold the pains we may have taken to attain it.

And there is this anchor for the beginner, that his work is cumulative: every act directed towards attainment builds up a destiny which must some day come to fruition. May all attain!

Yoga for Yellowbellies. Second Lecture

This wide-ranging lecture from *Eight Lectures on Yoga* on the relationship between Yoga and Science includes Crowley's vision of the Sun-
Sponge (sections 18, 19, and 20). He begins by stating "Knowledge is
Impossible," and concludes that Science is a failure, opening the field
to a Yoga of neither Science nor Knowledge.

Mr chairman, Your Royal Highness, Your Grace, my lords,
ladies and gentlemen.

Do what thou wilt shall be the whole of the Law.

In my last lecture I led you into the quag of delusion; I smothered
you in the mire of delusion; I brought you to thirst in the desert of
delusion; I left you wandering in the jungle of delusion, a prey to all
the monsters which are thoughts. It came into my mind that it was
up to me to do something about it.

We have constantly been discussing mysterious entities as if we
knew something about them, and this (on examination) always
turned out not to be the case.

2. Knowledge itself is impossible, because if we take the simplest
proposition of knowledge, S is P, we must attach some meaning to S
and P, if our statement is to be intelligible. (I say nothing as to
whether it is true!) and this involves definition. Now the original
proposition of identity, A = A, tells us nothing at all, unless the
second A gives us further information about the first A. We shall
therefore say that A is BC. Instead of one unknown we have two
unknowns; we have to define B as DE, C as FG. Now we have four
unknowns, and very soon we have used up the alphabet. When we
come to define Z, we have to go back and use one of the other letters,
so that all our arguments are arguments in a circle.

3. Any statement which we make is demonstrably meaningless.
And yet we do mean something when we say that a cat has four legs.
And we all know what we mean when we say so. We give our assent

113

to, or withhold it from, the proposition on the grounds of our experience. But that experience is not intellectual as above demonstrated. It is a matter of immediate intuition. We cannot have any warrant for that intuition, but at the same time any intellectual argument which upsets it does not in the faintest degree shake our conviction.

4. The conclusion to be drawn from this is that the instrument of mind is not intellectual, not rational. Logic is merely destructive, a self-destructive toy. The toy, however, is in some ways also instructive, even though the results of its use will not bear examination. So we make a by-law that the particular sorites which annihilate logic are out of bounds, and we go on reasoning within arbitrarily appointed limits. It is subject to these conditions that we may proceed to examine the nature of our fundamental ideas; and this is necessary, because since we began to consider the nature of the results of meditation, our conceptions of the backgrounds of thought are decided in quite a different manner; not by intellectual analysis, which, as we have seen, carries no conviction, but by illumination, which does carry conviction. Let us, therefore, proceed to examine the elements of our normal thinking.

5. I need hardly recapitulate the mathematical theorem which you all doubtless laid to heart when you were criticising Einstein's theory of relativity. I only want to recall to your minds the simplest element of that theorem; the fact that in order to describe anything at all, you must have four measurements. It must be so far east or west, so far north or south, so far up or down, from a standard point, and it must be after or before a standard moment. There are three dimensions of space and one of time.

6. Now what do we mean by space? Henri Poincaré, one of the greatest mathematicians of the last generation, thought that the idea of space was invented by a lunatic, in a fantastic (and evidently senseless and aimless) endeavour to explain to himself his experience of his muscular movements. Long before that, Kant had told us that space was subjective, a necessary condition of thinking; and while every one must agree with this, it is obvious that it does not tell us much about it.

7. Now let us look into our minds and see what idea, if any, we can form about space. Space is evidently a continuum. There cannot be any difference between any parts of it because it is wholly *where*. It is pure background, the area of possibilities, a condition of quality

and so of all consciousness. It is therefore in itself completely void. Is that right, sir?

8. Now suppose we want to fulfill one of these possibilities. The simplest thing we can take is a point, and we are told that a point has neither parts nor magnitude, but only position. But, as long as there is only one point, position means nothing. No possibility has yet been created of any positive statement. We will therefore take two points, and from these we get the idea of a line. Our Euclid tells us that a line has length but no breadth. But, as long as there are only two points, length itself means nothing; or, at the most, it means separateness. All we can say about two points is that there are two of them.

9. Now we take a third point, and at last we move to a more positive idea. In the first place, we have a plane surface, though that in itself still means nothing, in the same way as length means nothing when there are only two points there. But the introduction of the third point has given a meaning to our idea of length. We can say that the line AB is longer than the line BC, and we can also introduce the idea of an angle.

10. A fourth point, provided that it is not in the original plane, gives us the idea of a solid body. But, as before, it tells us nothing about the solid body as such, because there is no other solid body with which to compare it. We find also that it is not really a solid body at all as it stands, because it is merely an instantaneous kind of illusion. We cannot observe, or even imagine, anything, unless we have time for the purpose.

11. What, then, is time? It is a phantasm, exactly as tenuous as space, but the possibilities of differentiation between one thing and another can only occur in one way instead of in three different ways. We compare two phenomena in time by the idea of sequence.

12. Now it will be perfectly clear to all of you that this is all nonsense. In order to conceive the simplest possible object, we have to keep on inventing ideas, which even in the proud moment of invention are seen to be unreal. How are we to get away from this world of phantasmagoria to the common universe of sense? We shall require quite a lot more acts of imagination. We have got to endow our mathematical conceptions with three ideas which Hindu philosophers call Sat, Chit and Ananda, which are usually translated Being, Knowledge, and Bliss. This really means: Sat, the tendency to conceive of an object as real; Chit, the tendency to pretend that it

is an object of knowledge; and Ananda, the tendency to imagine that we are affected by it.

13. It is only after we have endowed the object with these dozen imaginary properties, each of which, besides being a complete illusion, is an absurd, irrational, and self-contradictory notion, that we arrive at even the simplest object of experience. And this object must, of course, be constantly multiplied. Otherwise our experience would be confined to a single object incapable of description.

14. We have also got to attribute to ourselves a sort of divine power over our nightmare creation, so that we can compare the different objects of our experience in all sorts of different manners. Incidentally, this last operation of multiplying the objects stands evidently invalid, because (after all) what we began with was absolutely Nothingness. Out of this we have somehow managed to obtain, not merely one, but many; but, for all that, our process has followed the necessary operation of our intellectual machine. Since that machine is the only machine that we possess, our arguments must be valid in some sense or other conformable with the nature of this machine. What machine? That is a perfectly real object. It contains innumerable parts, powers and faculties. And they are as much a nightmare as the external universe which it has created. Gad, sir, Patanjali is right!

15. Now how do we get over this difficulty of something coming from Nothing? Only by enquiring what we mean by Nothing. We shall find that this idea is totally inconceivable to the normal mind. For if Nothing is to be Nothing, it must be Nothing in every possible way. (Of course, each of these ways is itself an imaginary something, and there are Aleph-Zero—a transfinite number—of them.) If, for example, we say that Nothing is a square triangle, we have had to invent a square triangle in order to say it. But take a more homely instance. We know what we mean by saying "There are cats in the room." We know what we mean when we say "No cats are in the room." But if we say "*No* cats are *not* in the room," we evidently mean that *some* cats *are* in the room. This remark is not intended to be a reflection upon this distinguished audience.

16. So then, if Nothing is to be really the absolute Nothing, we mean that Nothing does not enter into the category of existence. To say that absolute Nothing exists is equivalent to saying that everything exists which exists, and the great Hebrew sages of old time noted this fact by giving it the title of the supreme idea of

reality (behind their tribal God, Jehovah, who, as we have previously shown, is merely the Yoga of the 4 Elements, even at his highest,—the Demiourgos) Eheieh-Asher-Eheieh,—I am that I am.

17. If there is any sense in any of this at all, we may expect to find an almost identical system of thought all over the world. There is nothing exclusively Hebrew about this theogony. We find, for example, in the teachings of Zoroaster and the neo-Platonists very similar ideas. We have a Pleroma, the void, a background of all possibilities, and this is filled by a supreme Light-God, from whom derive in turn the seven Archons, who correspond closely to the seven planetary deities, Aratron, Bethor, Phaleg and the rest. These in their turn constitute a Demiurge in order to create matter; and this Demiurge is Jehovah. Not far different are the ideas both of the classical Greeks and the neo-Platonists. The differences in the terminology, when examined, appear as not much more than the differences of local convenience in thinking. But all these go back to the still older cosmogony of the ancient Egyptians, where we have Nuit, Space, Hadit, the point of view; these experience congress, and so produce Heru-Ra-Ha, who combines the ideas of Ra-Hoor-Khuit and Hoor-paar-Kraat. These are the same twin Vau and Hé final which we know. Here is evidently the origin of the system of the Tree of Life.

18. We have arrived at this system by purely intellectual examination, and it is open to criticism; but the point I wish to bring to your notice to-night is that it corresponds closely to one of the great states of mind which reflect the experience of Samadhi.

There is a vision of peculiar character which has been of cardinal importance in my interior life, and to which constant reference is made in my Magical Diaries. So far as I know, there is no extant description of this vision anywhere, and I was surprised on looking through my records to find that I had given no clear account of it myself. The reason apparently is that it is so necessary a part of myself that I unconsciously assume it to be a matter of common knowledge, just as one assumes that everyone knows that one possesses a pair of lungs, and therefore abstains from mentioning the fact directly, although perhaps alluding to the matter often enough.

It appears very essential to describe this vision as well as possible, considering the difficulty of language, and the fact that the phenomena involved logical contradictions, the conditions of consciousness being other than those obtaining normally.

The vision developed gradually. It was repeated on so many occasions that I am unable to say at what period it may be called complete. The beginning, however, is clear enough in my memory.

19. I was on a Great Magical Retirement in a cottage overlooking Lake Pasquaney in New Hampshire. I lost consciousness of everything but an universal space in which were innumerable bright points, and I realised that this was a physical representation of the universe, in what I may call its essential structure. I exclaimed: "Nothingness, with twinkles!" I concentrated upon this vision, with the result that the void space which had been the principal element of it diminished in importance. Space appeared to be ablaze, yet the radiant points were not confused, and I thereupon completed my sentence with the exclamation: "But *what* Twinkles!"

20. The next stage of this vision led to an identification of the blazing points with the stars of the firmament, with ideas, souls, etc. I perceived also that each star was connected by a ray of light with each other star. In the world of ideas, each thought possessed a necessary relation with each other thought; each such relation is of course a thought in itself; each such ray is itself a star. It is here that logical difficulty first presents itself. The seer has a direct perception of infinite series. Logically, therefore, it would appear as if the entire space must be filled up with a homogeneous blaze of light. This is not, however, the case. The space is completely full, yet the monads which fill it are perfectly distinct. The ordinary reader might well exclaim that such statements exhibit symptoms of mental confusion. The subject demands more than cursory examination. I can do no more than refer the critic to Bertrand Russell's *Introduction to Mathematical Philosophy*, where the above position is thoroughly justified, as also certain positions which follow.

I want you to note in particular the astonishing final identification of this cosmic experience with the nervous system as described by the anatomist.

21. At this point we may well be led to consider once more what we call the objective universe, and what we call our subjective experience. What is Nature? Immanuel Kant, who founded an epoch-making system of subjective idealism, is perhaps the first philosopher to demonstrate clearly that space, time, causality (in short, all conditions of existence) are really no more than conditions of thought. I have tried to put it more simply by defining all possible predicates as so many dimensions. To describe an object properly it

is not sufficient to determine its position in the space-time continuum of four dimensions, but we must enquire how it stands in all the categories and scales, its values in all *kinds* of possibility. What do we know about it in respect of its greenness, its hardness, its mobility, and so on? And then we find out that what we imagine to be the description of the object is in reality nothing of the sort.

22. All that we recorded is the behaviour of our instruments. What did our telescopes, spectroscopes, and balances tell us? And these again are dependent upon the behaviour of our senses; for the reality of our instruments, of our organs of sense, is just as much in need of description and demonstration as are the most remote phenomena. And we find ourselves forced to the conclusion that anything we perceive is only perceived by us as such *because of our tendency so to perceive it.* And we shall find that in the fourth stage of the great Buddhist practice, Mahasatipatthana, we become directly and immediately aware of this fact instead of digging it out of the holts of these interminable sorites which badger us! Kant himself put it, after his fashion: "The laws of nature are the laws of our own minds." Why? It is not the contents of the mind itself that we can cognise, but only its structure. But Kant has not gone to this length. He would have been extremely shocked if it had ever struck him that the final term in his sorites was "Reason itself is the only reality." On further examination, even this ultimate truth turns out to be meaningless. It is like the well known circular definition of an obscene book, which is: one that arouses certain ideas in the mind of the kind of person in whom such ideas are excited by that kind of book.

23. I notice that my excellent chairman is endeavouring to stifle a yawn and to convert it into a smile, and he will forgive me for saying that I find the effect somewhat sinister. But he has every right to be supercilious about it. These are indeed "old, fond paradoxes to amuse wives in ale-houses." Since philosophy began, it has always been a favourite game to prove your axioms absurd.

You will all naturally be very annoyed with me for indulging in these fatuous pastimes, especially as I started out with a pledge that I would deal with these subjects from the hard-headed scientific point of view. Forgive me if I have toyed with these shining gossamers of the thought-web! I have only been trying to break it to you gently. I proceed to brush away with a sweep of my lily-white hand all this tenuous, filmy stuff, "such stuff as dreams are made of." We will get down to modern science.

24. For general reading there is no better introduction than *The Bases of Modern Science*, by my old and valued friend the late J. W. N. Sullivan. I do not want to detain you too long with quotations from this admirable book. I would much rather you got it and read it yourself; you could hardly make better use of your time. But let us spend a few moments on his remarks about the question of geometry.

Our conceptions of space as a subjective entity have been completely upset by the discovery that the equations of Newton based on Euclidean Geometry are inadequate to explain the phenomena of gravitation. It is instinctive to us to think of a straight line; it is somehow axiomatic. But we learn that this does not exist in the objective universe. We have to use another geometry, Riemann's Geometry, which is one of the curved geometries. (There are, of course, as many systems of geometry as there are absurd axioms to build them on. Three lines make one ellipse: any nonsense you like: you can proceed to construct a geometry which is correct so long as it is coherent. And there is nothing right or wrong about the result: the only question is: which is the most convenient system for the purpose of describing phenomena? We found the idea of Gravitation awkward: we went to Riemann.)

This means that the phenomena are not taking place against a background of a flat surface; the surface itself is curved. What we have thought of as a straight line does not exist at all. And this is almost impossible to conceive; at least it is quite impossible for myself to visualise. The nearest one gets to it is by trying to imagine that you are a reflection on a polished door-knob.

25. I feel almost ashamed of the world that I have to tell you that in the year 1900, four years before the appearance of Einstein's world-shaking paper, I described space as "finite yet boundless," which is exactly the description in general terms that he gave in more mathematical detail[1] You will see at once that these three words do describe a curved geometry; a sphere, for instance, is a finite object, yet you can go over the surface in any direction without ever coming to an end. I said above that Riemann's Geometry was not quite sufficient to explain the phenomena of nature. We have to postulate different kinds of curvature in different parts of the continuum. And even then we are not happy!

1. *Tannhäuser*, written in Mexico, O.F., August, 1900. See also my *Berashith*, written Delhi, April, 1901.

26. Now for a spot of Sullivan! "The geometry is so general that it admits of different degrees of curvature in different parts of space-time. It is to this curvature that gravitational effects are due. The curvature of space-time is most prominent, therefore, around large masses, for here the gravitational effects are most marked. If we take matter as fundamental, we may say that it is the presence of matter that causes the curvature of space-time. But there is a different school of thought that regards matter as due to the curvature of space-time. That is, we assume as fundamental a space-time continuum manifest to our senses as what we call matter. Both points of view have strong arguments to recommend them. But, whether or not matter may be derived from the geometrical peculiarities of the space-time continuum, we may take it as an established scientific fact that gravitation has been so derived. This is obviously a very great achievement, but it leaves quite untouched another great class of phenomena, namely, electro-magnetic phenomena. In this space-time continuum of Einstein's the electro-magnetic forces appear as entirely alien. Gravitation has been absorbed, as it were, into Riemannian geometry, and the notion of force, so far as gravitational phenomena are concerned, has been abolished. But the electro-magnetic forces still flourish undisturbed. There is no hint that they are manifestations of the geometrical peculiarities of the space-time continuum. And it can be shown to be impossible to relate them to anything in Riemann's Geometry. Gravitation can be shown to correspond to certain geometrical peculiarities of a Reimannian space-time. But the electro-magnetic forces lie completely outside this scheme."

27. Here is the great quag into which mathematical physics has led its addicts. Here we have two classes of phenomena, all part of a unity of physics. Yet the equations which describe and explain the one class are incompatible with those of the other class! This is not a question of philosophy at all, but a question of fact. It does not do to consider that the universe is composed of particles. Such a hypothesis underlies one class of phenomena, but it is nonsense when applied to the electro-magnetic equations, which insist upon our abandoning the idea of particles for that of waves.

Here is another Welsh rabbit for supper!

"Einstein's finite universe is such that its radius is dependent upon the amount of matter in it. Were more matter to be created, the volume of space would increase. Were matter to be annihilated, the volume of space would decrease. Without matter, space would not exist. Thus the mere existence of space, besides its metrical properties, depends upon the existence of matter. With this conception it becomes possible to regard all motion, including rotation, as purely relative."

Where do we go from here, boys?

28. "The present tendency of physics is towards describing the universe in terms of mathematical relations between unimaginable entities."

We have got a long way from Lord Kelvin's too-often and too-unfairly quoted statement that he could not imagine anything of which he could not construct a mechanical model. The Victorians were really a little inclined to echo Dr. Johnson's gross imbecile stamp on the ground when the ideas of Bishop Berkeley penetrated to the superficial strata of the drink-sodden grey cells of that beef-witted brute.

29. Now, look you, I ask you to reflect upon the trouble we have taken to calculate the distance of the fixed stars, and hear Professor G. N. Lewis, who "suggests that two atoms connected by a light ray may be regarded as in actual physical contact. The 'interval' between two ends of a light-ray is, on the theory of relativity, zero, and Professor Lewis suggests that this fact should be taken seriously. On this theory, light is not propagated at all. This idea is in conformity with the principle that none but observable factors should be used in constructing a scientific theory, for we can certainly never observe the passage of light in empty space. We are only aware of light when it encounters matter. Light which never encounters matter is purely hypothetical. If we do not make that hypothesis, then there is no empty space. On Professor Lewis's theory, when we observe a distant star, our eye as truly makes physical contact with that star as our finger makes contact with a table when we press it."

30. And did not all of you think that my arguments were arguments in a circle? I hope you did, for I was at the greatest pains to tell you so. But it is not a question of argument in Mr. Sullivan's book; it is a question of facts. He was talking about human values. He was asking whether science could possibly be cognizant of them. Here he comes, the great commander! Cheer, my comrades, cheer!

"But although consistent materialists were probably always rare, the humanistically important fact remained that science did not find it necessary to include values in its description of the universe. For it appeared that science, in spite of this omission, formed a closed system. If values form an integral part of reality, it seems strange that science should be able to give a consistent description of phenomena which ignores them.

"At the present time, this difficulty is being met in two ways. On the one hand, it is pointed out that science remains within its own domain by the device of cyclic definition, that is to say, the abstractions with which it begins are all it ever talks about. It makes no fresh contacts with reality, and therefore never encounters any possibly disturbing factors. This point of view is derived from the theory of relativity, particularly from the form of presentation adopted by Eddington. This theory forms a closed circle. The primary terms of the theory, 'point-events,' 'potentials,' 'matter' (etc.—there are ten of them), lie at various points on the circumference of the circle. We may start at any point and go round the circle, that is, from any one of these terms we can deduce the others. The primary entities of the theory are defined in terms of one another. In the course of this exercise we derive the laws of Nature studied in physics. At a certain point in the chain of deductions, at 'matter,' for example, we judge that we are talking about something which is an objective concrete embodiment of our abstractions. But matter, as it occurs in physics, is no more than a particular set of abstractions, and our subsequent reasoning is concerned only with these abstractions. Such other characteristics as the objective reality may possess never enter our scheme. But the set of abstractions called matter in relativity theory do not seem to be adequate to the whole of our scientific knowledge of matter. There remain quantum phenomena."

Ah!

"So we leave her, so we leave her,
Far from where her swarthy kindred roam—kindred roam
In the Scarlet Fever, Scarlet Fever,
Scarlet Fever Convalescent Home."

31. So now, no less than that chivalrous gentleman, His Grace, the Most Reverend the Archbishop of Canterbury, who in a recent broadcast confounded for ever all those infidels who had presumed to doubt the possibility of devils entering into swine, we have met the dragon science and conquered. We have seen that, however we

attack the problem of mind, whether from the customary spiritual standpoint, or from the opposite corner of materialism, the result is just the same.

One last quotation from Mr. Sullivan. "The universe may ultimately prove to be irrational. The scientific adventure may have to be given up."

But that is all *he* knows about science, bless his little heart! We do not give up. "You lied, d'Ormea, I do not repent!" The results of experiment are still valid for experience, and the fact that the universe turns out on enquiry to be unintelligible only serves to fortify our ingrained conviction that experience itself is reality.

32. We may then ask ourselves whether it is not possible to obtain experience of a higher order, to discover and develop the faculty of mind which can transcend analysis, stable against all thought by virtue of its own self-evident assurance. In the language of the Great White Brotherhood (whom I am here to represent) you cross the abyss. "Leave the poor old stranded wreck"—Ruach—"and pull for the shore" of Neschamah. For above the abyss, it is said, as you will see if you study the Supplement of the fifth number of the First Volume of *The Equinox,* an idea is only true in so far as it contains its contradictory in itself.

33. It is such states of mind as this which constitute the really important results of Samyama, and these results are not to be destroyed by philosophical speculation, because they are not susceptible of analysis, because they have no component parts, because they exist by virtue of their very Unreason—*"certum est quia ineptum!"* They cannot be expressed, for they are above knowledge. To some extent we can convey our experience to others familiar with that experience to a less degree by the aesthetic method. And this explains why all the good work on Yoga—alchemy, magick and the rest—not doctrinal but symbolic—the word of God to man is given in Poetry and Art.

In my next lecture I shall endeavour to go a little deeper into the technique of obtaining these results, and also give a more detailed account of the sort of thing that is likely to occur in the course of the preliminary practices.

Love is the law, love under will.

Trance

From *Little Essays Toward Truth*. Note that the magician's Words about Transcendence in his Magical Record are "authentic stigma."

The word *Trance* implies a passing beyond: scil., the conditions which oppress. The whole and sole object of all true Magical and Mystical training is to become free from every kind of limitation. Thus, body and mind, in the widest sense, are the obstacles in the Path of the Wise: the paradox, tragic enough as it seems, is that they are also the means of progress. How to get rid of them, to pass beyond or to transcend them, is the problem, and this is as strictly practical and scientific as that of eliminating impurities from a gas, or of adroitly using mechanical laws. Here is the inevitable logical flaw in the sorites of the Adept, that he is bound by the very principles which it is his object to overcome: and on him who seeks to discard them arbitrarily they haste to take a terrible revenge!

It is in practice, not in theory, that this difficulty suddenly disappears. For when we take rational steps to suspend the operation of the rational mind, the inhibition does not result in chaos, but in the apprehension of the Universe by means of a faculty to which the laws of the Reason do not apply; and when, returning to the normal state, we seek to analyse our experience, we find that the description abounds in rational absurdities.

On further consideration, however, it becomes gradually clear—gradually, because the habit of Trance must be firmly fixed before its fulminating impressions are truly intelligible—that there are not two kinds of Thought, or of Nature, but one only. The Law of the Mind is the sole substance of the Universe, as well as the sole means by which we apprehend it. There is thus no true antithesis between the conditions of Trance and those of ratiocination and perception; the fact that Trance is not amenable to the rules of argument is impertinent. We say that in Chess a Knight traverses the diagonal

125

of a rectangle measuring three squares by two, neglecting its motion as a material object in space. We have described a definite limited relation in terms of a special sense which works by an arbitrary symbolism: when we analyse any example of our ordinary mental processes, we find the case entirely similar. For what we 'see,' 'hear,' etc., depends upon idiosyncrasies, for one thing, and upon conventional interpretation for another. Thus we agree to call grass green, and to avoid walking over the edge of precipices, without any attempt to make sure than any two minds have exactly identical conceptions of what these things may mean; and just so we agree upon the moves in Chess. By the rules of the game, then, we must think and act, or we risk every kind of error; but we may be perfectly well aware that the rules are arbitrary, and that it is after all only a game. The constant folly of the traditional mystic has been to be so proud of himself for discovering the great secret that the Universe is no more than a toy invented by himself for his amusement that he hastens to display his powers by deliberately misunderstanding and misusing the toy. He has not grasped the fact that just because it is no more than a projection of his own Point-of-View, it is integrally Himself that he offends!

Here lies the error of such Pantheism as that of Mansur el-Hallaj, whom Sir Richard Burton so delightfully (twits in the *Kasîdah*) with his impotence—

> "Mansur was wise, but wiser they who smote
>   him with the hurléd stones;
> And though his blood a witness bore, no
>   Wisdom-Might could mend his bones."

God was in the stones no less than within his tarband-wrapping; and when the twain crashed together, one point of perception of the fact was obscured—which was in no wise his design!

To us, however, this matter is not one for regret; it is (like every phenomenon) an Act of Love. And the very definition of such Act is the Passing Beyond of two Events into a Third, and their withdrawal into a Silence or Nothingness by simultaneous reaction. In this sense it may be said that the Universe is a constant issue into Trance; and in fact the proper understanding of any Event by means of the suitable Contemplation should produce the type of Trance appropriate to the complex Event-Individual in the case.

Now all Magick is useful to produce Trance; for (α) it trains the mind in the discipline necessary to Yoga; (β) it exalts the spirit to the impersonal and divine sublimity which is the first condition of success; (γ) it enlarges the scope of the mind, assuring it full mastery of every subtler plane of Nature, thus affording it adequate material for ecstatic consummation of the Eucharist of Existence.

The essence of the idea of Trance is indeed contained in that of Magick, which is pre-eminently the transcendental Science and Art. Its method is, in one chief sense, Love, the very key of Trance; and, in another, the passing beyond normal conditions. The verbs to transcend, to transmit, to transcribe, and their like, are all of cardinal virtue in Magick. Hence "Love is the law, love under will" is the supreme epitome of Magical doctrine, and its universal Formula. Nor need any man fear to state boldly that every Magical Operation soever is only complete when it is characterised (in one sense or another) by the occurrence of Trance. It was ill done to restrict the use of the word to the supersession of dualistic human consciousness by the impersonal and monistic state of Samadhi. Fast bubbles the fountain of Error from the morass of Ignorance when distinction is forcibly drawn "between any one thing and any other thing." Yea, verily, and Amen! it is the first necessity as it is the last attainment of Trance to abolish every form and every order of dividuality so fast as it presents itself. By this ray may ye read in the Book of your own Magical Record the authentic stigma of your own success.

Liber Liberi vel Lapidis Lazuli (selections)

Excerpted here is the "Prologue" and four sections from "Liber Liberi vel Lapidis Lazuli," one of the inspired Holy Books. This book, which does not necessarily concern Yoga, describes in many different ways the struggles involved in the crossing of the abyss, violent Transcendence of reason, confrontation with Death. (Note the use of "God" as a poetic convenience for Beyond, or for the aspirant's desire to attain Godhead.)

PROLOGUE OF THE UNBORN

1. Into my loneliness comes—

2. The sound of a flute in dim groves that haunt the uttermost hills.

3. Even from the brave river they reach to the edge of the wilderness.

4. And I behold Pan.

5. The snows are eternal above, above—

6. And their perfume smokes upward into the nostrils of the stars.

7. But what have I to do with these?

8. To me only the distant flute, the abiding vision of Pan.

9. On all sides Pan to the eye, to the ear;

10. The perfume of Pan pervading, the taste of him utterly filling my mouth, so that the tongue breaks forth into a weird and monstrous speech.

11. The embrace of him intense on every centre of pain and pleasure.

12. The sixth interior sense aflame with the inmost self of Him,

13. Myself flung down the precipice of being

14. Even to the abyss, annihilation.

15. An end of loneliness, as to all.

16. Pan! Pan! Io Pan! Io Pan!

128

I

1. My God, how I love Thee!

2. With the vehement appetite of a beast I hunt Thee through the Universe.

3. Thou art standing as it were upon a pinnacle at the edge of some fortified city. I am a white bird, and perch upon Thee.

4. Thou art My Lover: I see Thee as a nymph with her white limbs stretched by the spring.

5. She lies upon the moss; there is none other but she:

6. Art Thou not Pan?

7. I am He. Speak not, O my God! Let the work be accomplished in silence.

8. Let my cry of pain be crystallized into a little white fawn to run away into the forest!

9. Thou art a centaur, O my God, from the violet-blossoms that crown Thee to the hoofs of the horse.

10. Thou art harder than tempered steel; there is no diamond beside Thee.

11. Did I not yield this body and soul?

12. I woo thee with a dagger drawn across my throat.

13. Let the spout of blood quench Thy blood-thirst, O my God!

14. Thou art a little white rabbit in the burrow Night.

15. I am greater than the fox and the hole.

16. Give me Thy kisses, O Lord God!

17. The lightning came and licked up the little flock of sheep.

18. There is a tongue and a flame; I see that trident walking over the sea.

19. A phoenix hath it for its head; below are two prongs. They spear the wicked.

20. I will spear Thee, O Thou little grey god, unless Thou beware!

21. From the grey to the gold; from the gold to that which is beyond the gold of Ophir.

22. My God! but I love Thee!

23. Why hast Thou whispered so ambiguous things? Wast Thou afraid, O goat-hoofed One, O horned One, O pillar of lightning?

24. From the lightning fall pearls; from the pearls black specks of nothing.

25. I based all on one, one on naught.

26. Afloat in the aether, O my God, my God!

27. O Thou great hooded sun of glory, cut off these eyelids!

28. Nature shall die out; she hideth me, closing mine eyelids with fear, she hideth me from My destruction, O Thou open eye.

29. O ever-weeping One!

30. Not Isis my mother, nor Osiris my self; but the incestuous Horus given over to Typhon, so may I be!

31. There thought; and thought is evil.

32. Pan! Pan! Io Pan! it is enough.

33. Fall not into death, O my soul! Think that death is the bed into which you are falling!

34. O how I love Thee, O my God! Especially is there a vehement parallel light from infinity, vilely diffracted in the haze of this mind.

35. I love Thee.

I love Thee.

I love Thee.

36. Thou art a beautiful thing whiter than a woman in the column of this vibration.

37. I shoot up vertically like an arrow, and become that Above.

38. But it is death, and the flame of the pyre.

39. Ascend in the flame of the pyre, O my soul! Thy God is like the cold emptiness of the utmost heaven, into which thou radiatest thy little light.

40. When Thou shall know me, O empty God, my flame shall utterly expire in Thy great N. O. X.

41. What shalt Thou be, my God, when I have ceased to love Thee?

42. A worm, a nothing, a niddering knave!

43. But Oh! I love Thee.

44. I have thrown a million flowers from the basket of the Beyond at Thy feet, I have anointed Thee and Thy Staff with oil and blood and kisses.

45. I have kindled Thy marble into life—ay! into death.

46. I have been smitten with the reek of Thy mouth, that drinketh never wine but life.

47. How the dew of the Universe whitens the lips!

48. Ah! trickling flow of the stars of the mother Supernal, begone!

49. I Am She that should come, the Virgin of all men.

50. I am a boy before Thee, O Thou satyr God.

51. Thou wilt inflict the punishment of pleasure—Now! Now! Now!

52. Io Pan! Io Pan! I love Thee. I love Thee.

53. O my God, spare me!

54. Now!

It is done! Death.

55. I cried aloud the word—and it was a mighty spell to bind the Invisible, an enchantment to unbind the bound: yea, to unbind the bound.

V

1. O my beautiful God! I swim in Thy heart like a trout in the mountain torrent.

2. I leap from pool to pool in my joy; I am goodly with brown and gold and silver.

3. Why, I am lovelier than the russet autumn woods at the first snowfall.

4. And the crystal cave of my thought is lovelier than I.

5. Only one fish-hook can draw me out; it is a woman kneeling by the bank of the stream. It is she that pours the bright dew over herself, and into the sand so that the river gushes forth.

6. There is a bird on yonder myrtle; only the song of that bird can draw me out of the pool of Thy heart, O my God!

7. Who is this Neopolitan boy that laughs in his happiness? His lover is the mighty crater of the Mountain of Fire. I saw his charred limbs borne down the slopes in a stealthy tongue of liquid stone.

8. And Oh! the chirp of the cicada!

9. I remember the days when I was cacique in Mexico.

10. O my God, wast Thou then as now my beautiful lover?

11. Was my boyhood then as now Thy toy, Thy joy?

12. Verily, I remember those iron days.

13. I remember how we drenched the bitter lakes with our torrent of gold; how we sank the treasurable image in the crater of Citlaltepetl.

14. How the good flame lifted us even unto the lowlands, setting us down in the impenetrable forest.

15. Yea, Thou wast a strange scarlet bird with a bill of gold. I was Thy mate in the forests of the lowland; and ever we heard from afar the shrill chant of mutilated priests and the insane clamour of the Sacrifice of Maidens.

16. There was weird winged God that told us of his wisdom.

17. We attained to be starry grains of gold dust in the sands of a slow river.

18. Yea, and that river was the river of space and time also.

19. We parted thence; ever to the smaller, ever to the greater, until now, O sweet God, we are ourselves, the same.

20. O God of mine, Thou art like a little white goat with lightning in his horns!

21. I love Thee, I love Thee.

22. Every breath, every word, every thought, every deed is an act of love with Thee.

23. The beat of my heart is the pendulum of love.

24. The songs of me are the soft sighs:

25. The thoughts of me are very rapture:

26. And my deeds are the myriads of Thy children, the stars and the atoms.

27. Let there be nothing!

28. Let all things drop into this ocean of love!

29. Be this devotion a potent spell to exorcise the demons of the Five!

30. Ah God, all is gone! Thou dost consummate Thy rapture. Falútil! Falútli!

31. There is a solemnity of the silence. There is no more voice at all.

32. So shall it be unto the end. We who were dust shall never fall away into the dust.

33. So shall it be.

34. Then, O my God, the breath of the Garden of Spices. All these have a savour averse.

35. The cone is cut with an infinite ray; the curve of hyperbolic life springs into being.

36. Farther and farther we float; yet we are still. It is the chain of systems that is falling away from us.

37. First falls the silly world; the world of the old grey land.

38. Falls it unthinkably far, with its sorrowful bearded face presiding over it; it fades to silence and woe.

39. We to silence and bliss, and the face is the laughing face of Eros.

40. Smiling we greet him with the secret signs.

41. He leads us into the Inverted Palace.

42. There is the Heart of Blood, a pyramid reaching its apex down beyond the Wrong of the Beginning.

43. Bury me unto Thy Glory, O beloved, O princely lover of this harlot maiden, within the Secretest Chamber of the Palace!

44. It is done quickly; yea, the seal is set upon the vault.

45. There is one that shall avail to open it.

46. Nor by memory, nor by imagination, nor by prayer, nor by fasting, nor by scourging, nor by drugs, nor by ritual, nor by meditation; only by passive love shall he avail.

47. He shall await the sword of the Beloved and bare his throat for the stroke.

48. Then shall his blood leap out and write me runes in the sky; yea, write me runes in the sky.

VI

1. Thou wast a priestess, O my God, among the Druids; and we knew the powers of the oak.

2. We made us a temple of stones in the shape of the Universe, even as thou didst wear openly and I concealed.

3. There we performed many wonderful things by midnight.

4. By the waning moon did we work.

5. Over the plain came the atrocious cry of wolves.

6. We answered; we hunted with the pack.

7. We came even unto the new Chapel and Thou didst bear away the Holy Graal beneath Thy Druid vestments.

8. Secretly and by stealth did we drink of the informing sacrament.

9. Then a terrible disease seized upon the folk of the grey land; and we rejoiced.

10. O my God, disguise Thy glory!

11. Come as a thief, and let us steal away the Sacraments!

12. In our groves, in our cloistral cells, in our honeycomb of happiness, let us drink, let us drink!

13. It is the wine that tinges everything with the true tincture of infallible gold.

14. There are deep secrets in these songs. It is not enough to hear the bird; to enjoy song he must be the bird.

15. I am the bird, and Thou art my song, O my glorious galloping God!

16. Thou reinest in the stars; thou drivest the constellations seven abreast through the circus of Nothingness.

17. Thou Gladiator God!

18. I play upon mine harp; Thou fightest the beasts and the flames.

19. Thou takest Thy joy in the music, and I in the fighting.

20. Thou and I are beloved of the Emperor.

21. See! he has summoned us to the Imperial dais.

The night falls; it is a great orgy of worship and bliss.

22. The night falls like a spangled cloak from the shoulders of a prince upon a slave.

23. He rises a free man!

24. Cast thou, O prophet, the cloak upon these slaves!

25. A great night, and scarce fires therein; but freedom for the slave that its glory shall encompass.

26. So also I went down into the great sad city.

27. There dead Messalina bartered her crown for poison from the dead Locusta; there stood Caligula, and smote the seas of forgetfulness.

28. Who wast Thou, O Caesar, that Thou knewest God in an horse?

29. For lo! we beheld the White Horse of the Saxon engraven upon the earth; and we beheld the Horses of the Sea that flame about the old grey land, and the foam from their nostrils enlightens us!

30. Ah! but I love thee, God!

31. Thou art like a moon upon the ice-world.

32. Thou art like the dawn of the utmost snows upon the burnt-up flats of the tiger's land.

33. By silence and by speech do I worship Thee.

34. But all is in vain.

35. Only Thy silence and Thy speech that worship me avail.

36. Wail, O ye folk of the grey land, for we have drunk your wine, and left ye but the bitter dregs.

37. Yet from these we will distil ye a liquor beyond the nectar of the Gods.

38. There is value in our tincture for a world of Spice and gold.

39. For our red powder of projection is beyond all possibilities.

40. There are few men; there are enough.

41. We shall be full of cup-bearers, and the wine is not stinted.

42. O dear my God! what a feast Thou hast provided.

43. Behold the lights and the flowers and the maidens!

44. Taste of the wines and the cakes and the splendid meats!

45. Breathe in the perfumes and the clouds of little gods like wood-nymphs that inhabit the nostrils!

46. Feel with your whole body the glorious smoothness of the marble coolth and the generous warmth of the sun and the slaves!

47. Let the Invisible inform all the devouring Light of its disruptive vigour!

48. Yea! all the world is split apart, as an old grey tree by the lightning!

49. Come, O ye gods, and let us feast.

50. Thou, O my darling, O my ceaseless Sparrow-God, my delight, my desire, my deceiver, come Thou and chirp at my right hand!

51. This was the tale of the memory of Al A'in the priest; yea, of Al A'in the priest.

VII

1. By the burning of the incense was the Word revealed, and by the distant drug.

2. O meal and honey and oil! O beautiful flag of the moon, that she hangs out in the centre of bliss!

3. These loosen the swathings of the corpse; these unbind the feet of Osiris, so that the flaming God may rage through the firmament with his fantastic spear.

4. But of pure black marble is the sorry statue, and the changeless pain of the eyes is bitter to the blind.

5. We understand the rapture of that shaken marble, torn by the throes of the crowned child, the golden rod of the golden God.

6. We know why all is hidden in the stone, within the coffin, within the mighty sepulchre, and we too answer Olalám! Imál! Tutúlu! as it is written in the ancient book.

7. Three words of that book are as life to a new aeon; no god has read the whole.

8. But Thou and I, O God, have written it page by page.

9. Ours is the elevenfold reading of the Elevenfold word.

10. These seven letters together make seven diverse words; each word is divine, and seven sentences are hidden therein.

11. Thou art the Word, O my darling, my lord, my master!

12. O come to me, mix the fire and the water, all shall dissolve.

13. I await Thee in sleeping, in waking. I invoke Thee no more; for Thou art in me, O Thou who hast made me a beautiful instrument tuned to Thy rapture.

14. Yet art Thou ever apart, even as I.

15. I remember a certain holy day in the dusk of the year, in the

dusk of the Equinox of Osiris, when first I beheld Thee visibly; when first the dreadful issue was fought out; when the Ibis-headed One charmed away the strife.

16. I remember Thy first kiss, even as a maiden should. Nor in the dark byways was there another: Thy kisses abide.

17. There is none other beside Thee in the whole Universe of Love.

18. My God, I love Thee, O Thou goat with gilded horns!

19. Thou beautiful bull of Apis! Thou beautiful serpent of Apep! Thou beautiful child of the Pregnant Goddess!

20. Thou hast stirred in Thy sleep, O ancient sorrow of years! Thou has raised Thine head to strike, and all is dissolved into the Abyss of Glory.

21. An end to the letters of the words! An end to the sevenfold speech.

22. Resolve me the wonder of it all into the figure of a gaunt swift camel striding over the sand.

23. Lonely is he, and abominable; yet hath he gained the crown.

24. Oh rejoice! rejoice!

25. My God! O my God! I am but a speck in the star-dust of ages; I am the Master of the Secret of Things.

26. I am the Revealer and the Preparer. Mine is the Sword—and the Mitre and the Wingèd Wand!

27. I am the Initiator and the Destroyer. Mine is the Globe—and the Bennu Bird and the Lotus of Isis my daughter!

28. I am the One beyond these all; and I bear the symbols of the mighty darkness.

29. There shall be a sigil as of a vast black brooding ocean of death and the central blaze of darkness, radiating its night upon all.

30. It shall swallow up that lesser darkness.

31. But in that profound who shall answer: What is?

32. Not I.

33. Not Thou, O God!

34. Come, let us no more reason together; let us enjoy! Let us be ourselves, silent, unique, apart.

35. O lonely woods of the world! In what recesses will ye hide our love?

36. The forest of the spears of the Most High is called Night, and Hades, and the Day of Wrath; but I am His captain, and I bear His cup.

37. Fear me not with my spearmen! They shall slay the demons with their petty prongs. Ye shall be free.

38. Ah, slaves! ye will not—ye know not how to will.

39. Yet the music of my spears shall be a song of freedom.

40. A great bird shall sweep from the Abyss of Joy, and bear ye away to be my cup-bearers.

41. Come, O my God, in one last rapture let us attain to the Union with the Many!

42. In the silence of Things, in the Night of Forces, beyond the accursèd domain of the Three, let us enjoy our love!

43. My darling! My darling! away, away beyond the Assembly and the Law and the Enlightenment unto an Anarchy of Solitude and Darkness!

44. For even thus must we veil the brilliance of our Self.

45. My darling! My darling!

46. O my God, but the love in Me bursts over the bonds of Space and Time; my love is spilt among them that love not love.

47. My wine is poured out for them that never tasted wine.

48. The fumes thereof shall intoxicate them and the vigour of my love shall breed mighty children from their maidens.

49. Yea! without draught, without embrace:—and the Voice answered Yea! these things shall be.

50. Then I sought a Word for Myself; nay, for myself.

51. And the Word came: O Thou! it is well. Heed naught! I love thee! I love Thee!

52. Therefore had I faith unto the end of all; yea, unto the end of all.

PART III

Sex and Magick

MAGICK AND WOMAN

The Great Work is the uniting of opposites. It may mean the uniting of the soul with God, of the microcosm with the macrocosm, of the female with the male, of the ego with the non-ego—or what not.
                                                            Magick Without Tears

Seeing that Every Act is an Orgasm, their total issue cannot be but Birth.
                                            "Silence," Little Essays Toward Truth

Thou and I will Kiss, and atone for the wrong of the Beginning.
                                                    "Liber Liberi vel Lapidis Lazuli"

Hold! Hold! Bear up in thy rapture; fall not in swoon of the excellent kisses! Harder! Hold up thyself! Lift thine head! Breathe not so deep—die!
                                                            The Book of the Law

In her blood I inscribe the secret riddles of the Sphinx of the gods, that none shall understand—save only the pure and the voluptuous, the chaste and the obscene, the androgyne and the gynander. . . .
                                                    "Liber Cordis Cincti Serpente"

Those persons who have supposed that the use of these symbols implied worship of the generative organs, merely attributed to the sages of every time and country minds of a calibre equal to their own.
                                                                        Magick

It is no secret that Aleister Crowley wrote Magick. And no particular secret that he produced erotica. As with other fields he entered, he produced it in abundance: *White Stains, Leah Sublime, Snowdrops From a Curate's Garden, The Bagh-i-Muattar* (the last a ribald poetry and prose paeon to placing "spud" in the "crimson mud" of young boys).[1] Sex Magick, though, he tries to hide, never admitting the Magick (or even the Sex).

Crowley's instructionary essays on Sex Magick are, unlike the rest of his work, written exclusively for private study by the highest level

1. *The Scented Garden of Abdullah the Satirist of Shiraz*, or *The Bagh-I-Muattar* (reprinted privately: no place of origin, listing of publisher or pub. date), p. 38.

officials of the Ordo Templi Orientis (O.T.O.), his magical order whose course of study climaxed with such workings. Sex Magick (if we might drop the formalities) has no public posture. It crouches behind (Free)masonry, slouches so it does not reveal its size. Sex Magick maintains a low profile through silence and special instruction to students not to reveal its workings. "Energized Enthusiasm," Crowley's paper on "it" for *The Equinox,* cuts off; it tantalizingly omits a description of procedures. And even though after many years the specifics were published, they remain arcanely abbreviated, Written in an arch style and utilizing a battery of obscure alchemic terms. Sex Magick couches itself in a flurry of Words unfurry, and here are just a few of a veritable rash: Lion (male), Eagle (female), Lingam (penis), Yoni (vagina), Red Tincture, or Coagulated Blood (sperm), White Tincture, or Gluten (vaginal secretions), and Elixir of Life (the mixture of the Red and White).

Crowley's ultimate paper on sex, "The Book of the Unveiling of Sangraal" (or "Liber Agape"), was in this way so muddled and riddled that he wrote a second paper, "De Arte Magica," in order to at least mention his topic. But while the first lies buried in a treasure house of symbol, the second still insists on hinting around. Talking about homosexual Magick, "rites analogous" to strict and straight Sex Magick, Crowley skirts the issue: "It is said by certain Initiates that to obtain Spiritual gifts, and to aid Nature, the Sacrament should be as it were a Nuptial of the Folk of Earth; but that Magick is of the Demon, and that by a certain perversion of the Office, may be created Elementals fit to perform the Will of the Magician."[2] The point buried here is that anal sex may be better than vaginal in order "to aid Nature"; copulate in the anus to "f . . ." with the "earth."

It is a curious affair, this vagueness. This Magick that does not resemble Magick and Sex that does not resemble Sex. Modesty never became Crowley, and in terms of keeping magical secrets, he flaunted the fact that he published Golden Dawn materials in his magazine against that Order's orders. Though the curtain has been drawn as tightly as possible, the physical workings of Sexual Magick are not complex, and hardly surprising or shocking. Crowley's activities included mentally meditating on his penis—masturbating—while thinking of gods and angels; consecrating talismans with combinations of semen, vaginal juices and menstrual blood; prolonging and intensify-

---

2. "De Arte Magica," *The Works of Aleister Crowley, Volume I* (reprinted Keighley, Great Britain: Kadath Press, 1986), p. 39.

ing sex through visualization and meditation; and, perhaps most mundanely, beseeching gods for information, money and material possessions during sex. These areas of research were limited only by Crowley's physical stamina which, based on his private diaries, was indeed great.

What can be made, then, of a grown man preoccupied with sex to the point that it came to rule his "profession," but who chose to hide his habits in the closet? In explaining away the dirty secrets of Sex Magick one could trace a glistening line through history (as has been done), concluding that Crowleyan sex systems are a collage of received ideas whirled around in the magical Cup. In which case Sex Magick makes sense and cannot be said to be obscene because it has always been digestible, even agreeable, as part of ancient Buddhist and Hindu Tantrism and "primitive" fertility cults. Or, out of desperation, one might find Crowley's life so difficult to explain, so pathetic and perverse, that no possibility is left but to psychoanalyze Crowley's character, calling him a sex addict with a hard habit to break. John Symonds says that Crowley "lacked integration" and that "he was in the grip of unconscious forces."[3] Even Crowley doubts himself a bit, saying in his autohagiography that he suffers from "congenital masochism."[4]

In these ways one reduces Crowley's size, abbreviating Sex Magick to S. M. The alternative is to chart a long and tortured course through all of his writings to put the Magick back in S. M. Crowley begins with Love: "Love is the law, love under will. Nor let the fools mistake love; for there are love and love."[5] Love under Will, a Love not secular, but the conjunction of coition raised to the level of the sacred, as in the workings of an orgy, is an essential part of Crowley's Law. "*Orgia,* only used in the plural and connected with Ergon (work), means sacred rites . . . and *Orgazio* means, therefore, to celebrate Orgies, or ceremonies, or to celebrate any sacred rites."[6] This Love that is not Love (and nothing is what it seems in Sex Magick) partakes of Magick, but initially takes place on a physical rather than a spiritual plane, or perhaps in a different room of the house.

Sex Magick indulges in a Love that is not Love in seeking the same

3. *The Confessions of Aleister Crowley* (New York: Hill and Wang, 1970), p. 22.
4. *The Confessions of Aleister Crowley,* p. 44.
5. *Liber AL: The Book of the Law* (reprinted Berkeley: O. T. O., 1982), Chapter I, Verse 57.
6. "Concerning Blasphemy," reprinted in *The Equinox, Volume III, Number 10* (New York: Thelema Publications, 1986), p. 222.

path as Ceremonial Magick, a path which includes such steps as "the Knowledge and Conversation of the Holy Guardian Angel," general "spiritual attainment," "further insight into Nature and her laws," and "the establishment of the Kingdom of Ra-Hoor-Khuit upon the earth" (as explained in the prophetic work *The Book of the Law*).[7] As one might imagine (or fantasize) Sex Magick simplifies in many ways the practices of more traditional forms of magic. Perhaps the culmination of a Magick that belies its ancestor's worn-out equipment, S. M. needs no temple, altar, or costumes. With one exception then, Sex Magick is easier (more portable) than ritual magic and that exception is Woman. Woman is central to the Sex Magick of the O.T.O.'s highest workings and necessary for creation of the important Elixir of Life (the consistency and pungency of the Elixir determines whether the operation has been successful). Though Crowley practiced both masturbatory and homosexual Magick, he concludes that "the Lion and the Eagle are best in combination."[8] This is forecast in *The Book of the Law*, which posits the conjunction of the masculine Hadit, "the wingèd secret flame," and the feminine Nuit, "the stooping starlight,"[9] who must come together as the infinitely great heavens and the infinitely small star to bring forth the New Aeon of Horus.

Yet Woman can be only an "assistant"; she doesn't have a penis or the semen that creates. "For the Gluten is but a menstruum or solvent, and containeth nothing in itself."[10] She is a dark place for hiding, a body in which the rapture of the Man-God can take place. "Man is the guardian of the Life of God; woman but a temporary expedient; a shrine indeed for the God, but not the God."[11] Their difference is "indicated by that of their respective orgasms, the female undulatory, the male catastrophic."[12] The Man explodes with semen—he makes something—while the Woman implodes without creating. Thus the formula: Love under Will. ". . . Though She be love, her function is but passive. . . . And thus they err with grievous error and dire who prate of Love as the Formula of Magick; Love is unbalanced, void, vague,

7. "De Arte Magica," p. 46.
8. "De Arte Magica," p. 40.
9. *Liber AL: The Book of the Law*, Chapter I, Verse 16.
10. "De Arte Magica," p. 40.
11. "The Book of the Unveiling of Sangraal," *The Secret Rituals of the O.T.O.* (reprinted New York: Samuel Weiser, 1973), p. 221.
12. *Magick Without Tears* (St. Paul: Llewellyn Publications, 1973), pp. 130–131.

undirected, sterile, nay, more, a very Shell, the prey of abject arts demonic: Love must be *'under will.'*"[13]

Woman unspecifies since she doesn't shine with her own light, cannot project her own Will. She appears black and mysterious, abject and demonic, vague in her void. She performs best as a blank, an unwitting partner, when it comes to the operation of Sex Magick. "It is better and easier that the other party should be in ignorance of the sacred character of the Office."[14] In her lies open possibility, opportunity, Unknown and Unknowable. Man acts both cautious and yearning when it comes to the Unknown. On the other hand, he must seek it out, because "perfect is no man in himself without his fulfillment in all possibility."[15] She is exciting, stimulating. "I will make me a little boat of my tongue, and explore the unknown rivers."[16] But because she is excitement, driving man past reason and logic, "therefore also hath she no Nature of Truth."[17] She is abyss. "In the place of her face is a gory hole,"[18] Crowley wrote in his youth. The "all possibility" of excitement deludes Man, covers her hole(s). She projects nothing but image, a mask. "Yea! I love the Mask through which glitter Her unfathomable eyes."[19] The mask concealing not Woman but Ape—the figure which represents the limit of Knowledge. "I saw the Woman. O my God, I beheld the image thereof, even as a lovely shape that concealeth a black monkey, even as a figure that draweth with her hands small images of men down into hell."[20]

But the more one Unknows Woman, unconfronts Her, unshapes Her, enters her dark cavern, the "Deeper and deeper into the mire of things! Farther and farther into the neverending Expansion of the Abyss. . . . I contract ever as she ever expandeth."[21] His Wand, his Phallus, his Will, for example is a "binding and a limitation," while her Cup, her Yoni, her

13. "Love," *Little Essays Toward Truth* (Malton, Canada: Dove Press, approximately 1970), p. 70.
14. "De Arte Magica," p. 39.
15. "Chastity," *Little Essays Toward Truth,* p. 61.
16. "Liber Cordis Cincti Serpente," reprinted in *The Holy Books of Thelema* (York Beach, Maine: Samuel Weiser, 1983), p. 70.
17. *Liber Aleph vel CXI: The Book of Wisdom or Folly* (reprinted Seattle: Aeon Press, 1985), p. 75.
18. *The Confessions of Aleister Crowley,* p. 82.
19. *The Magical Record of the Beast 666: The Journals of Aleister Crowley* (Quebec: Next Step Publications, 1972), p. 211.
20. "Vel Ararita," reprinted in *The Holy Books of Thelema,* p. 220.
21. "Vel Ararita," p. 227.

Unknowledge is "an expansion—into the Infinite."[22] And with contraction—as the penis feels like it shrinks in the face of the looming black hole—the desire to be destroyed is born. "Slay thyself in the fervour of thine abandonment unto Our Lady. Let thy flesh hang loose upon thy bones, and thine eyes glare with thy quenchless lust unto the Infinite, with the passion for the Unknown, for Her that is beyond Knowledge the accursed one."[23] In "De Arte Magica," Crowley goes so far as to suggest that physical death at the moment of orgasm, *"Mores Justi,"* might be (im)proper, as Death and Love are twins.[24] On the other hand, evil for Crowley is typified by the workings of the "Black Brothers," and defined as that which refuses to let itself be killed by Woman, refuses to destroy itself in Love.[25]

Woman the destroyer, essentially Unknowable—the destroyer of the known—is however known within the bounds of community (the ties that bind together), where she is named by "type," or by the role she projects. At one extreme, Babalon, the sinner, the Dominatrix whore, destroys according to desire and direction, taking man straight to hell. "I want my crown crushed by Her feet; I want my face fouled by Her spittle. I want my heart torn by Her boot-heel, my mind to Her skirt-hem's rustle, my soul to Her privy."[26] Under such conditions, the guardian of the life of God, the keeper of the creative Love under Will, suffocates. "I drown in delight at the thought that I who have been Master of the Universe should lie beneath Her feet, Her slave, Her victim, eager to be abased, passionately athirst for suffering, swooning at Her cruelty, craving Her contempt; 'tis joy to be splashed with the mire of Her Triumph, to bleed under Her whip's lash, to choke as Her heel treads my throat."[27]

In another class, the classier perfect Golden Goddess, the Saint, the Virgin daughter of the King presents herself in a slightly different, more classically passive way. "The chaste man, the true Knight-Errant of the Stars, imposes continually his essential virility upon the throbbing Womb of the King's Daughter."[28] Yet her creamy-white, speechless abyss can serve as the engine of destruction: "I wish thee more than

22. *Magick* (reprinted New York: Samuel Weiser, 1974), p. 78.
23. "Liber Cheth vel Vellum Abiegni," reprinted in *Gems from the Equinox* (St. Paul: Llewellyn Publications, 1974), p. 604.
24. "De Arte Magica," p. 44.
25. "De Lege Libellum," reprinted in *Gems from the Equinox,* p. 135.
26. *The Magical Record of the Beast 666: The Journals of Aleister Crowley,* p. 178.
27. *The Magical Record of the Beast 666: The Journals of Aleister Crowley,* p. 177.
28. "Chastity," p. 60.

this, that . . . thou mayst find a Virgin like unto this to draw thee with her Simplicity, and her embroidered Silence. . . ."[29]

Equally fit for duty are the Golden Goddess or Babalon. Such terms barely stick to Woman as they contaminate each other. "Many have arisen, being wise. They have said, 'Seek out the glittering Image in the place every golden, and unite yourselves with It.' Many have arisen, being foolish. They have said, 'Stoop down unto the darkly splendid world, and be wedded to that Blind Creature of the Slime.' I who am beyond Wisdom and Folly, arise and say unto you: achieve both weddings!"[30] The goddess slips to slime, the slime turns to gold. In order to Unknow woman more and more, Crowley prescribes chastity for prostitutes, and "unchastity" for prudes.[31] "In low grades of initiation, dogmatic quarrels are inflamed . . . when Saint John distinguishes between the Whore BABALON and the Woman clothed with the Sun."[32]

Putting oneself in a kind of drugged trance during sex ("Erotocomatose Lucidity," as Crowley calls it[33]) constitutes one way of unknowing, uncaring, self-destroying. Another is to make love to "disgusting" women, who have such low self-esteem that they are nothing but bodies with holes. "To this end take chiefly all such things as are naturally repulsive. For what is pleasant is assimilated easily and without ecstacy: it is in the transfiguration of the loathsome and abhorred into The Beloved that the Self is shaken to the root in Love."[34] This can bring Crowley away from Woman, into the arms of a Man or even Animal. "History teacheth us that the supreme masters of the world seek ever the vilest and most horrible creatures for their concubines, overstepping even the limited laws of sex and species in their necessity to transcend normality."[35]

And so Crowley poses the limit of Woman. At a certain point, this expedient, this convenience is no longer necessary. A dog will do. Woman must finally be seen as not a woman, or women, but only the idea of "Woman" as distinct from "Man." A Woman that is not a woman, whose generative organs are just the figure of her vagina as laid

29. *Liber Aleph vel CXI: The Book of Wisdom or Folly,* p. 80.
30. "Liber Tzaddi vel Hamus Hermeticus," reprinted in *Gems from the Equinox,* p. 661.
31. "Thien Tao," *Konx Om Pax* (reprinted Yogi Publication Society, no place of origin/pub. date), p. 62.
32. *Magick,* p. 343.
33. "De Arte Magica," pp. 43–44.
34. "De Lege Libellum," p. 120.
35. "De Lege Libellum," p. 121.

against his figural penis. As a figure—whether Babalon or Golden Goddess—she is radically separate, different, an other. A gap where he has something tangible (even rock hard) in need of softening.

The Knowledge and Conversation of the Holy Guardian Angel is one specific task of Sex Magick that demonstrates the slippery construction Woman, the relative arbitrariness of the Other—in this case a holy Angel which is not an Angel. On the face of it (without trying to read between the lines) converting one's special Angel by identifying that Angel with the Woman to whom you make love initiates contact with beings on other planes, hooks one into the spiritual switchboard, "contributes occult puberty."[36] But pull the sheet off the ghost and there is nothing; not Angel/Woman, but the magician's face (or penis) reflected in the Other, "the unconscious Creature Self—the Spiritual Phallus."[37] To "know" this Angel "being" is to Unknow the magician's Other, his double, and to see his Self constituted by this Other, realizing that he is no better than his own *doppelgänger.* "For the body of Man is but his Shadow."[38] Through the Magick of Sex, he (un)sees himself in fleeting images in his Woman's eyes and through Her womb. "I manifested mine whole Magical Self in her Mind. Thus then in Her, as in a Mirror, have I been able to interpret myself to myself."[39] To uninterpret himself: it may be named Woman, but it spells Man.

At the moment when his Self must be traced through her—the Other—at the moment of orgasm, he is both lost and found. He reaches orgasm—he reaches puberty—and recedes as a thing of no substance. And so he dies "the death of his old mind",[40] the mind that conceived of a "thing" called "Self." To reach orgasm during the operation of Conversation is to return from the Hell of Self into the Silence of Nothing—as No One—through the relatively unimportant unvehicle of "the borneless one," Angel, Other, Woman.

Having come this far, physically using up this Woman, it is perhaps time to relax, smoke a cigarette, and broaden the view, returning to the Qabalistic paths. Paths shared by both Ceremonial Magick and Sexual Magick. "Berashith" 's story of the conjunction of the infinitely great and the infinitely small and of the creation of the universe can easily be retold

36. "Liber Samekh Theurgia Goetia Summa Congressus Cum Daemone," reprinted in *Gems from the Equinox*, p. 335.
37. Ibid.
38. *Liber Aleph vel CXI: The Book of Wisdom or Folly*, p. 55.
39. *Liber Aleph vel CXI: The Book of Wisdom or Folly*, p. 47.
40. "Liber Samekh Theurgia Goetia Summa Congressus Cum Daemone," p. 347.

as a sexual adventure. Expounding to Crowley on the problematics of creation during Crowley's homosexual "Paris Workings," Mercury [the Roman equivalent of the Egyptian Thoth, the "god" who invented Writing] tells Crowley that the planes of existence result from the Phallus being seduced away from the Yoni, a *coitus interruptus* on a cosmic scale. A spillage from a long, tubular vessel. "Every drop of semen which Hermes [the Greek version of Thoth] sheds is a world. . . . People upon the worlds are like maggots upon an apple, all forms of life bred by the world are in the nature of parasites. All worlds are excreta, they represent wasted semen. Therefore all is blasphemy."[41] The infinitely great, the dark and silent skies of Nuit, makes love to the infinitely small, the Will of a star Man, Hadit. It is only by this break in their act of Love that we exist and that tragedy takes place. This version of beginnings neatly (or messily) reverses the Biblical story of creation. In the Bible, God Wills the world into existence and his creatures—a woman and a man—later fall from perfect grace; in Crowley's story the fall comes with creation, with a penis releasing into the air.

Recovering from this trauma, the inevitable Qabalistic creation, Man rejoins with Woman. "For I am divided for love's sake, for the chance of union. This is the creation of the world, that the pain of division is as nothing, and the joy of dissolution of all."[42] At this Crowleyan creation is more than a terrible tragedy. It is also a set-up, an artifice—perhaps not as sad as first thought, perhaps even desirable. In Writing on Sex Magick to his "magical child," Crowley urges him "to create by Artifice a Conflict in thyself, that thou mayst take thy Pleasure in its Resolution."[43] The play of Nuit and Hadit, for example, amounts to a love play of opposites—the "Drama or Commemoration of the whole Mystery of By-coming."[44] The world as artifice was created so that it could be "un-created" through the S. M. pleasures of the Yoni, wherein the conflicts and divisions of pleasure and pain, domination and submission, passion and detachment, chastity and virility, are explored, reunited, burst apart. "Bind thyself, and thou shalt be for ever free."[45] And it doesn't hurt a bit. "All Pain is but sharp Sauce to the Dish of Pleasure."[46]

41. *The Paris Working,* quoted in Francis King, *The Magical World of Aleister Crowley* (New York: Coward, McCann & Geoghegan, Inc., 1978), p. 84.
42. *Liber AL: The Book of the Law,* Chapter I, Verses 29–30.
43. *Liber Aleph vel CXI: The Book of Wisdom or Folly,* p. 69.
44. Ibid.
45. "Liber III vel Jugorum," reprinted in *Gems from the Equinox,* p. 208.
46. *Liber Aleph vel CXI: The Book of Wisdom or Folly,* p. 33.

Semen cannot be indiscriminately spilled during the hijinx. "To you that are Adepts it is ruin absolute."[47] The loss of the Semen during Sex Magick brings the world too much into focus, leaves a mess on the rug. "Unless 'all you have and all you are' is identical with the Universe, its annihilation would leave a surplus."[48] Losing Semen is also similar to retaining a single thought of Self during the Conversation of the Holy Guardian Angel, a retention which means being cast into the world where the Self is constituted for eternity. Therefore, Crowley urges extreme caution: "The Elixir being then prepared solemnly and in silence, do thou consume it utterly."[49] Whatever is created during the act of Sex Magick must be eaten, recycled. He admires (though does not practice himself) the ability of Hindu masters to withhold their Semen, recirculating it within the body to prevent its straying.

But this seemingly physical grounding of Sex Magick omits the relationship of these practices to the Word. Just as magical speech and ritual are tied up in language so is the magician's Phallus. "He [the Magus, one of the three chief grades in Crowleyan Magick] is the Logos [the Word]; and He is phallic. This doctrine is of the utmost Qabalistic importance."[50] The Word—Speech—is Phallocentric, and the Phallus-Word (Semen) spits the World. Not just to a shared path, a creation myth which might be spoken both horizontally and vertically, but something more. Something that will reopen the case of the Yoni. When the Phallus (the Word) is let loose (no longer spilling within the Yoni), the blasphemy of worlds, of selves—of even Man and Woman—results. It should come as no surprise that the grade of Magus is attributed to the second Sephira on the Tree of Life, Chokmah, because we have already seen how Chokmah is the Word. In like manner, the first letter ("Y") of the Hebrew formula of the Tetragrammaton (the formula of creation "YHVH"), also rests with Chokmah and represents the Masculine and the Father. Chokmah registers therefore as the Father/Phallus/Logos (Creative Love under Will). The second letter ("H") positions itself at Binah, Writing—the Feminine and passive vehicle of the Will, the Mother. Binah serves reservedly as Mother/ Yoni/Writing (always already to be spoken by the Father, Written through). The *coitus interruptus* of which we spoke is thus creation unmediated, Word without Writing. A directly creative and communi-

---

47. "Of the Secret Marriages of Gods with Men," reprinted in *The Secret Rituals of the O.T.O.*, p. 201.
48. *Magick Without Tears*, p. 109.
49. "The Book of the Unveiling of Sangraal," p. 225.
50. "Chastity," p. 59.

cative side of Speech heard independent of its more ambivalent sex partner. The Outside Word deludes—a power delusion that Crowley says can be suffered by he who attains the dangerous grade of Magus, who can see only power in orgasm (i.e., he can form a planet but blows his orgasm).

Sex Magick aims its all-possible shot of Semen carefully, aims to recognize that break from Writing and put us in our place—back in bed—by acknowledging a world created by the Logos of the Father only through the Unknowable Mother, Writing. "Yea, blessed be She, blessed be Her Name, and the Name of Her Name, unto the Ages!"[51] Man is only an "impulse" until he joins with Woman; there literally is no Logos until it is interpreted through Writing. S. M. devotes itself to a sexual economy that makes us all—Man and Woman—effects of Sex Writing. Back in the Yoni with Crowley, we note in part a restaging of the act. Climaxing outside may generate the heavens, but climaxing inside produces another sort of orgasm. "Every 'act of love under will' has the dual result [1] the creation of a child combining the qualities of its parents, [2] the withdrawal by ecstasy into Nothingness."[52] The double-shooting Phallus Writes not one, but two children. "The Universe is conserved by the duplex action involved in the formula. The disappearance of Father and Mother is precisely compensated by the emergence of Son and Daughter."[53]

As there can be no way out of Language, we are stuck in the Bed; Writing and Sex Magick the same. Caught in the act the two children, previously unidentified to protect their names, now display themselves as the two final letters of the Tetragrammaton, "V" and "H". "V" is the boy child of the union: the Logos unbridled, an emanation in time and space, the creation of the planets, stars, et al. "H" is the girl child: the withdrawal into nothingness, the ecstasic Writing of orgasm that annihilates the world, an "ecstasy rising into silence."[54] This final "H", little "H", finds herself seated by the Qabalists at the bottom of the Tree of Life, in the material world of the tenth Sephira, Malkuth, identified with the dirt of earth. Malkuth, the home of little "H" (traditionally attributed as female) is different from the other Sephiroth, in that when light shines into it from the ninth Sephira Malkuth has nowhere else to reflect it. Malkuth is the bottom: simply receiving.

With Malkuth comes consummation, as little "H" replaces the mother

51. *Liber Aleph vel CXI: The Book of Wisdom or Folly*, p. 79.
52. *Magick Without Tears*, p. 63.
53. "Love," *Little Essays Toward Truth*, pp. 66–67.
54. *Eight Lectures on Yoga* (reprinted Phoenix: Falcon Press, 1985), p. 43.

in her Father's bed, to become a "compensation which cancels" the son, creation. Her mud of the world begins the "absorption" of the world.[55] Father (the Logos of creation who paradoxically resides in the place of nothingness) and Daughter (the created earth who paradoxically continues to represent the Writing of Woman) keep things all in the family. "This therefore closeth the Circle of my Speech, for now I am returned to that which I spake aforetime concerning the general Method of Love, and thy Development by that Way."[56] The second child, the little girl, makes love to Daddy, and the earth fuses with heaven. When her earthy little orgasm roars, the world quivers with anticipation.

Which is the closed economy, the Path, the Letters of Love: another Woman, another Unknown, another Poison. "She [little "H"] is mysterious, being at once the Flower of the Three Others, and their Poison."[57] A "subtle" Poison indeed, acting as Antidote to the created world. Crushed and destroyed, the Man unites with his beloved. "Therefore, must thou seek ever those Things which are to thee poisonous, and that in the highest Degree, and make them thine by Love."[58] We have seen how the Dominatrix Babalon and the Golden Goddess destroy the Man Crowley, and how the Holy Guardian Angel destroys the idea of Man (or Self) as separate from Other. Now, under Writing, Man bows to its pressures, loses mastery over objects, collapses under the stabbings of his own pen in the body of another. Given the closed economy—the tightening of the vagina around the penis so that not a single drop is lost—Father, Mother, Son and Daughter each in turn (in reverse order) disappear.

Beyond the Father on the Tree of Life lies only the first Sephira, Kether, the Crown, the Negative Nothing. Where Known and Unknown, Writing and Logos, trade roles and change positions, juggling passive and active, masculine and feminine. "Both God and the Soul are male or female as convenience requires."[59] The feminine, as opposed to Woman, is already a part of every Man, and vice versa. The Aeon of Horus is the Aeon of "two sexes in one person,"[60] when "it is therefore incumbent on the male magician to cultivate those female virtues in

55. *Eight Lectures on Yoga*, p. 43.
56. *Liber Aleph vel CXI: The Book of Wisdom or Folly*, p. 49.
57. *Liber Aleph vel CXI: The Book of Wisdom or Folly*, p. 59.
58. *Liber Aleph vel CXI: The Book of Wisdom or Folly*, p. 13.
59. "Of the Secret Marriages of Gods with Men," p. 198.
60. *Magick*, p. 171.

which he is deficient, and this task he must of course accomplish without in anyway impairing his virility."[61] "I am hard and strong and male; but come Thou! I shall be soft and weak and feminine."[62]

To the point where nothing stays what it seems: a Man is no longer a Man, his Semen no longer Semen (as the Angel that is not Angel, the Woman not Woman, the Love not Love). "The divine consciousness . . . feeds upon a certain secretion, as I believe. This secretion is analogous to semen, but not identical with it. . . . So closely is this secretion connected with the sexual economy that it appears to me at times as if it might be a by-product of that process which generates semen."[63] This by-product may be some kind of spiritual Semen or mental Semen, though it may be best not to get too bogged down in "sementics" within a system of secrets that denies everything and proves nothing. His emissions "consist," instead, of a "red powder of projection [the Red Tincture] . . . beyond all possibilities."[64]

A longing Love confession: "This shall regenerate the world, the little world my sister, my heart & my tongue, unto whom I send this kiss."[65] A kiss that is not, in this case, still a kiss, as the Semen which is not Semen, the Angel not Angel, the Woman not Woman, the Love not Love. The kiss in question a reference to the text—*The Book of the Law*—in which it writhes. Dripping with the promise withheld in Crowley's O. T. O. sex directives: sex books without the language of sex. Here: sexy words that are still not sex, but texts. Like a "Lover's Alphabet" of poems, one for each Love Letter, left unfinished by Crowley.[66] Or bedtime stories.

61. *Magick,* p. 151.
62. "Liber Liberi vel Lapidis Lazuli," reprinted in *The Holy Books of Thelema,* p. 20.
63. "Energized Enthusiasm," reprinted in *Gems from the Equinox,* p. 617.
64. "Liber Liberi vel Lapidis Lazuli," p. 31.
65. *Liber AL: The Book of the Law,* Chapter I, Verse 53.
66. *The Confessions of Aleister Crowley,* p. 333.

De Arte Magica

Crowley signs this Sex Magick instruction book, like the others written for the elite of the O.T.O., with the name "Baphomet," the goat-headed god said to have been worshipped by the fallen Christian Knights Templar during the Middle Ages. This wide-ranging text is intended to be a comment on "The Book of the Unveiling of Sangraal," as he states, but goes into a number of areas that the other never suggests. Section IX concerns Sex Magick performed during a woman's period. Crowley commentator Kenneth Grant has made much of this in his books on Crowley. (Note: Briah, Yetzirah and Assiah refer to the three "worlds" of Qabalistic creation—spiritual, angelic and earthly.)

Baphomet X° Rex Summus Sanctissimus O.T.O. National Grand Master General ad vitam of Ireland, Iona and all the Britains, in the Name of the Secret Master, Aumn. Greeting and Peace to Out Most Holy, Most Illuminated, Most Illustrious, and Most Dear Brother, his Excellency Sir James Thomas Windram X° O.T.O., Our Viceroy in the Union of South Africa, and sendeth these for his pleasure and instruction, and for communication at utmost extremity of need to selected Initiates of the Sanctuary of the Gnosis IX° who have either (a) shewn by power their fitness for that degree, or (b) shewn by wisdom their suitability to ward the Arcanum Arcanorum. Also to certain trusty bretheren of the VIII°, VII°, and VI° chosen for this moment of peril.

For at this hour the clouds gather again upon the face of the Sun our Father, all Those Who Know may perish in the world-war; even as it is written in the Ritual of the V°:

"It is the hour when the Veil of the Temple was rent in twain,
When darkness began to overspread the earth,
When the altar was thrown down,

154

The star called Wormwood fell upon the earth,
When the Blazing Star was eclipsed,
The Sacred Tau was defiled with blood and water,
Despair the tribulation visited us,
And the Word was lost."

Now therefore that the floods menace the Earth, and the Winter of Civilisation is upon us, it is fitting that an Ark of the Sanctuary be builded wherein the sacred Phallus may be hidden, a Field sown wherein the Germ of Life may be preserved; so that although the Tradition be destroyed in the destruction of the Brains that bear it, it shall be possible for those that may be worthy coming after us to recover the Lost Word.

I

Of Ararat

The supreme secret of the O.T.O. is written in detail in the Book called *Agape* and is also written plainly in Liber CCCXXXIII, Cap. XXXVI.

But now also do We think it fitting to add Our own comment to this book *Agape* which We wrote in Our own words for the proper setting-forth of this Secret taught Us at Our Initiation to the IX° by the O.H.O. And this Book has received His official approbation in every word thereof.

But in this comment do We not set forth the Secret itself (rather on the contrary guarding it by certain subtilties even from the conjecture of the unworthy) but only Our own ideas as to its right use, with other matters germane, thinking that those into whose hands it may come may thereby understand more fully the utter importance of this Secret as having been the Pivot of Our working for so long a period, and further that it may aid such persons to attain perfectly the mastery of this Holy and Imperial Art.

II

Of the Importance of the Secret

This secret is the true Key to Magick; that is, by the right use of this secret man may impose his Will on Nature herself, as will appear hereafter in this comment.

In this way, although all recorded Knowledge were destroyed, it would be possible for an adept of this secret to restore it.

III

Of the Mind of the Adept

In Our holiest isle Ierne is found a being called Leprechaun. This creature, once seen, is easy to catch; and once caught must lead his captor to great treasure, provided that never for an eye-wink doth he relax vigilance; and the Leprechaun by all manner of tricks doth seek ever to divert the attention of him that hath made him prisoner.

Now this is a Magical Apologue or Fable of the utmost abyss of Truth.

For in the preparation of the Sacrament, and in its consummation also, the mind of the Initiate must be concerned absolutely in one rushing flame of will upon the determined object of his operation.

For there is no act more easy and natural to man than this preparation, none which requires less auxiliary. And yet by far the most part of mankind is ignorant and incapable of its proper performance; so that it is said that perfection in it as both science and art requires no less study than the most abstruse of philosophies, and no less practice than the most difficult of dexterities. But it is utterly in vain unless this first condition be fulfilled; and so difficult is this, not only because of the Overcoming of the Bodily Trance, but because of the wandering nature of the mind itself. And thereafter only by long and hard training preliminary in the art of meditation, and by constant practice and experience, can this Act become fruitful in Magick.

IV

Of Times and Seasons

Although no instruction has been given on this matter, yet it is evident, not only from considerations of the nature of things, but from Our own experience of these two years, that the fruitfulness of this Sacrament varies constantly, as it seems without rational cause.

Nor have We fully understood the best conditions. But it is Our Opinion that the Adept should suffer inward premonition whether the hour be propitious or no.

Yet it hath also been observed, and that often, that by extreme violence to Nature results are obtained equal to those garnered when Nature herself urges vehemently to the Act by enthusiasm.

But mediocre states of body and mind are to be avoided. As it is written: "I would thou wert cold or hot; but because thou art lukewarm I shall spew thee out of My mouth."

Nor is it necessarily to be disregarded as superstition to assert that certain hours of the day and certain aspects of the stars are more favourable than others, but rather to be criticised and investigated according to the methods of true science.

V

Of Bodily States

There is here a certain difficulty, in that the body being full of meat and wine is more apt for the preparation, as it is said, *Sine Cereri et Baccho Venus friget,* while for the consummation the body should be empty of all gross nutriment, so that the Elixir may be sucked up eagerly, and, running nobly into every part, revivify the whole.

It will in Our opinion be best if a full meal be taken not less than three hours before the beginning of the Ceremony, and after that no food, although stimulants whether of wine or subtler agents may be continued, so as to raise the body from excitement to excitement, and thus fit it for the proper exaltation suitable to the Work.

But in all this men may differ, and there is no rule but what may be engraven upon her Tracing Board by the burin of Experience.

VI

Of Operations of this Art, whether they should be Single or Multiple

We have doubt also in this matter whether, if an operation fail, it be wise to reiterate.

A Single Act implieth perfection, and full faith, in the Adept, if he repeat, that is Fear, and argueth imperfection in the first Trial.

Yet possibly for great cosmic operations it may be well to perform a series of Sacraments; but in this case the series should be arranged beforehand, and carried out regularly. As for example the 16 operations of Jupiter done in the city of Paris during the passage of the Sun from 10° Capricorn to 22° Aquarius An Ix.

In Our experience, repetitions undertaken because of apparent failure have sometimes seemed fatal, actually stopping what might reasonably have been expected to occur, and which has occurred only some time after the cessation of such attempts.

But we have also noted that in such cases the result hath been great and favourable, as if the repeated operations had built a dam restraining the natural current of the favourable forces, thus keeping them back so as to make them more effective in the end. But this may be false interpretation of the observed phenomena.

And, again, a series of such Sacraments has been futile until one last Work has landed in Success.

Yet this again may be coincidence, the result of the first working, but delayed.

The Adept will develop Intuition in all these questions; it is likely that the personal equation is very important, and that no absolute Rule Catholic, always everywhere, and by all men to be observed, exists.

VII

Of certain unknown Inhibitions,
and their Effect

We have marked subtly and regularly, the conditions and results of divers Workings of this Art, and this is the marvel now the Result follows swift and perfect, now again a group of lesser Results sympathetic to the Result willed, now but slight movements imitative of that Result, and now not only perfect failure, but the sudden reversal of all hopes in despair and ruin.

More plainly, if X be the Object of the Work, the result is sometimes X, sometimes x x x x, sometimes $\sqrt{(x)}$, sometimes $-\sqrt{(x)}$, or $-$x x x x, or $-$X.

In the concrete, suppose that one worketh this Art to obtain a great sum. Then at one time that sum will arrive that same night or within (say) 48 hours after, or an event occur involving the gain of that sum; at another time there will merely arise a group of circumstances favourable; at another time again a lesser sum will arrive; but also these may be reversed, in the worst case the loss of the sum proposed or the occurrence of an event which might involve that loss, or at least disappoint some reasonable expectation of that gain.

In the particular case of employing this Sacrament for the Elixer of Life, its misuse might cause premature old age, disease, or even death, as it is said; but We do not think that these results would follow the miscarriage of any other operation; We think that retribution is to be the evil and adverse reflection of reward, and on its plane. Adepts will then shew prudence by experimenting thoroughly in minor operations, where failure does not imply irreparable disaster, until they have the knowledge and Experience of this Art which will give a reasonable confidence.

VIII

Of a Theory of this Art Magical

The theory of this Art appears to Us to involve certain cosmic hypotheses to which it is perhaps not impossible to assent at least tentatively, but which are certainly unproven.

The idea of Prana in some form more mystical than that which identifieth it with the Motion of the physicist is perhaps inherent.

In the mere consummation of the Sacrament for health and vitality is no violation of reason, but at most an exaggeration of anticipation; for the Matter of the Sacrament is indubitably a Microcosm; but in the extension of this Sacrament to validity in Magick is an hiatus comparable to that which exists in the theory of Astrology. Even granting that an angle of 120° subtended at the eye of the observer on Earth between Sol and Saturn (exempli gratia) is accompanied by certain fortunes, this may be casual and not causal.

However, in this matter We have no doubt of the efficacy of the process, and are therefore fain to toy with any hypothesis, investigating as probability may determine us to do.

Thus we may assume an Ether or Akasa, inflamed or stressed by a particular Prana. And all stresses in this Akasa being of one kind ultimately, though mediately diverse, it may be as easy to arrest the course of the Earth as to destroy a worm. For the Work is taking place in a World of Causes fluid and not solid, in Yetzirah (or even Briah) rather than in Assiah.

It will be impossible or very difficult to move infantry from one wing of the engaged line to the other, but in the Quarters of the Staff it is indifferent whether that body, being at the base, is pushed forward to either. One cannot easily oxidize gold precipitated from the chloride, but having the chloride, it is easy to prepare the oxide rather than the metal.

And in all these matters reason must be the guide, and experience the teacher, so that the adept seek not to perform things impossible in Nature, and so blaspheme the Sacrament and bring it to contempt.

Yet let this be said, that to the consumate and sublime Initiate it may seem that of Himself was it written: "With God all things are possible."

However, God Himself is not found to interfere arbitrarily with the course of Nature, but to work within His laws.

Let the Adept act not otherwise.

IX

Of the Course of the Moon,
and her Influence

It is said that the second party is useless, even dangerous, when the influence of the Moon first shews itself. [Yet the motion of the Earth implying great causes in Briah and Yetzirah, must be difficult to check, unless by Briatic forces of much intensity.] But on the second day and after, though perhaps not on the last day, the Sacrament is more efficacious than at any other time, as is figured by our ancient Brethren the Alchemists in their preference of the Red Tincture to the White.

This We also believe, though We hold it hitherto not proven.

X

Of the Second Party to this Art,
whether Initiation is Desirable

If the other party to the Sacrament be also of the Ninth degree an Initiate of the Sanctuary of the Gnosis, it seems to Us urgent that the Object of both be one only, also that the general interest and nature of them be but one; else cometh division the enemy of Will, and utter failure following. And, the whole being considered carefully, We do opine that it is better and easier that the other party should be in ignorance of the sacred character of the Office.

It is enough if that assistant be formed by Nature signally for the physical task, robust, vigorous, eager, sensible, hot and healthy; flesh, nerve and blood being tense, quick, and lively, easily enflamed, and nigh inextinguishable.

XI

Of certain Rites analogous
to that of the IX°

It is said by certain Initiates that to obtain Spiritual gifts, and to aid Nature, the Sacrament should be as it were a Nuptial of the Folk of Earth; but that Magick is of the Demon, and that by a certain Perversion of the Office, may be created Elementals fit to perform the Will of the Magician.

Now herein is a difficulty, since in this case the Matter of the Sacrament cannot exist, for that there is no White Eagle to generate the Gluten.

Howbeit, We hold that in this rite is great efficacy; it may be that for certain operations it is equal or superior to that explained to Initiates of the IX°.

But We hold that in this case the Priest must be an Initiate, for that it is his will which determineth the magical character of his Lion; so that if he hath no purpose but that of the goddess Adonai he cannot raise agape to her Lord Thelema, nor will the Intention of the Priestess, although a lofty Initiate, replace this essential Power of the Priest over that of which he is but the vehicle and guardian.

For this reason the Ninth degree is not so easy to be made effective by Woman initiates.

Of what may be the result of a development parallel to that indicated above among the Noble and Chaste Ladies of the Order, it is at present impossible for Us to declare; but a priori it seems that, though the Lion and the Eagle are best in combination, the Lion is more likely to be able to dispense with the assistance of the Eagle, than the Eagle to make shift in the absence of the Lion. For the Gluten is but a menstruum or solvent, and containeth nothing in itself. The tradition also of certain lesser initiations confirmeth this. Yet considerations of divinity and of philosophy, and even of physics, do assure that our Way excelleth others even as spring tides exceed the neap. Water burneth the skin not at all, and the Oil of Vitriol but slowly but add a drop of water to the drop of Oil, and instantly cometh Heat and a pang intense and sharp. This is but analogy, yet just, and pleasing to the philosopher.

XII

Of the Choice of an Assistant

With regard to the choice of one to serve this Sacrament, man is so confused in mind, and so easily deceived as to this matter, that it seems to Us not unreasonable to allow full sway to the Caprice of the Moment. For this caprice so-called is in truth perhaps the Voice of the Sub-Consciousness; that is, it *is* the deliberate choice of the Holy Phallus itself. "The Phallus is the physiological basis of the Over-soul." For this very reason are these many men led astray, lost in unchastity and ruin.

But let the conscious Will be devoted wholly to the Great Work, then shall the Subconscious Will choose inevitably the Appointed Vehicle of the Work.

It is for this reason that already in the Seventh Degree the Sir Knights are sworn to Chastity. And this Chastity is an Abstinence from all gross sexual acts of every kind.

Moreover, this is further to be observed in the choice, that the second party must be consenting enthusiastically to co-operate physically with the Priest, so that the Lion be perfectly dissolved in a full portion of the Gluten. And whether this preparation be truly and duly done is known by the appearance of the Matter of the Sacrament, and also by its taste. For not idly is it written in the *Book of Judges,* "What is sweeter than honey, and what is stronger than a lion?" And that this secret is here manifested by the Holy Ghost is clear from the rejoinder of Samson, "If ye had not plowed with my heifer, ye had not found out my riddle."

XIII

Of certain Jewish theories

Among the Jews are certain instructed Initiates of their Qabalah who hold, as We understand, the view that in the Zraa or Semen itself lies a creative force inherent which cannot be baulked. Thus they say that before Eve was made, the dreams of Adam produced Lilith, a demon, and that from his intercourse with her sprang evil races.

Now then they mine the Roads of the Harbour of conjugal love with many restrictions; as these (1) it must be an holy act, preceded by ablutions, and by prayer (2) all lustful thoughts must be rigidly excluded (3) the purpose must be solely that of procreation (4) the blessing of God must be most earnestly invoked, so that the child shall be under His special protection.

In other language, this is their theory: the act of love causes a magical disturbance in the Aether or Akasa of such a nature as to attract or create a disincarnate human spirit.

All other sexual acts involving emission of semen therefore attract or excite other spirits, incomplete and therefore evil. Thus nocturnal pollutions bring succubi, which are capable of separate existence, and of vampirising their creator.

But voluntarily sterile acts create demons, and (if done with concentration and magical intention), such demons as may subserve that intention. Thus, as Levi testifieth, to graft a tree successfully, the graft is fixed by a woman while the man copulateth with her *per vas nefandum.*

We also narrate for the sake of completeness their method— perfected by modern Adepts—let us here give honour and worship to the name of Our lay-sister Ida Nelidoff—of attaining spiritual ecstasy by sexual means. And this method We have called Eroto-comatose Lucidity.

XIV

Of the Consummation of the Element Diune, whether Quantity be as important as Quality, and whether its waste be Sacrilege

It is said by the O.H.O. that of this perfect medicine a single dewdrop sufficeth, and this may be true. Yet it is humbly and with all deference and worship Our opinion that every drop generated (so far as may be possible) should be consumed. Firstly, that this most precious of all the gifts of Nature be not lost or profaned—indeed the Roman heresy hath appointed most excellent instructions for the treatment in all respects of the consecrated Host.

Let the adepts of this degree study *Missale Romanum—Ritus servandus in celebratione Missae* and *De defectibus in celebratione Missarum occurrentibus*—and gather therefrom the ceremonial adjuncts, the mental attitude, and so forth as a guide to their own working in this higher Sacrament.

And also do We think that the Consummation should be complete on this consideration, that if indeed it be the contained Prana that operateth the miracle, then the Quantity is as important as the Quality, just as in working with electricity amperage is as important as voltage.

And this We believe especially to be true in the case of great miracles; for We hold that it is the pitting of the David Spirit against the Goliah Matter. And although this proportion be small, it is not indefinitely small.

But it may be that the Action of this Divine Substance is catalytic, and capable of transmuting an unlimited quantity of base and blind matter into the plastic and docile image of the Will. And this theory is certainly more in accordance with the tradition of the Stone and of the Medicine.

XV

Of Eroto-comatose Lucidity

The Candidate is made ready for the Ordeal by general athletic training, and by feasting. On the appointed day he is attended by one or more chosen and experienced attendants whose duty is (a) to exhaust him sexually by every known means (b) to rouse him sexually by every known means. Every device and artifice of the courtesan is to be employed, and every stimulant known to the physician. Nor should the attendants reck of danger, but hunt down ruthlessly their appointed prey.

Finally the Candidate will sink into a sleep of utter exhaustion, resembling coma, and it is now that delicacy and skill must be exquisite. Let him be roused from this sleep by stimulation of a definitely and exclusively sexual type. Yet if convenient, music wisely regulated will assist.

The attendants will watch with assiduity for signs of waking; and, the moment these occur, all stimulation must cease instantly, and the Candidate be allowed to fall again into sleep; but no sooner has this happened than the former practice is resumed. This alternation is to continue indefinitely until the Candidate is in a state which is neither sleep nor waking, and in which his Spirit, set free by perfect exhaustion of the body, and yet prevented from entering the City of Sleep, communes with the Most High and the Most Holy Lord God of its being, maker of heaven and earth.

The Ordeal terminates by failure—the occurrence of sleep invincible—or by success, in which ultimate waking is followed by a final performance of the sexual act. The Initiate may then be allowed to sleep, or the practice may be renewed and persisted in until death ends all. The most favourable death is that occurring during the orgasm, and is called *Mors Justi*.

As it is written: Let me die the death of the Righteous, and let my last end be like his!

XVI

Of certain Hindu theories

Like the Jews, the wise men of India have a belief that a certain particular Prana, or force, resides in the Bindu, or semen. But all their theory of magick and meditation being reverbatory, so that their "communing with God" is but a "communing with Self", and all their artifice directed to development of the powers in their own bodies and minds, as opposed to the Western idea of extending those powers to bear sway over others, we find naturally that just as they seek to restrain the breath altogether, or to avoid its violent extrusion from the nostrils, lest the Prana thereof be lost to them, and as they even practice to suck up water into the rectum, so that in defaecation they may be able to retain the Apana, or particular virtue thereof, and replace it in the Svadistthana-cakkra, so also much more do they extravagantly labour to retain the prime Prana of life, the Bindu.

Therefore they stimulate to the maximum its generation by causing a consecrated prostitute to excite the organs, and at the same time vigorously withhold by will. After some little exercise they claim that they can deflower as many as eighty virgins in a night without losing a single drop of the Bindu. Nor is this ever to be lost, but reabsorbed through the tissues of the body. The organs thus act as a siphon to draw constantly fresh supplies of life from the cosmic reservoir, and flood the body with their fructifying virtue.

The Initiate is asked to compare and contrast this chapter with chapter XIV, observing in particular, underlying both systems, this one postulate: in the semen itself exists a physical force which can be turned to the magical or mystical Ends of the Adept.

Initiates will notice also that these heathen philosophers have made also one further march towards the truth when they say that the Sun and Moon must be united before the reabsorption (see almost any Tantra, in particular Shiva Sanhita). But the full glory of the Sun, the simple and most efficacious and most Holy Sacrament, is reserved for the Elect, the Illuminated, the Initiates of the Sanctuary of the Gnosis.

XVII

Of a suggested Course of Experiment

Here is a series of Operations of this Art Magick of the IX° suggested for the Use of any Initiate as he begins his Working.

   I. Sex-force and sex-attraction
      (To ensure the regular course of these operations)
  II. Understanding the Mysteries of the IX° and Wisdom in their use
      (To ensure the right performance of these operations)
 III. Increase of the O.T.O.

(As a duty, and to ensure a suitable heir to the Secret. This is especially important if the Initiate be of the X°)

IV. (If necessary) Ease of circumstances
(To ensure leisure for these operations, and to enlarge the field of choice of second parties)

V. Establishment of a protective bodyguard of invisible warriors
(To secure freedom from interruption in the course of these operations. This may include preservation of the health)

VI. The Knowledge and Conversation of the Holy Guardian Angel

VII. Spiritual attainment: e.g. devotion to Nuit-Babalon-Baphomet

VIII. Further insight into Nature and her laws

IX. The foundation of an Abbey of O.T.O.

X. The establishment of the Kingdom of Ra-Hoor-Khuit upon the earth. Also divers matters, as the Rejuvenation of one's own body, if desired, the power of healing, and the like.

It will be seen that these few operations appear to fill every Lotus of the Universe with their Buddhas. But it may be that each operation must be worked in detail, with digital probe rather than palmary grasp, so that each practical act of the Initiate might need a separate consecration.

Or for great operations like the X in the above list it might be arranged to make a specially elaborate Sacrament every Sunday (for example) in the year, the intervening days being devoted to the details of the Building.

But the Initiate will soon develop a Method of his own for extracting the most efficiently the honey from this Comb.

XVIII

Of a certain other method of Magick not included in the instruction of O.T.O.

It may not be altogether inappropriate to allude to a method of vampirism commonly practised.

The Vampire selects the victim, stout and vigorous as may be, and, with the magical intention of transferring all that strength to himself, exhausts the quarry by a suitable use of the body, most usually the mouth, without himself entering in any other way into the matter. And this is thought by some to partake of the nature of Black Magic.

The exhaustion should be complete; if the work be skilfully executed, a few minutes should suffice to produce a state resembling, and not far removed from, coma.

Experts may push this practice to the point of the death of the victim, thus not merely obtaining the physical strength, but imprisoning and enslaving the soul. This soul then serves as a familiar spirit.

The practice was held to be dangerous. (It was used by the late Oscar Wilde, and by Mr. and Mrs. "Horos"; also in a modified and marred form by S. L. Mathers and his wife, and by E. W. Berridge.

The ineptitude of the three latter saved them from the fate of the three former.)

XIX

Of the Adept of this Art

In armour of leaping flame let the Adept rage through the Universe, majestic and irresistible as the Sun.

Let no eye behold him unblasted; let him strike upon the necks of the ungodly.

Let him be a mighty light of comfort, and the Father of all fertility.

Let him send forth rain in due season, and the earth grow green at his coming.

Let his planets whirl upon his wheel; let him send forth his comets as angels unto his brethren; and let him give light to all his realm.

Let no eye behold him unblasted; let him strike upon the necks of the ungodly.

XX

Of the Thesaurus of the O.T.O.

Remember these chief treasures to be preserved:

1. This Secret of the IX°.
2. The Secret of the VIII° concerning Universal Brotherhood: in the Macrocosm the Sun lord of all life; in the Microcosm the Phallus

lord of all-life; indubitable, undeniable, a basis for the faith of all men.

3. The secret of the VII°: our particular method of instruction, selection, governance, and initiation.
4. The secret of the VI°, the history of the Temple, the mystery of Baphomet, our war on those never wholly subdued foes of humanity, tyranny and superstition.
5. The secret of the V°: the mystery of the Rose and Cross; and the One Law Do What Thou Wilt.
6. The secret of the lesser degrees: the cycle of existence—ex nihil nihil fit.
7. The secret of these things reverenced: the Sun, the Moon, the Phallus, the Tree, the Ancestor, the Fire, the Lion, the Snake, and the Mountain. [Of these is Discourse in Our Epistle *De Natura Deorum*.]

XXI

Valediction

Now therefore all is said, most
Holy, most Illuminated, most
Illustrious and most Dear
Brother. In the Name of the
Secret Master Hail and fare well.

Given from the Throne of
Ireland Iona and All the Britains
this day of Jupiter An X
Sol in 0° Libra 35'21"
Luna in Sagittarius 28'6'
Valley of London.

Liber A'ash vel Capricorni Pneumatici

"The Book of Creation, or of the Goat of the Spirit," a Holy Book in the name of Baphomet. Crowley says in his syllabus to his writings that this text contains "the true secret of all practical magick," and its sexually suggestive character is apparent enough. "Whom I love I chastise with many rods."

---

0. Gnarled Oak of God! In thy branches is the lightning nested! Above thee hangs the Eyeless Hawk.

1. Thou art blasted and black! Supremely solitary in that heath of scrub.

2. Up! The ruddy clouds hang over thee! It is the storm.

3. There is a flaming gash in the sky.

4. Up.

5. Thou art tossed about in the grip of the storm for an aeon and an aeon and an aeon. But thou givest not thy sap; thou fallest not.

6. Only in the end shalt thou give up thy sap when the great God F. I. A. T. is enthroned on the day of Be-with-Us.

7. For two things are done and a third thing is begun. Isis and Osiris are given over to incest and adultery. Horus leaps up thrice armed from the womb of his mother. Harpocrates his twin is hidden within him. Set is his holy covenant, that he shall display in the great day of M. A. A. T., that is being interpreted the Master of the Temple of A ∴ A ∴ whose name is Truth.

8. Now in this is the magical power known.

9. It is like the oak that hardens itself and bears up against the storm. It is weather-beaten and scarred and confident like a sea-captain.

10. Also it straineth like a hound in the leash.

11. It hath pride and great subtlety. Yea, and glee also!

12. Let the magus act thus in his conjuration.

13. Let him sit and conjure; let him draw himself together in that

170

forcefulness; let him rise next swollen and straining; let him dash back the hood from his head and fix his basilisk eye upon the sigil of the demon. Then let him sway the force of him to and fro like a satyr in silence, until the Word burst from his throat.

14. Then let him not fall exhausted, although the might have been ten thousandfold the human; but that which floodeth him is the infinite mercy of the Genitor-Genetrix of the Universe, whereof he is the Vessel.

15. Nor do thou deceive thyself. It is easy to tell the live force from the dead matter. It is no easier to tell the live snake from the dead snake.

16. Also concerning vows. Be obstinate, and be not obstinate. Understand that the yielding of the Yoni is one with the lengthening of the Lingam. Thou art both these; and thy vow is but the rustling of the wind on Mount Meru.

17. Now shalt thou adore me who am the Eye and the Tooth, the Goat of the Spirit, the Lord of Creation. I am the Eye in the Triangle, the Silver Star that ye adore.

18. I am Baphomet, that is the Eightfold Word that shall be equilibrated with the Three.

19. There is no act or passion that shall not be a hymn in mine honour.

20. All holy things and all symbolic things shall be my sacraments.

21. These animals are sacred unto me; the goat, and the duck, and the ass, and the gazelle, the man, the woman and the child.

22. All corpses are sacred unto me; they shall not be touched save in mine eucharist. All lonely places are sacred to me; where one man gathereth himself together in my name, there will I leap forth in the midst of him.

23. I am the hideous god; and who mastereth me is uglier than I.

24. Yet I give more than Bacchus and Apollo; my gifts exceed the olive and the horse.

25. Who worshippeth me must worship me with many rites.

26. I am concealed with all concealments; when the Most Holy Ancient One is stripped and driven through the marketplace I am still secret and apart.

27. Whom I love I chastise with many rods.

28. All things are sacred to me; no thing is sacred from me.

29. For there is no holiness where I am not.

30. Fear not when I fall in the fury of the storm; for mine acorns are blown afar by the wind; and verily I shall rise again, and my children about me, so that we shall uplift our forest in Eternity.

31. Eternity is the storm that covereth me.

32. I am Existence, the Existence that existeth not save through its own Existence, that is beyond the Existence of Existences, and rooted deeper than the No-Thing-Tree in the Land of No-Thing.

33. Now therefore thou knowest when I am within thee, when my hood is spread over thy skull, when my might is more than the penned Indus, and resistless as the Giant Glacier.

34. For as thou art before a lewd woman in Thy nakedness in the bazaar, sucked up by her slyness and smiles, so art thou wholly and no more in part before the symbol of the beloved, though it be but a Pisacha or a Yantra or a Deva.

35. And in all shalt thou create the Infinite Bliss, and the next link of the Infinite Chain.

36. This chain reaches from Eternity to Eternity, ever in triangles—is not my symbol a triangle?—ever in circles—is not the symbol of the Beloved a circle? Therein is all progress base illusion, for every circle is alike and every triangle alike!

37. But the progress is progress, and progress is rapture, constant, dazzling, showers of light, waves of dew, flames of the hair of the Great Goddess, flowers of the roses that are about her neck, Amen!

38. Therefore lift up thyself as I am lifted up. Hold thyself in as I am master to accomplish. At the end, be the end far distant as the stars that lie in the navel of Nuit, do thou slay thyself as I at the end am slain, in the death that is life, in the peace that is mother of war, in the darkness that holds light in his hand, as a harlot that plucks a jewel from her nostrils.

39. So therefore the beginning is delight and the end is delight, and delight is in the midst, even as the Indus is water in the cavern of the glacier, and water among the greater hills and the lesser hills and through the ramparts of the hills and through the plains, and water at the mouth thereof when it leaps forth into the mighty sea, yea, into the mighty sea.

(The Interpretation of this Book will be given to members of the Grade of Dominus Liminis on application, each to his Adeptus.)

Liber Cheth vel Vallum Abiegni

This Holy Book describes coitus with Babalon—within her "Holy Graal"—in which the magician destroys Life, Knowledge, Truth, Death, Love, and End. At the End, though, is still the Beginning, and the "white ash" of Hermes, who Writes.

---

1. This is the secret of the Holy Graal, that is the sacred vessel of our Lady the Scarlet Woman, Babalon the Mother of Abominations, the bride of Chaos, that rideth upon our Lord the Beast.

2. Thou shalt drain out thy blood that is thy life into the golden cup of her fornication.

3. Thou shalt mingle thy life with the universal life. Thou shalt keep not back one drop.

4. Then shall thy brain be dumb, and thy heart beat no more, and all thy life shall go from thee; and thou shalt be cast out upon the midden, and the birds of the air shall feast upon thy flesh, and thy bones shall whiten in the sun.

5. Then shall the winds gather themselves together, and bear thee up as it were a little heap of dust in a sheet that hath four corners, and they shall give it unto the guardians of the abyss.

6. And because there is no life therein, the guardians of the abyss shall bid the angels of the winds pass by. And the angels shall lay thy dust in the City of the Pyramids, and the name thereof shall be no more.

7. Now therefore that thou mayest achieve this ritual of the Holy Graal, do thou divest thyself of all thy goods.

8. Thou hast wealth; give it unto them that have need thereof, yet no desire toward it.

9. Thou hast health; slay thyself in the fervour of thine abandonment unto Our Lady. Let thy flesh hang loose upon thy bones, and thine eyes glare with thy quenchless lust unto the Infinite, with thy

passion for the Unknown, for Her that is beyond Knowledge the accursed one.

10. Thou hast love; tear thy mother from thine heart, and spit in the face of thy father. Let thy foot trample the belly of thy wife, and let the babe at her breast be the prey of dogs and vultures.

11. For if thou dost not this with thy will, then shall We do this despite thy will. So that thou attain to the Sacrament of the Graal in the Chapel of Abominations.

12. And behold! if by stealth thou keep unto thyself one thought of thine, then shalt thou be cast out into the abyss for ever; and thou shalt be the lonely one, the eater of dung, the afflicted in the Day of Be-with-Us.

13. Yea! verily this is the Truth, this is the Truth, this is the Truth. Unto thee shall be granted joy and health and wealth and wisdom when thou art no longer thou.

14. Then shall every gain be a new sacrament, and it shall not defile thee; thou shalt revel with the wanton in the market-place, and the virgins shall fling roses upon thee, and the merchants bend their knees and bring thee gold and spices. Also young boys shall pour wonderful wines for thee, and the singers and the dancers shall sing and dance for thee.

15. Yet shalt thou not be therein, for thou shalt be forgotten, dust lost in dust.

16. Nor shall the aeon itself avail thee in this; for from the dust shall a white ash be prepared by Hermes the Invisible.

17. And this is the wrath of God, that these things should be thus.

18. And this is the grace of God, that these things should be thus.

19. Wherefore I charge you that ye come unto me in the Beginning; for if ye take but one step in this Path, ye must arrive inevitably at the end thereof.

20. This Path is beyond Life and Death; it is also beyond Love; but that ye know not, for ye know not Love.

21. And the end thereof is known not even unto Our Lady or to the Beast whereon She rideth; nor unto the Virgin her daughter nor unto Chaos her lawful Lord; but unto the Crowned Child is it known? It is not known if it be known.

22. Therefore unto Hadit and unto Nuit be the glory in the End and the Beginning; yea, in the End and the Beginning.

Liber Tzaddi vel Hamus Hermeticus

Literally "The Book of the Hermetic Fish-Hook," "Liber Tzaddi" is an invitation to the magician to lose himself in Love, detaching through attachment to all "things."

---

0. In the name of the Lord of Initiation, Amen.

1. I fly and I alight as an hawk: of mother-of-emerald are my mighty-sweeping wings.

2. I swoop down upon the black earth; and it gladdens into green at my coming.

3. Children of Earth! rejoice! rejoice exceedingly; for your salvation is at hand.

4. The end of sorrow is come; I will ravish you away into mine unutterable joy.

5. I will kiss you, and bring you to the bridal: I will spread a feast before you in the house of happiness.

6. I am not come to rebuke you, or to enslave you.

7. I bid you not turn from your voluptuous ways, from your idleness, from your follies.

8. But I bring you joy to your pleasure, peace to your languor, wisdom to your folly.

9. All that ye do is right, if so be that ye enjoy it.

10. I am come against sorrow, against weariness, against them that seek to enslave you.

11. I pour you lustral wine, that giveth you delight both at the sunset and the dawn.

12. Come with me, and I will give you all that is desirable upon the earth.

13. Because I give you that of which Earth and its joys are but as shadows.

14. They flee away, but my joy abideth even unto the end.

15. I have hidden myself beneath a mask: I am a black and terrible God.

16. With courage conquering fear shall ye approach me: ye shall lay down your heads upon mine altar, expecting the sweep of the sword.

17. But the first kiss of love shall be radiant on your lips; and all my darkness and terror shall turn to light and joy.

18. Only those who fear shall fail. Those who have bent their backs to the yoke of slavery until they can no longer stand upright; them will I despise.

19. But you who have defied the law; you who have conquered by subtlety or force; you will I take unto me, even I will take you unto me.

20. I ask you to sacrifice nothing at mine altar; I am the God who giveth all.

21. Light, Life, Love; Force, Fantasy, Fire; these do I bring you: mine hands are full of these.

22. There is joy in the setting-out; there is joy in the journey; there is joy in the goal.

23. Only if ye are sorrowful, or weary, or angry, or discomforted; then ye may know that ye have lost the golden thread, the thread wherewith I guide you to the heart of the groves of Eleusis.

24. My disciples are proud and beautiful; they are strong and swift; they rule their way like mighty conquerors.

25. The weak, the timid, the imperfect, the cowardly, the poor, the tearful—these are mine enemies, and I am come to destroy them.

26. This also is compassion: an end to the sickness of earth. A rooting-out of the weeds: a watering of the flowers.

27. O my children, ye are more beautiful than the flowers: ye must not fade in your season.

28. I love you; I would sprinkle you with the divine dew of immortality.

29. This immortality is no vain hope beyond the grave: I offer you the certain consciousness of bliss.

30. I offer it at once, on earth; before an hour hath struck upon the bell, ye shall be with Me in the Abodes that are beyond Decay.

31. Also I give you power earthly and joy earthly; wealth, and health, and length of days. Adoration and love shall cling to your feet, and twine around your heart.

32. Only your mouths shall drink of a delicious wine—the wine of

Iacchus; they shall reach ever to the heavenly kiss of the Beautiful God.

33. I reveal unto you a great mystery. Ye stand between the abyss of height and the abyss of depth.

34. In either awaits you a Companion; and that Companion is Yourself.

35. Ye can have no other Companion.

36. Many have arisen, being wise. They have said "Seek out the glittering Image in the place ever golden, and unite yourselves with It."

37. Many have arisen, being foolish. They have said, "Stoop down unto the darkly splendid world, and be wedded to that Blind Creature of the Slime."

38. I who am beyond Wisdom and Folly, arise and say unto you: achieve both weddings! Unite yourselves with both!

39. Beware, beware, I say, lest ye seek after the one and lose the other!

40. My adepts stand upright; their head above the heavens, their feet below the hells.

41. But since one is naturally attracted to the Angel, another to the Demon, let the first strengthen the lower link, the last attach more firmly to the higher.

42. Thus shall equilibrium become perfect. I will aid my disciples; as fast as they acquire this balanced power and joy so faster will I push them.

43. They shall in their turn speak from this Invisible Throne; their words shall illumine the worlds.

44. They shall be masters of majesty and might; they shall be beautiful and joyous; they shall be clothed with victory and splendour; they shall stand upon the firm foundation; the kingdom shall be theirs; yea, the kingdom shall be theirs.

In the name of the Lord of Initiation. Amen.

Love

This is from one of Crowley's last books, *Little Essays Toward Truth*, which consists of a series of 16 interrelated pieces. "Love" distinguishes between sexual love and magical love, and explains *The Book of the Law*'s mandate of "Love under Will" in terms of the "Formula of Tetragrammaton" (the spelling of the name of God, "YHVH").

"**N**ow the Magus is Love, and bindeth together That and This in his Conjuration."

The Formula of Tetragrammaton is the complete mathematical expression of Love. Its essence is this: any two things unite, with a double effect; firstly, the destruction of both, accompanied by the ecstasy due to the relief of the strain of separateness; secondly, the creation of a third thing, accompanied by the ecstasy of the realisation of existence, which is Joy until with development it becomes aware of its imperfection, and loves.

This formula of Love is universal; all the laws of Nature are its servitors. Thus, gravitation, chemical affinity, electrical potential, and the rest—and these are alike mere aspects of the general law—are so many differently-observed statements of the unique tendency.

The Universe is conserved by the duplex action involved in the formula. The disappearance of Father and Mother is precisely compensated by the emergence of Son and Daughter. It may therefore be considered as a perpetual-motion-engine which continually develops rapture in each of its phases.

The sacrifice of Iphigenia at Aulis may be taken as typical of the formula: the mystical effect is the assumption of the maid to the bosom of the goddess; while, for the magical, the destruction of her earthly part, the fawn, composes the rage of Æolus, and bids the Danaids set sail.

Now it cannot be too clearly understood, or too acutely realised by

178

means of action, that the intensity of the Joy liberated varies with the original degree of opposition between the two elements of the union. Heat, light, electricity are phenomena expressive of the fullness of passion, and their value is greatest when the diversity of the Energies composing the marriage is most strenuous. One obtains more from the explosion of Hydrogen and Oxygen than from the dull combination of substances indifferent to each other. Thus, the union of Nitrogen and Chlorine is so little satisfying to either molecule, that the resulting compound disintegrates with explosive violence at the slightest shock. We might say, then, in the language of Thelema, that such an act of love is not "love under will." It is, so to speak, a black magical operation.

Let us consider, in a figure, the "feelings" of a molecule of Hydrogen in the presence of one of Oxygen or of Chlorine. It is made to suffer intensely by the realisation of the extremity of its deviation from the perfect type of monad by the contemplation of an element so supremely opposed to its own nature at every point. So far as it is egoist, its reaction must be scorn and hatred; but as it understands by the true shame that is put upon its separateness by the presence of its opposite, these feelings turn to anguished yearning. It begins to crave the electric spark which will enable it to assuage its pangs by the annihilation of all those properties which constitute its separate existence, in the rapture of union, and at the same time to fulfil its passion to create a perfect type of Peace.

We see the same psychology everywhere in the physical world. A stronger and more elaborate illustration might well have been drawn, were the purpose of this essay less catholic, from the structure of the atoms themselves, and their effort to resolve the agony of their agitation in the beatific Nirvana of the 'noble' gases.

The process of Love under Will is evidently progressive. The Father who has slain himself in the womb of the Mother finds himself again, with her, and transfigured, in the Son. This Son acts as a new Father; and it is thus that the Self is constantly aggrandized, and able to counterpoise an ever greater Not-Self, until the final act of Love under Will which comprehends the Universe in Sammasamadhi.

The passion of Hatred is thus really directed against oneself; it is the expression of the pain and shame of separateness; and it only appears to be directed against the opposite by psychological transference. This thesis the School of Freud has made sufficiently clear.

There is then little indeed in common between Love and such tepid passions as regard, affection, or kindliness; it is the uninitiate, who, to his damnation in a hell of cabbage soup and soap-suds, confuses them.

Love may best be defined as the passion of Hatred inflamed to the point of madness, when it takes refuge in Self-destruction.

Love is clear-sighted with the lust of deadly rage, anatomizing its victim with keen energy, seeking where best to strike home mortally to the heart; it becomes blind only when its fury has completely overpowered it, and thrust it into the red maw of the furnace of self-immolation.

We must further distinguish Love in this magical sense from the sexual formula, symbol and type though that be thereof. For the pure essence of Magick is a function of ultimate atomic conscious-ness, and its operations must be refined from all confusion and contamination. The truly magical operations of Love are therefore the Trances, more especially those of Understanding; as will readily have been appreciated by those who have made a careful Qabalistic study of the nature of Binah. For she is omniform as Love and as Death, the Great Sea whence all Life springs, and whose black womb re-absorbs all. She thus resumes in herself the duplex process of the Formula of Love under Will; for is not Pan the All-Begetter in the heart of the Groves at high noon, and is not Her "hair the trees of Eternity" the filaments of All-Devouring Godhead "under the Night of Pan?"

Yet let it not be forgotten that though She be love, her function is but passive; she is the vehicle of the Word, of Chokmah, Wisdom, the All-Father, who is the Will of the All-One. And thus they err with grievous error and dire who prate of Love as the Formula of Magick; Love is unbalanced, void, vague, undirected, sterile, nay, more, a very Shell, the prey of abject arts demonic: Love must be *"under will."*

The Formula of Tetragrammaton[1]

Chapter III of *Magick in Theory and Practice,* this essay goes into detail concerning "YHVH."

T his formula is of most universal aspect, as all things are necessarily comprehended in it; but its use in a magical ceremony is little understood.

The climax of the formula is in one sense before even the formulation of the Yod. For the Yod is the most divine aspect of the Force—the remaining letters are but a solidification of the same thing. It must be understood that we are here speaking of the whole ceremony considered as a unity, not merely of that formula in which *Yod* is the God invoked, *Hé* the Archangel, and so on. In order to understand the ceremony under this formula, we must take a more extended view of the functions of the four weapons that we have hitherto done.

The formation of the *Yod* is the formulation of the first creative force, of that father who is called "self-begotten," and unto whom it is said: "Thou hast formulated thy Father, and made fertile thy Mother." The adding of the *Hé* to the *Yod* is the marriage of that Father to the great co-equal Mother, who is a reflection of Nuit as He is of Hadit. Their union brings forth the son *Vau* who is the heir. Finally the daughter *Hé* is produced. She is both the twin sister and the daughter of *Vau*.[2]

His mission is to redeem her by making her his bride; the result of this is to set her upon the throne of her mother, and it is only she whose youthful embrace can reawaken the eld of the All-Father. In this complex family relationship[3] is symbolised the whole course of

---

1. יהוה; Yod, Hé, Vau, Hé, the Ineffable Name (Jehovah) of the Hebrews. The four letters refer respectively to the four "elements", Fire, Water, Air, Earth, in the order named.
2. There is a further mystery herein, far deeper, for initiates.
3. The formula of Tetragrammaton, as ordinarily understood, ending with the appearance of the daughter, is indeed a degradation.

181

the Universe. It will be seen that (after all) the Climax is at the end. It is the second half of the formula which symbolises the Great Work which we are pledged to accomplish. The first step of this is the attainment of the Knowledge and Conversation of the Holy Guardian Angel, which constitutes the Adept of the Inner Order.

The re-entry of these twin spouses into the womb of the mother is that initiation described in Liber 418, which gives admission to the Inmost Order of the A ∴ A ∴. Of the last step we cannot speak.

It will now be recognised that to devise a practical magical ceremony to correspond to Tetragrammaton in this exalted sense might be difficult if not impossible. In such a ceremony the Rituals of purification alone might occupy many incarnations.

It will be necessary, therefore, to revert to the simpler view of Tetragrammaton, remembering only that the *Hé* final is the Throne of the Spirit, of the Shin of Pentagrammaton.

The Yod will represent a swift and violent creative energy; following this will be a calmer and more reflective but even more powerful flow of will, the irresistible force of a mighty river. This state of mind will be followed by an expansion of the consciousness; it will penetrate all space, and this will finally undergo a crystallization resplendent with interior light. Such modifications of the original Will may be observed in the course of the invocations when they are properly performed.

The peculiar dangers of each are obvious—that of the first is a flash in the pan—a misfire; that of the second, a falling into dreaminess or reverie; that of the third, loss of concentration. A mistake in any of these points will prevent, or injure the proper formation of, the fourth.

In the expression which will be used in Chapter XV: "Enflame thyself", etc., only the first stage is specified; but if that is properly done the other stages will follow as if by necessity. So far is it written concerning the formula of Tetragrammaton.

Liber Cordis Cincti Serpente (selections)

"The Book of the Heart Girt with a Serpent" describes in its constantly shifting imagery the Knowledge and Conversation of the Holy Guardian Angel. "Liber Samekh," not included in this volume, but reprinted in *Magick* and *Gems from the Equinox*, is a much more technical treatise on this working.

I

1. I am the Heart; and the Snake is entwined
About the invisible core of the mind.
Rise, O my snake! It is now the hour
Of the hooded and holy ineffable flower.
Rise, O my snake, into brilliance of bloom
On the corpse of Osiris afloat in the tomb!
O heart of my mother, my sister, mine own,
Thou art given to Nile, to the terror Typhon!
Ah me! but the glory of ravening storm
Enswathes thee and wraps thee in frenzy of form.
Be still, O my soul! that the spell may dissolve
As the wands are upraised, and the aeons revolve.
Behold! in my beauty how joyous Thou art,
O Snake that caresses the crown of mine heart!
Behold! we are one, and the tempest of years
Goes down to the dusk, and the Beetle appears.
O Beetle! the drone of Thy dolorous note
Be ever the trance of this tremulous throat!
I await the awaking! The summons on high
From the Lord Adonai, from the Lord Adonai!

2. Adonai spake unto V. V. V. V. V., saying: There must ever be division in the word.

3. For the colours are many, but the light is one.

4. Therefore thou writest that which is of mother of emerald, and of lapis-lazuli, and of turquoise, and of alexandrite.

183

5. Another writeth the words of topaz, and of deep amethyst, and of gray sapphire, and of deep sapphire with a tinge as of blood.

6. Therefore do ye fret yourselves because of this.

7. Be not contented with the image.

8. I who am the Image of an Image say this.

9. Debate not of the image, saying Beyond! Beyond!

One mounteth unto the Crown by the moon and by the Sun, and by the arrow, and by the Foundation, and by the dark home of the stars from the black earth.

10. Not otherwise may ye reach unto the Smooth Point.

11. Nor is it fitting for the cobbler to prate of the Royal matter. O cobbler! mend me this shoe, that I may walk. O king! if I be thy son, let us speak of the Embassy to the King thy Brother.

12. Then was there silence. Speech had done with us awhile.

There is a light so strenuous that it is not perceived as light.

13. Wolf's bane is not so sharp as steel; yet it pierceth the body more subtly.

14. Even as evil kisses corrupt the blood, so do my words devour the spirit of man.

15. I breathe, and there is infinite dis-ease in the spirit.

16. As an acid eats into steel, as a cancer that utterly corrupts the body; so am I unto the spirit of man.

17. I shall not rest until I have dissolved it all.

18. So also the light that is absorbed. One absorbs little, and is called white and glistening; one absorbs all and is called black.

19. Therefore, O my darling, art thou black.

20. O my beautiful, I have likened thee to a jet Nubian slave, a boy of melancholy eyes.

21. O the filthy one! the dog! they cry against thee.

Because thou art my beloved.

22. Happy are they that praise thee; for they see thee with Mine eyes.

23. Not aloud shall they praise thee; but in the night watch one shall steal close, and grip thee with the secret grip; another shall privily cast a crown of violets over thee; a third shall greatly dare, and press mad lips to thine.

24. Yea! the night shall cover all, the night shall cover all.

25. Thou wast long seeking Me; thou didst run forward so fast that I was unable to come up with thee.

O thou darling fool! What bitterness thou didst crown thy days withal.

26. Now I am with thee; I will never leave thy being.

27. For I am the soft sinuous one entwined about thee, heart of gold!

28. My head is jewelled with twelve stars; My body is white as milk of the stars; it is bright with the blue of the abyss of stars invisible.

29. I have found that which could not be found; I have found a vessel of quicksilver.

30. Thou shalt instruct the servant in his ways, thou shalt speak often with him.

31. (The scribe looketh upwards and crieth) Amen! Thou hast spoken it, Lord God!

32. Further Adonai spake unto V. V. V. V. V. and said:

33. Let us take our delight in the multitude of men!

Let us shape unto ourselves a boat of mother-of-pearl from them, that we may ride upon the river of Amrit!

34. Thou seest yon petal of amaranth, blown by the wind from the low sweet brows of Hathor?

35. (The Magister saw it and rejoiced in the beauty of it.) Listen!

36. (From a certain world came an infinite wail.)

That falling petal seemed to the little ones a wave to engulph their continent.

37. So they will reproach thy servant, saying: Who hath set thee to save us?

38. He will be sore distressed.

39. All they understand not that thou and I are fashioning a boat of mother-of-pearl. We will sail down the river of Amrit even to the yew-groves of Yama, where we may rejoice exceedingly.

40. The joy of men shall be our silver gleam, their woe our blue gleam—all in the mother-of-pearl.

41. (The scribe was wroth thereat. He spake:

O Adonai and my master, I have borne the inkhorn and the pen without pay, in order that I might search this river of Amrit, and sail thereon as one of ye. This I demand for my fee, that I partake of the echo of your kisses.)

42. (And immediately it was granted unto him.)

43. (Nay; but not therewith as he content. By an infinite abasement unto shame did he strive. Then a voice:)

44. Thou strivest ever; even in the yielding thou strivest to yield—and lo! thou yieldest not.

45. Go thou unto the outermost places and subdue all things.

46. Subdue thy fear and thy disgust. Then—yield!

47. There was a maiden that strayed among the corn, and sighed; then grew a new birth, a narcissus, and therein she forgot her sighing and her loneliness.

48. Even instantly rode Hades heavily upon her, and ravished her away.

49. (Then the scribe knew the narcissus in his heart; but because it came not to his lips, therefore was he shamed and spake no more.)

50. Adonai spake yet again with V. V. V. V. V. and said:

The earth is ripe for vintage; let us eat of her grapes, and be drunken thereon.

51. And V. V. V. V. V. answered and said: O my lord, my dove, my excellent one, how shall this word seem unto the children of men?

52. And He answered him: Not as thou canst see.

It is certain that every letter of this cipher hath some value; but who shall determine the value? For it varieth ever, according to the subtlety of Him that made it.

53. And He answered Him: Have I not the key thereof?

I am clothed with a body of flesh; I am one with the Eternal and Omnipotent God.

54. Then said Adonai: Thou hast the Head of the Hawk, and thy Phallus is the Phallus of Asar. Thou knowest the white, and thou knowest the black, and thou knowest that these are one. But why seekest thou the knowledge of their equivalence?

55. And he said: That my Work may be right.

56. And Adonai said: The strong brown reaper swept his swathe and rejoiced. The wise man counted his muscles, and pondered, and understood not, and was sad.

Reap thou, and rejoice!

57. Then was the Adept glad, and lifted his arm.

Lo! an earthquake, and plague, and terror on the earth!

A casting down of them that sate in high places; a famine upon the multitude!

58. And the grape fell ripe and rich into his mouth.

59. Stained is the purple of thy mouth, O brilliant one, with the white glory of the lips of Adonai.

60. The foam of the grape is like the storm upon the sea; the ships tremble and shudder; the shipmaster is afraid.

61. That is thy drunkenness, O holy one, and the winds whirl away the soul of the scribe into the happy haven.

62. O Lord God! let the haven be cast down by the fury of the storm! Let the foam of the grape tincture my soul with Thy light!

63. Bacchus grew old, and was Silenus; Pan was ever Pan for ever and ever more throughout the aeons.

64. Intoxicate the inmost, O my lover, not the outermost!

65. So it was—ever the same! I have aimed at the peeled wand of my God, and I have hit; yea, I have hit.

IV

1. O crystal heart! I the Serpent clasp Thee; I drive home mine head into the central core of Thee, O God my beloved.

2. Even as on the resounding wind-swept heights of Mitylene some god-like woman casts aside the lyre, and with her locks aflame as an aureole, plunges into the wet heart of the creation, so I, O Lord my God!

3. There is a beauty unspeakable in this heart of corruption, where the flowers are aflame.

4. Ah me! but the thirst of Thy joy parches up this throat, so that I cannot sing.

5. I will make me a little boat of my tongue, and explore the unknown rivers. It may be that the everlasting salt may turn to sweetness, and that my life may no longer athirst.

6. O ye that drink of the brine of your desire, ye are nigh to madness! Your torture increaseth as ye drink, yet still ye drink. Come up through the creeks to the fresh water; I shall be waiting for you with my kisses.

7. As the bezoar-stone that is found in the belly of the cow, so is my lover among lovers.

8. A honey boy! Bring me Thy cool limbs hither! Let us sit awhile in the orchard, until the sun go down! Let us feast on the cool grass! Bring wine, ye slaves, that the cheeks of my boy may flush red.

9. In the garden of immortal kisses, O thou brilliant One, shine forth! Make Thy mouth an opium-poppy, that one kiss is the key to the infinite sleep and lucid, the sleep of Shi-loh-am.

10. In my sleep I beheld the Universe like a clear crystal without one speck.

11. There are purse-proud penniless ones that stand at the door of the tavern and prate of their feats of wine-bibbing.

12. There are purse-proud penniless ones that stand at the door of the tavern and revile the guests.

13. The guests dally upon couches of mother-of-pearl in the garden; the noise of the foolish men is hidden from them.

14. Only the inn-keeper feareth lest the favour of the king be withdrawn from him.

15. Thus spake the Magister V. V. V. V. V. unto Adonai his God, as they played together in the starlight over against the deep black pool that is in the Holy Place of the Holy House beneath the Altar of the Holiest One.

16. But Adonai laughed, and played more languidly.

17. Then the scribe took note, and was glad. But Adonai had no fear of the Magician and his play.

For it was Adonai who had taught all his tricks to the Magician.

18. And the Magister entered into the play of the Magician. When the Magician laughed he laughed; all as a man should do.

19. And Adonai said: Thou art enmeshed in the web of the Magician. This He said subtly, to try him.

20. But the Magister gave the sign of the Magistry, and laughed back on Him: O Lord, O beloved, did these fingers relax on Thy curls, or these eyes turn away from Thine eye?

21. And Adonai delighted in him exceedingly.

22. Yea, O my master, thou art the beloved of the Beloved One; the Bennu Bird is set up in Philae not in vain.

23. I who was the priestess of Ahathoor rejoice in your love. Arise, O Nile-God, and devour the holy place of the Cow of Heaven! Let the milk of the stars be drunk up by Sebek the dweller of Nile!

24. Arise, O serpent Apep, Thou art Adonai the beloved one! Thou art my darling and my lord, and Thy poison is sweeter than the kisses of Isis the mother of the Gods!

25. For Thou art He! Yeah, Thou shalt swallow up Asi and Asar, and the children of Ptah. Thou shalt pour forth a flood of poison to destroy the works of the Magician. Only the Destroyer shall devour Thee; Thou shalt blacken his throat, wherein his spirit abideth. Ah, serpent Apep, but I love Thee!

26. My God! Let Thy secret fang pierce to the marrow of the little secret bone that I have kept against the Day of Vengeance of Hoor-Ra. Let Kheph-Ra sound his sharded drone! let the jackals of Day and Night howl in the wilderness of Time! let the Towers of the Universe totter, and the guardians hasten away! For my Lord hath revealed Himself as a mighty serpent, and my heart is the blood of His body.

27. I am like a love-sick courtesan of Corinth. I have toyed with kings and captains, and made them my slaves. To-day I am the slave of the little asp of death; and who shall loosen our love?

28. Weary, weary! saith the scribe, who shall lead me to the sight of the Rapture of my master?

29. The body is weary and the soul is sore weary and sleep weighs down their eyelids; yet ever abides the sure consciousness of ecstasy, unknown, yet known in that its being is certain. O Lord, be my helper, and bring me to the bliss of the Beloved!

30. I came to the house of the Beloved, and the wine was like fire that flieth with green wings through the world of waters.

31. I felt the red lips of nature and the black lips of perfection. Like sisters they fondled me their little brother; they decked me out as a bride; they mounted me for Thy bridal chamber.

32. They fled away at Thy coming; I was alone before Thee.

33. I trembled at Thy coming, O my God, for Thy messenger was more terrible than the Death-star.

34. On the threshold stood the fulminant figure of Evil, the Horror of emptiness, with his ghastly eyes like poisonous wells. He stood, and the chamber was corrupt; the air stank. He was an old and gnarled fish more hideous than the shells of Abaddon.

35. He enveloped me with his demon tentacles; yea, the eight fears took hold upon me.

36. But I was anointed with the right sweet oil of the Magister; I slipped from the embrace as a stone from the sling of a boy of the woodlands.

37. I was smooth and hard as ivory; the horror gat no hold. Then at the noise of the wind of Thy coming he was dissolved away, and the abyss of the great void was unfolded before me.

38. Across the waveless sea of eternity Thou didst ride with Thy captains and Thy hosts; with Thy chariots and horsemen and spearmen didst Thou travel through the blue.

39. Before I saw Thee Thou wast already with me; I was smitten through by Thy marvellous spear.

40. I was stricken as a bird by the bolt of the thunderer; I was pierced as the thief by the Lord of the Garden.

41. O my Lord, let us sail upon the sea of blood!

42. There is a deep taint beneath the ineffable bliss; it is the taint of generation.

43. Yea, though the flower wave bright in the sunshine, the root is deep in the darkness of earth.

44. Praise to thee, O beautiful dark earth, thou art the mother of a million myriads of myriads of flowers.

45. Also I beheld my God, and the countenance of Him was a thousandfold brighter than the lightning. Yet in his heart I beheld the slow and dark One, the ancient one, the devourer of His children.

46. In the height and the abyss, O my beautiful, there is no thing, verily, there is no thing at all, that is not altogether and perfectly fashioned for Thy delight.

47. Light cleaveth unto Light, and filth to filth; with pride one contemneth another. But not Thou, who art all, and beyond it; who art absolved from the Division of the Shadows.

48. O day of Eternity, let Thy wave break in foamless glory of sapphire upon the laborious coral of our making!

49. We have made us a ring of glistening white sand, strewn wisely in the midst of the Delightful Ocean.

50. Let the palms of brilliance flower upon our island; we shall eat of their fruit, and be glad.

51. But for me the lustral water, the great ablution, the dissolving of the soul in that resounding abyss.

52. I have a little son like a wanton goat; my daughter is like an unfledged eaglet; they shall get them fins, that they may swim.

53. That they may swim, O my beloved, swim far in the warm honey of Thy being, O blessed one, O boy of beatitude!

54. This heart of mine is girt about with the serpent that devoureth his own coils.

55. When shall there be an end, O my darling, O when shall the Universe and the Lord thereof be utterly swallowed up?

56. Nay! who shall devour the Infinite? who shall undo the Wrong of the Beginning?

57. Thou criest like a white cat upon the roof of the Universe; there is none to answer Thee.

58. Thou art like a lonely pillar in the midst of the sea; there is none to behold Thee, O Thou who beholdest all!

59. Thou dost faint, thou dost fail, thou scribe; cried the desolate Voice; but I have filled thee with a wine whose savour thou knowest not.

60. It shall avail to make drunken the people of the old gray

sphere that rolls in the infinite Far-off; they shall lap the wine as dogs that lap the blood of a beautiful courtesan pierced through by the Spear of a swift rider through the city.

61. I too am the Soul of the desert; thou shalt seek me yet again in the wilderness of sand.

62. At thy right hand a great lord and a comely; at thy left hand a woman clad in gossamer and gold and having the stars in her hair. Ye shall journey far into a land of pestilence and evil; ye shall encamp in the river of a foolish city forgotten; there shall ye meet with Me.

63. There will I make Mine habitation; as for bridal will I come bedecked and anointed; there shall the Consummation be accomplished.

64. O my darling, I also wait for the brilliance of the hour ineffable, when the universe shall be like a girdle for the midst of the ray of our love, extending beyond the permitted end of the endless One.

65. Then, O thou heart, will I the serpent eat thee wholly up; yea, I will eat thee wholly up.

PART IV

Liber AL: The
Book of the Law

MAGICK AND LAW

For instance, one may wish to obtain the knowledge put forth in this book. Not knowing that such a book exists, one might yet induce some one who knows it to offer a copy.

Magick

The verbs to transcend, to transmit, to transcribe, and their like, are all of cardinal virtue in Magick.

"Trance," Little Essays Toward Truth

Everyone knows the eccentricities of fountain pens.

Magick

. . . the Beast had agreed to follow the instructions communicated to Him only in order to show that "nothing would happen if you broke all the rules." Poor fool! The way of mastery is to break all the rules. . . .

"New Comment" on The Book of the Law

The dawn-meditation was highly graced by the K[nowledge] & C[onversation] of the H[oly] G[uardian] A[ngel]. And I came thence to ask the meaning of the word "Who". I can't define it.

The Magical Record of the Beast

Hadst thou a name, thou were errovacably lost.

The Vision and the Voice

All words are sacred and all prophets true.

The Book of the Law

The Book of the Law, which is technically known by the name of *Liber AL vel Legis,* and less formally as *Liber Legis, Liber AL* or even *AL* (AL is Hebrew for "God"), is a book of Laws about the Nature of Law (or the Law of Nature). Though it bears the name of Aleister Crowley, he is, he asserts, merely the Master to claim its authority, and not its author. It is an "Exorcism of Art,"[1] a direct Word from the gods, and entitled by title and text to protection of its contents—its infallibility. "The letters?

1. From Crowley's invocation of *The Book of the Law,* quoted in John Symonds, *The Great Beast* (London: River, 1951), p. 59.

Change them not in style or value."[2] *The Book of the Law* attempts to both embody Law and empower Law; it is a written body of Lawful Law.

The history of *The Book of the Law* is part of the Law. When it comes to the Law, once is never enough. The Law asserts itself, desires to hear its right to reign endlessly recounted.

This history, Aleister Crowley's story, his-story, is a tale well told and retold. *The Confessions* (his autohagiography) focuses around this central event, and *The Equinox of the Gods* is his book-length version of the story. His commentary and writings bear frequent reference to *The Book of the Law* and its transmission; for example, one of the volumes of his magical journal *The Equinox* (part of the ongoing record "The Temple of Solomon the King") includes an extended retelling. And the four most noted writers on Crowley to date—John Symonds, Israel Regardie, Kenneth Grant and Francis King—have each had several chances again to set the facts in order.[3]

Once more Writing the story of the Law, the Law of this story: *The Book of the Law* was transcribed in Cairo in April of 1904, while Crowley lived there, passing himself off as a Persian prince under the assumed name of Chioa Khan. Rose, his wife, began to experience premonitions of a Book, which Crowley at first dismissed as "pure rubbish."[4] A series of coincidences convinced Crowley that Rose possessed special knowledge. He felt certain enough to follow her instructions: on April 8, 9, and 10, beginning at noon and ending an hour later, he sat in his room and wrote what he heard. "I was being treated like a hypnotized imbecile, only worse, for I was perfectly aware of what I was doing."[5]

Recapping: Aleister Crowley, who was also Chioa Khan, acted under order of his wife, Rose, also known by her spiritual name Ouarda, to receive the word of Crowley's Holy Guardian Angel, named Aiwaz (as originally spelled) or Aiwass (as Crowley would later spell it, for numerological reasons), who, in turn, is acting for the minister of the god Horus in the guise of the Child, Hoor-paar-Kraat, who, bringing matters full circle, has emerged on this earth in the form of Aleister Crowley as Ra-Hoor-Khuit, Hoor's double, now taking the form of the

2. *Liber AL: The Book of the Law* (reprinted Berkeley: O. T. O., 1982), Chapter II, Verse 54.
3. Citations for these books are all included in the second part of the bibliography.
4. *The Confessions of Aleister Crowley* (New York: Hill and Wang, 1970), p. 394.
5. "New Comment" to *The Book of the Law*, reprinted in *The Law is For All* (Phoenix: Falcon Press, 1982), p. 170.

Crowned and Conquering Child and spreading his Word concerning a new Aeon.

In one sense, then, Horus is dictating the Book to his incarnate self—("Because of me in Thee which Thou knewest not"[6]—though the lines of this transmission divide, add, multiply. The Book is spoken by three voices: Nuit (the endless firmament), Hadit (the star in the firmament), and Ra-Hoor-Khuit. Through these multiple voices, though, Crowley still manages to speak. "My own inspiration, not any alien advice or intellectual consideration, is to be the energizing force of this work."[7] Law is dependent on Voice, and if *Liber AL* is not the infallible word of Horus, if it is part Crowleyan "inspiration", then how can it be Law? Dr. Regardie and John Symonds both say that Crowley wrote *AL,* while Kenneth Grant sides with divine writing. Crowley usually (but not always) claims Horus as sole author, though at times he might also claim himself for Horus. "In the new Aeon the Hierophant is Horus . . . therefore the Candidate will be Horus too."[8] Perhaps Crowley hears an echo or is cut, schiz. "In the text of the Book itself are thorns for the flesh of the most ardent swain as he buries his face in the roses; some of the ivy that clings about the Thyrse of this Dionysus is Poison Ivy. The question arises, especially on examining the original manuscript in my handwriting: 'Who wrote these words?' "[9]

Ivy creeps, slinks, twists around, poison or no. Candidates for copyright of the *Law* start to blur. "It is rare that a severed antenna twitches,"[10] and Crowley has made himself a veritable switching center for overlapping signals, interference patterns in the air, even errors of Law. *The Book of the Law* blindly records the proceedings. During day one of the transmission Aiwass instructs Crowley to take a particular line and "write this in whiter words."[11] Ouarda later supplies the language for the substitution. "To write whiter": either to clarify (and why clarify a god?) or to make more opaque, to obliterate a single writer with whiter. Both the first and second day transmissions include lines by Crowley—sentences, he concludes, that he thought during the

6. *Liber AL: The Book of the Law,* Chapter II, Verse 12.
7. *The Equinox of the Gods* (reprinted New York: Gordon Press, 1974), p. 126.
8. "Liber Samekh Theurgia Goetia Summa Congressus Cum Daemone," reprinted in *Gems from the Equinox* (St. Paul: Llewellyn Publications, 1974), p. 335.
9. *The Equinox of the Gods,* pp. 96–97.
10. Quoted in John Symonds, *The Great Beast,* p. 193.
11. Visible on p. 6 of the original manuscript, which is reproduced most recently in *The Holy Books of Thelema* (York Beach: Samuel Weiser, 1983) and *The Law is For All.*

transmission. "Who am I, and what shall be the sign?" is one such line,[12] posing the problem of Crowley's place within this Book, signed by the hands of more or less than one. "Ah! Ah! What do I feel? Is the word exhausted?"[13] injects Crowley's feelings directly into the text. Finally, on the third day, the prayer on the Egyptian tablet known as the Stélé of Revealing is left out of *Liber AL*'s transmitted text; Crowley translates this tablet—housed as luck would have it in a Cairo museum—and makes poetic paraphrases of the Stélé for subsequent inclusion. The Stélé is another source for the Book—a real steal by Horus, a revealingly concealing source.

"The Book of the Law is Written and Concealed. Aum. Ha."[14] So ends *Liber AL*. All is not yet in plain sight. The book's hidden treasures are far from exposed. The signals cease, the voices stop, but there is yet more to be said—and not by Horus, but Crowley. Still finding the Word of Law far from exhausted at the end of *The Book of the Law,* Crowley spends the rest of his life writing hundreds of pages of Commentary on *Liber AL,* as demanded by Ra-Hoor-Khuit.[15] Somehow, Aiwass' exceptional truth—an "English in itself"[16] or even "wordless gesture"[17]—needs to be supplemented. Crowley is both vessel bound by *AL*'s Law—irrefutable—and privileged interpreter of the Book's contents. Writing as the priest Ankh-F-N-Khonsu: "All questions of the Law are to be decided only by appeal to my writings."[18] "My award is . . . absolute without appeal."[19] *AL*'s final truth lies not in appeal back to the Book, but in the Comment, a second level of law operating in the name of the first—a first which we had been promised was "for all" and that furthermore could be divined even within Crowley's Comment "each for himself."[20] The supplement of the Comment is dangerous indeed in its implication for total Law.

We may go so far as to say that Crowley and his Comment may even be an obstruction of Justice, of Law: "I will make easy to you the abstruction from the ill-ordered house in the Victorious City."[21]

12. *Liber AL: The Book of the Law,* Chapter I, Verse 26.
13. *Liber AL: The Book of the Law,* Chapter II, Verse 69.
14. *Liber AL: The Book of the Law,* Chapter III, Verse 75.
15. *Liber AL: The Book of the Law,* Chapter III, Verses 40–41.
16. *The Equinox of the Gods,* p. 117.
17. *The Equinox of the Gods,* p. 125.
18. Single page "Comment," reprinted with *Liber AL: The Book of the Law,* p. 47.
19. *The Equinox of the Gods,* p. 127.
20. "Comment," p. 47.
21. *Liber AL: The Book of the Law,* Chapter III, Verse 11.

This line, like many others in *Liber AL,* confused Crowley. How to read this Word, "abstruction"? In his "Old Comment," Crowley says it means he must "construct" a replica of the Stélé of Revealing, per a previous verse, but he reconsiders this opinion. The Word, says Crowley, "suggests an idea otherwise inexpressible is conveyed in this manner."[22] If Crowley had written *AL* himself, "I should not have . . . acquiesced in the horror 'abstruction'."[23] To say the least it is abstruse, but perhaps it can be read as "obstruct" so that Crowley, the vessel, must perforce take up the role of Crowley, the obstruction—interposing himself in the clear channel, turning Law into an "ill-ordered house." And yet he cannot see this, for the obstruction cannot see himself in the way, but in this way the obstruction creates Law, becomes the Law. Crowley—the abstruction vessel that rests in perpetual agitation between Aiwass and the reader, conveying the "inexpressible" by abstruction. This is the unlogic of *The Book of the Law* and its Comment. The "o" of obstruction, the "o" of Nothing, turned into the "a" of abstruction. "O" for "A," nothing into something, All, Law. A–L. The humble scribe of *Liber AL* is no mean Artist, but an Artist of Interruption, who receives Law in his own image.

And if *The Book of the Law,* being so contaminated by Crowley's Comment and his subjective readers, is not now THE Law—the proclamation of Ra-Hoor-Khuit, with instruction as to how men must reach their maximum potential, and perhaps become gods—it may be merely Crowley's Law, or law, or not, or nothing. Crowley's answer: "It does not matter to the theory whether the communicating spirit so-called is an objective entity or a concealed portion of the diviner's mind."[24] *The Book of the Law* says, "Nothing is a secret key of this law."[25] The wavering on this point, the sense of doubt, this problem of Law and of the interpretation of the various commentaries, is known to Crowley. It is part of Law. Not only is it visible in the history of *AL,* it is an unknowability—of Not/Nothing—embedded in the text and its name, and their Qabalistic reading. This reading was performed Not by Crowley, but by his student/interpreter Charles Stansfeld Jones (or Frater Achad) in his *Liber 31.* Achad's research proves an exception to Crowley's iron rule over it. Achad is the one that "cometh after him"

22. *The Equinox of the Gods,* p. 129.
23. *The Equinox of the Gods,* p. 106.
24. *Magick* (reprinted New York: Samuel Weiser, 1974), p. 267.
25. *Liber AL: The Book of the Law,* Chapter I, Verse 46.

mentioned in *AL*[26], Crowley's "child and that strangely" who it was prophecized will reveal some of the Book's riddles. According to Achad, "AL" is "God," and "All"—the Law; the reverse, "LA," is Hebrew for "Not." Both words are equivalent numerologically, adding to 31. The Book hints at this relationship in lines pregnant with double meaning: "The fool readeth this Book of the Law, and its comment; & he understandeth it not."[27] As Crowley notes, "He [Achad] understood it—this Book—not. That is, he understood that this Book was, so to speak, a vesture or veil upon the idea of 'not'."[28] The Law of Not. The Law is Not. The veil of Law tied in Nots, Not just circuitous like vines. Not upholding the Law, but rather the shuttling back and forth between the authors, the speakers, Law and the Law of Nothing—in the vessel, on the circuit. (Crowley's Yoga diary in India also contains this revelation: "There is *not* an intelligence directing law."[29]) Or, in a similar vein, Law is now Naughty Law. To enter into Law may be to Transgress. "I notice that Language itself testifies to the soundness of my ontological theories; for the adjective of Naught is Naughty!"[30]

We do not need to read Naughty Books on the straight and narrow, left to Right, left to Right, according to the traditional rules and Laws of interpretation. The Law of the Linear can be upset by many things, including the pun, a doubling up that stops smooth flow, for example, in the line, "There is a splendour in my name hidden and glorious, as the sun of midnight is ever the son."[31] In this case the relationship between sun and son is both hidden and exposed by pun. That which is associated with god, giving life—a sun— is confused by Language with that which receives life from a father—the son. Read Horus for god and Crowley for son and you can see how the pun can keep the Law undone.[32] "[There are] many such cases of double entendre, paranomasia in one language or another, sometimes two at once, numerical-literal puzzles, and even (on one occasion) an illuminating connexion

---

26. *Liber AL: The Book of the Law*, Chapter III, Verse 47.
27. *Liber AL: The Book of the Law*, Chapter III, Verse 63.
28. *The Equinox of the Gods*, p. 99.
29. *The Confessions of Aleister Crowley*, p. 262.
30. *The Magical Record of the Beast 666: The Journals of Aleister Crowley* (Quebec: Next Step Publications, 1972), p. 135.
31. *Liber AL: The Book of the Law*, Chapter III, Verse 74.
32. Of course, the "sun of midnight" may be the moon, in which case it is a son of the sun, reflecting its light. But with Words and puns there are no suns—no first lights—and meaning reflects from no point of origin.

of letters in various lines by a slashing scratch."[33] *Liber AL vel Legis* is a numbered series of scratches, slashes and breaks, in and between lines. Many varying editions of *The Book of the Law* have been published, based on new readings of the sloppily handwritten text, and who is to say which Law is Lawful?

AL is Law Fully Naughty. Fragments, curt commands, a forest of exclamation marks (the "stops" are supplied by Crowley per Aiwass' instruction). Nonstop stops, starts and turnabouts. A "connexion" of breaks and a break of "connexions." Crowley himself cites regular "changes of speaker" as well as "curious deformities of grammar and syntax, defects of rhythm," "rambling and unintelligible" passages.[34] Such "jumbles of matter, such abrupt jerks from subject to subject" subject one to the problem of the subject in *AL*. In this veritable collage, which subject speaks? These regularly irregular devices are similar in effect to sexual climax. Speaking of the style of his precursor, the French magician Eliphas Levi (Crowley felt that he was the reincarnation of Levi), Crowley says, "It is evidently the supreme enjoyment to strike a chord composed of as many conflicting elements as possible. The pleasure seems to be derived from gratifying the sense of power, the power to compel every possible element of thought to contribute to the spasm."[35] Again, the problem of the Law, this time raised in the name of Power. Power (or Law) in writing approaches impossibility when Power means pushing the audience to a readerly orgasm and a loss of Self/Subject. In the abyss of orgasm, in the chasm of spasm, the reader can Not perceive Law, cannot distinguish Law from Nothing. *Liber AL*'s Law voids Law, releases the Law of the Void.

The Law of Space. From which a disembodied voice commands, "If this be not right; if ye confound the space-marks, saying: They are one; or saying, They are many; . . . then expect the direful judgments of Ra Hoor Khuit!"[36] *The Book of the Law* marks space, spaces out its marks, using every mark in the Book—every bookmark—to keep it open, to leave space between the Words, the lines, the speakers in the text. *AL*'s textual strategies acknowledge the gaps, preventing the Law from being reduced to One, to One Self, to one voice, whether Horus or Crowley; or from being added together as compendium—*AL* as All—a

33. *The Equinox of the Gods*, p. 98.
34. *The Equinox of the Gods*, pp. 105–106.
35. *Magick*, p. 186.
36. *Liber AL: The Book of the Law*, Chapter I, Verse 52.

complete set of Selves. Rather, Self leaks, leaving a mark. "Clearly this Self is also not-Self, for Self, as a word, implies 'space-marks'."[37] Marking the threshold of closure—the drive to totalize, to turn word to Law. Law's Space proliferates infinitely. Mapped out in all directions of voice. The marks, the stops, the slashing scratches punctuate the whole *Book of Law*.

Such punctures open up another textbook—one whose surfaces delimit the Law and delineate the Laws of Chance, a second and more freewheeling Language. "Paste the [handwritten manuscript] sheets from right to left and from top to bottom: then behold!" instructs Aiwass.[38] The pattern of pages reveals new meaning—hidden Law. So does even the ink and paper, since Aiwass instructs Crowley to reproduce both as exactly as possible in printing. "For in the chance shape of the letters and their position to one another: in these are mysteries that no Beast shall divine."[39] (Aiwass means that many of the mysteries of the Book will remain unsolved even by Crowley, the Master of the Comment—the Beast). By Aiwass' authority, the surface marking of the paper is as significant as (or more than, or no less than) the word of the gods. And other alternate, Qabalistic or Chance readings of the Book could, as Crowley says, occupy a lifetime or more. Crowley seasonally sought special counsel from the *AL* by divining words of power, "placing the thumb at random within the leaves."[40] The interpretation of *The Book of the Law* now seems an endless, pointless task. The Law as written is too flexible for Law—may Not be trustable as often as Not, as Chance.

Is *AL*, then, all blind alleys and no exists, a playful but random dialing of numbers, and an existential maze or trap designed to lose the casual traveler and make him grind his teeth searching for the word of Horus? Because, as Crowley says, if *The Book of the Law* is Not as good as its word—if it is Not "valid absolutely" as Law—then it must be "an appalling proof that no kind or degree of evidence soever is sufficient to establish any possible proposition, since the closest concatenation of circumstances may be no more than the jetsam of chance, and the most comprehensive plans of purpose a puerile pantomime."[41] But no! no!—the answer to these critics must be framed

---

37. *The Magical Record of the Beast 666: The Journals of Aleister Crowley*, p. 122.
38. *Liber AL: The Book of the Law*, Chapter III, Verse 73.
39. *Liber AL: The Book of the Law*, Chapter III, Verse 47.
40. *Magick*, p. 268.
41. *The Equinox of the Gods*, pp. 132–133.

in the double negative, just as *AL* often doubles its voice and cries out, as in "But exceed! exceed!"[42] Crowley writes with "the Double Wand of Power",[43] "the Double Gift of Tongues, the Word of Double Power,"[44] the Power that doubles back on itself, the double-trouble mark that undermines the mind of reason, the doubling up in laughter, the double reading represented by the Ape of Thoth, the doubling of the child Horus. Permitting himself to both Write blind in the unquestioning service of the Law and Aiwass, and yet also be the maker of these marks, automatically. Neither lordly Law nor nihilist Nought can reign in such a rain of marks. "Nor shall they who cry aloud in their folly that thou meanest nought avail; they shall reveal it: thou availest: they are the slaves of because: They are not of me."[45] Those on the side of Because are seen as aligned with *either* absolute Law or, in this passage, absolute Nothing, with *either* pure Self/Me or pure babble. With personal scrawl of pen, or the heaviness of ink. With the tried and true story of the *Liber AL* as word from Horus, or Crowley's random order of backward pages.

Frater Achad's reading, then, is Not so much a complete rereading, a locating of the "new symbols" of the Alphabet,[46] or even an inducement to total babble, as these both end up as Nothing more than Law. It is the initiation of a displacement, a ceaseless displacement, of both Law and Not. "They shall reveal it," meaning that those who suggest that *Liber AL* is Nothing have already revealed its Law. Believe in Nothing, and you find it always already the Law. Believe in the Law, and you find it always already Nothing. This may be a ceaseless "failure" to pin the book down to one position or the other, but "then this circle squared in its failure is a key also."[47]

The paradox of Law and Nothing is embodied in the Crowleyan reading of *AL*'s most repeated line: "Do what thou wilt shall be the whole of the Law."[48] A summary statement for a book that forecloses the possibility of summary, it sticks in the throat and refuses to settle. If you simply "Do what thou wilt," then Law is the sort of frontier justice practiced in wide open spaces. The law of Nothing, amorality, where

---

42. *Liber AL: The Book of the Law*, Chapter II, Verse 71.
43. *Liber AL: The Book of the Law*, Chapter III, Verse 72.
44. *The Book of Lies* (reprinted New York: Samuel Weiser, 1978), p. 148.
45. *Liber AL: The Book of the Law*, Chapter II, Verse 54.
46. *Liber AL: The Book of the Law*, Chapter II, Verse 55.
47. *Liber AL: The Book of the Law*, Chapter III, Verse 47.
48. *Liber AL: The Book of the Law*, Chapter I, Verse 40.

everything is legitimized—it all becomes self-expression—because "The word of Sin is Restriction."[49] And the Law of no Law is, in its own way, whole, founded on such rocks as self-pleasure and personal inclination.

Yet it is some other voice, Law, which is saying, "Do what thou wilt," and that makes everything permissible. Crowleyan Will is postordained by Law; what you Will is what you Will Do, Did. Each person has a path to set, an orbit to follow " 'unassuaged of purpose'. . . . Any purpose in the will would damper it; clearly the 'lust of result' is a thing from which it must be delivered."[50] Will has no purpose, no desire for action; It lives by and sets at the same time its own logic and laws. One can do no more than to act freely, because such an act has already been cited in the statutes of Law. "Do what thou wilt is absolute in a sense, just because it concurs in relativity."[51]

AL's Law and Will are locked together mortally—they do Not fight, though they wrestle in such a way as to always occupy each other's space. *Liber AL* warns its reader not to choose sides, not to engage in such matches. "The tearing asunder *is* a crushing together," as Crowley is told in the wilderness.[52] The tearing apart—the freedom, the freedom of Transgression, the Transgression of freedom—is crush controlled. The full weight of the Law, therefore, is Nothing—Nothing but a complex weaving of something/Nothing. Where the Will is Not: "O if everyman did No Matter What, provided that it is the one thing that he will not and cannot do!"[53] Where the puzzle of Law *v.* Will is no longer a debate or a puzzle, but a pattern. "One may be unable to tell when a thread of a particular colour will be woven into the carpet of Destiny. It is only when the carpet is finished and seen from a proper distance that the position of that particular strand is seen to be necessary. From this one is tempted to break a lance on that most ancient battlefield, free-will and destiny."[54]

And when *Liber AL vel Legis* is Not Law but the flickering effects of the patterns Will and Law, Chance and Law, Not and Law, Comment and Law, Crowley and Law—the flickering when *AL* looks at its mirror

49. *Liber AL: The Book of the Law,* Chapter I, Verse 41.
50. "Liber II," reprinted in *The Equinox, Volume III, Number 10* (New York: Thelema Publications, 1986), pp. 25–26.
51. *The Magical Record of the Beast 666: The Journals of Aleister Crowley,* p. 143.
52. *The Vision and the Voice* (reprinted Dallas: Sangreal Foundation, 1972), p. 210.
53. *The Book of Lies,* p. 130.
54. *Magick,* p. 65.

image, LA—the Book will risk everything. By returning for the first time to what has been avoided: namely, a truly Lawful reading of *The Book of the Law*. Not opposing another reading to a more black and white reading of the Book, but rather detecting the flicker within. So that "not only 'Black is White', but 'The Whiteness of Black is the *essential* of its Blackness.' "[55]

On the face of it, the message of *The Book of the Law* is that any one thing must be brought together with its opposite in order to disappear into a third, and that by this operation the magician will manifest himself as god. The first section of *AL*, concerning the Nuit, represents the age of the Egyptian goddess Isis, the pre-Christian era of pantheism. The second section, concerning Hadit, represents the age of the god Osiris, the Christian era of one God. Isis and Osiris are the parents of Horus, who in different forms is both Hoor-paar-Kraat, the god to whom Aiwass reports, and Ra-Hoor-Khuit, of whom the third section of *AL* concerns, the Crowned and Conquering Child of the new Aeon, when God emerges from within. In the new Aeon pantheism flickers against theism, the gods of the fields flicker with the supreme and separate god, the female Nuit flickers with the male Hadit, her Silence flickers against his Speech.

In the new Aeon, the Writer of the text of Law, Hoor-paar-Kraat (the crippled child-dwarf who is also "silence"),[56] flickers with the embodiment of Law, the God of Law, Ra-Hoor-Khuit. And then Crowley, the embodiment of Horus, becomes both the God of Law, and the Writing of the God of Law. "I wrenched DOG backwards to find GOD; now GOD barks."[57] Supreme God and Crippled God, Law and Not Law folded in upon each other, a flashing which is dazzling to the I. As dazzling as the Qabalist's conception of the Writing of (Not) God, "The Ante Primal Triad which is Not-God. Nothing is. Nothing becomes. Nothing is not."[58]

Then let Writing take hold, again! again! "I see thee hate the hand & the pen; but I am stronger."[59] "Write, and find ecstasy in writing!"[60] Let Crowley declare "a feast for the three days of the writing of the Book of

55. *Magick,* p. 39.
56. Kenneth Grant, *Aleister Crowley & the Hidden God* (New York: Samuel Weiser, 1974), p. 210.
57. *The Book of Lies,* p. 136.
58. *The Book of Lies,* p. 10.
59. *Liber AL: The Book of the Law,* Chapter II, Verse 11.
60. *Liber AL: The Book of the Law,* Chapter II, Verse 66.

the Law."[61] A feast Not just for the Book, but for Writing itself. The Law is a Book about to be written, the Law of continuous Writing of Law/Nothing, God/Not God, of weaving and flickering, as it has always been, as it must always become. "The history of [*The Book of the Law*] must one day be told by a more vivid voice. Properly considered, it is a history of a continuous miracle."[62] "For the writing of the Book goes on eternally; there is no way of closing the record until the goal of all has been attained."[63] "All" here should not be read literally, but in the same light as Law. All is Not possible, as Aiwass reveals, nor even desirable: "All is not aught."[64] Crowley elaborates: "This phrase is . . . an excessively neat cipher or hieroglyph of the great key to this Book. All (AL) is not aught (LA)."[65] All is Naught, which is a miracle of miracles: the miracle of *Liber AL*'s Lawful treasures flickering with the monsters of its void. Good or ill, the Law is for All. Let the Book never close!

"The Tables of the Law? Bah!"[66] "Nevertheless, behold, o my Son, this Mystery. His true Word was LA ALLH that is to say: (There is) No God, and LA AL is that Mystery of Mysteries which thine own Eye pierced in thine Initiation."[67] "For I am perfect, being Not."[68] "There is division hither homeward; there is a word not known."[69] Division: Aleister, Al, AL, LA, Law, Awe, Aum. Word Not known.

61. *Liber AL: The Book of the Law*, Chapter II, Verse 38.
62. *The Equinox of the Gods*, p. 135.
63. *Magick*, p. 110.
64. *Liber AL: The Book of the Law*, Chapter III, Verse 2.
65. *The Law is For All*, p. 267.
66. "Laughter," *Little Essays Toward Truth* (reprinted Malton, Canada: Dove Press, approximately 1970), p. 30.
67. Liber Aleph vel CXI: *The Book of Wisdom or Folly* (reprinted Seattle: Aeon Press, 1985), p. 41.
68. *Liber AL: The Book of the Law*, Chapter II, Verse 15.
69. *Liber AL: The Book of the Law*, Chapter III, Verse 2.

Liber AL vel Legis, or The Book of the Law

(Note: The excerpt from *The Equinox of the Gods* which follows *Liber AL* in this book (see page 222) is Crowley's line-by-line comment on the book's "voice" and, given the difficulties involved in following *AL*'s text, might bear consulting during the reading of *AL*.)

---

1. Had! The manifestation of Nuit.

2. The unveiling of the company of heaven.

3. Every man and every woman is a star.

4. Every number is infinite; there is no difference.

5. Help me, o warrior lord of Thebes, in my unveiling before the Children of men!

6. Be thou Hadit, my secret centre, my heart & my tongue!

7. Behold! it is revealed by Aiwass the minister of Hoor-paar-kraat.

8. The Khabs is in the Khu, not the Khu in the Khabs.

9. Worship then the Khabs, and behold my light shed over you!

10. Let my servants be few & secret: they shall rule the many & the known.

11. These are fools that men adore; both their Gods & their men are fools.

12. Come forth, o children, under the stars, & take your fill of love!

13. I am above you and in you. My ecstasy is in yours. My joy is to see your joy.

14. Above, the gemmèd azure is
    The naked splendour of Nuit;
She bends in ecstasy to kiss
    The secret ardours of Hadit.
The wingèd globe, the starry blue,
Are mine, O Ankh-af-na-khonsu!

15. Now ye shall know that the chosen priest & apostle of infinite space is the prince-priest the Beast; and in his woman called the

Scarlet Woman is all power given. They shall gather my children into their fold: they shall bring the glory of the stars into the hearts of men.

16. For he is ever a sun, and she a moon. But to him is the winged secret flame, and to her the stooping starlight.

17. But ye are not so chosen.

18. Burn upon their brows, o splendrous serpent!

19. O azure-lidded woman, bend upon them!

20. The key of the rituals is in the secret word which I have given unto him.

21. With the God & the Adorer I am nothing: they do not see me. They are as upon the earth; I am Heaven, and there is no other God than me, and my lord Hadit.

22. Now, therefore, I am known to ye by my name Nuit, and to him by a secret name which I will give him when at last he knoweth me. Since I am Infinite Space, and the Infinite Stars thereof, do ye also thus. Bind nothing! Let there be no difference made among you between any one thing & any other thing; for thereby there cometh hurt.

23. But whoso availeth in this, let him be the chief of all!

24. I am Nuit, and my word is six and fifty.

25. Divide, add, multiply, and understand.

26. Then saith the prophet and slave of the beauteous one: Who am I, and what shall be the sign? So she answered him, bending down, a lambent flame of blue, all-touching, all penetrant, her lovely hands upon the black earth, & her lithe body arched for love, and her soft feet not hurting the little flowers: Thou knowest! And the sign shall be my ecstasy, the consciousness of the continuity of existence, the omnipresence of my body.

27. Then the priest answered & said unto the Queen of Space, kissing her lovely brows, and the dew of her light bathing his whole body in a sweet-smelling perfume of sweat: O Nuit, continuous one of Heaven, let it be ever thus; that men speak not of Thee as One but as None; and let them speak not of thee at all, since thou art continuous!

28. None, breathed the light, faint & faery, of the stars, and two.

29. For I am divided for love's sake, for the chance of union.

30. This is the creation of the world, that the pain of division is as nothing, and the joy of dissolution all.

31. For these fools of men and their woes care not thou at all! They

feel little; what is, is balanced by weak joys; but ye are my chosen ones.

32. Obey my prophet! follow out the ordeals of my knowledge! seek me only! Then the joys of my love will redeem ye from all pain. This is so; I swear it by the vault of my body; by my sacred heart and tongue; by all I can give, by all I desire of ye all.

33. Then the priest fell into a deep trance or swoon, & said unto the Queen of Heaven; Write unto us the ordeals; write unto us the rituals; write unto us the law!

34. But she said: the ordeals I write not: the rituals shall be half known and half concealed: the Law is for all.

35. This that thou writest is the threefold book of Law.

36. My scribe Ankh-af-na-khonsu, the priest of the princes, shall not in one letter change this book; but lest there be folly, he shall comment thereupon by the wisdom of Ra-Hoor-Khu-it.

37. Also the mantras and spells; the obeah and the wanga; the work of the wand and the work of the sword; these he shall learn and teach.

38. He must teach; but he may make severe the ordeals.

39. The word of the Law is θελημα.

40. Who calls us Thelemites will do no wrong, if he look but close into the word. For there are therein Three Grades, the Hermit, and the Lover, and the man of Earth. Do what thou wilt shall be the whole of the Law.

41. The word of Sin is Restriction. O man! refuse not thy wife, if she will! O lover, if thou wilt, depart! There is no bond that can unite the divided but love: all else is a curse. Accursed! Accursed be it to the aeons! Hell.

42. Let it be that state of manyhood bound and loathing. So with thy all; thou hast no right but to do thy will.

43. Do that, and no other shall say nay.

44. For pure will, unassuaged of purpose, delivered from the lust of result, is every way perfect.

45. The Perfect and the Perfect are one Perfect and not two; nay, are none!

46. Nothing is a secret key of this law. Sixty-one the Jews call it; I call it eight, eighty, four hundred & eighteen.

47. But they have the half: unite by thine art so that all disappear.

48. My prophet is a fool with his one, one, one; are not they the Ox, and none by the Book?

49. Abrogate are all rituals, all ordeals, all words and signs. Ra-Hoor-Khuit hath taken his seat in the East at the Equinox of the Gods; and let Asar be with Isa, who also are one. But they are not of me. Let Asar be the adorant, Isa, the sufferer; Hoor in his secret name and splendour is the Lord initiating.

50. There is a word to say about the Hierophantic task. Behold! there are three ordeals in one, and it may be given in three ways. The gross must pass through fire; let the fine be tried in intellect, and the lofty chosen ones in the highest; Thus ye have star & star, system & system; let not one know well the other!

51. There are four gates to one palace; the floor of that palace is of silver and gold; lapis lazuli & jasper are there; and all rare scents; jasmine & rose, and the emblems of death. Let him enter in turn or at once the four gates; let him stand on the floor of the palace. Will he not sink? Amn. Ho! warrior, if thy servant sink? But there are means and means. Be goodly therefore: dress ye all in fine apparel; eat rich foods and drink sweet wines and wines that foam! Also, take your fill and will of love as ye will, when, where and with whom ye will! But always unto me.

52. If this be not aright; if ye confound the space-marks, saying: They are one; or saying, They are many; if the ritual be not ever unto me: then expect the direful judgments of Ra Hoor Khuit!

53. This shall regenerate the world, the little world my sister, my heart & my tongue, unto whom I send this kiss. Also, o scribe and prophet, though thou be of the princes, it shall not assuage thee nor absolve thee. But ecstasy be thine and joy of earth: ever To me! To me!

54. Change not as much as the style of a letter; for behold! thou, o prophet, shalt not behold all these mysteries hidden therein.

55. The child of thy bowels, *he* shall behold them.

56. Expect him not from the East, nor from the West; for from no expected house cometh that child. Aum! All words are sacred and all prophets true; save only that they understand a little; solve the first half of the equation, leave the second unattacked. But thou hast all in the clear light, and some, though not all, in the dark.

57. Invoke me under my stars! Love is the law, love under will. Nor let the fools mistake love; for there are love and love. There is the dove, and there is the serpent. Choose ye well! He, my prophet, hath chosen, knowing the law of the fortress, and the great mystery of the House of God.

All these old letters of my Book are aright; but צ is not the Star. This also is secret: my prophet shall reveal it to the wise.

58. I give unimaginable joys on earth: certainty, not faith, while in life, upon death; peace unutterable, rest, ecstasy; nor do I demand aught in sacrifice.

59. My incense is of resinous woods & gums; and there is no blood therein: because of my hair the trees of Eternity.

60. My number is 11, as all their numbers who are of us. The Five Pointed Star, with a Circle in the Middle, & the circle is Red. My colour is black to the blind, but the blue & gold are seen of the seeing. Also I have a secret glory for them that love me.

61. But to love me is better than all things: if under the night-stars in the desert thou presently burnest mine incense before me, invoking me with a pure heart, and the Serpent flame therein, thou shalt come a little to lie in my bosom. For one kiss wilt thou then be willing to give all; but whoso gives one particle of dust shall lose all in that hour. Ye shall gather goods and store of women and spices; ye shall wear rich jewels; ye shall exceed the nations of the earth in splendour & pride; but always in the love of me, and so shall ye come to my joy. I charge you earnestly to come before me in a single robe, and covered with a rich headdress. I love you! I yearn to you! Pale or purple, veiled or voluptuous, I who am all pleasure and purple, and drunkenness of the innermost sense, desire you. Put on the wings, and arouse the coiled splendour within you: come unto me!

62. At all my meetings with you shall the priestess say—and her eyes shall burn with desire as she stands bare and rejoicing in my secret temple—To me! To me! calling forth the flame of the hearts of all in her love-chant.

63. Sing the rapturous love-song unto me! Burn to me perfumes! Wear to me jewels! Drink to me, for I love you! I love you!

64. I am the blue-lidded daughter of Sunset; I am the naked brilliance of the voluptuous night-sky.

65. To me! To me!

66. The Manifestation of Nuit is at an end.

1. Nu! the hiding of Hadit.

2. Come! all ye, and learn the secret that hath not yet been revealed. I, Hadit, am the complement of Nu, my bride. I am not extended, and Khabs is the name of my House.

3. In the sphere I am everywhere the centre, as she, the circumference, is nowhere found.

4. Yet she shall be known & I never.

5. Behold! the rituals of the old time are black. Let the evil ones be cast away; let the good ones be purged by the prophet! Then shall this Knowledge go aright.

6. I am the flame that burns in every heart of man, and in the core of every star. I am Life, and the giver of Life, yet therefore is the knowledge of me the knowledge of death.

7. I am the Magician and the Exorcist. I am the axle of the wheel, and the cube in the circle. "Come unto me" is a foolish word: for it is I that go.

8. Who worshipped Heru-pa-kraath have worshipped me; ill, for I am the worshipper.

9. Remember all ye that existence is pure joy; that all the sorrows are but as shadows; they pass & are done; but there is that which remains.

10. O prophet! thou hast ill will to learn this writing.

11. I see thee hate the hand & the pen; but I am stronger.

12. Because of Me in Thee which thou knewest not.

13. For why? Because thou wast the knower, and me.

14. Now let there be a veiling of this shrine: now let the light devour men and eat them up with blindness!

15. For I am perfect, being Not; and my number is nine by the fools; but with the just I am eight, and one in eight: Which is vital, for I am none indeed. The Empress and the King are not of me; for there is a further secret.

16. I am The Empress & the Hierophant. Thus eleven, as my bride is eleven.

17. Hear me, ye people of sighing!
　　　The sorrows of pain and regret
　　Are left to the dead and the dying,
　　　The folk that not know me as yet.

18. These are dead, these fellows; they feel not. We are not for the poor and sad: the lords of the earth are our kinsfolk.

19. Is a God to live in a dog? No! but the highest are of us. They shall rejoice, our chosen: who sorroweth is not of us.

20. Beauty and strength, leaping laughter and delicious languor, force and fire, are of us.

21. We have nothing with the outcast and the unfit: let them die in

their misery. For they feel not. Compassion is the vice of kings: stamp down the wretched & the weak: this is the law of the strong: this is our law and the joy of the world. Think not, o king, upon that lie: That Thou Must Die: verily thou shalt not die, but live. Now let it be understood: If the body of the King dissolve, he shall remain in pure ecstasy for ever. Nuit! Hadit! Ra-Hoor-Khuit! The Sun, Strength & Sight, Light; these are for the servants of the Star & the Snake.

22. I am the Snake that giveth Knowledge & Delight and bright glory, and stir the hearts of men with drunkenness. To worship me take wine and strange drugs whereof I will tell my prophet, & be drunk thereof! They shall not harm ye at all. It is a lie, this folly against self. The exposure of innocence is a lie. Be strong, o man! lust, enjoy all things of sense and rapture: fear not that any God shall deny thee for this.

23. I am alone: there is no God where I am.

24. Behold! these be grave mysteries; for there are also of my friends who be hermits. Now think not to find them in the forest or on the mountain; but in beds of purple, caressed by magnificent beasts of women with large limbs, and fire and light in their eyes, and masses of flaming hair about them; there shall ye find them. Ye shall see them at rule, at victorious armies, at all the joy; and there shall be in them a joy a million times greater than this. Beware lest any force another, King against King! Love one another with burning hearts; on the low men trample in the fierce lust of your pride, in the day of your wrath.

25. Ye are against the people, O my chosen!

26. I am the secret Serpent coiled about to spring: in my coiling there is joy. If I lift up my head, I and my Nuit are one. If I droop down mine head, and shoot forth venom, then is rapture of the earth, and I and the earth are one.

27. There is great danger in me; for who doth not understand these runes shall make a great miss. He shall fall down into the pit called Because, and there he shall perish with the dogs of Reason.

28. Now a curse upon Because and his kin!

29. May Because be accursed for ever!

30. If Will stops and cries Why, invoking Because, then Will stops & does nought.

31. If Power asks why, then is Power weakness.

32. Also reason is a lie; for there is a factor infinite & unknown; & all their words are skew-wise.

33. Enough of Because! Be he damned for a dog!

34. But ye, o my people, rise up & awake!

35. Let the rituals be rightly performed with joy & beauty!

36. There are rituals of the elements and feasts of the times.

37. A feast for the first night of the Prophet and his Bride!

38. A feast for the three days of the writing of the Book of the Law.

39. A feast for Tahuti and the child of the Prophet—secret, O Prophet!

40. A feast for the Supreme Ritual, and a feast for the Equinox of the Gods.

41. A feast for fire and a feast for water; a feast for life and a greater feast for death!

42. A feast every day in your hearts in the joy of my rapture!

43. A feast every night unto Nu, and the pleasure of uttermost delight!

44. Aye! feast! rejoice! there is no dread hereafter. There is the dissolution, and eternal ecstasy in the kisses of Nu.

45. There is death for the dogs.

46. Dost thou fail? Art thou sorry? Is fear in thine heart?

47. Where I am these are not.

48. Pity not the fallen! I never knew them. I am not for them. I console not: I hate the consoled & the consoler.

49. I am unique & conqueror. I am not of the slaves that perish. Be they damned & dead! Amen. (This is of the 4: there is a fifth who is invisible, & therein am I as a babe in the egg.)

50. Blue am I and gold in the light of my bride: but the red gleam is in my eyes; & my spangles are purple & green.

51. Purple beyond purple: it is the light higher than eyesight.

52. There is a veil: that veil is black. It is the veil of the modest woman; it is the veil of sorrow, & the pall of death: this is none of me. Tear down that lying spectre of the centuries: veil not your vices in virtuous words: these vices are my service; ye do well, & I will reward you here and hereafter.

53. Fear not, o prophet, when these words are said, thou shalt not be sorry. Thou art emphatically my chosen; and blessed are the eyes that thou shalt look upon with gladness. But I will hide thee in a mask of sorrow: they that see thee shall fear thou art fallen: but I lift thee up.

54. Nor shall they who cry aloud their folly that thou meanest nought avail; thou shall reveal it: thou availest: they are the slaves

of because: They are not of me. The stops as thou wilt; the letters? change them not in style or value!

55. Thou shalt obtain the order & value of the English Alphabet; thou shalt find new symbols to attribute them unto.

56. Begone! ye mockers; even though ye laugh in my honour ye shall laugh not long: then when ye are sad know that I have forsaken you.

57. He that is righteous shall be righteous still; he that is filthy shall be filthy still.

58. Yea! deem not of change: ye shall be as ye are, & not other. Therefore the kings of the earth shall be Kings for ever: the slaves shall serve. There is none that shall be cast down or lifted up: all is ever as it was. Yet there are masked ones my servants: it may be that yonder beggar is a King. A King may choose his garment as he will: there is no certain test: but a beggar cannot hide his poverty.

59. Beware therefore! Love all, lest perchance is a King concealed! Say you so? Fool! If he be a King, thou canst not hurt him.

60. Therefore strike hard & low, and to hell with them, master!

61. There is a light before thine eyes, o prophet, a light undesired, most desirable.

62. I am uplifted in thine heart; and the kisses of the stars rain hard upon thy body.

63. Thou art exhaust in the voluptuous fullness of the inspiration; the expiration is sweeter than death, more rapid and laughterful than a caress of Hell's own worm.

64. Oh! thou art overcome: we are upon thee; our delight is all over thee: hail! hail: prophet of Nu! prophet of Had! prophet of Ra-Hoor-Khu! Now rejoice! now come in our splendour & rapture! Come in our passionate peace, & write sweet words for the Kings!

65. I am the Master: thou art the Holy Chosen One.

66. Write, & find ecstasy in writing! Work, & be our bed in working! Thrill with the joy of life & death! Ah! thy death shall be lovoely: whso seeth it shall be glad! Thy death shall be the seal of the promise of our agelong love. Come! lift up thine heart & rejoice! We are one: we are none.

67. Hold! Hold! Bear up in thy rapture; fall not in swoon of the excellent kisses!

68. Harder! Hold up thyself! Lift thine head! breathe not so deep—die!

69. Ah! Ah! What do I feel? Is the word exhausted?

70. There is help & hope in other spells. Wisdom says: be strong! Then canst thou bear more joy. Be not animal; refine thy rapture! If thou drink, drink by the eight and ninety rules of art: if thou love, exceed by delicacy; and if thou do aught joyous, let there be subtlety therein!

71. But exceed! exceed!

72. Strive ever to more! and if thou art truly mine—and doubt it not, an if thou art ever joyous!—death is the crown of all.

73. Ah! Ah! Death! Death! thou shalt long for death. Death is forbidden, o man, unto thee.

74. The length of thy longing shall be the strength of its glory. He that lives long & desires death much is ever the King among the Kings.

75. Aye! listen to the numbers & the words:

76. 4 6 3 8 A B K 2 4 A L G M O R 3 Y X 24 89 R P S T O V A L. What meaneth this, o prophet? Thou knowest not; nor shalt thou know ever. There cometh one to follow thee: he shall expound it. But remember, o chosen one, to be me; to follow the love of Nu in the star-lit heaven; to look forth upon men, to tell them this glad word.

77. O be thou proud and mighty among men!

78. Lift up thyself! for there is none like unto thee among men or among Gods! Lift up thyself, o my prophet, thy stature shall surpass the stars. They shall worship thy name, foursquare, mystic, wonderful, the number of the man; and the name of thy house 418.

79. The end of the hiding of Hadit; and blessing & worship to the prophet of the lovely Star!

1. Abrahadabra; the reward of Ra Hoor Khut.

2. There is division hither homeward; there is a word not known. Spelling is defunct; all is not aught. Beware! Hold! Raise the spell of Ra-Hoor-Khuit!

3. Now let it be first understood that I am a god of War and of Vengeance. I shall deal hardly with them.

4. Choose ye an island!

5. Fortify it!

6. Dung it about with enginery of war!

7. I will give you a war-engine.

8. With it ye shall smite the peoples; and none shall stand before you.

9. Lurk! Withdraw! Upon them! this is the Law of the Battle of Conquest: thus shall my worship be about my secret house.

10. Get the stélé of revealing itself; set it in thy secret temple—and that temple is already aright disposed—& it shall be your Kiblah for ever. It shall not fade, but miraculous colour shall come back to it day after day. Close it in locked glass for a proof to the world.

11. This shall be your only proof. I forbid argument. Conquer! That is enough. I will make easy to you the abstruction from the ill-ordered house in the Victorious City. Thou shalt thyself convey it with worship, o prophet, though thou likest it not. Thou shalt have danger & trouble. Ra-Hoor-Khu is with thee. Worship me with fire & blood; worship me with swords & with spears. Let the woman be girt with a sword before me: let blood flow to my name. Trample down the Heathen; be upon them, o warrior, I will give you of their flesh to eat!

12. Sacrifice cattle, little and big: after a child.

13. But not now.

14. Ye shall see that hour, o blesséd Beast, and thou the Scarlet Concubine of his desire!

15. Ye shall be sad thereof.

16. Deem not too eagerly to catch the promises; fear not to undergo the curses. Ye, even ye, know not this meaning all.

17. Fear not at all; fear neither men, nor Fates, nor gods, nor anything. Money fear not, nor laughter of the folk folly, nor any other power in heaven or upon the earth or under the earth. Nu is your refuge as Hadit your light; and I am the strength, force, vigour, of your arms.

18. Mercy let be off: damn them who pity! Kill and torture; spare not; be upon them!

19. That stélé they shall call the Abomination of Desolation; count well its name, & it shall be to you as 718.

20. Why? Because of the fall of Because, that he is not there again.

21. Set up my image in the East: thou shalt buy thee an image which I will show thee, especial, not unlike the one thou knowest. And it shall be suddenly easy for thee to do this.

22. The other images group around me to support me: let all be worshipped, for they shall cluster to exalt me. I am the visible object of worship; the others are secret; for the Beast & his Bride are they: and for the winners of the Ordeal x. What is this? Thou shalt know.

23. For perfume mix meal & honey & thick leavings of red wine: then oil of Abramelin and olive oil, and afterward soften & smooth down with rich fresh blood.

24. The best blood is of the moon, monthly: then the fresh blood of a child, or dropping from the host of heaven: then of enemies; then of

the priest or of the worshippers: last of some beast, no matter what.

25. This burn: of this make cakes & eat unto me. This hath also another use; let it be laid before me, and kept thick with perfumes of your orison: it shall become full of beetles as it were and creeping things sacred unto me.

26. These slay, naming your enemies; & they shall fall before you.

27. Also these shall breed lust & power of lust in you at the eating thereof.

28. Also ye shall be strong in war.

29. Moreover, be they long kept, it is better; for they swell with my force. All before me.

30. My altar is of open brass work: burn thereon in silver or gold!

31. There cometh a rich man from the West who shall pour his gold upon thee.

32. From gold forge steel!

33. Be ready to fly or to smite!

34. But your holy place shall be untouched throughout the centuries: though with fire and sword it be burnt down & shattered, yet an invisible house there standeth, and shall stand until the fall of the Great Equinox; when Hrumachis shall arise and the double-wanded one assume my throne and place. Another prophet shall arise, and bring fresh fever from the skies; another woman shall awake the lust & worship of the Snake; another soul of God and beast shall mingle in the globèd priest; another sacrifice shall stain The tomb; another king shall reign; and blessing no longer be poured To the Hawk-headed mystical Lord!

35. The half of the word of Heru-ra-ha, called Hoor-pa-kraat and Ra-Hoor-Khut.

36. Then said the prophet unto the God:

37. I adore thee in the song—

> I am the Lord of Thebes, and I
>> The inspired forth-speaker of Mentu;
> For me unveils the veilèd sky,
>> The self-slain Ankh-af-na-khonsu
> Whose words are truth. I invoke, I greet
>> Thy presence, O Ra-Hoor-Khuit!
> Unity uttermost showed!
>> I adore the might of Thy breath,
> Supreme and terrible God,
>> Who makest the gods and death

To tremble before Thee:—
I, I adore thee!

Appear on the throne of Ra!
Open the ways of the Khu!
Lighten the ways of the Ka!
The ways of the Khabs run through
To stir me or still me!
Aum! let it fill me!

38. So that thy light is in me; & its red flame is as a sword in my hand to push thy order. There is a secret door that I shall make to establish thy way in all the quarters, (these are the adorations, as thou hast written), as it is said:

The light is mine; its rays consume
Me: I have made a secret door
Into the House of Ra and Tum,
Of Khephra and of Ahathoor.
I am thy Theban, O Mentu,
The prophet Ankh-af-na-khonsu!

By Bes-na-Maut my breast I beat;
By wise Ta-Nech I weave my spell.
Show thy star-splendour, O Nuit!
Bid me within thine House to dwell,
O wingèd snake of light, Hadit!
Abide with me, Ra-Hoor-Khuit!

39. All this and a book to say how thou didst come hither and a reproduction of this ink and paper for ever—for in it is the word secret & not only in the English—and thy comment upon this the Book of the Law shall be printed beautifully in red ink and black upon beautiful paper made by hand; and to each man and woman that thou meetest, were it but to dine or to drink at them, it is the Law to give. Then they shall chance to abide in this bliss or no; it is no odds. Do this quickly!

40. But the work of the comment? That is easy; and Hadit burning in thy heart shall make swift and secure thy pen.

41. Establish at thy Kaaba a clerk-house: all must be done well and with business way.

42. The ordeals thou shalt oversee thyself, save only the blind ones. Refuse none, but thou shalt know & destroy the traitors. I am

Ra-Hoor-Khuit; and I am powerful to protect my servant. Success is thy proof: argue not; convert not; talk not overmuch! Them that seek to entrap thee, to overthrow thee, them attack without pity or quarter; & destroy them utterly. Swift as a trodden serpent turn and strike! Be thou yet deadlier than he! Drag down their souls to awful torment: laugh at their fear: spit upon them!

43. Let the Scarlet Woman beware! If pity and compassion and tenderness visit her heart; if she leave my work to toy with old sweetnesses; then shall my vengeance be known. I will slay me her child: I will alienate her heart: I will cast her out from men: as a shrinking and despised harlot shall she crawl though dusk wet streets, and die cold and an-hungered.

44. But let her raise herself in pride! Let her follow me in my way! Let her work the work of wickedness! Let her kill her heart! Let her be loud and adulterous! Let her be covered with jewels, and rich garments, and let her be shameless before all men!

45. Then will I lift her to pinnacles of power: then will I breed from her a child mightier than all the kings of the earth. I will fill her with joy: with my force shall she see & strike at the worship of Nu: she shall achieve Hadit.

46. I am the warrior Lord of the Forties: the Eighties cower before me, & are abased. I will bring you to victory & joy: I will be at your arms in battle & ye shall delight to slay. Success is your proof; courage is your armour; go on, go on, in my strength; & ye shall turn not back for any!

47. This book shall be translated into all tongues: but always with the original in the writing of the Beast; for in the chance shape of the letters and their position to one another: in these are mysteries that no Beast shall divine. Let him not seek to try: but one cometh after him, whence I say not, who shall discover the Key of it all. Then this line drawn is a key: then this circle squared in its failure is a key also. And Abrahadabra. It shall be his child & that strangely. Let him not seek after this; for thereby alone can he fall from it.

48. Now this mystery of the letters is done, and I want to go on to the holier place.

49. I am in a secret fourfold word, the blasphemy against all gods of men.

50. Curse them! Curse them! Curse them!

51. With my Hawk's head I peck at the eyes of Jesus as he hangs upon the cross.

52. I flap my wings in the face of Mohammed & blind him.

53. With my claws I tear out the flesh of the Indian and the Buddhist, Mongol and Din.

54. Bahlasti! Ompehda! I spit on your crapulous creeds.

55. Let Mary inviolate be torn upon wheels: for her sake let all chaste women be utterly despised among you!

56. Also for beauty's sake and love's!

57. Despise also all cowards; professional soldiers who dare not fight, but play: all fools despise!

58. But the keen and the proud, the royal and the lofty; ye are brothers!

59. As brothers fight ye!

60. There is no law beyond Do what thou wilt.

61. There is an end of the word of the God enthroned in Ra's seat, lightening the girders of the soul.

62. To Me do ye reverence! to me come ye through tribulation of ordeal, which is bliss.

63. The fool readeth this Book of the Law, and its comment; & he understandeth it not.

64. Let him come through the first ordeal, & it will be to him as silver.

65. Through the second, gold.

66. Through the third, stones of precious water.

67. Through the fourth, ultimate sparks of the intimate fire.

68. Yet to all it shall seem beautiful. Its enemies who say not so, are mere liars.

69. There is success.

70. I am the Hawk-Headed Lord of Silence & of Strength; my nemyss shrouds the night-blue sky.

71. Hail! ye twin warriors about the pillars of the world! for your time is nigh at hand.

72. I am the Lord of the Double Wand of Power; the wand of the Force of Coph Nia—but my left hand is empty, for I have crushed an Universe; & nought remains.

73. Paste the sheets from right to left and from top to bottom: then behold!

74. There is a splendour in my name hidden and glorious, as the sun of midnight is ever the son.

75. The ending of the words is the Word Abrahadabra.

The Book of the Law is Written
and Concealed.
Aum. Ha.

From *The Equinox of the Gods*

This brief section from *The Equinox of the Gods,* Crowley's late-in-life remembrances and reflections on the importance of *Liber AL,* suggests a reading of *The Book of the Law* as a kind of running dialogue (or even struggle) between Horus and Crowley.

CHAPTER I

Verse 1. Nuit is the speaker. She invokes her lover and then begins to give a title to her speech in the end of verse 1–20.

In verses 3 and 4, she begins her discourse. So far her remarks have been addressed to no one in particular.

Verse 4 startled my intelligence into revolt.

In verse 5 she explains that she is speaking, and appeals to me personally to help her to unveil by taking down her message.

In verse 6 she claims me for her chosen, and I think that I then became afraid lest I should be expected to do too much. She answers this fear in verse 7 by introducing Aiwaz as the actual speaker in articulate human accents on her behalf.

In verse 8 the oration continues, and we now see that it is addressed to mankind in general. This continues till verse 13.

Verse 14 is from the Stélé. It seems to have been written in by me as a kind of appreciation of what she had just said.

Verse 15 emphasizes that it is mankind in general that is addressed; for the Beast is spoken of in the third person, though his was the only human ear to hear the words.

Verses 18–19 seem to be almost in the nature of a quotation from some hymn. It is not quite natural for her to address herself as she appears to do in verse 19.

Verse 26. The question "Who am I and what shall be the sign?" is my own conscious thought. In the previous verses I have been called to an exalted mission, and I naturally feel nervous. This thought is then entered in the record by Aiwaz as if it were a story that he was telling; and he develops this story after her answer, in order to bring back the thread of the chapter to the numerical mysteries of Nuith begun in verses 24–25, and now continued in verse 28.

Another doubt must have arisen in my mind at verse 30; and this doubt is interpreted and explained to me personally in verse 31.

The address to mankind is resumed in verse 32, and Nuith emphasizes the point of verse 30 which has caused me to doubt. She confirms this with an oath, and I was convinced. I thought to myself, "in this case let us have written instructions as to the technique," and Aiwaz again makes a story out of my request as in verse 26.

In verse 35 it seems that she is addressing me personally, but in verse 36 she speaks of me in the third person.

Verse 40. The word "us" is very puzzling. It apparently means "All those who have accepted the Law whose word is Thelema." Among these she includes herself.

There is now no difficulty for a long while. It is a general address dealing with various subjects, to the end of verse 52.

From verses 53–56 we have a strictly personal address to me.

In verse 57 Nuith resumes her general exhortation. And I am spoken of once more in the third person.

Verse 61. The word "Thou" is not a personal address. It means any single person, as opposed to a company. The "Ye" in the third sentence indicates the proper conduct for worshippers as a body. The "you," in sentence 4, of course applies to a single person; but the plural form suggests that it is a matter of public worship as opposed to the invocation in the desert of the first sentence of this verse.

There is no further difficulty in this chapter.

Verse 66 is the statement of Aiwaz that the words of verse 65, which were spoken diminuendo down to pianissimo, indicated the withdrawal of the goddess.

CHAPTER II

Hadith himself is evidently the speaker from the start. The remarks are general. In verse 5 I am spoken of in the third person.

After verse 9 he notices my vehement objections to writing statements to which my conscious self was obstinately opposed.

Verse 10, addressed to me, notes that fact; and in verse 11 he declares that he is my master, and that the reason for this is that he is my secret self, as explained in verses 12–13.

The interruption seems to have added excitement to the discourse, for verse 14 is violent.

Verses 15 & 16 offer a riddle, while verse 17 is a sort of parody of poetry.

Verse 18 continues his attack on my conscious mind. In verses 15–18 the style is complicated, brutal, sneering and jeering. I feel the whole passage as a contemptuous beating down of the resistance of my mind.

In verse 19 he returns to the exalted style with which he began until I interfered.

The passage seems addressed to what he calls his chosen or his people, though it is not explained exactly what he means by the words.

This passage from verse 19 to verse 52 is of sustained and matchless eloquence.

I must have objected to something in verse 52, for verse 53 is directed to encourage me personally as to having transmitted this message.

Verse 54 deals with another point as to the intelligibility of the message.

Verse 55 instructed me to obtain the English Qabalah; it made me incredulous, as the task seemed an impossible one, and probably his perception of this criticism inspired verse 56, though "ye mockers" applies evidently to my enemies, referred to in verse 54.

Verse 57 brings us back to the subject begun in verse 21. It is a quotation from the Apocalypse verbatim, and is probably suggested by the matter of verse 56.

There is no real change in the essence of anything, however its combinations vary.

Verses 58–60 conclude the passage.

Verse 61. The address is now strictly personal. During all this time Hadith had been breaking down my resistance with his violently expressed and varied phrases. As a result of this, I attained to the trance described in these verses from 61–68.

Verse 69 is the return to consciousness of myself. It was a sort of gasping question as a man coming out of Ether might ask "Where am I?" I think that this is the one passage in the whole book which was not spoken by Aiwaz; and I ought to say that these verses 63–68 were written without conscious hearing at all.

Verse 70 does not deign to reply to my questions, but points out the way to manage life. This continues until verse 74, and seems to be addressed not to me personally but to any man, despite the use of the word "Thou."

Verse 75 abruptly changes the subject, interpolating the riddle of verse 76 with its prophecy. This verse is addressed to me personally, and continues to the end of verse 78 to mingle lyrical eloquence with literal and numerical puzzles.

Verse 79 is the statement of Aiwaz that the end of the chapter has come. To this he adds his personal compliment to myself.

CHAPTER III

Verse 1 appears to complete the triangle begun by the first verses of the two previous chapters. It is a simple statement involving no particular speaker or hearer. The omission of the "i" in the name of God appears to have alarmed me, and in verse 2 Aiwaz offers a hurried explanation in a somewhat excited manner, and invokes Ra-Hoor-Khuit.

Verse 3 is spoken by Ra-Hoor-Khuit. "Them" evidently refers to some undescribed enemies, and "ye" to those who accept his formula. This passage ends with verse 9. Verse 10 and verse 11 are addressed to me personally and the Scarlet Woman, as shown in the continuation of this passage which seems to end with verse 33, though it is left rather vague at times as to whether the Beast, or the Beast and his Concubine, or the adherents of Horus, generally, are exhorted.

Verse 34 is a kind of poetical peroration, and is not addressed in particular to anybody. It is a statement of events to come.

Verse 35 states simply that section one of this chapter is completed.

I seem to have become enthusiastic, for there is a kind of interlude reported by Aiwaz of my song of adoration translated from the Stélé; the incident parallels that of Chapter I, verse 26, &c.

It is to be noted that the translations from the Stélé in verses 37–38 were no more than instantaneous thoughts to be inserted afterwards.

Verse 38 begins with my address to the God in the first sentence, while in the second is his reply to me. He then refers to the hieroglyphs of the Stélé, and bids me quote my paraphrases. This order was given by a species of wordless gesture, not visible nor audible, but sensible in some occult manner.

Verses 39–42 are instructions for me personally.

Verses 43–45 indicate the proper course of conduct for the Scarlet Woman.

Verse 46 is again more general—a sort of address to soldiers before battle.

Verse 47 is again mostly personal instruction, mixed up with prophecies, proof of the praeterhuman origin of the Book, and other matters.

I observe that this instruction, taken with those not to change "so much as the style of a letter," etc., imply that my pen was under the physical control of Aiwaz; for his dictation did not include directions as to the use of capitals, and the occasional mis-spellings are most assuredly not mine!

Verse 48 impatiently dismisses such practical matters as a nuisance.

Verses 49–59 contain a series of declarations of war; and there is no further difficulty as to speaker or hearer to the end of the chapter, although the subject changes repeatedly in an incomprehensible manner. Only in verse 75 do we find a peroration on the whole book, presumably by Aiwaz, ending by his formula of withdrawal.

On Certain Technical Difficulties Connected with the Literary Form of the Book

This section from *The Equinox of the Gods* explores in some detail the very charged issues of authorship, double entendre (under which Crowley frames the paradox of "Not"), punning, and number puzzles.

I

Certain very serious questions have arisen with regard to the method by which this Book was obtained. I do not refer to those doubts—real or pretended—which hostility engenders, for all such are dispelled by study of the text; no forger could have prepared so complex a set of numerical and literal puzzles as to leave himself (a) devoted to the solution for years after, (b) baffled by a simplicity which when disclosed leaves one gasping at its profundity, (c) enlightened only by progressive initiation, or by "accidental" events apparently disconnected with the Book, which occurred long after its publication, (d) hostile, bewildered, and careless even in the face of independent testimony as to the power and clarity of the Book, and of the fact that by Its light other men have attained the loftiest summits of initiation in a tithe of the time which history and experience would lead one to expect, and (e) angrily unwilling to proceed with that part of the Work appointed for him which is detailed in Chapter III, even when the course of events on the planet, war, revolution, and the collapse of the social and religious systems of civilization, proved plainly to him that whether he liked it or no, Ra Hoor Khuit was indeed Lord of the Aeon, the Crowned and Conquering Child whose innocence meant no more than inhuman cruelty and wantonly senseless destructiveness as he avenged Isis our mother the Earth and the Heaven for the murder and

227

mutilation of Osiris, Man, her son. The War of 1914–18 and its sequels have proved even to the dullest statesmen, beyond wit of even the most subtly sophistical theologians to gloze, that death is not an unmixed benefit either to the individual or the community: that force and fire of leaping manhood are more useful to a nation than cringing respectability and emasculate servility; that genius goes with courage, and the sense of shame and guilt with "Defeatism."

For these reasons and many more I am certain, I the Beast, whose number is Six Hundred and Sixty and Six, that this Third Chapter of the Book of the Law is nothing less than the authentic Word, the Word of the Aeon, the Truth about Nature at this time and on this planet. I wrote it, hating it and sneering at it, secretly glad that I could use it to revolt against this Task most terrible that the Gods have thrust remorselessly upon my shoulders, their Cross of burning steel that I must carry even to my Calvary, the place of a skull, there to be eased of its weight only that I be crucified thereon. But, being lifted up, I will draw the whole world unto me; and men shall worship me the Beast, Six Hundred and Three-score and Six, celebrating to Me their Midnight Mass every time soever when they do that they will, and on Mine altar slaying to Me that victim I most relish, their Selves; when Love designs and Will executes the Rite whereby (an they know it or know not) their God in man is offered to me The Beast, their God, the Rite whose virtue, making their God of their throned Beast, leaves nothing, howso bestial, undivine.

On such lines my own "conversion" to my own "religion" may yet take place, though as I write these words all but twelve weeks of Sixteen years are well nigh past.

II

This long digression is but to explain that I, myself, who issue Liber Legis, am no fanatic partisan. I will obey my orders (III, 42) "Argue not, convert not;" even though I shirk some others. I shall not deign to answer sceptical enquiries as to the origin of the Book. "Success is your proof." I, of all men on this Earth reputed mightiest in Magick, by mine enemies more than by my friends, have striven to lose this Book, to forget it, defy it, criticise it, escape it, these nigh sixteen years; and It holds me to the course It sets, even as the Mountain of Lodestone holds the ship, or Helios by invisible bonds controls his planets; yea, or as BABALON grips between her thighs the Great Wild Beast she straddles!

So much for the sceptics; put your heads in the Lion's mouth; so may you come to certainty, whether I be stuffed with straw!

But, in the text of the Book itself, are thorns for the flesh of the most ardent swain as he buries his face in the roses; some of the ivy that clings about the Thyrse of this Dionysus is Poison Ivy. The question arises, especially on examining the original manuscript in My handwriting: "Who wrote these words?"

Of course I wrote them, ink on paper, in the material sense; but they are not My words, unless Aiwaz be taken to be no more than my subconscious self, or some part of it: in that case, my conscious self being ignorant of the Truth in the Book and hostile to most of the ethics and philosophy of the Book, Aiwaz is a severely suppressed part of me.[1] If so, the theorist must suggest a reason for this explosive yet ceremonially controlled manifestation, and furnish an explanation of the dovetailing of Events in subsequent years with His word written and published. In any case, whatever "Aiwaz" is, "Aiwaz" is an Intelligence possessed of power and knowledge absolutely beyond human experience; and therefore Aiwaz is a Being worthy, as the current use of the word allows, of the title of a God, yea verily and amen, of a God. Man has no such fact recorded, by proof established in surety beyond cavil of critic, as this Book, to witness the existence of an Intelligence praeterhuman and articulate, purposefully interfering in the philosophy, religion, ethics, economics and politics of the Planet.

The proof of His praeterhuman Nature—call Him a Devil or a God or even an Elemental as you will—is partly external, depending on events and persons without the sphere of Its influence, partly internal, depending on the concealment of (a) certain Truths, some previously known, some not known, but for the most part beyond the scope of my mind at the time of writing, (b) of an harmony of letters and numbers subtle, delicate and exact, and (c) of Keys to all life's mysteries, both pertinent to occult science and otherwise, and to all the Locks of Thought; the concealment of these three galaxies of glory, I say, in a cipher

1. Such a theory would further imply that I am unknown to myself, possessed of all sorts of praeternatural knowledge and power. The law of Parsimony of Thought (Sir W. Hamilton) appears in rebuttal. Aiwaz calls Himself "the minister of Hoor-paar-Kraat," the twin of Heru-Ra-Ha. This is the dual form of Horus, child of Isis and Osiris.

simple and luminous, but yet illegible for over Fourteen years, and translated even then not by me, but by my mysterious Child according to the Foreknowledge written in the Book itself, in terms so complex that the exact fulfilment of the conditions of His birth, which occurred with incredible precision, seemed beyond all possibility, a cipher involving higher mathematics, and a knowledge of the Hebrew, Greek and Arabic Qabalahs as well as the True Lost Word of the Freemason, is yet veiled within the casual silk-stuff of ordinary English words, nay, even in the apparently accidental circumstance of the characters of the haste-harried scrawl of My pen.

Many such cases of double entendre, paranomasia in one language or another, sometimes two at once, numerical-literal puzzles, and even (on one occasion) an illuminating connexion of letters in various lines by a slashing scratch, will be found in the Qabalistic section of the Commentary.

III

As an example of the first method above mentioned, we have, Cap. III, "The fool readeth this Book—and he understandeth it not." This has a secret reverse-sense, meaning: The fool (Parzival = Fra. O.I.V.V.I.O.) understandeth it (being a Magister Templi, the Grade attributed to Understanding) not (i.e. to be 'not').

This Parzival, adding to 418, is (in the legend of the Graal) the son of Kamuret, adding to 666, being the son of me The Beast by the Scarlet Woman Hilarion. This was a Name chosen by her when half drunk, as a theft from Theosophical legend, but containing many of our letter-number Keys to the Mysteries; the number of the petals in the most sacred lotus. It adds to 1001, which also is Seven times Eleven times Thirteen, a series of factors which may be read as The Scarlet Woman's Love by Magick producing Unity, in Hebrew Achad. For 7 is the number of Venus, and the secret seven-lettered Name of my concubine B A B A L O N is written with Seven Sevens, thus:

$$77 + \frac{7+7}{7} + 77 = 156, \text{ the number of BABALON.}$$

418 is the number of the Word of the Magical Formula of this Aeon. (666 is I, the Beast.)

Parzival had also the name Achad as a Neophyte of A ∴ A ∴, and it was Achad whom Hilarion bare to Me. And Achad means Unity, and the letter of Unity is Aleph, the letter of The Fool in the Tarot. Now this Fool invoked the Magical Formula of the Aeon by taking as his Magick, or True, Name, one which added also to 418.

He took it for his Name on Entering the Gnosis where is Understanding, and he understood it—this Book—not. That is, he understood that this Book was, so to speak, a vesture or veil upon the idea of "not." In Hebrew "not" is LA, 31, and AL is God, 31, while there is a third 31 still deeplier hidden in the double letter ST, which is a graphic glyph of the sun and moon conjoined to look like a foreshortened Phallus, thus—when written in Greek capitals. This S or Sigma is like a phallus, thus, σ, when writ small; and like a serpent or spermatozoon when writ final, thus, ς. This T or Theta is the point in the circle, or phallus in the kteis, and also the Sun just as C is the Moon, male and female.

But Sigma in Hebrew is Shin, 300, the letter of Fire and of the "spirit of the Gods" which broods upon the Formless Void in the Beginning, being by shape a triple tongue of flame, and by meaning a tooth, which is the only part of the secret and solid foundation of Man that is manifested normally. Teeth serve him to fight, to crush, to cut, to rend, to bite and grip his prey; they witness that he is a fierce, dangerous, and carnivorous animal. But they are also the best witness to the mastery of Spirit over Matter, the extreme hardness of their substance being chiselled and polished and covered with a glistening film by Life no less easily and beautifully than it does with more naturally plastic types of substance.

Teeth are displayed when our Secret Self—our Subconscious Ego, whose Magical Image is our individuality expressed in mental and bodily form—our Holy Guardian Angel—comes forth and declares our True Will to our fellows, whether to snarl or to sneer, to smile or to laugh.

Teeth serve us to pronounce the dental letters which in their deepest nature express decision, fortitude, endurance, just as gutturals suggest the breath of Life itself free-flowing, and labials the duplex vibrations of action and reaction. Pronounce T, D, S or N, and you will find them all continuously forcible exhalations whose difference is determined solely by the position of the tongue, the teeth being bared as when a wild beast turns to bay. The sibilant sound of S or Sh is our English word, and also the Hebrew word,

Hush, a strongly aspirated S, and suggests the hiss of a snake. Now this hiss is the common sign of recognition between men when one wants to call another's attention without disturbing the silence more than necessary. (Also we have Hist, our Double letter.) This hiss means: "Attention! A man!" For in all Semitic and some Aryan languages, ISh or a closely similar word means "a man." Say it: you must bare your clenched teeth as in defiance, and breathe harshly out as in excitement.

Hiss! Sh! means "Keep silent! there's danger if you are heard. Attention! There's a man somewhere, deadly as a snake. Breathe hard; there's a fight coming."

This Sh is then the forcible subtle creative Spirit of Life, fiery and triplex, continuous, Silence of pure Breath modified into sound by two and thirty obstacles, as the Zero of Empty Space, though it contain all Life, only takes form according (as the Qabalists say) to the two and thirty "Paths" of Number and Letter which obstruct it.

Now the other letter, Theta or Teth, has the value of Nine, which is that of AVB, the Secret Magick of Obeah, and of the Sephira Yesod, which is the seat in man of the sexual function by whose Magick he overcomes even Death, and that in more ways than one, ways that are known to none but the loftiest and most upright Initiates, baptised by the Baptism of Wisdom, and communicants at that Eucharist where the Fragment of the Host in the Chalice becomes whole.[2]

This T is the letter of Leo, the Lion, the house of heaven sacred to the Sun. (Thus also we find in it the number 6, whence 666). And Teth means a Serpent, the symbol of the magical Life of the Soul, lord of "the double wand" of life and death. The serpent is royal, hooded, wise, silent save for an hiss when need is to disclose his Will; he devours his tail—the glyph of Eternity, of Nothingness and of Space; he moves wavelike, one immaterial essence travelling through crest and trough, as a man's soul through lives and deaths. He straightens out; he is the Rod that strikes, the Light-radiance of the Sun or the Life-radiance of the Phallus.

The sound of T is tenuous and sharply final; it suggests a spontaneous act sudden and irrevocable, like the snake's bite, the lion's snap, the Sun's stroke, and the Lingam's.

---

2. The Chalice is not presented to laymen. Those who understand the reason for this and other details of the Mass, will wonder at the perfection with which the Roman Communion has preserved the form, and lost the substance, of the Supreme Magical Ritual of the True Gnosis.

Now in the Tarot the Trump illustrating this letter Sh is an old form of the Stélé of Revealing, Nuith with Shu and Seb, the pantacle or magical picture of the old Aeon, as Nuit with Hadit and Ra Hoor Khuit is of the new. The number of this Trump is XX. It is called the Angel, the messenger from Heaven of the new Word. The Trump giving the picture of T is called Strength. It shows the Scarlet Woman, BABALON, riding (or conjoined with) me The Beast; and this card is my special card, for I am Baphomet, "the Lion and the Serpent," and 666, the "full number" of the Sun.[3]

So then, as Sh, XX, shows the Gods of the Book of the Law and T, XI, shows the human beings in that Book, me and my concubine, the two cards together illustrate the whole Book in pictorial form.

Now XX + XI = XXXI, 31, the third 31, which we needed to put with LA, 31 and AL, 31, that we might have 31 × 3 = 93, the Word of the Law, θελημα, Will, and ἀγαπη, Love which under Will, is the Law. It is also the number of Aiwaz, the Author of the Book, of the Lost Word whose formula does in sober truth "raise Hiram," and of many another close-woven Word of Truth.

Now then this Two-in-One letter ☾ ☉, is the third Key to this Law; and on the discovery of that fact, after years of constant seeking, what sudden splendours of Truth, sacred as secret, blazed in the midnight of my mind! Observe now: "this circle squared in its failure is a key also." Now I knew that in the value of the letters of ALHIM, "the Gods," the Jews had concealed a not quite correct value of π, the ratio of a circle's circumference to its diameter, to 4 places of decimals: 3.1415; nearer would be 3.1416. If I prefix our Key, 31, putting ☾ ☉, Set or Satan, before the old Gods, I get 3.141593, π correct to Six places, Six being my own number and that of Horus the Sun. And the whole number of this new Name is 395,[4] which on analysis yields an astounding cluster of numerical "mysteries."

IV

Now for an example of the 'paronomasia' or pun. Chapter III, 17—"Ye, even ye, know not this meaning all." (Note how the peculiar grammar suggests a hidden meaning.) Now YE is in Hebrew Yod Hé, the man and the woman; The Beast and BABA-

---

3. The "magical numbers" of the Sun are, according to tradition, 6, (6 × 6) 36, (666 ÷ 6) 111, and Σ (1-36) 666.
4. Shin 300 Teth 9 Aleph 1 Lamed 30 He 5 Yod 10 Mem 40. Note that 395 is to be reversed, 593 being the correction required! Note also the 31 and the 93 in this value of π.

LON, whom the God was addressing in his verse. Know suggests 'no' which gives LA, 31; 'not' is LA, 31, again, by actual meaning; and 'all' refers to AL, 31, again. (Again, ALL is 61, AIN, "nothing.")

V

Then we have numerical problems like this. "Six and fifty. Divide, add, multiply and understand." $6 \div 50$ gives 0.12, a perfect glyph-statement of the metaphysics of the Book.

The external evidence for the Book is accumulating yearly: the incidents connected with the discovery of the true spelling of Aiwaz are alone sufficient to place it beyond all quaver of doubt that I am really in touch with a Being of intelligence and power immensely subtler and greater than aught we can call human.

This has been the One Fundamental Question of Religion. We know of invisible powers, and to spare! But is there any Intelligence of Individuality (of the same general type as ours) independent of our human brain-structure? For the first time in history, yes! Aiwaz has given us proof: the most important gate toward Knowledge swings wide.

I, Aleister Crowley, declare upon my honour as a gentleman that I hold this revelation a million times more important than the discovery of the Wheel, or even of the Laws of Physics or Mathematics. Fire and Tools made Man master of his planet: Writing developed his mind; but his Soul was a guess until the Book of the Law proved this.

I, a master of English, was made to take down in three hours, from dictation, sixty-five 8″ × 10″ pages of words not only strange, but often displeasing to me in themselves; concealing in cipher propositions unknown to me, majestic and profound; foretelling events public and private beyond my control, or that of any man.

This Book proves: there is a Person thinking and acting in a praeterhuman manner, either without a body of flesh, or with the power of communicating telepathically with men and inscrutably directing their actions.

VI

I write this therefore with a sense of responsibility so acute that for the first time in my life I regret my sense of humour and the literary practical jokes which it has caused me to perpetrate. I am glad, though, that care was taken of the MS. itself and of diaries and letters of the period, so that the physical facts are as plain as can be desired.

My sincerity and seriousness are proved by my life. I have fought this Book and fled it; I have defiled it and I have suffered for its sake. Present or absent to my mind, it has been my Invisible Ruler. It has overcome me; year after year extends its invasion of my being. I am the captive of the Crowned and Conquering Child.

The point then arises: How did the Book of the Law come to be written? The description in The Equinox, I, VII, might well be more detailed; and I might also elucidate the problem of the apparent changes of speaker, and the occasional lapses from straightforward scribecraft in the MS.

I may observe that I should not have left such obvious grounds for indictment as these had I prepared the MS. to look pretty to a critical eye; nor should I have left such curious deformities of grammar and syntax, defects of rhythm, and awkwardness of phrase. I should not have printed passages, some rambling and unintelligible, some repugnant to reason by their absurdity, others again by their barbaric ferocity abhorrent to heart. I should not have allowed such jumbles of matter, such abrupt jerks from subject to subject, disorder ravaging reason with disconnected sluttishness. I should not have tolerated the discords, jarred and jagged, of manner, as when a sublime panegyric of Death is followed first by a cipher and then by a prophecy, before, without taking breath, the author leaps to the utmost magnificence of thought both mystical and practical, in language so concise, simple, and lyrical as to bemuse our very amazement. I should not have spelt "Ay" "Aye," or acquiesced in the horror "abstruction."

Compare with this Book my "jokes," where I pretend to edit the MS. of another: "Alice," "Amphora," "Clouds without Water." Observe in each case the technical perfection of the "discovered" or "translated" MS., smooth skilled elaborate art and craft of a Past Master Workman; observe the carefully detailed tone and style of the prefaces, and the sedulous creation of the personalities of the imaginary author and the imaginary editor.

Note, moreover, with what greedy vanity I claim authorship even of all the other A ∴ A ∴ Books in Class A, though I wrote them inspired beyond all I know to be I. Yet in these Books did Aleister Crowley, the master of English both in prose and in verse, partake insofar as he was That. Compare those Books with the Book of the Law![5] The style is simple and sublime; the imagery is gorgeous and faultless; the rhythm is subtle and intoxicating; the theme is

5. See Liber LXV, I, Equinox III, and Liber VII Equinox III, II, especially.

interpreted in faultless symphony. There are no errors of grammar, no infelicities of phrase. Each Book is perfect in its kind.

I, daring to snatch credit for these, in that brutal Index to The Equinox Volume One, dared nowise to lay claim to have touched the Book of the Law, not with my littlest finger-tip.

I, boasting of my many Books; I, swearing each a masterpiece; I attack the Book of the Law at a dozen points of literature. Even so, with the same breath, I testify, as a Master of English, that I am utterly incapable, even when most inspired, of such English as I find in that Book again and again.

Terse, yet sublime, are these verses of this Book; subtle yet simple; matchless for rhythm, direct as a ray of light. Its imagery is gorgeous without decadence. It deals with primary ideas. It announces revolutions in philosophy, religion, ethics, yea, in the whole nature of Man. For this it needs no more than to roll sea-billows solemnly forth, eight words, as *"Every man and every woman is a star,"* or it bursts in a mountain torrent of monosyllables as *"Do what thou wilt shall be the whole of the Law."*

Nuith cries: *"I love you,"* like a lover; when even John reached only to the cold impersonal proposition "God is love." She woos like a mistress; whispers *"To me!"* in every ear; Jesus, with needless verb, appeals vehemently to them "that labour and are heavy laden." Yet he can promise no more than "I will give you rest," in the future; while Nuit, in the present, says: *"I give unimaginable joys on earth,"* making life worth while; *"certainty, not faith, while in life, upon death,"* the electric light Knowledge for the churchyard corpse-candle Faith, making life fear-free, and death itself worth while: *"peace unutterable, rest, ecstasy,"* making mind and body at ease that soul may be free to transcend them when It will.

I have never written such English; nor could I ever, that well I know. Shakespeare could not have written it: still less could Keats, Shelley, Swift, Sterne or even Wordsworth. Only in the Books of Job and Ecclesiastes, in the work of Blake, or possibly in that of Poe, is there any approach to such succinct depth of thought in such musical simplicity of form, unless it be in Greek and Latin poets. Nor Poe nor Blake could have sustained their effort as does this our Book of the Law; and the Hebrews used tricks of verse, mechanical props to support them.

How then—back once more to the Path!—how then did it come to be written?

De Lege Lebellum

Originally published in *The Equinox,* "De Lege Lebellum" is one of Crowley's most intriguing and well written essays. It takes a slightly more straightforward approach from a broader perspective in its analysis of *Liber AL,* suggesting that Liberty, Love, Life and Light are *The Book of the Law*'s chief concerns.

THE LAW

Do what thou wilt shall be the whole of the Law.

IN RIGHTEOUSNESS OF HEART come hither, and listen: for it is I, TO MEΓ A ΘHPION, who gave this Law unto everyone that holdeth himself holy. It is I, not another, that willeth your whole Freedom, and the arising within you of full Knowledge and Power.

Behold! the Kingdom of God is within you, even as the Sun standeth eternal in the heavens, equal at midnight and at noon. He riseth not: he setteth not: it is but the shadow of the earth which concealeth him, or the clouds upon her face.

Let me then declare unto you this Mystery of the Law, as it hath been made known unto me in divers places, upon the mountains and in the deserts, but also in great cities, which thing I speak for your comfort and good courage. And so be it unto all of you.

Know first, that from the Law spring four Rays or Emanations: so that if the Law be the centre of your own being, they must needs fill you with their secret goodness. And these four are Light, Life, Love, and Liberty.

By Light shall ye look upon yourselves, and behold All Things that are in Truth One Thing only, whose name hath been called No Thing for a cause which later shall be declared unto you. But the substance of Light is Life, since without Existence and Energy it were naught. By Life therefore are you made yourselves, eternal and incorruptible, flaming forth as suns, self-created and self-supported, each the sole centre of the Universe.

Now by the Light ye beheld, by Love ye feel. There is an ecstacy of pure knowledge, and another of pure Love. And this Love is the force that uniteth things diverse, for the contemplation in Light of their Oneness. Know that the Universe is not at rest, but in extreme motion whose sum is Rest. And this understanding that Stability is Change, and Change Stability, that Being is Becoming, and Becoming Being, is the Key to the Golden Palace of this Law.

Lastly, by Liberty is the power to direct your course according to your Will. For the extent of the Universe is without bounds, and ye are free to make your pleasure as ye will, seeing that the diversity of being is infinite also. For this also is the Joy of the Law, that no two stars are alike, and ye must understand also that this Multiplicity is itself Unity, and without it Unity could not be. And this is an hard saying against Reason: ye shall comprehend, when, rising above Reason, which is but a manipulation of the Mind, ye come to pure Knowledge by direct perception of the Truth.

Know also that these four Emanations of the Law flame forth upon all paths: ye shall use them not only in these Highways of the Universe whereof I have written, but in every By-path of your daily life.

Love is the law, love under will.

I

OF LIBERTY

IT IS OF LIBERTY that I would first write unto you, for except ye be free to act, ye cannot act. Yet all four gifts of the Law must in some degree be exercised, seeing that these four are one. But for the Aspirant that cometh unto the Master, the first need is freedom.

The great bond of all bonds is ignorance. How shall a man be free to act if he know not his own purpose? You must therefore first of all discover which star of all the stars you are, your relation to the other stars about you, and your relation to, and identity with, the Whole.

In our Holy Books are given sundry means of making this discovery, and each must make it for himself, attaining absolute conviction by direct experience, not merely reasoning and calculating what is probable. And to each will come the knowledge of his finite will, whereby one is a poet, one prophet, one worker in steel, another in jade. But also to each be the knowledge of his infinite Will, his destiny to perform the Great Work, the realization of his True Self. Of this Will let me therefore speak clearly unto all, since it pertaineth unto all.

Understand now that in yourselves is a certain discontent. Analyse well its nature: at the end is in every case one conclusion. The ill springs from the belief in two things, the Self and the Not-Self, and the conflict between them. This also is a restriction of the Will. He who is sick is in conflict with his own body: he who is poor is at odds with society: and so for the rest. Ultimately, therefore, the problem is how to destroy this perception of duality, to attain to the apprehension of unity.

Now then let us suppose that you have come to the Master, and that He has declared to you the Way of this attainment. What hindereth you? Alas! there is yet much Freedom afar off.

Understand clearly this: that if you are sure of your Will, and sure of your means, then any thoughts or actions which are contrary to those means are contrary also to that Will.

If therefore the Master should enjoin upon you a Vow of Holy Obedience, compliance is not a surrender of the Will, but a fulfilment thereof.

For see, what hindereth you? It is either from without or from within, or both. It may be easy for the strong-minded seeker to put his heel upon public opinion, or to tear from his heart the objects which he loves, in a sense: but there will always remain in himself many discordant affections, as also the bond of habit, and these also must he conquer.

In our holiest Book it is written: "Thou hast no right but to do thy will. Do that, and no other shall say nay." Write it also in your heart and in your brain: for this is the key of the whole matter.

Here Nature herself be your preacher: for in every phenomenon of force and motion doth she proclaim aloud this truth. Even in so small a matter as driving a nail into a plank, hear this same sermon. Your nail must be hard, smooth, fine-pointed, or it will not move swiftly in the direction willed. Imagine then a nail of tinder-wood with twenty points—it is verily no longer a nail. Yet nigh all mankind are like unto this. They wish a dozen different careers; and the force which might have been sufficient to attain eminence in one is wasted on the others: they are null.

Here then let me make open confession, and say thus: though I pledged myself almost in boyhood to the Great Work, though to my aid came the most puissant forces in the whole Universe to hold me to it, though habit itself now constraineth me in the right direction, yet I have not fulfilled my Will: I turn aside daily from the appointed task. I waver. I falter. I lag.

Let this then be of great comfort to you all, that if I be so imperfect—and for very shame I have not emphasized that imperfection—if I, the chosen one, still fail, then how easy for yourselves to surpass me! Or, should you only equal me, then even so how great attainment should be yours!

Be of good cheer, therefore, since both my failure and my success are arguments of courage for yourselves.

Search yourselves cunningly, I pray you, analysing your inmost thoughts. And first you shall discard all those gross obvious hindrances to your Will: idleness, foolish friendships, waste employments or enjoyments, I will not enumerate the conspirators against the welfare of your State.

Next, find the minimum of daily time which is in good sooth necessary to your natural life. The rest you shall devote to the True Means of your Attainment. And even these necessary hours you shall consecrate to the Great Work, saying consciously always while at these Tasks that you perform them only in order to preserve your body and mind in health for the right application to that sublime and single Object.

It shall not be very long before you come to understand that such a life is the true Liberty. You will feel distractions from your Will as being what they are. They will no longer appear pleasant and attractive, but as bonds, as shames. And when you have attained this point, know that you have passed the Middle Gate of this Path. For you will have unified your Will.

Even thus, were a man sitting in a theatre where the play wearies him, he would welcome every distraction, and find amusement in any accident: but if he were intent upon the play, every such incident would annoy him. His attitude to these is then an indication of his attitude towards the play itself.

At first the habit of attention is hard to acquire. Persevere, and you will have spasms of revulsion periodically. Reason itself will attack you, saying: how can so strict a bondage be the Path of Freedom?

Persevere. You have never yet known Liberty. When the temptations are overcome, the voice of Reason silenced, then will your soul bound forward unhampered upon its chosen course, and for the first time will you experience the extreme delight of being Master of Yourself, and therefore of the Universe.

When this is fully attained, when you sit securely in the saddle, then you may enjoy also all those distractions which first pleased you and then angered you. Now they will do neither any more: for they are your slaves and toys.

Until you have reached this point, you are not wholly free. You must kill out desire, and kill out fear. The end of all is the power to live according to your own nature, without danger that one part may develop to the detriment of the whole, or concern lest that danger should arise.

The sot drinks, and is drunken: the coward drinks not, and shivers: the wise man, brave and free, drinks, and gives glory to the Most High God.

This then is the Law of Liberty: you possess all Liberty in your own right, but you must buttress Right with Might: you must win Freedom for yourself in many a war. Woe unto the children who sleep in the Freedom that their forefathers won for them!

"There is no law beyond Do what thou wilt:" but it is only the greatest of the race who have the strength and courage to obey it.

O man! behold thyself! With what pains wast thou fashioned! What ages have gone to thy shaping! The history of the planet is woven into the very substance of thy brain! Was all this for naught? Is there no purpose in thee? Wast thou made thus that thou shouldst eat, and breed, and die? Think it not so! Thou dost incorporate so many elements, thou art the fruit of so many aeons of labour, thou art fashioned thus as thou art, and not otherwise, for some colossal End.

Nerve thyself, then, to seek it and to do it. Naught can satisfy thee but the fulfilment of thy transcendent Will, that is hidden within thee. For this, then, up to arms! Win thine own Freedom for thyself! Strike hard!

II

OF LOVE

IT IS WRITTEN THAT "Love is the law, love under will." Herein is an Arcanum concealed, for in the Greek Language Αγαπη, Love, is of the same numerical value as Θελημα, Will. By this we understand that the Universal Will is of the nature of Love.

Now Love is the enkindling in ecstacy of Two that will to become One. It is thus an Universal formula of High Magick. For see now how all things, being in sorrow caused by dividuality, must of necessity will Oneness as their medicine.

Here also is Nature monitor to them that seek Wisdom at her breast: for in the uniting of elements of opposite polarities is there a glory of heat, of light, and of electricity. Thus also in mankind do we behold the spiritual fruit of poetry and all genius, arising from the seed of what is but an animal gesture, in the estimation of such as are schooled in Philosophy. And it is to be noted strongly that the most violent and divine passions are those between people of utterly unharmonious natures.

But now I would have you to know that in the mind are no such limitations in respect of species as prevent a man falling in love with an inanimate object, or an idea. For to him that is in any wise advanced upon the Way of Meditation it appears that all objects save the One Object are distasteful, even as appeared formerly in respect of his chance wishes to the Will. So therefore all objects must be grasped by the mind, and heated in the sevenfold furnace of Love, until with explosion of ecstacy they unite, and disappear, for they, being imperfect, are destroyed utterly in the creation of the Perfection of Union, even as the persons of the Lover and the Beloved are fused into the spiritual gold of Love, which knoweth no person, but comprehendeth all.

Yet since each star is but one star, and the coming together of any two is but one partial rapture, so must the aspirant to our holy Science and Art increase constantly by this method of assimilating ideas, that in the end, become capable of apprehending the Universe in one thought, he may leap forth upon It with the massed violence of his Self, and destroying both these, become that Unity whose name is No Thing. Seek ye all therefore constantly to unite yourselves in rapture with each and every thing that is, and that by utmost passion and lust of Union. To this end take chiefly all such things as are naturally repulsive. For what is pleasant is assimilated easily and without ecstacy: it is in the transfiguration of the loathsome and abhorred into The Beloved that the Self is shaken to the root in Love.

Thus in human love also we see that mediocrities among men mate with null women: but History teacheth us that the supreme masters of the world seek ever the vilest and most horrible creatures for their concubines, overstepping even the limiting laws of sex and species in their necessity to transcend normality. It is not enough in such natures to excite lust or passion: the imagination itself must be enflamed by every means.

For us, then, emancipated from all base law, what shall we do to satisfy our Will to Unity? No less a mistress than the Universe: no lupanar more cramped than Infinite Space: no night of rape that is not coëval with Eternity!

Consider that as Love is mighty to bring forth all Ecstacy, so absence of Love is the greatest craving. Whoso is balked in Love suffereth indeed, but he that hath not activity that passion in his heart towards some object is weary with the ache of craving. And this state is called mystically "Dryness." For this there is, as I believe, no cure but patient persistence in a Rule of life.

But this Dryness hath its virtue, in that hereby the soul is purged of those things that impeach the Will: for when the drouth is altogether perfect, then is it certain that by no means can the Soul be satisfied, save by the Accomplishment of the Great Work. And this is in strong souls a stimulus to the Will. It is the Furnace of Thirst that burneth up all dross within us.

But to each act of Will is a particular Dryness corresponding: and as Love increaseth within you, so doth the torment of His absence. Be this also unto you for a consolation in the ordeal! Moreover, the more fierce the plague of impotence, the more swiftly and suddenly is to wont to abate.

Here is the method of Love in Meditation. Let the Aspirant first practice and then discipline himself in the Art of fixing the attention upon any thing whatsoever at will, without permitting the least imaginable distraction.

Let him also practice the art of the Analysis of Ideas, and that of refusing to allow the mind its natural reaction to them, pleasant or unpleasant, thus fixing himself in Simplicity and Indifference. These things being achieved in their ripe season, be it known to you that all ideas will have become equal to your apprehension, since each is simple and each indifferent: any one of them remaining in the mind at Will without stirring or striving, or tending to pass on to any other. But each idea will possess one special quality common to all: this, that no one of any of them is The Self, inasmuch as it is perceived by The Self as Something Opposite.

When this is thorough and profound in the impact of its realization, then is the moment for the aspirant to direct his Will to Love upon it, so that his whole consciousness findeth focus upon that One Idea. And at the first it may be fixed and dead, or lightly held. This may then pass into dryness, or into repulsion. Then at last by pure persistence in that Act of Will to Love, shall Love himself arise, as a bird, as a flame, as a song, and the whole Soul shall wing a fiery path of music unto the Ultimate Heaven of Possession.

Now in this method there are many roads and ways, some simple and direct, some hidden and mysterious, even as it is with human love whereof no man hath made so much as the first sketches for a Map: for Love is infinite in diversity even as are the Stars. For this cause do I leave Love himself master in the heart of every one of you: for he shall teach you rightly if you but serve him with diligence and devotion even to abandonment.

Nor shall you take umbrage or surprise at the strange pranks that he shall play: for He is a wayward boy and wanton, wise in the Wiles of Aphrodite Our Lady His sweet Mother: and all His jests and cruelties are spices in a confection cunning as no art may match.

Rejoice therefore in all His play, not remitting in any wise your own ardour, but glowing with the sting of His whips, and making of Laughter itself a sacrament adjuvant to Love, even as in the Wine of Rheims is sparkle and bite, like as they were ministers to the High Priest of its Intoxication.

It is also fit that I write to you of the importance of Purity in Love. Now this matter concerneth not in any wise the object or the method of the practice: the one thing essential is that no alien element should intrude. And this is of most particular pertinence to the aspirant in that primary and mundane aspect of his work wherein he establisheth himself in the method through his natural affections.

For know, that all things are masks or symbols of the One Truth, and nature serveth alway to point out the higher perfection under the veil of the lower perfection. So then all the Art and Craft of human love shall serve you as an hieroglyphic: for it is written that That which is above is like that which is below: and That which is below is like that which is above.

Therefore also doth it behoove you to take well heed lest in any manner you fail in this business of purity. For though each act is to be complete on its own plane, and no influence of any other plane is to be brought in for interference or admixture, for that such is all impurity, yet each act should in itself be so complete and perfect that it is a mirror of the perfection of every other plane, and thereby becometh partaker of the pure Light of the highest. Also, since all acts are to be acts of Will in Freedom on every plane, all planes are in reality but one: and thus the lowest expression of any function of that Will is to be at the same time an expression of the highest Will, or only true Will, which is that already implied in the acceptance of the Law.

Be it also well understood of you that it is not necessary or right to shut off natural activity of any kind, as certain false folk, eunuchs of the spirit, most foully teach, to the destruction of many. For in every thing soever inhereth its own perfection proper to it, and to neglect the full operation and function of any one part bringeth distortion and degeneration to the whole. Act therefore in all ways, but transforming the effect of all these ways to the One Way of the Will. And this is possible, because all ways are in actual Truth One Way, the Universe being itself One and One Only, and its appearance as Multiplicity that cardinal illusion which it is the very object of Love to dissipate.

In the achievement of Love are two principles, that of mastering and that of yielding. But the nature of these is hard to explain, for they are subtle, and are best taught by Love Himself in the course of the Operations. But it is to be said generally that the choice of one formula or the other is automatic, being the work of that inmost Will which is alive within you. Seek not then to determine consciously this decision, for herein true instinct is not liable to err.

But now I end, without further words: for in our Holy Books are written many details of the actual practices of Love. And those are the best and truest which are most subtly written in symbol and image, especially in Tragedy and Comedy, for the whole nature of these things is in this kind, Life itself being but the fruit of the flower of Love.

It is then of Life that I must needs now write to you, seeing that by every act of Will in Love you are creating it, a quintessence more mysterious and joyous than you deem, for this which men call life is but a shadow of that true Life, your birthright, and the gift of the Law of Thelema.

III

OF LIFE

SYSTOLE AND DIASTOLE: these are the phases of all component things. Of such also is the life of man. Its curve arises from the latency of the fertilized ovum, say you, to a zenith whence it declines to the nullity of death? Rightly considered, this is not wholly truth. The life of man is but one segment of a serpentine curve which reaches out to infinity, and its zeros but mark the changes from the plus to minus, and minus to plus, coefficients of its equation. It is for this cause, among many others, that wise men in old time chose the Serpent as the Hieroglyph of Life.

Life then is indestructible as all else is. All destruction and construction are changes in the nature of Love, as I have written to you in the former chapter proximate. Yet even as the blood in one pulse-throb of the wrist is not the same blood as that in the next, so individuality is in part destroyed as each life passeth; nay, even with each thought.

What then maketh man, if he dieth and is reborn a changeling with each breath? This: the consciousness of continuity given by memory, the conception of his Self as something whose existence, far from being threatened by these changes, is in verity assured by them. Let then the aspirant to the sacred Wisdom consider his Self no more as one segment of the Serpent, but as the whole. Let him extend his consciousness to regard both birth and death as incidents trivial as systole and diastole of the heart itself, and necessary as they to its function.

To fix the mind in this apprehension of Life, two modes are

preferred, as preliminary to the greater realizations to be discussed in their proper order, experiences which transcend even those attainments of Liberty and Love of which I have hitherto written, and this of Life which I now inscribe in this little book which I am making for you so that you may come unto the Great Fulfilment.

The first mode is the acquisition of the Magical Memory so-called, and the means as described with accuracy and clearness in certain of our Holy Books. But for nearly all men this is found to be a practice of exceeding difficulty. Let then the aspirant follow the impulse of his own Will in the decision to choose this or no.

The second mode is easy, agreeable, not tedious, and in the end as certain as the other. But as the way of error in the former lieth in Discouragement, so in the latter are you to be ware of False Paths. I may say indeed generally of all Works, that there are two dangers, the obstacle of Failure, and the snare of Success.

Now this second mode is to dissociate the beings which make up your life. Firstly, because it is easiest, you should segregate that Form which is called the Body of Light (and also by many other names) and set yourself to travel in this Form, making systematic exploration of those worlds which are to other material things what your own Body of Light is to your own material form.

Now it will occur to you in these travels that you come to many Gates which you are not able to pass. This is because your Body of Light is itself as yet not strong enough, or subtle enough, or pure enough: and you must then learn to dissociate the elements of that Body by a process similar to the first, your consciousness remaining in the higher and leaving the lower. In this practice do you continue, bending your Will like a great Bow to drive the Arrow of your consciousness through heavens even higher and holier. But the continuance in this Way is itself of vital value: for it shall be that presently habit herself shall persuade you that the body which is born and dieth within so little a space as one cycle of Neptune in the Zodiac is no essential of your Self, that the Life of which you are become partaker, while itself subject to the Law of action and reaction, ebb and flow, systole and diastole, is yet insensible to the afflictions of that life which you formerly held to be your sole bond with Existence.

And here must you resolve your Self to make the mightiest endeavours: for so flowered are the meadows of this Eden, and so sweet the fruit of its orchards, that you will love to linger among them, and to take delight in sloth and dalliance therein. Therefore I write to you with energy that you should not do thus to the hindrance of your true progress, because all these enjoyments are dependent upon duality, so that their true name is Sorrow of Illusion, like that of the normal life of man, which you have set out to transcend.

Be it according to your Will, but learn this, that (as it is written) they only are happy who have desired the unattainable. It is then best, ultimately, if it be your Will to find alway your chiefest pleasure in Love, that is, in Conquest, and in Death, that is, in Surrender, as I have written to you already. Thus then you shall delight in these delights aforesaid, but only as toys, holding your manhood firm and keen to pierce to deeper and holier ecstacies without arrest of Will.

Furthermore, I would have you to know that in this practice, pursued with ardour unquenchable, is this especial grace, that you will come as it were by fortune into states which transcend the practice itself, being of the nature of those Works of Pure Light of which I will to write to you in the chapter following after this. For there be certain Gates which no being who is still conscious of dividuality, that is, of the Self and not-Self as opposites, may pass through: and in the storming of Those Gates by fiery assault of lust celestial, your flame will burn vehemently against your gross Self, though it be already divine beyond your present imagining, and devour it in a mystical death, so that in the Passing of the Gate all is dissolved in formless Light of Unity.

Now then, returning from these states of being, and in the return also there is a Mystery of Joy, you will be weaned from the Milk of Darkness of the Moon, and made partaker of the Sacrament of Wine that is the blood of the Sun. Yet at the first there may be shock and conflict, for the old thought persists by force of its habit: it is for you to create by repeated act the true right habit of this consciousness of the Life which abideth in Light. And this is easy, if you will be strong: for the true Life is so much more vivid and quintessential than the false that (as I rudely estimate) one hour of the former makes an impression on the memory equal to one year of the latter. One single experience, in duration it may be but a few seconds of terrestrial time, is sufficient to destroy the belief in the reality of our vain life on earth: but this wears gradually away if the consciousness, through shock or fear, adhere not to it, and the Will strive not continually to repetition of that bliss, more beautiful and terrible than death, which it hath won by virtue of Love.

There be moreover many other modes of attaining the apprehension of true Life, and these two following are of much value in breaking up the ice of your mortal error in the vision of your being. And of these the first is the constant contemplation of the Identity of Love and Death, and the understanding of the dissolution of the body as an Act of Love done upon the Body of the Universe, as also it is written at length in our Holy Books. And with this goeth, as it were sister with twin brother, the practice of mortal love as a sacrament symbolical of that great Death: as it is written "Kill thyself": and again "Die daily."

And the second of these lesser modes is the practice of the mental apprehension and analysis of ideas, mainly as I have already taught you, but with especial emphasis in choice of things naturally repulsive, in particular, death itself, and its phenomena ancillary. Thus the Buddha bade his disciples to meditate upon Ten Impurities, that is, upon ten cases of death of decomposition, so that the Aspirant, identifying himself with his own corpse in all these imagined forms, might lose the natural horror, loathing, fear or disgust which he might have had for them. Know this, that every idea of every sort becomes unreal, phantastic, and most manifest illusion, if it be subjected to persistent investigation, with concentration. And this is particularly easy to attain in the case of all bodily impressions, because all material things, and especially those of which we are first conscious, namely, our own bodies, are the grossest and most unnatural of all falsities. For there is in us all, latent, that Light wherein no error may endure, and It already teaches our instinct to reject first of all those veils which are most closely wrapt about It. Thus also in meditation it is (for many men) most profitable to concentrate the Will to Love upon the sacred centres of nervous force: for they, like all things, are apt images or true reflexions of their semblables in finer spheres: so that, their gross natures being dissipated by the dissolving acid of the Meditation, their finer souls appear (so to speak) naked, and display their force and glory in the consciousness of the aspirant.

Yea, verily, let your Will to Love burn eagerly toward this creation in yourselves of the true Life that rolls its waves across the shoreless sea of Time! Live not your petty lives in fear of the hours! The Moon and Sun and Stars by which ye measure Time are themselves but servants of that Life which pulses in you, joyous drum-beat as you march triumphant through the Avenue of the Ages. Then, when each birth and death of yours are recognized in this perception as mere milestones on your ever-living Road, what of the foolish incidents of your mean lives? Are they not grains of sand blown by the desert wind, or pebbles that you spurn with your winged feet, or grassy hollows where you press the yielding and elastic turf and moss with lyrical dances? To him who lives in Life naught matters: his is eternal motion, energy, delight of never-failing Change: unwearied, you pass on from aeon to aeon, from star to star, the Universe your playground, its infinite variety of sport ever old and ever new. All those ideas which bred sorrow and fear are known in their truth, and thus become the seed of joy: for you are certain beyond all proof that you can never die; that, though you change, change is part of your own nature: the Great Enemy is become the Great Ally.

And now, rooted in this perfection, your Self become the very Tree of Life, you have a fulcrum for your lever: you are ready to understand that this pulsation of Unity is itself Duality, and therefore, in the highest and most sacred sense, still Sorrow and Illusion; which having comprehended, aspire yet again, even unto the Fourth of the Gifts of the Law, unto the End of the Path, even unto Light.

IV

OF LIGHT

I PRAY YOU, be patient with me in that which I shall write concerning Light: for here is a difficulty, ever increasing, in the use of words. Moreover, I am myself carried away constantly and overwhelmed by the sublimity of this matter, so that plain speech may whirl into lyric, when I would plod peaceably with didactic, expression. My best hope is that you may understand by virtue of the sympathy of your intuition, even as two lovers may converse in language as unintelligible to others as it seemeth silly, wanton, and dull, or as in that other intoxication given by Ether the partakers commune with infinite wit, or wisdom, as the mood taketh them, by means of a word or a gesture, being initiated to apprehension by the subtlety of the drug. So may I that am inflamed with love of this Light, and drunken on the wine Ethereal of this Light, communicate not so much with your reason and intelligence, but with that principle hidden in yourself which is ready to partake with me. Even so may man and woman become mad with love, no word being spoken between them, because of the induction (as it were) of their souls. And your understanding will depend upon your ripeness for perception of my Truth. Moreover, if so be that Light in you be ready to break forth, then Light will interpret to you these dark words in the language of Light, even as a string inanimate, duly adjusted, will vibrate to its peculiar tone, struck on another cord. Read, therefore, not only with the eye and brain, but with the rhythm of the Life which you have attained by your Will to Love quickened to dancing measure by these words, which are the movements of the wand of my Will to Love, and so to enkindle your Life to Light.

In this mood did I interrupt myself in the writing of this my little book, and for two days and nights sleeplessly have I made consideration, wrestling vehemently with my spirit, lest by haste or carelessness I might fail toward you.

In exercise of Will and of Love are implied motion and change, but in Life is gained an Unity which moveth and changeth only in pulse or in phase, and is even as music. Yet in the attainment of this Life you will already have experienced that the Quintessence thereof is pure Light, an ecstacy formless, and without bound or mark. In this Light naught exists, for It is homogeneous: and therefore have men called it Silence, and Darkness, and Nothing. But in this, as in all other effort to name it, is the root of every falsity and misapprehension, since all words imply some duality. Therefore, though I call it Light, it is not Light, nor absence of Light. Many also have sought to describe it by contradictions, since through transcendent negation of all speech it may by some natures be attained. Also by images and symbols have men striven to express it: but always in vain. Yet those that were ready to apprehend the nature of this Light have understood by sympathy: and so shall it be with you who read this little book, loving it. However, be it known unto you that the best of all instruction on this matter, and the Word best suited to the Aeon of Horus, is written in *The Book of the Law*. Yet also the Book *Ararita* is right worthy in the Work of the Light, as *Trigrammaton* in that of Will, *Cordis Cincti Serpente* in the Way of Love, and *Liberi* in that of Life. All these Books also concern all these Four Gifts, for in the end you will see that every one is inseparable from every other.

I wish to write to you with regard to the number 93, the number of Θελημα. For it is not only the number of its interpretation Αγαπη, but also that of a Word unknown to you unless you be Neophyte of our Holy Order of the A ∴ A ∴ which word representeth in itself the arising of the Speech from the Silence, and the return thereunto in the End. Now this number 93 is thrice 31, which is in Hebrew LA, that is to say NOT, and so it denieth extension in the three dimensions of Space. Also I would have you to meditate most closely upon the name NU that is 56, which we are told to divide, add, multiply, and understand. By division cometh forth 0.12, as if it were written Nuith! Hadith! Ra-Hoor-Khuith! before the Dyad. By addition ariseth Eleven, the number of True Magick: and by multiplication Three Hundred, the Number of the Holy Spirit or Fire, the letter Shin, wherein all things are consumed utterly. With these considerations, and a full understanding of the mysteries of the Numbers 666 and 418, you will be armed mightily in this Way of far flight. But you should also consider all numbers in their scales. For there is no means of resolution better than this of pure mathematics, since already therein are gross ideas made fine, and all is ordered and ready for the Alchemy of the Great Work.

I have already written to you of how, in the Will of Love, Light ariseth as the secret part of Life. And in the first, the little, Loves, the attained Life is still personal: later, it becometh impersonal and universal. Now then is Will arrived, may I say so, at its magnetic pole, whence the lines of force point alike every way and no way: and Love also is no more a work, but a state. These qualities are become part of the Universal Life, which proceedeth infinitely with the enjoyment of the Will, and of Love as inherent therein. These things therefore, in their perfection, have lost their names, and their natures. Yet these were the Substance of Life, its Father and Mother: and without their operation and impact Life itself will gradually cease its pulsations. But since the infinite energy of the whole Universe is therein, what then is possible but that it return to its own First Intention, dissolving itself little by little into that Light which is its most secret and most subtle Nature?

For this Universe is in Truth Zero, being an equation whereof

Zero is the sum. Whereof this is the proof, that if not, it would be unbalanced, and something would have come from Nothing, which is absurd. This Light or Nothing is then the Resultant or Totality thereof in pure Perfection; and all other states, positive or negative, are imperfect, since they omit their opposites.

Yet, I would have you consider that this equality or identity of equation between all things and No thing is most absolute, so that you will remain no more in the one than you did in the other. And you will understand this greatest Mystery very easily in the light of those other experiences which you will have enjoyed, wherein motion and rest, change and stability, and many other subtle opposites, have been redeemed to identify by the force of your holy meditation.

The greatest gift of the Law, then, cometh forth by the most perfect practice of the Three Lesser Gifts. And so thoroughly must you travail in this Work that you are able to pass from one side of the equation to the other at will: nay, to comprehend the whole at once, and for ever. This then your time-and-space-bound soul shall travel according to its nature in its orbit, revealing the Law to them that walk in chains, for that this is your particular function.

Now here is the Mystery of the Origin of Evil. Firstly, by Evil we mean that which is in opposition to our own wills: it is therefore a relative, and not an absolute, term. For everything which is the greatest evil of some one is the greatest good of some other, just as the hardness of the wood which wearieth the axeman is the safety of him that ventureth himself upon the sea in a ship built of that wood. And this is a truth easy to apprehend, being superficial, and intelligible to the common mind.

All evil is thus relative, or apparent, or illusory: but, returning to philosophy, I will repeat that its root is always in duality. Therefore the escape from this apparent evil is to seek the Unity, which you shall do as I have already shewn you. But I will now make mention of that which is written concerning this in *The Book of the Law*.

The first step being Will, Evil appears as by this definition, "all that hinders the execution of the Will." Therefore is it written: "The word of Sin is Restriction." It should also be noted that in *The Book of the Thirty Aethyrs [Book 418]* Evil appears as Choronzon whose number is 333, which in Greek importeth Impotence and Idleness: and the nature of Choronzon is Dispersion and Incoherence.

Then in the Way of Love Evil appears as "all that which tends to prevent the Union of any two things." Thus *The Book of the Law* sayeth, under the figure of the Voice of Nuit: "take your fill and will of love as ye will, when, where and with whom ye will! But always unto me." For every act of Love must be "under will," that is, in accordance with the True Will, which is not to rest content with things partial and transitory, but to proceed firmly to the End. So also, in *The Book of the Thirty Aethyrs,* the Black Brothers are those who shut themselves up, unwilling to destroy themselves by Love.

Thirdly, in the Way of Life Evil appears under a subtler form as "all that which is not impersonal and universal." Here *The Book of the Law,* by the Voice of Hadit, informeth us: "In the sphere I am everywhere the centre". And again: "I am Life and the giver of Life" [. . .] " 'Come unto me' is a foolish word: for it is I that go." "For I am perfect, being Not". For this Life is in every place and time at once, so that in It these limitations no longer exist. And you will have seen this for yourself, that in every act of Love time and space disappear with the creation of the Life by its virtue, as also doth personality itself. For the third time, then, in even subtler sense, "The word of Sin is Restriction."

Lastly, in the Way of Light this same versicle is the key to the conception of Evil. But here Restriction is in the failure to solve the Great Equation, and, later, to prefer one expression or phase of the Universe to the other. Against this we are warned in *The Book of the Law* by the Word of Nuit, saying: "None" [. . .] "and two. For I am divided for love's sake, for the chance of union", and therefore, "If this be not aright: if ye confound the space marks, saying: They are one: or saying, They are many;" [. . .] "then expect the direful judgments" [. . .]

Now therefore by the favour of Thoth am I come to the end of this my book: and do you arm yourselves accordingly with the Four Weapons: the Wand for Liberty, the Cup for Love, the Sword for Life, the Disk for Light: and with these work all wonders by the Art of High Magick under the Law of the New Aeon, whose Word is Θελημα.

The Wand

Part of a longer essay in *Book 4,* "The Wand," representing the Will and the Logos (the Word), is one of Crowley's most succinct statements on the problem of "Will" and "Law."

The Magical Will is in its essence twofold, for it presupposes a beginning and an end; to will to be a thing is to admit that you are not that thing.

Hence to will anything but the supreme thing, is to wander still further from it—**any will but that to give up the self to the Beloved is Black Magick**—yet this surrender is so simple an act that to our complex minds it is the most difficult of all acts; and hence training is necessary. Further, the Self surrendered must not be less than the All-Self; one must not come before the altar of the Most High with an impure or an imperfect offering. As it is written in Liber LXV, "To await Thee is the end, not the beginning."

This training may lead through all sorts of complications, varying according to the nature of the student, and hence it may be necessary for him at any moment to will all sorts of things which to others might seem unconnected with the goal. Thus it is not *à priori* obvious why a billiard player should need a file.

Since, then, we may want *anything,* let us see to it that our will is strong enough to obtain anything we want without loss of time.

It is therefore necessary to develop the will to its highest point, even though the last task but one is the total surrender of this will. Partial surrender of an imperfect will is of no account in Magick.

The will being a lever, a fulcrum is necessary; this fulcrum is the main aspiration of the student to attain. All wills which are not dependent upon this principal will are so many leakages; they are like fat to the athlete.

The majority of the people in this world are ataxic; they cannot

255

coördinate their mental muscles to make a purposed movement. They have no real will, only a set of wishes, many of which contradict others. The victim wobbles from one to the other (and it is no less wobbling because the movements may occasionally be very violent) and at the end of life the movements cancel each other out. Nothing has been achieved; except the one thing of which the victim is not conscious: the destruction of his own character, the confirming of indecision. Such an one is torn limb from limb by Choronzon.

How then is the will to be trained? All these wishes, whims, caprices, inclinations, tendencies, appetites, must be detected, examined, judged by the standard of whether they help or hinder the main purpose, and treated accordingly.

Vigilance and courage are obviously required. I was about to add self-denial, in deference to conventional speech; but how could I call that self-denial which is merely denial of those things which hamper the self? It is not suicide to kill the germs of malaria in one's blood.

Now there are very great difficulties to be overcome in the training of the mind. Perhaps the greatest is forgetfulness, which is probably the worst form of what the Buddhists call ignorance. Special practices for training the memory may be of some use as a preliminary for persons whose memory is naturally poor. In any case **the Magical Record prescribed for Probationers by the A ∴ A ∴ is useful and necessary.**

Above all the practices of Liber III must be done again and again, for these practices develop not only vigilance but those inhibiting centres in the brain which are, according to some psychologists, the mainspring of the mechanism by which civilized man has raised himself above the savage.

So far it has been spoken, as it were, in the negative. Aaron's rod has become a serpent, and swallowed the serpents of the other Magicians; it is now necessary to turn it once more into a rod.[1]

This Magical Will is the wand in your hand by which the Great Work is accomplished, by which the Daughter is not merely set upon the throne of the Mother, but assumed into the Highest.[2]

---

1. As everyone knows, the word used in Exodus for a Rod of Almond is סמקדד, adding to 463. Now 400 is Tau, the path leading from Malkuth to Yesod. Sixty is Samekh, the path leading from Yesod to Tiphereth; and 3 is Gimel, the path leading thence to Kether. The whole rod therefore gives the paths from the Kingdom to the Crown.

2. In one, the best, system of Magick, the Absolute is called the Crown, God is called the Father, the Pure Soul is called the Mother, the Holy Guardian Angel is called the

The Magick Wand is thus the principal weapon of the Magus; and the *name* of that wand is the Magical Oath.

The will being twofold is in Chokmah, who is the Logos, the word; hence some have said that **the word is the will.** Thoth the Lord of Magic is also the Lord of Speech; Hermes the messenger bears the Caduceus.

Word should express will: hence **the Mystic Name of the Probationer is the expression of his highest Will.**

There are, of course, few Probationers who understand themselves sufficiently to be able to formulate this will to themselves, and therefore at the end of their probation they choose a new name.

It is convenient therefore for the student to express his will by taking Magical Oaths.

Since such an oath is irrevocable it should be well considered; and it is better not to take any oath permanently; because with increase of understanding may come a perception of the incompatibility of the lesser oath with the greater.

This is indeed almost certain to occur, and it must be remembered that as the whole essence of the will is its one-pointedness,[3] a dilemma of this sort is the worst in which the Magus can find himself.

Another great point in this consideration of Magick Vows is to keep them in their proper place. They must be taken for a clearly defined purpose, a clearly understood purpose, and they must never be allowed to go beyond it.

It is a virtue in a diabetic not to eat sugar, but only in reference to his own condition. It is not a virtue of universal import. Elijah said on one occasion: "I do well to be angry;" but such occasions are rare.

Moreover, one man's meat is another man's poison. An oath of poverty might be very useful for a man who was unable intelligently to use his wealth for the single end proposed; to another it would be simply stripping himself of energy, causing him to waste his time over trifles.

There is no power which cannot be pressed into the service of the Magical Will: it is only the temptation to value that power for itself which offends.

Son, and the Natural Soul is called the Daughter. The Son purifies the Daughter by wedding her; she thus becomes the Mother, the uniting of whom with the Father absorbs all into the Crown. See Liber CDXVIII.

3. The Top of the Wand is in Kether—which is one; and the Qliphoth of Kether are the Thaumiel, opposing heads that rend and devour each other.

One does not say: "Cut it down; why cumbereth it the ground?" unless repeated prunings have convinced the gardener that the growth must always be a rank one.

"If thine hand offend thee, cut it off!" is the scream of a weakling. If one killed a dog the first time it misbehaved itself, not many would pass the stage of puppyhood.

The best vow, and that of most universal application, is the vow of Holy Obedience; for not only does it lead to perfect freedom, but is a training in that surrender which is the last task.

It has this great value, that it never gets rusty. If the superior to whom the vow is taken knows his business, he will quickly detect which things are really displeasing to his pupil, and familiarize him with them.

Disobedience to the superior is a contest between these two wills in the inferior. The will expressed in his vow, which is the will linked to his highest will by the fact that he has taken it in order to develop that highest will, contends with the temporary will, which is based only on temporary considerations.

The Teacher should then seek gently and firmly to key up the pupil, little by little, until obedience follows command without reference to what that command may be; as Loyola wrote: "perinde ac cadaver."

No one has understood the Magical Will better than Loyola; in his system the individual was forgotten. The will of the General was instantly echoed by every member of the Order; hence the Society of Jesus became the most formidable of the religious organizations of the world.

That of the Old Man of the Mountains was perhaps the next best.

The defect in Loyola's system is that the General was not God, and that owing to various other considerations he was not even necessarily the best man in the Order.

To become General of the Order he must have willed to become General of the Order; and because of this he could be nothing more.

To return to the question of the development of the Will. It is always something to pluck up the weeds, but the flower itself needs tending. Having crushed all volitions in ourselves, and if necessary in others, which we find opposing our real Will, that Will itself will grow naturally with greater freedom. But it is not only necessary to purify the temple itself and consecrate it; invocations must be made. Hence it is necessary to be constantly doing things of a positive, not merely of a negative nature, to affirm that Will.

Renunciation and sacrifice are necessary, but they are comparatively easy. There are a hundred ways of missing, and only one of hitting. To avoid eating beef is easy; to eat nothing but pork is very difficult.

Levi recommends that at times the Magical Will itself should be cut off, on the same principle as one can always work better after a "complete change." Levi is doubtless right, but he must be understood as saying this "for the hardness of men's hearts." The turbine is more efficient than a reciprocating engine; and his counsel is only good for the beginner.

Ultimately the Magical Will so identifies itself with the man's whole being that it becomes unconscious, and is as constant a force as gravitation. One may even be surprised at one's own acts, and have to reason out their connection. But let it be understood that when the Will has thus really raised itself to the height of Destiny, the man is no more likely to do wrong than he is to float off into the air.

One may be asked whether there is not a conflict between this development of the Will and Ethics.

The answer is Yes.

In the Grand Grimoire we are told "to buy an egg without haggling"; and attainment, and the next step in the path of attainment, is that pearl of great price, which when a man hath found he straightway selleth all that he hath, and buyeth that pearl.

With many people custom and habit—of which ethics is but the social expression—are the things most difficult to give up: and **it is a useful practice to break any habit just to get into the way of being free from that form of slavery.** Hence we have practices for breaking up sleep, for putting our bodies into strained and unnatural positions, for doing difficult exercises of breathing—all these, apart from any special merit they may have in themselves for any particular purpose, have the main merit that the man forces himself to do them despite any conditions that may exist. Having conquered internal resistance one may conquer external resistance more easily.

In a steamboat the engine must first overcome its own inertia before it can attack the resistance of the water.

When the will has thus ceased to be intermittent, it becomes necessary to consider its size. Gravitation gives an acceleration of thirty-two feet per second on this planet, on the moon very much less. And a Will, however single and however constant, may still be of no particular use, because the circumstances which oppose it may be altogether too strong, or because it is for some reason unable to get into touch with them. It is useless to wish for the moon. If one does so, one must consider by what means that Will may be made effective.

And though a man may have a tremendous Will in one direction it need not always be sufficient to help him in another; it may even be stupid.

There is the story of the man who practised for forty years to walk across the Ganges; and, having succeeded, was reproached by his Holy Guru, who said: "You are a great fool. All your neighbours have been crossing every day on a raft for two pice."

This occurs to most, perhaps to all, of us in our careers. We spend infinite pains to learn something, to achieve something, which when gained does not seem worth even the utterance of the wish.

But this is a wrong view to take. The discipline necessary in order to learn Latin will stand us in good stead when we wish to do something quite different.

At school our masters punished us; when we leave school, if we have not learned to punish ourselves, we have learned nothing.

In fact the only danger is that we may value the achievement in itself. The boy who prides himself on his school knowledge is in danger of becoming a college professor.

So the Guru of the water-walking Hindu only meant that it was now time to be dissatisfied with what he had done—and to employ his powers to some better end.

And, incidentally, since the divine Will is one, it will be found that there is no capacity which is not necessarily subservient to the destiny of the man who possesses it.

One may be unable to tell when a thread of a particular colour will be woven into the carpet of Destiny. It is only when the carpet is finished and seen from a proper distance that the position of that particular strand is seen to be necessary. From this one is tempted to break a lance on that most ancient battlefield, free-will and destiny.

But even though every man is "determined" so that every action is merely the passive resultant of the sum-total of the forces which have acted upon him from eternity, so that his own Will is only the echo of the Will of the Universe, yet that consciousness of "free-will" is valuable; and if he really understands it as being the partial and individual expression of that internal motion in a Universe whose sum is rest, by so much will he feel that harmony, that totality. And though the happiness which he experiences may be criticised as only one scale of a balance in whose other scale is an equal misery, there are those who hold that misery consists only in the feeling of separation from the Universe, and that consequently all may cancel out among the lesser feelings, leaving only that infinite bliss which is one phase of the infinite consciousness of that ALL. Such speculations are somewhat beyond the scope of the present remarks. It is of no particular moment to observe that the elephant and flea can be no other than they are; but we do perceive that one is bigger than the other. That is the fact of practical importance.

We do know that persons can be trained to do things which they could not do without training—and anyone who remarks that you cannot train a person unless it is his destiny to be trained is quite unpractical. Equally it is the destiny of the trainer to train. There is a fallacy in the determinist argument similar to the fallacy which is the root of all "systems" of gambling at Roulette. The odds are just over three to one against red coming up twice running; but after red has come up once the conditions are changed.

It would be useless to insist on such a point were it not for the fact that many people confuse Philosophy with Magick. Philosophy is the enemy of Magick. Philosophy assures us that after all nothing matters, and that *che sarà sarà.*

In practical life, and Magick is the most practical of the Arts of life, this difficulty does not occur. It is useless to argue with a man who is running to catch a train that he may be destined not to catch it; he just runs, and if he could spare breath would say "Blow destiny!"

It has been said earlier that the real Magical Will must be toward the highest attainment, and this can never be until the flowering of the Magical Understanding. The Wand must be made to grow in length as well as in strength; it need not do so of its own nature.

The ambition of every boy is to be an engine-driver. Some attain it, and remain there all their lives.

But in the majority of cases the Understanding grows faster than the Will, and long before the boy is in a position to attain his wish he has already forgotten it.

In other cases the Understanding never grows beyond a certain point, and the Will persists without intelligence.

The business man (for example) has wished for ease and comfort, and to this end goes daily to his office and slaves under a more cruel taskmaster than the meanest of the workmen in his pay; he decides to retire, and finds that life is empty. The end has been swallowed up in the means.

Only those are happy who have desired the unattainable.

All possessions, the material and the spiritual alike, are but dust.

Love, sorrow, and compassion are three sisters who, if they seem freed from this curse, are only so because of their relation to the Unsatisfied.

Beauty is itself so unattainable that it escapes altogether; and the true artist, like the true mystic, can never rest. To him the Magician is but a servant. His wand is of infinite length; it is the creative Mahalingam.

The difficulty with such an one is naturally that his wand being very thin in proportion to its length is liable to wobble. Very few artists are conscious of their real purpose, and in very many cases we have this infinite yearning supported by so frail a constitution that nothing is achieved.

The Magician must build all that he has into his pyramid; and if that pyramid is to touch the stars, how broad must be the base! There is no knowledge and no power which is useless to the Magician. One might almost say there is no scrap of material in the whole Universe with which he can dispense. His ultimate enemy is the great Magician, the Magician who created the whole illusion of the Universe; and to meet him in battle, so that nothing is left either of him or of yourself, you must be exactly equal to him.

At the same time let the Magician never forget that every brick must tend to the summit of the pyramid—the sides must be perfectly smooth; there must be no false summits, even in the lowest layers.

This is the practical and active form of that obligation of a Master of the Temple in which it is said: "I will interpret every phenomenon as a particular dealing of God with my soul."

In Liber CLXXV many practical devices for attaining this one-pointedness are given, and though the subject of that book is devotion to a particular Deity, its instructions may be easily generalized to suit the development of any form of will.

This will is then the active form of understanding. The Master of the Temple asks, on seeing a slug: "What is the purpose of this message from the Unseen? How shall I interpret this Word of God Most High?" The Magus thinks: "How shall I use this slug?" And in this course he must persist. Though many things useless, so far as he can see, are sent to him, one day he will find the one thing he needs, while his Understanding will appreciate the fact that none of those other things were useless.

So with these early practices of renunciation it will now be clearly understood that they were but of temporary use. They were only of value as training. The adept will laugh over his early absurdities— the disproportions will have been harmonized; and the structure of his soul will be seen as perfectly organic, with no one thing out of its place. He will see himself as the positive Tau with its ten complete squares within the triangle of the negatives; and this figure will become one, as soon as from the equilibrium of opposites he has attained to the identity of opposites. . . .

PART V

The Book of Lies

MAGICK AND LIES

Nature is false; but I'm a bit of a liar myself.

But note that a good Qabalist cannot err.

Awake from dream, the truth is known: awake from waking, the Truth is—The Unknown.

!

?

All this is true and false, and it is true and false to say that it is true and false.

The Book of Lies

Not wishing to Lie, one can safely say that *The Book of Lies* is the least important book written by Aleister Crowley, and the most important. Its significance relative to, for example, *The Book of the Law* is clearly explained in his *Confessions. AL*'s reception occupies an entire chapter of Crowley's autohagiography, while the Writing of *The Book of Lies* takes up two paragraphs, less space than that afforded many of his volumes of poetry. According to the story, *The Book of the Law* was dictated by god to the scribe Crowley in a quiet room, after the reception of a number of special portents. With *Lies* he relates that it one day "occured" to him to write the book, a volume in "epigrammatic and sometimes humorous form."[1] The 91 chapters were written during meals—both lunch and dinner—"by the aid of the god Dionysus" (a far cry from Horus). Within the text itself Crowley sometimes signals the jest of this less than perfectly prepared tale: Chapter 34—"The Smoking Dog"—for example, came to him "at breakfast at 'Au Chien qui Fume'."[2] Chapter 61—"The Fool's Knot"—was composed "dining with friends, in about a minute and a half. That is how you must know the Qabalah."[3]

Though *The Book of Lies* may have been composed between courses, Crowley maintains that without it he would never have turned

1. *The Confessions of Aleister Crowley* (New York: Hill and Wang, 1970), p. 709.
2. *The Book of Lies* (reprinted New York: Samuel Weiser, Inc., 1978), p. 79.
3. *The Book of Lies*, p. 133.

his magical attentions so intently to sex. After the publication of *The Book of Lies*, the head of the O.T.O. (to which Crowley already belonged but regarded at that time as merely a "convenient compendium" of masonic lore) accused him of revealing the O.T.O. secrets of Sex Magick within its pages. "It instantly flashed upon me," Crowley reports.[4] He suddenly understood the significance of the suggestive passage—Chapter 36, "The Star Sapphire"—and Magick changed.[5] But Francis King points out that one must be wary of any story told about a book of Lies. The confrontation with the O.T.O. is said to have taken place in 1912, while the title page of *The Book of Lies* reads 1913. Two possible Lies: Crowley lied on the title page (which within a book of Lies means he told the Truth) or he lied about the confrontation. He may also have Lied about which book or text upset the O.T.O.[6]

When Crowley's Lies proliferate, should the reader continue to listen, should he or she take it lying down? Or break down by taking a break from these intentionally misleading questions and probing the title-page: "The Book of Lies which is also falsely called BREAKS, the wanderings or falsifications of the one thought of Frater Perdurabo (Aleister Crowley) which thought is itself untrue."[7] First consider that "Breaks" is a "false" title for a book full of Lies. Either "Breaks" falsely relates to *The Book of Lies*, or else, given that "Breaks" is a Lie within Lies (Lies might be Lying about Breaks), "Breaks" therefore might be what Crowley would call "relatively true."[8]

Not able to disentangle this web of interrelationships, the original problem can be rephrased: given only two choices, what do we prefer to call this volume—a Break or a Lie? For Crowley, a Lie would be exactly that which would show his lack of respect for "Truth" and its necessary ties to belief, objecthood, and reality. On the other hand, a Break Breaks reality's hold, shocking us into recognition of our consciousness (as we have seen with Yoga). It acknowledges "a lie grafted upon a lie, a lie multiplied by a lie."[9] If we are to believe Lies, "Breaks" is a cheat. The term "Break" seems to devalue the rigorous contradictory power of Lies; perhaps this "Lie" is just a tough

4. *The Confessions of Aleister Crowley*, p. 710.
5. Francis King, *The Magical World of Aleister Crowley*, (New York: Coward, McCann & Geoghegan, Inc., 1978), p. 80
6. Francis King, *The Magical World of Aleister Crowley*, p. 81
7. *The Book of Lies*, p. 3.
8. *The Book of Lies*, p. 4.
9. *The Book of Lies*, p. 62.

Break or a slight Break from accepted behavior rather than a Sin. Conversely, to call "Breaks" *The Book of Lies* is bad for the Breaks, since a Lie firms up a Break, gives it a rotten name and thereby grants its existence.

The phrase "falsifications of the one thought" leads to belief that Lies Break thought into different streams running in varied directions, one thought correct and the others not—facilitating a world of Truth and Lies, of True and False where once there was Unbroken Truth. In this case, say goodbye to Lie. But if the one thought "is itself untrue," and this perverse mechanism of the Lie can enable one to Break from belief in Truth *before* the Lie—well, one might side with Lie. And then there are the Breaks: also Breaking our belief in the Unbroken Truth while additionally rupturing the very fabric that fancies Lie and Truth distinguished.

So which came first, the Lie or the Break? Crowley plays chicken and the subsequent text breaks *The Book of Lies* into figures—shadowy characters who negotiate Lies and Breaks: the Hermit, Pan, the Fool, and Frater Perdurabo.

The Hermit

The Hermit figures in several chapters of the book, and while not as important as other, more brightly shining stars, still has a special light to shed on Lie. In the Tarot, according to Crowley, the Hermit carries a lamp through the lower regions of the world, the lower branches of the Tree of Life, illuminating the path wherever he goes. The Hermit is also attributed to the Hebrew letter "Yod", which, as we have seen, represents the Logos in the Qabalah, the Father in Sex Magick.[10] He can reveal "the fluidic essence of Light",[11] spermatozoon.

Though he holds the lamp—the "Truth" of the Father, Logos and Sperm which would reveal each of them as conditional formulations— he walks through the world, the "Abyss of Hallucinations,"[12] cloaked and concealed. Hidden like the leopard by the sun, he can "resemble

---

10. *The Book of Thoth (Egyptian Tarot)* (reprinted New York: U.S. Game Systems, Inc. 1979), p. 88.
11. *The Book of Thoth (Egyptian Tarot)*, p. 89.
12. *The Book of Lies,* p. 30.

all that surroundeth," and "take . . . pleasure among the living."[13] Hidden within a world of Law and Reason, "the Bond of the Great Lie."[14] The Hermit, who has not yet crossed the abyss, must reside in that which is reasonable, that which sorts the "Universe" or "Consciousness."[15] He might be counterposed to the Sorcerer, who also has not crossed the abyss, he by his own choice, and believes that he rules over the world, only to find "with all this he was but himself."[16] The Sorcerer conjures the Lie which thinks the Truth. The Hermit is the Truth of the Lie and the Lie of the Truth, embodied within the formulae of Lie and Truth. Not yet Breaking, he walks a tightrope. "Were I an hermit, how could I support the pain of consciousness, the curse of thought? even were I THAT, there still were one sore spot—The Abyss that stretches between THAT and NOT."[17]

Pan

Pan the goat, sits as the Devil in the Tarot. The Devil, when attributed to the Tree of Life, balances human consciousness and bliss.[18] Therefore Pan, like the Hermit, can take pleasure in the world. But given the Truth and the Lie, the Law and the Sin, he might just grin and begin with the Sin, and indulge. Indulgence presents itself to Pan in the form of the Body of the Scarlet Woman, Laylah (Arabic for Darkness), unbroken, all-absorbing Sin who provides the "Food of Falsity."[19] Crowley compares Laylah to the nursery rhyming Margery Daw, the "silly slut" who sells her bed "to lie upon dirt."[20] She lies naked in her hut waiting for Pan.

The three letters in Pan's name, according to Crowleyan Qabalism,

13. *The Book of Lies*, p. 48.
14. *The Book of Lies*, p. 30.
15. *The Book of Lies*, p. 30.
16. *The Book of Lies*, p. 64.
17. *The Book of Lies*, p. 158.
18. *The Book of Thoth (Egyptian Tarot)*, p. 105
19. *Liber Aleph vel CXI: The Book of Wisdom and Folly*, (reprinted Seattle: Aeon Press, 1985), p. 75.
20. *The Book of Lies*, p. 137.

reveal Pan as more than indulgence, as instead a Duality of Energy and Death—the energy that engenders consciousness and the world, and the Death of it too.[21] "Love Alway Yieldeth: Love Alway Hardeneth" is a sexy anagram for this double work of Living and Dying, Hardening and Softening.[22] The Energy of indulgence leads directly to Pan's Death; the Comedy of Pan, according to Crowley, means that he who hunts finds himself already the hunted.[23] To kill is to be killed. Laylah reveals to Pan "the night before His threshold!"[24] and Pan gives himself to Laylah in order to destroy himself—to destroy Sin—in order to Break. Loving Laylah is a "giving" which is a "spending" of a "man."[25] "Let there be no more! Let me be Thine; let me be Thou; let me be neither Thou nor I; let there be love in night and night in love."[26] Through Laylah, Pan enters the Night of Pan, where he still sees the engendered Tree (like the Hermit), though transparently[27]—plummeting through Darkness in Light, the Light in the Dark, or Night thrown into the abyss. A Night of Fire, destroying himself in himself. "O ye who dwell in the City of the Pyramids beneath the Night of PAN, remember that ye shall see no more light but That of the great fire that shall consume your dust to ashes!"[28]

When Truth and Lie talk themselves to Death, the Tongue of prayer buries itself in Laylah's dark vagina, in the 69th position, and cannot speak a Lie. "Holy, Holy, Holy are these Truths that I utter, knowing them to be but falsehoods, broken mirrors, troubled waters; hide me, O our Lady, in thy Womb! for I may not endure the rapture."[29] As Chapter 69 of *The Book of Lies* suggests: to "Succeed" means using the tongue to suck seed.[30] In Laylah, the tongue returns to "the Silence of the Night" where there can be no Truth and Lie, no Lie that is not Truth, no Sin that is not permissible to the Body and where the Energy of Pan's Sin undermines the body of Law, beyond "the babble of the apes" in the province of Body without Law.[31] "Blessed, unutterably

21. *The Book of Lies*, p. 13.
22. *The Book of Lies*, p. 66.
23. *The Book of Lies*, p. 78.
24. *The Book of Lies*, p. 68.
25. *The Book of Lies*, p. 160.
26. *The Book of Lies*, p. 68.
27. *The Book of Thoth* (*Egyptian Tarot*), p. 105.
28. *The Book of Lies*, p. 144.
29. *The Book of Lies*, p. 32.
30. *The Book of Lies*, p. 148.
31. *The Book of Lies*, p. 146.

blessed, is this last of the illusions; let me play the man, and thrust it from me!"[32]

The Fool

The wise Fool runs the Path of Aleph—the Path leading from Kether to Chokmah, from Chokmah to Kether. The Fool barely lives in this world; he is always on the verge of renouncing it. "He rideth upon the chariot of eternity; the white and the black are harnessed to his car."[33] In the guise of Parsifal— "the Pure Fool"—he compares to the highest magical grade, Ipsissimus.[34] He does not live by life's rules because he can no longer comprehend them, and he cannot be held to them.

He wanders the countryside, preferring it to company. Crowley's advice in Chapter 23 of The Book of Lies applies: "What man is at ease in his Inn? Get out. Wide is the world and cold. Get out. Thou hast become an in-itiate. Get out."[35] He achieves a peculiar kind of "self mastery" by losing himself in foolish acts. Parsifal can kill an innocent Swan and then come face to face with those who would jail him for the crime. "Perceiving that I was but a Pure Fool, they let me pass."[36] And I laid my head against the Head of the Swan, and laughed, saying: Is there not joy ineffable in this aimless winging? Is there not weariness and impatience for who would attain to some goal? And the swan was ever silent. Ah! but we floated in the infinite Abyss. Joy! Joy!"[37]

Though he commits Sins, he does not indulge himself like Pan. "I have burst the bonds of Love and of Power and of Worship."[38] Parsifal, in fact, is the chaste knight. (Though, as Crowley notes, he did not shy away from sex. In the Fool and Parsifal's system, "One cannot 'find the Lady' by any other way than that of the Knight-Errant, of the Great

---

32. *The Book of Lies*, p. 32.
33. "Liber Arcanorum," reprinted in *Gems from the Equinox* (St. Paul: Llewellyn Publications, 1974), pp. 667–668.
34. *The Book of Lies*, p. 133.
35. *The Book of Lies*, p. 56.
36. *The Book of Lies*, p. 44.
37. "Liber Cordis Cincti Serpente," reprinted in *The Holy Books of Thelema* (York Beach, Maine: Samuel Weiser, 1983), p. 60.
38. "Liber Cordis Cincti Serpente," p. 69.

Fool."[39]. He prefers to think his way out of thinking, and into naïvety. Writing Chapter 39 of *The Book of Lies*, Crowley found himself away from his usual reference books and invented the word "Looby" ("booby" and "lout") to describe the Parsifal figure. The Looby forces himself to unbelieve in everything (both "truisms" and "absurdity") through "unreason," without which he would forever be trapped within the "Lies of a Looby."[40] (On a related note, the important Magick "Act of Truth" involves seeking the "absurd"—freeing the mind through belief in an impossible possibility[41]). When the True and the False are both incorporated into the Fool's system of beliefs, the Fool can't be fooled by Lies. He Breaks into laughter and the system Breaks (dissolves). "The Universal Joke . . . often proves the chief ingredient of the Universal Solvent."[42] "The Universe is the Practical Joke" at which some weep and others laugh,[43] yet even laughter Breaks at the thought. "And in Himself He neither laughed nor wept. Nor did He mean what He said."[44]

Frater Perdurabo

Frater Perdurabo ("I will endure unto the end"[45]) was one of the many magical names Crowley used, and as Frater P. or even P. he weaves as one with the Hermit, Pan, and the Fool, and shares characteristics with each. Perdurabo prefers like Pan to abide in rugged and barren terrain. Perdurabo, like the Fool, is connected to Zero, Nothing—the Fool numbers Zero in the Tarot arcanum, and "O, the last letter of Perdurabo, is Naught."[46] P. earned the grade Master of the Temple at the time of the writing of *The Book of Lies*, placing him just beyond the abyss but below the grade of Magus. Unencumbered by the Magus' pride, P. always moves. He grapples as "The Mountaineer" who "leapt from rock to rock

39. "Understanding," *Little Essays Toward Truth* (Malton, Canada: Dove Press, approximately 1970), p. 57.
40. *The Book of Lies*, p. 88.
41. *Magick Without Tears* (St. Paul: Llewellyn Publications, 1973) p. 154.
42. "Laughter," *Little Essays Toward Truth*, p. 30.
43. *The Book of Lies*, p. 38.
44. *The Book of Lies*, p. 38.
45. *The Book of Lies*, p. 25.
46. *The Book of Lies*, p. 25.

of the moraine without ever casting his eyes upon the ground."[47] (Crowley reports of his own mountain climbing experiences: "People used to say that I didn't climb them, that I oozed over them!"[48]) He lumbers as a camel crossing the desert, and as a charioteer. He pauses poised as avalanche, ready to fall. Prone to put himself at risk, he can be violent to others as well. He might yell in order to explain Yoga. He hunts and slays animals for sport. If you don't agree with him he exclaims, "D'ye want a clip on the jaw?"[49]

P. does not plan to act, does not prejudge his action, does not act, he *Does*. "So let me worry along, please, with the accent on the 'along'."[50] He Does unconsciously, with perfect indifference, without morals, delivered from the result. "Behold how sad a thing it is, quoth the Ape of Thoth, for one to be so holy that he cannot chop a tree and cook his food without preparing upon it a long and tedious Morality!"[51] Frater P. sees the world and its materials as the place of free play; "it is Pure Chance that rules the Universe."[52] He climbs mountains without worry, risks life and limb without thought, strikes without reason. He is as a blind man, and blind he loses sight of himself, which perfectly defines himself, Perdurabo. The Charioteer "is only himself when lost to himself when in the Charioting."[53] Perdurabo is as No Man—NEMO—who will pass away in the Doing, with pleasure.

When it comes to ideas and words, too, Perdurabo Does—Does not insist—wandering silently across them. *The Book of Lies*, remember, is "the wanderings or falsifications of the one thought of Frater Perdurabo." So he interprets statements only "in the most ordinary and commonplace way, without any mystical sense",[54] in the same manner that the wandering rock climber and camel might treat their rocks and sand. A rock cannot be either Lie or Truth. It's a rock! For P., ideas such as "Many" and "Naught" (and "Many," for instance, can stand for Pan, and "Naught," for instance, can stand for the Fool), are nothing but themselves—ideas. "They are They!" and nothing "deeper" or more meaningful, material on its surface.[55] And like rocks, unrestrained by concepts, liable to Break and to Break what gets in their way.

47. *The Book of Lies*, p. 74.
48. *Magick Without Tears*, p. 223.
49. *The Book of Lies*, p. 170.
50. *Magick Without Tears*, p. 222.
51. "Liber CCC: Khabs Am Pekht," reprinted in *Gems from the Equinox*, p. 110.
52. *The Book of Lies*, p. 54.
53. *The Book of Lies*, p. 26.
54. *The Book of Lies*, p. 93.
55. *The Book of Lies*, p. 176.

The double authorship of *The Book of Lies* by both Aleister Crowley and Frater Perdurabo might cause one to wonder about the thinker of these great thoughts. Which one of them wrote it, which one is Lying? Yet Frater P., who writes to rock the boat and fails to file his copyright, cannot stomach the rhetoric of the true and false author. "There is still some meaning in the term 'Forger', as used in general speech. . . . This seems to me a pity."[56] While the book is (tentatively), signed by P., "so wrote not FRATER PERDURABO, but the Imp Crowley in his Name. . . . And yet who knoweth which is Crowley and which is FRATER PERDURABO?"[57]

The Lie that Spells the Truth

The ways of life encountered in *The Book of Lies* which Break and Lie are: Silent Passage, to quietly bend the Break, carrying the Truth of Lies and the Lie of Truth within the world of Truth and Lies; Pandemonium, to smother Lies by Breaking deliriously to excess; Foolishness, to reverse the Lie through a kind of Broken Truth; and Endurance, to wander across the Broken field of Truth and Lie.

Stretching a point, those figures—the Hermit, Pan, the Fool, and Perdurabo—squeeze into the scheme forecast in a key verse of *The Book of the Law:* "For there are therein Three Grades, the Hermit, and the Lover, and the man of Earth."[58] In which case the True model for Man has been discharged by *The Book of Lies*. But "this counsels a course of action hardly distinguishable from hypocrisy; but the distinction is obvious to any clear thinker, though not altogether so to Frater P."[59] If the reader believes to have Broken the Lie thereby—setting the terms for action, settling the differences between the Truth and Lie, the relationship between Lie and Break—he or she may instead have threatened the Lie and re-established some form of Truth. He who seeks to reveal the "Arcanum," according to Crowley, has "only profaned it."[60]

56. "Concerning Blasphemy," reprinted in *The Equinox, Volume III, Number 10* (New York: Thelema Publications, 1986), p. 220.
57. *The Book of Lies*, p. 122.
58. *Liber AL: The Book of Law*, (reprinted Berkeley: O.T.O., 1982), Chapter I, Verse 40.
59. *The Book of Lies*, p. 49.
60. "Liber LXI: vel Causae," reprinted in *Gems from the Equinox*, p. 9.

Crowley's working method in *The Book of Lies* is "the transvaluation of values" or "the method of contradiction"[61], a Crowleyan scepticism which at each and every point must continue to reverse itself. Only through constant Doubt—Lies to Truth, Truth to Lies—can he break with what has been established in the name of order. "I slept with Faith, and found a corpse in my arms on awaking. I drank and danced all night with Doubt, and found her a virgin in the morning."[62]

To Lie is already to Break. To Break is already to Lie. And Truth includes both "Nakedness" and "Veils."[63] "The prose of this chapter combines, and of course denies, all of these meanings, both singly and in combination."[64] The first two pages of *The Book of Lies* consist of an exclamation point and a question mark. Writing marks for a kind of hysteria followed by doubt, an ending of categories and still a question left to ask. Enclosing the Lie in Break, or Break in Lie misses the mark. Once Lying and Breaking, Crowley continues to run on in this fashion, unable to apply the Breaks. "The slaves of reason call this book Abuse-of-Language; they are right.[65]

"It is certain that every letter of this cipher hath some value; but who shall determine the value? For it varieth ever, according to the subtlety of Him that made it."[66] Reaching out to him who made it, who is not Frater P. nor Crowley, not Hermit nor Pan nor the Fool, he states that he searches for the state "beyond the Word and the Fool."[67] He yearns for the Unbroken Truth. "He piles contradiction upon contradiction, and thus a higher degree of rapture, with every sentence, until his armoury is exhausted, and, with the word Amen, he enters the supreme state."[68] Yet who can find the final Truth in *The Book of Lies*? "Amen" is the final word of *The Book of Lies*—the full text of Chapter 91—but supplanted in this resting place by a later comment: "The chapter consists of an analysis of this word, but gives no indication of the result of this analysis, as if to imply this: The final Mystery is always insoluble."[69]

61. *The Book of Lies*, p. 95.
62. *The Book of Lies*, p. 100.
63. *Liber Aleph vel CXI: The Book of Wisdom or Folly*, p. 116.
64. *The Book of Lies*, p. 163.
65. *The Book of Lies*, p. 58.
66. "Liber Cordis Cincti Serpente," p. 57.
67. "Vel Ararita," reprinted in *The Holy Books of Thelema*, p. 229.
68. *The Book of Lies*, p. 33.
69. *The Book of Lies*, p. 192.

When the Lying stops, Writing continues. Chapter 89: "I am annoyed about the number 89. I shall avenge myself by writing nothing in this chapter. That, too, is wise; for since I am annoyed, I could not write even a reasonably decent lie."[70] The Lie buried in this chapter is this statement that Crowley will Write nothing, because by the time he Writes that he will not Lie he has already Written the Lie, the Break, that separates. One (more) last word, then, as another character, "Bowley," in the story "Ali Sloper": "Certainly, I am never—very seldom—very very seldom—aware of what I am going to write, am writing, have written. I know, for example, roughly, that we have been talking about Truth to-night. But Heaven help me if I should try to reproduce the arguments or apportion the speeches! A great deal of my verse is the mere reflection of my rapture—a rapture, may be, of dissimilar nature."[71]

70. *The Book of Lies*, p. 188.
71. "Ali Sloper," *Konx Om Pax* (reprinted Yogi Publication society, no place of origin/pub. date), p. 50.

The Book of Lies (selections)

This selection of two-thirds of the chapters from *The Book of Lies* amply demonstrates the book's scope. Beyond the interests noted in my introductory essay to this section, *The Book of Lies* addresses Qabalah, Yoga, Sex and the message of *The Book of the Law*. As such, it encapsulates in delightfully playful and cryptic ways each major area of Crowley's thought.

ΚΕΦΑΛΗ Η ΟΥΚ ΕΣΤΙ ΚΕΦΑΛΗ
O!

THE ANTE PRIMAL TRIAD WHICH IS
NOT-GOD
Nothing is.
Nothing becomes.
Nothing is not.

THE FIRST TRIAD WHICH IS GOD
I AM.
I utter The Word.
I hear The Word

THE ABYSS
The Word is broken up.
There is Knowledge.
Knowledge is Relation.
These fragments are Creation.
The broken manifests Light.

THE SECOND TRIAD WHICH IS GOD
GOD the Father and Mother is concealed in Generation.
GOD is concealed in the whirling energy of Nature.
GOD is manifest in gathering: harmony: consideration: the Mirror of the Sun and of the Heart.

THE THIRD TRIAD
Bearing: preparing.
Wavering: flowing: flashing.
Stability: begetting.

278

THE TENTH EMANATION
The world.

1

KEΦAΛH A
THE SABBATH OF THE GOAT

O! the heart of N.O.X. the Night of Pan.
ΠAN: Duality: Energy: Death.
Death: Begetting: the supporters of O!
To beget is to die; to die is to beget.
Cast the Seed into the Field of Night.
Life and Death are two names of A.
Kill thyself.
Neither of these alone is enough.

2

KEΦAΛH B
THE CRY OF THE HAWK

Hoor hath a secret fourfold name: it is Do What
  Thou Wilt.
Four Words: Naught—One—Many—All.
          Thou—Child!
          Thy Name is holy.
          Thy Kingdom is come.
          Thy Will is done.
          Here is the Bread.
          Here is the Blood.
  Bring us through Temptation!
  Deliver us from Good and Evil!
That Mine as Thine be the Crown of the Kingdom,
  even now.
          ABRAHADABRA.
These ten words are four, the Name of the One.

3

ΚΕΦΑΛΗ Γ
THE OYSTER

The Brothers of A ∴ A ∴ are one with the Mother of
the Child.

The Many is as adorable to the One as the One is to
the Many. This is the Love of These; creation-
parturition is the Bliss of the One; coition-
dissolution is the Bliss of the Many.

The All, thus interwoven of These, is Bliss.

Naught is beyond Bliss.

The Man delights in uniting with the Woman; the
woman in parting from the Child.

The Brothers of A ∴ A ∴ are Women: the Aspirants
to A ∴ A ∴ are Men.

5

ΚΕΦΑΛΗ Ε
THE BATTLE OF THE ANTS

That is not which is.

The only Word is Silence.

The only Meaning of that Word is not.

Thoughts are false.

Fatherhood is unity disguised as duality.

Peace implies war.

Power implies war.

Harmony implies war.

Victory implies war.

Glory implies war.

Foundation implies war.

Alas! for the Kingdom wherein all these are at war.

6

ΚΕΦΑΛΗ F
CAVIAR

The Word was uttered: the One exploded into one
  thousand million worlds.
Each world contained a thousand million spheres.
Each sphere contained a thousand million planes.
Each plane contained a thousand million stars.
Each star contained a many thousand million things.
Of these the reasoner took six, and, preening, said:
  This is the One and the All.
These six the Adept harmonised, and said: This is the
  Heart of the One and the All.
These six were destroyed by the Master of the
  Temple; and he spake not.
The Ash thereof was burnt up by the Magus into
  The Word.
Of all this did the Ipsissimus know Nothing.

7

ΚΕΦΑΛΗ Z
THE DINOSAURS

None are They whose number is Six: else were they
  six indeed.
Seven are these Six that live not in the City of the
  Pyramids, under the Night of Pan.
There was Lao-tzu.
There was Siddartha.
There was Krishna
There was Tahuti.
There was Mosheh.
There was Dionysus.
There was Mahmud.
But the Seventh men called PERDURABO; for
  enduring unto The End, at The End was Naught
  to endure.
Amen.

8

ΚΕΦΑΛΗ Η
STEEPED HORSEHAIR

Mind is a disease of semen.
All that a man is or may be is hidden therein.
Bodily functions are parts of the machine; silent,
    unless in dis-ease.
But mind, never at ease, creaketh "I".
This I persisteth not, posteth not through generations,
    changeth momently, finally dead.
Therefore is man only himself when lost to himself
    in The Charioting.

9

ΚΕΦΑΛΗ Θ
THE BRANKS

Being is the Noun; Form is the adjective.
Matter is the Noun; Motion is the Verb.
Wherefore hath Being clothed itself with Form?
Wherefore hath Matter manifested itself in Motion?
Answer not, O silent one! For THERE is no "wherefore",
    no "because".
The name of THAT is not known; the Pronoun
    interprets, that is, misinterprets, It.
Time and Space are Adverbs.
Duality begat the Conjunction.
The Conditioned is Father of the Preposition.
The Article also marketh Division; but the Interjection
    is the sound that endeth in the Silence.
Destroy therefore the Eight Parts of Speech; the
    Ninth is nigh unto Truth.
This also must be destroyed before thou enterest
    into The Silence.
Aum.

10

ΚΕΦΑΛΗ Ι
WINDLESTRAWS

The Abyss of Hallucinations has Law and Reason;
  but in Truth there is no bond between the Toys of
  the Gods.
This Reason and Law is the Bond of the Great Lie.
Truth! Truth! Truth! crieth the Lord of the Abyss
  of Hallucinations.
There is no Silence in that Abyss: for all that men
  call Silence is Its Speech.
This Abyss is also called "Hell", and "The Many".
  Its name is "Consciousness", and "The Universe",
  among men.
But THAT which neither is silent, nor speaks, rejoices
  therein.

11

ΚΕΦΑΛΗ ΙΑ
THE GLOW-WORM

Concerning the Holy Three-in-Naught.
Nuit, Hadit, Ra-Hoor-Khuit, are only to be understood
  by the Master of the Temple.
They are above The Abyss, and contain all contradic-
  tions in themselves.
Below them is a seeming duality of Chaos and
  Babalon; these are called Father and Mother, but
  it is not so. They are called Brother and Sister,
  but it is not so. They are called Husband and
  Wife, but it is not so.
The reflection of All is Pan; the Night of Pan is the
  Annihilation of the All.
Cast down through The Abyss is the Light, the Rosy
  Cross, the rapture of Union that destroys, that is
  The Way. The Rosy Cross is the Ambassador of Pan.
How infinite is the distance from This to That! Yet
  All is Here and Now. Nor is there any There or Then;

for all that is, what is it but a manifestation, that is,
a part, that is, a falsehood, of THAT which is not?
Yet THAT which is not neither is nor is not That
which is!
Identity is perfect; therefore the Law of Identity is
but a lie. For there is no subject, and there is no
predicate; nor is there the contradictory of either
of these things.
Holy, Holy, Holy are these Truths that I utter,
knowing them to be falsehoods, broken mirrors,
troubled waters; hide me, O our Lady, in Thy
Womb! for I may not endure the rapture.
In this utterance of falsehood upon falsehood, whose
contradictories are also false, it seems as if That
which I uttered not were true.
Blessed, unutterably blessed, is this last of the
illusions; let me play the man, and thrust it from
me! Amen.

13

ΚΕΦΑΛΗ ΙΓ
PILGRIM TALK

O thou that settest out upon The Path, false is the
Phantom that thou seekest. When thou hast it
thou shalt know all bitterness, thy teeth fixed in
the Sodom-Apple.
Thus hast thou been lured along That Path, whose
terror else had driven thee far away.
O thou that stridest upon the middle of The Path, no
phantoms mock thee. For the stride's sake thou
stridest.
Thus art thou lured along That Path, whose fascina-
tion else had driven thee far away.
O thou that drawest toward the End of The Path,
effort is no more. Faster and faster dost thou fall;
thy weariness is changed into Ineffable Rest.
For there is no Thou upon That Path: thou hast
become The Way.

14

ΚΕΦΑΛΗ ΙΔ
ONION-PEELINGS

The Universe is the Practical Joke of the General
    at the Expense of the Particular, quoth FRATER
    PERDURABO, and laughed.
But those disciples nearest to him wept, seeing the
    Universal Sorrow.
Those next to them laughed, seeing the Universal
    Joke.
Below these certain disciples wept.
Then certain laughed.
Others next wept.
Others next laughed.
Next others wept.
Next others laughed.
Last came those that wept because they could not
    see the Joke, and those that laughed lest they
    should be thought not to see the Joke, and thought
    it safe to act like FRATER PERDURABO.
But though FRATER PERDURABO laughed
    openly, He also at the same time wept secretly;
    and in Himself He neither laughed nor wept.
Nor did He mean what He said.

15

ΚΕΦΑΛΗ ΙΕ
THE GUN-BARREL

Mighty and erect is this Will of mine, this Pyramid
    of fire whose summit is lost in Heaven. Upon it
    have I burned the corpse of my desires.
Mighty and erect is this $\Phi\alpha\lambda\lambda o\varsigma$ of my Will. The
    seed thereof is That which I have borne within me
    from Eternity; and it is lost within the Body of
    Our Lady of the Stars.
I am not I; I am but an hollow tube to bring down
    Fire from Heaven.
Mighty and marvellous is this Weakness, this
    Heaven which draweth me into Her Womb, this
    Dome which hideth, which absorbeth, Me.
This is The Night wherein I am lost, the Love
    through which I am no longer I.

16

ΚΕΦΑΛΗ ΙΣ
THE STAG-BEETLE

Death implies change and individuality; if thou be
  THAT which hath no person, which is beyond the
  changing, even beyond changelessness, what hast
  thou to do with death?
In birth of individuality is ecstasy; so also is its
  death.
In love the individuality is slain; who loves not love?
Love death therefore, and long eagerly for it.
Die Daily.

17

ΚΕΦΑΛΗ ΙΖ
THE SWAN

There is a Swan whose name is Ecstasy: it wingeth
  from the Deserts of the North; it wingeth through
  the blue; it wingeth over the fields of rice; at its
  coming they push forth the green.
In all the Universe this Swan alone is motionless: it
  seems to move, as the Sun seems to move; such
  is the weakness of our sight.
O fool! criest thou?
Amen. Motion is relative: there is Nothing that is
  still.
Against this Swan I shot an arrow; the white breast
  poured forth blood. Men smote me; then, perceiving
  that I was but a Pure Fool, they let me pass.
Thus and not otherwise I came to the Temple of the
  Graal.

18

ΚΕΦΑΛΗ ΙΗ
DEWDROPS

Verily, love is death, and death is life to come.

Man returneth not again; the stream floweth not
uphill; the old life is no more; there is a new life
that is not his.

Yet that life is of his very essence; it is more He
than all that he calls He.

In the silence of a dewdrop is every tendency of his
soul, and of his mind, and of his body; it is the
Quintessence and the Elixir of his being. Therein
are the forces that made him and his father and his
father's father before him.

This is the Dew of Immortality.

Let this go free, even as It will; though art not its
master, but the vehicle of It.

19

ΚΕΦΑΛΗ ΙΘ
THE LEOPARD AND THE DEER

The spots of the leopard are the sunlight in the
glade; pursue thou the deer stealthily at thy
pleasure.

The dappling of the deer is the sunlight in the glade;
concealed from the leopard do thou feed at thy
pleasure.

Resemble all that surroundeth thee; yet be Thyself
—and take thy pleasure among the living.

This is that which is written—Lurk!—in The Book
of The Law.

21

ΚΕΦΑΛΗ ΚΑ
THE BLIND WEBSTER

It is not necessary to understand; it is enough to
   adore.
The god may be of clay: adore him; he becomes
   GOD.
We ignore what created us; we adore what we create.
   Let us create nothing but GOD!
That which causes us to create is our true father and
   mother; we create in our own image, which is
   theirs.
Let us create therefore without fear; for we can
   create nothing that is not GOD.

22

ΚΕΦΑΛΗ ΚΒ
THE DESPOT

The waiters of the best eating-houses mock the whole
   world; they estimate every client at his proper
   value.
This I know certainly, because they always treat me
   with profound respect. Thus they have flattered
   me into praising them thus publicly.
Yet it is true; and they have this insight because
   they serve, and because they can have no personal
   interest in the affairs of those whom they serve.
An absolute monarch would be absolutely wise and
   good.
But no man is strong enough to have no interest.
   Therefore the best king would be Pure Chance.
It is Pure Chance that rules the Universe; therefore,
   and only therefore, life is good.

23

ΚΕΦΑΛΗ ΚΓ(23)
SKIDOO

What man is at ease in his Inn?
Get out.
Wide is the world and cold.
Get out.
Thou has become an in-itiate.
Get out.
But thou canst not get out by the way thou camest
    in. The Way out is THE WAY.
Get out.
For OUT is Love and Wisdom and Power.
Get OUT.
If thou hast T already, first get UT.
Then get O.
And so at last get OUT.

24

ΚΕΦΑΛΗ ΚΔ
THE HAWK AND THE BLINDWORM

This book would translate Beyond-Reason into the
    words of Reason.
Explain thou snow to them of Andaman.
The slaves of reason call this book Abuse-of-
    Language: they are right.
Language was made for men to eat and drink, make
    love, do barter, die. The wealth of a language consists
    in its Abstracts; the poorest tongues have
    wealth of Concretes.
Therefore have Adepts praised silence; at least it
    does not not mislead as speech does.
Also, Speech is a symptom of Thought.
Yet, silence is but the negative side of Truth; the
    positive side is beyond even silence.
Nevertheless, One True God crieth *hriliu!*
    And the laughter of the Death-rattle is akin.

25

ΚΕΦΑΛΗ ΚΕ
THE STAR RUBY

Facing East, in the centre, draw deep deep deep thy
breath, closing thy mouth with thy right forefinger prest against thy lower lip. Then dashing
down the hand with a great sweep back and out,
expelling forcibly thy breath, cry: ΑΠΟ ΠΑΝΤΟC
ΚΑΚΟΔΑΙΜΟΝΟC.

With the same forefinger touch thy forehead, and
say COI, thy member, and say ΩΦΑΛΛΕ, thy
right shoulder, and say ICXYPOC, thy left
shoulder, and say EYXAPICTOC; then clasp
thine hands, locking the fingers, and cry ΙΑΩ.

Advance to the East. Imagine strongly a Pentagram,
aright, in thy forehead. Drawing the hands to the
eyes, fling it forth, making the sign of Horus, and
roar XAOC. Retire thine hand in the sign of Hoor
pa kraat.

Go round to the North and repeat; but scream
ΒΑΒΑΛΟΝ.

Go round to the West and repeat; but say ΕΡΩC.

Go round to the South and repeat; but bellow
ΨΥΧΗ.

Completing the circle widdershins, retire to the
centre, and raise thy voice in the Paian, with these
words IO ΠΑΝ with the signs of N.O.X.

Extent the arms in the form of a Tau, and say low
but clear: ΠΡΟ ΜΟΥ ΙΥΓΓΕC ΟΠΙCΩ ΜΟΥ
ΤΕΛΕΤΑΡΧΑΙ ΕΠΙ ΔΕΞΙΑ CYNOXEC
ΕΠΑΡΙCΤΕΡΑ ΔΑΙΜΟΝΕC ΦΛΕΓΕΙ ΓΑΡ
ΠΕΡΙ ΜΟΥ Ο ΑCΤΗΡ ΤΩΝ ΠΕΝΤΕ ΚΑΙ ΕΝ
ΤΗΙ CΤΗΛΗΙ Ο ΑCΤΗΡ ΤΩΝ ΕΞ ΕCΤΗΚΕ.

Repeat the Cross Qabalistic, as above, and end as
thou didst begin.

26

ΚΕΦΑΛΗ ΚF
THE ELEPHANT AND THE TORTOISE

The Absolute and the Conditioned together make
  The One Absolute.
The Second, who is the Fourth, the Demiurge, whom
  all nations of Men call The First, is a lie grafted
  upon a lie, a lie multiplied by a lie.
Fourfold is He, the Elephant upon whom the
  Universe is poised: but the carapace of the
  Tortoise supports and covers all.
This Tortoise is sixfold, the Holy Hexagram.
These six and four are ten, 10, the One manifested
  that returns into the Naught unmanifest.
The All-Mighty, the All-Ruler, the All-Knower, the
  All-Father, adored by all men and by me
  abhorred, be thou accursed, be thou abolished, be
  thou annihilated, Amen!

27

ΚΕΦΑΛΗ ΚΖ
THE SORCERER

A Sorcerer by the power of his magick had subdued
  all things to himself.
Would he travel? He could fly through space more
  swiftly than the stars.
Would he eat, drink, and take his pleasure? There
  was none that did not instantly obey his bidding.
In the whole system of ten million times ten million
  spheres upon the two and twenty million planes he
  had his desire.
And with all this he was but himself.
Alas!

28

ΚΕΦΑΛΗ ΚΗ
THE POLE-STAR

Love is all virtue, since the pleasure of love is but
    love, and the pain of love is but love.
Love taketh no heed of that which is not and of that
    which is.
Absence exalteth love, and presence exalteth love.
Love moveth ever from height to height of ecstasy
    and faileth never.
The wings of love droop not with time, nor slacken
    for life or for death.
Love destroyeth self, uniting self with that which is
    not-self, so that Love breedeth All and None in
    One.
Is it not so? . . . No? . . .
Then thou art not lost in love; speak not of love.
Love Alway Yieldeth: Love Alway Hardeneth.
. . . . May be: I write it but to write Her name.

29

ΚΕΦΑΛΗ ΚΘ
THE SOUTHERN CROSS

Love, I love you! Night, night, cover us! Thou art
    night, O my love; and there are no stars but thine
    eyes.
Dark night, sweet night, so warm and yet so fresh,
    so scented yet so holy, cover me, cover me!
Let me be no more! Let me be Thine; let me be
    Thou; let me be neither Thou nor I; let there be
    love in night and night in love.
N. O. X. the night of Pan; and Laylah, the night
    before His threshold!

30

ΚΕΦΑΛΗ Λ
JOHN-A-DREAMS

Dreams are imperfections of sleep; even so is consciousness
the imperfection of waking.
Dreams are impurities in the circulation of the blood;
even so is consciousness a disorder of life.
Dreams are without proportion, without good
sense, without truth; so also is consciousness.
Awake from dream, the truth is known: awake
from waking, the Truth is—The Unknown.

31

ΚΕΦΑΛΗ ΛΑ
THE GAROTTE

IT moves from motion into rest, and rests from rest
into motion. These IT does alway, for time is not.
So that IT does neither of these things. IT does
THAT one thing which we must express by two
things neither of which possesses any rational
meaning.
Yet ITS doing, which is not-doing, is simple and yet
complex, is neither free nor necessary.
For all these ideas express Relation; and IT, com-
prehending all Relation in ITS simplicity, is out of
all Relation even with ITSELF.
All this is true and false; and it is true and false to
say that it is true and false.
Strain forth thine Intelligence, O man, O worthy
one, O chosen of IT, to apprehend the discourse
of THE MASTER; for thus thy reason shall at
last break down, as the fetter is struck from a
slave's throat.

32

ΚΕΦΑΛΗ ΛΒ
THE MOUNTAINEER

Consciousness is a symptom of disease.

All that moves well moves without will.

All skilfulness, all strain, all intention is contrary to
ease.

Practise a thousand times, and it becomes difficult;
a thousand thousand, and it becomes easy; a
thousand thousand times a thousand thousand,
and it is no longer Thou that doeth it, but It that
doeth itself through thee. Not until then is that
which is done well done.

Thus spoke FRATER PERDURABO as he leapt
from rock to rock of the moraine without ever
casting his eyes upon the ground.

34

ΚΕΦΑΛΗ ΛΔ
THE SMOKING DOG

Each act of man is the twist and double of an hare.

Love and Death are the greyhounds that course him.

God bred the hounds and taketh His pleasure in the
sport.

This is the Comedy of Pan, that man should think
he hunteth, while those hounds hunt him.

This is the Tragedy of Man when facing Love and
Death he turns to bay. He is no more hare, but
boar.

There are no other comedies or tragedies.

Cease then to be the mockery of God; in savagery of
love and death live thou and die!

Thus shall His laughter be thrilled through with
Ecstasy.

36

ΚΕΦΑΛΗ ΛΣ
THE STAR SAPPHIRE

Let the Adept be armed with his Magick Rood [and
provided with his Mystic Rose].

In the centre, let him give the L. V. X. signs; or if
he know them, if he will and dare do them, and
can keep silent about them, the signs of N. O. X.
being the signs of Puer, Vir, Puella, Mulier. Omit
the sign I. R.

Then let him advance to the East, and make the
Holy Hexagram, saying: PATER ET MATER
UNUS DEUS ARARITA.

Let him go round to the South, make the Holy
Hexagram, and say: MATER ET FILIUS UNUS
DEUS ARARITA.

Let him go round to the West, make the Holy
Hexagram, and say: FILIUS ET FILIA UNUS
DEUS ARARITA.

Let him go round to the North, make the Holy
Hexagram, and then say: FILIA ET PATER
UNUS DEUS ARARITA.

Let him then return to the Centre, and so to The Centre of
All [making the ROSY CROSS as he may know how]
saying: ARARITA ARARITA ARARITA.

In this the Signs shall be those of Set Triumphant
and of Baphomet. Also shall Set appear in the
Circle. Let him drink of the Sacrament and let him
communicate the same.]

Then let him say: OMNIA IN DUOS: DUO IN
UNUM: UNUS IN NIHIL: HAEC NEC
QUATUOR NEC OMNIA NEC DUO NEC
UNUS NEC NIHIL SUNT.

GLORIA PATRI ET MATRI ET FILIO ET FILIAE ET
SPIRITUI SANCTO EXTERNO ET SPIRITUI SANCTO
INTERNO UT ERAT EST ERIT IN SAECULA SAECULO-
RUM SEX IN UNO PER NOMEN SEPTEM IN UNO
ARARITA. Let him then repeat the signs of L.V.X. but not
the signs of N.O.X.: for it is not he that shall arise in the
Sign of Isis Rejoicing.

38

ΚΕΦΑΛΗ ΛΗ
LAMBSKIN

Cowan, skidoo!
Tyle!
Swear to hele all.
This is the mystery.
Life!
Mind is the traitor.
Slay mind.
Let the corpse of mind lie unburied on the edge of
   the Great Sea!
Death!
This is the mystery.
Tyle!
Cowan, skidoo!

39

ΚΕΦΑΛΗ ΛΘ
THE LOOBY

Only loobies find excellence in these words.
It is thinkable that A is not-A; to reverse this is but
   to revert to the normal.
Yet by forcing the brain to accept propositions of
   which one set is absurdity, the other truism, a
   new function of brain is established.
Vague and mysterious and all indefinite are the
   contents of this new consciousness; yet they are
   somehow vital. By use they become luminous.
Unreason becomes Experience.
This lifts the leaden-footed Soul to the Experience
   of THAT of which Reason is the blasphemy.
But without that Experience these words are the
   Lies of a Looby.
Yet a Looby to thee, and a Booby to me, a Balassius
   Ruby to GOD, may be!

42

ΚΕΦΑΛΗ ΜΒ
DUST-DEVILS

In the Wind of the mind arises the turbulence
    called I.
It breaks; down shower the barren thoughts.
All life is choked.
This desert is the Abyss wherein is the Universe.
    The Stars are but thistles in that waste.
Yet this desert is but one spot accursed in a world of
    bliss.
Now and again Travellers cross the desert; they come
    from the Great Sea, and to the Great Sea they go.
As they go they spill water; one day they will irrigate
    the desert, till it flower.
See! five footprints of a Camel! V. V. V. V. V.

44

ΚΕΦΑΛΗ ΜΔ
THE MASS OF THE PHŒNIX

*The Magician, his breast bare, stands before an altar
    on which are his Burin, Bell, Thurible, and two
    of the Cakes of Light. In the Sign of the Enterer he
    reaches West across the Altar, and cries:*
Hail Ra, that goest in Thy bark
Into the Caverns of the Dark!

*He gives the sign of Silence, and take the Bell, and
    Fire, in his hands.*
East of the Altar see me stand
With Light and Musick in mine hand!

*He strikes Eleven times upon the Bell 3 3 3 — 5 5 5 5 5 —
    3 3 3 and places the Fire in the Thurible.*
I strike the Bell: I light the flame:
I utter the mysterious Name.
                    ABRAHADABRA
He strikes Eleven times upon the Bell.

Now I begin to pray: Thou Child,
Holy Thy name and undefiled!
Thy reign is come: Thy will is done.
Here is the Bread; here is the Blood.
Bring me through midnight to the Sun!
Save me from Evil and from Good!
That Thy one crown of all the Ten
Even now and here be mine. AMEN.

He puts the first Cake on the Fire of the Thurible,
I burn the Incense-cake, proclaim
These adorations of Thy name.

*He makes them as in Liber Legis, and strikes again
Eleven times upon the Bell. With the Burin he then
makes upon his breast the proper sign.*

45

ΚΕΦΑΛΗ ΜΕ
CHINESE MUSIC

"Explain this happening!"
"It must have a 'natural' cause."
"It must have a 'supernatural' cause." } Let
   these two asses be set to grind corn.
May, might, must, should, probably, may be, we
   may safely assume, ought, it is hardly questionable,
   almost certainly—poor hacks! let them be
   turned out to grass!
Proof is only possible in mathematics, and mathematics
   is only a matter of arbitrary conventions.
And yet doubt is a good servant but a bad master; a
   perfect mistress, but a nagging wife.
"White is white" is the lash of the overseer; "white
   is black" is the watchword of the slave. The Master
   takes no heed.
The Chinese cannot help thinking that the octave has
   5 notes.
The more necessary anything appears to my mind,
   the more certain it is that I only assert a limitation.
I slept with Faith, and found a corpse in my arms on
   awaking; I drank and danced all night with Doubt,
   and found her a virgin in the morning.

46

ΚΕΦΑΛΗ ΜΓ
BUTTONS AND ROSETTES

The cause of sorrow is the desire of the One to the
Many, or of the Many to the One. This also is the
cause of joy.

But the desire of one to another is all of sorrow; its
birth is hunger, and its death satiety.

The desire of the moth for the star at least saves him
satiety.

Hunger thou, O man, for the infinite: be insatiable
even for the finite; thus at The End shalt thou
devour the finite, and become the infinite.

Be thou more greedy than the shark, more full of
yearning than the wind among the pines.

The weary pilgrim struggles on; the satiated pilgrim
stops.

The road winds uphill: all law, all nature must be
overcome.

Do this by virtue of THAT in thyself before which
law and nature are but shadows.

50

ΚΕΦΑΛΗ Ν
THE VIGIL OF ST. HUBERT

In the forest God met the Stag-beetle. "Hold! Worship
me!" quoth God. "For I am All-Great, All-
Good, All Wise. . . . The stars are but sparks from
the forges of My smiths. . . ."

"Yea, verily and Amen," said the Stag-beetle, "all
this do I believe, and that devoutly."

"Then why do you not worship Me?"

"Because I am real and you are only imaginary."

But the leaves of the forest rustled with the laughter
of the wind.

Said Wind and Wood: "They neither of them know
anything!"

51

ΚΕΦΑΛΗ ΝΑ
TERRIER-WORK

Doubt. Doubt.
Doubt thyself.
Doubt even if thou doubtest thyself.
Doubt all.
Doubt even if thou doubtest all.
It seems sometimes as if beneath all conscious doubt
    there lay some deepest certainty. O kill it! Slay the
    snake!
The horn of the Doubt-Goat be exalted!
Dive deeper, ever deeper, into the Abyss of Mind,
    until thou unearth the fox THAT. On, hounds!
    Yoicks! Tally-ho! Bring THAT to bay!
Then, wind the Mort!

55

ΚΕΦΑΛΗ ΝΕ
THE DROOPING SUNFLOWER

The One Thought vanished; all my mind was torn to
    rags:—nay! nay! my head was mashed into
    wood pulp, and thereon the Daily Newspaper was
    printed.
Thus wrote I, since my One Love was torn from me.
    I cannot work: I cannot think: I seek distraction
    here: I seek distraction there: but this is all my
    truth, that *I who love have lost; and how may I
    regain?*
I must have money to get to America.
O Mage! Sage! Gauge thy Wage, or in the Page of
    Thine Age is written Rage!
O my darling! We should not have spent Ninety
    Pounds in that Three Weeks in Paris! . . . Slash the
    Breaks on thine arm with a pole-axe!

56

ΚΕΦΑΛΗ ΝϜ
TROUBLE WITH TWINS

Holy, holy, holy, unto Five Hundred and Fifty Five
    times holy be OUR LADY of the STARS!
Holy, holy, holy, unto One Hundred and Fifty Six
    times holy be OUR LADY that rideth upon THE
    BEAST!
Holy, holy, holy, unto the Number of Times
    Necessary and Appropriate be OUR LADY
    Isis in Her Millions-of-Names, All-Mother,
    Genetrix-Meretrix!
Yet holier than all These to me is LAYLAH, night
    and death; for Her do I blaspheme alike the finite
    and The Infinite.
So wrote not FRATER PERDURABO, but the
    Imp Crowley in his Name.
For forgery let him suffer Penal Servitude for Seven
    Years; or at least let him do Pranayama all the
    way home—home? nay! but to the house of the
    harlot whom he loveth not. For it is LAYLAH that
    he loveth ....
And yet who knoweth which is
    Crowley, and which is
FRATER PERDURABO?

61

ΚΕΦΑΛΗ ΞΑ
THE FOOL'S KNOT

O Fool! begetter of both I and Naught, resolve this
    Naught-y Knot!
O! Ay! this I and O—IO!—IAO! For I owe "I"
    aye to Nibbana's Oe.
I Pay—Pé, the dissolution of the House of God—
    for Pé comes after O—after Ayin that triumphs
    over Aleph in Ain, that is O.
OP-us, the Work! the OP-ening of THE EYE!
Thou Naughty Boy, thou openest THE EYE OF
    HORUS to the Blind Eye that weeps! The Up-
    right One in thine Uprightness rejoiceth—Death
    to all Fishes!

63

ΚΕΦΑΛΗ ΞΓ
MARGERY DAW

I love LAYLAH.
I lack LAYLAH.
"Where is the Mystic Grace?" sayst thou?
Who told thee, man, that LAYLAH is not Nuit, and
    I Hadit?
I destroyed all things; they are reborn in other
    shapes.
I gave up all for One; this One hath given up its
    Unity for all?
I wrenched DOG backwards to find GOD; now GOD
    barks.
Think me not fallen because I love LAYLAH, and
    lack LAYLAH.
I am the Master of the Universe; then give me a
    heap of straw in a hut, and LAYLAH naked!
    Amen.

65

ΚΕΦΑΛΗ ΞΕ
SIC TRANSEAT—

"At last I lifted up mine eyes, and beheld; and lo!
    the flames of violet were become as tendrils of
    smoke, as mist at sunset upon the marsh-lands.
"And in the midst of the moon-pool of silver was the
    Lily of white and gold. In this Lily is all honey,
    in this Lily that flowereth at the midnight. In
    this Lily is all perfume; in this Lily is all music.
    And it enfolded me."
Thus the disciples that watched found a dead body
    kneeling at the altar. Amen!

66

ΚΕΦΑΛΗ ΞF
THE PRAYING MANTIS

"Say: God is One." This I obeyed: for a thousand
and one times a night for one thousand nights and
one did I affirm the Unity.
But "night" only means LAYLAH, and Unity and
GOD are not worth even her blemishes.
Al-lah is only sixty-six; but LAYLAH counteth
up to Seven and Seventy.
"Yea! the night shall cover all; the night shall cover
all."

67

ΚΕΦΑΛΗ ΞΖ
SODOM-APPLES

I have bought pleasant trifles, and thus soothed my
lack of LAYLAH.
Light is my wallet, and my heart is also light; and
yet I know that the clouds will gather closer for
the false clearing.
The mirage will fade; then will the desert be thirstier
than before.
O ye who dwell in the Dark Night of the Soul, beware
most of all of every herald of the Dawn!
O ye who dwell in the City of the Pyramids beneath
the Night of PAN, remember that ye shall see no
more light but That of the great fire that shall
consume your dust to ashes!

69

ΚΕΦΑΛΗ ΞΘ
THE WAY TO SUCCEED—AND THE WAY TO SUCK EGGS!

This is the Holy Hexagram.

Plunge from the height, O God, and interlock with Man!

Plunge from the height, O Man, and interlock with Beast!

The Red Triangle is the descending tongue of grace; the Blue Triangle is the ascending tongue of prayer.

This Interchange, the Double Gift of Tongues, the Word of Double Power—ABRAHADABRA!—is the sign of the GREAT WORK, for the GREAT WORK is accomplished in Silence. And behold is not that Word equal to Cheth, that is Cancer, whose Sigil is ♋?

This Work also eats up itself, accomplishes its own end, nourishes the worker, leaves no seed, is perfect in itself.

Little children, love one another!

70

ΚΕΦΑΛΗ Ο
BROOMSTICK-BABBLINGS

FRATER PERDURABO is of the Sanhedrim of the Sabbath, say men; He is the Old Goat himself, say women.

Therefore do all adore him; the more they detest him the more do they adore him.

Ay! let us offer the Obscene Kiss!

Let us seek the Mystery of the Gnarled Oak, and of the Glacier Torrent!

To Him let us offer up our babes! Around Him let us dance in the mad moonlight!

But FRATER PERDURABO is nothing but AN EYE; what eye none knoweth.

Skip, witches! Hop, toads! Take your pleasure!— for the play of the Universe is the pleasure of FRATER PERDURABO.

73

ΚΕΦΑΛΗ ΟΓ
THE DEVIL, THE OSTRICH, AND THE ORPHAN CHILD

Death rides the Camel of Initiation.

Thou humped and stiff-necked one that groanest in
Thine Asana, death will relieve thee!

Bite not, Zelator dear, but bide! Ten days didst
thou go with water in thy belly? Thou shalt go
twenty more with a firebrand at thy rump!

Ay! all thine aspiration is to death: death is the
crown of all thine aspiration. Triple is the cord of
silver moonlight; it shall hang thee, O Holy One,
O Hanged Man, O Camel-Termination-of-the-
third-person-plural for thy multiplicity, thou
Ghost of a Non-Ego!

Could but Thy mother behold thee, O thou UNT!

The Infinite Snake Ananta that surroundeth the
Universe is but the Coffin-Worm!

74

ΚΕΦΑΛΗ ΟΔ
CAREY STREET

When NOTHING became conscious, it made a bad
bargain.

This consciousness acquired individuality: a worse
bargain.

The Hermit asked for love; worst bargain of all.

And now he has let his girl go to America, to have
"success" in "life": blank loss.

Is there no end to this immortal ache

That haunts me, haunts me sleeping or awake?

If I had Laylah, how could I forget

Time, Age, and Death? Insufferable fret!

Were I an hermit, how could I support

The pain of consciousness, the curse of thought?

Even were I THAT, there still were one sore
spot—

The Abyss that stretches between THAT and
NOT.

Still, the first step is not so far away:—

The Mauretania sails on Saturday!

75

ΚΕΦΑΛΗ ΟΕ
PLOVERS' EGGS

Spring beans and strawberries are in: goodbye to the
 oyster!
If I really knew what I wanted, I could give up
 Laylah, or give up everything for Laylah.
But "what I want" varies from hour to hour.
This wavering is the root of all compromise, and so
 of all good sense.
With this gift a man can spend his seventy years in
 peace.
Now is this well or ill?
Emphasise *gift,* then *man,* then *spend,* then *seventy
 years,* and lastly *peace,* and change the intonations
 — each time reverse the meaning!
I would show you how; but—for the moment!
—I prefer to think of Laylah.

76

ΚΕΦΑΛΗ Ο*F*
PHAETON

No.
Yes.
Perhaps.
O!
Eye.
I.
Hi!
Y?
No.
Hail! all ye spavined, gelded, hamstrung horses!
Ye shall surpass the planets in their courses.
How? Not by speed, nor strength, nor power to stay,
But by the Silence that succeeds the Neigh!

79

KEΦAΛH OΘ
THE BAL BULLIER

Some men look into their minds into their memories,
and find naught but pain and shame.
These then proclaim "The Good Law" unto mankind.
These preach renunciation, "virtue", cowardice in
every form.
These whine eternally.
Smug, toothless, hairless Coote, debauch-emasculated
Buddha, come ye to me? I have a trick to
make you silent, O ye foamers-at-the-mouth!
Nature *is* wasteful; but how well She can afford it!
Nature *is* false; but I'm a bit of a liar myself.
Nature *is* useless; but then how beautiful she is!
Nature *is* cruel; but I too am a Sadist.
The game goes on; it may have been too rough for
Buddha, but it's (if anything) too dull for me.
Viens, beau négre! Donne-moi tes lèvres encore!

81

KEΦAΛH ΠA
LOUIS LINGG

I am not an Anarchist in *your* sense of the word:
your brain is too dense for any known explosive
to affect it.
I am not an Anarchist in your sense of the word:
fancy a Policeman let loose on Society!
While there exists the burgess, the hunting man, or
any man with ideals less than Shelley's and self-
discipline less than Loyola's—in short, any man
who falls far short of MYSELF—I am against
Anarchy, and for Feudalism.
Every "emancipator" has enslaved the free.

83

ΚΕΦΑΛΗ ΠΓ
THE BLIND PIG

Many becomes two: two one: one Naught. What
    comes to Naught?
What! shall the Adept give up his hermit life, and
    go eating and drinking and making merry?
Ay! shall he not do so? he knows that the Many is
    Naught; and having Naught, enjoys that Naught
    even in the enjoyment of the Many.
For when Naught becomes Absolute Naught, it
    becomes again the Many.
And this Many and this Naught are identical; they
    are not correlatives or phases of some one deeper
    Absence-of-Idea; they are not aspects of some
    further Light: they are They!
Beware, O my brother, lest this chapter deceive
    thee!

84

ΚΕΦΑΛΗ ΠΔ
THE AVALANCHE

Only through devotion to FRATER PERDURABO
    may this book be understood.
How much more then should He devote Himself to
    AIWASS for the understanding of the Holy Books
    of ΘΕΛΗΜΑ?
Yet must he labour underground eternally. The
    sun is not for him, nor the flowers, nor the voices
    of the birds; for he is past beyond all these. Yea,
    verily, oft-times he is weary; it is well that the
    weight of the Karma of the Infinite is with him.
Therefore is he glad indeed; for he hath finished THE
    WORK; and the reward concerneth him no whit.

89

ΚΕΦΑΛΗ ΠΘ
UNPROFESSIONAL CONDUCT

I am annoyed about the number 89.
I shall avenge myself by writing nothing in this
   chapter.
That, too, is wise; for since I am annoyed, I could
   not write even a reasonably decent lie.

90

ΚΕΦΑΛΗ Ρ
STARLIGHT

Behold! I have lived many years, and I have travelled
   in every land that is under the dominion of the
   Sun, and I have sailed the seas from pole to pole.
Now do I lift up my voice and testify that all is
   vanity on earth, except the love of a good woman,
   and that good woman LAYLAH. And I testify
   that in heaven all is vanity (for I have journeyed
   oft, and sojourned oft, in every heaven), except the
   love of OUR LADY BABALON. And I testify
   that beyond heaven and earth is the love of OUR
   LADY NUIT.
And seeing that I am old and well stricken in years,
   and that my natural forces fail, therefore do I rise
   up in my throne and call upon THE END.
For I am youth eternal and force infinite.
And at THE END is SHE that was LAYLAH, and
   BABALON, and NUIT, being . . .

91

ΚΕΦΑΛΗ ΡΑ
THE HEIKLE

A. M. E. N.

Laughter

An entry from *Little Essays Toward Truth*. Laughter renews, but leaves all unsettled, dissolving in uncertainty, "dancing." (Note: Osiris is the father of Horus in Egyptian mythology. When in paragraph three Crowley mentions "the formula of Osiris," he is saying that the magician accepts the Death of Man—himself—only to be reborn in the Aeon of Horus).

The common defect of all mystical systems previous to that of the Aeon whose Law is Thelema is that there has been no place for Laughter. But the sadness of the mournful Mother and the melancholy of the dying Man are swept into the limbo of the past by the confident smile of the immortal Child.

And there is no Vision more critical in the career of the Adept of Horus than the Universal Joke.

In this Trance he accepts fully the Formula of Osiris, and in the act transcends it; the spear of the Centurion passes harmlessly through his heart, and the sword of the Executioner strikes idly on his neck. He discovers that the Tragedy of which so many centuries have made such case is but a farce for children's pleasure. Punch is knocked down only to get up grinning with his gay "Root-too-too-tit! Here we are again!" Judy, the Beadle, the Hangman and the Devil are merely the companions of his playtime.

So, since (after all) the facts which he thought tragic are real enough, the essence of his solution is that they are not true, as he thought, of himself; they are just one set of phenomena, as interesting and as fatuously impotent to affect him as any other set. His personal grief was due to his passionate insistence on contemplating one insignificant congeries of Events as if it were the sole reality and importance in the infinite mass of Manifestation.

It is thus that the Perception of the Universal Joke leads directly to the Understanding of the Idea of Self as coterminous with the Universe, and at the same time one with it, creator of it, and aloof from it; which Triune State is, as is well known, one of the most

310

necessary stages of Samadhi. (It is the culmination of one of the two most important chapters of the Bhagavadgita.)

There is a further merit in this matter. In the idea of Laughter is inherent that of Cruelty, as has been shewn by many philosophers; and this is doubtless why it has been excluded by the Mystic Schools of Pitymongers from their dull curricula. The only answer is to shrug the shoulders in humorous contempt. For on this rock and no other have all their brave barks foundered one by one amid the ΑΝΛΡΙΘΜΟΝ ΓΕΛΑΣΜΑ of Ocean. Nature is full of cruelty; its highest points of joy and victory are marked by laughter. It is the true physiological explosion and relaxation of a tension which produces it. Notably, such drugs as Cannabis Indica and Anhalonium Lewinii, which do actually "loosen the girders of the soul which give her breathing," cause immediate laughter as one of their most characteristic effects.

Oh the huge wholesome contempt for the limiting self which springs from the sense of Gargantuan disproportion perceived in this Laughter! Truly it slays, with jolliest cannibal revels, that sour black-coated missionary the serious Ego, and plumps him into the pot. Te-he!—the Voice of Civilisation—the Messenger of the White Man's God—bubble, bubble, bubble! Throw in another handful of sage, brother! And the sweet-smelling smoke rises and veils with exquisite shy seduction the shameless bodies of the Stars!

Beyond all this for practical value—since the signpost at every turn of the Path of the Wise reads DANGER—yet springing directly from it by virtue of this very slaying of the Ego, is the use of Laughter as a safeguard of sanity. How easy for the charlatans of oratory to seduce the simple enthusiasm of the soul! What help have we unless we have the wit to know them as ridiculous? There is no limit to the abyss of Idiocy wherein the quacks would plunge us—our only saving reflex is the automatic joke of the Sense of Humour!

Robert Browning was not far from the Kingdom of God when he wrote:

> "Rejoice that man is hurled
> "From change to change unceasingly,
> "His soul's wings never furled";

and there is after all but little salt in the sneer of Juvenal's "Satur est cum dicit Horatius 'Evohe!' " For it is yet to be recorded that any man brought aid or comfort to his fellow by moping.

No, the Universal Joke, though it be not a true Trance, is most assuredly a means of Grace, and often proves the chief ingredient of the Universal Solvent.

Back then to Browning, to the brave last words he wrote while fourscore struck upon the timepiece of his years:

> "Greet the unseen with a cheer!
> "Bid him forward, breast and back as either
>   should be.
> " 'Strive and thrive,' cry 'Speed, fight on, fare ever.
> " 'There as here!' "

Amen.

> "Were the world understood,
> "Ye would see it was good,
> "A dance to a delicate measure!"

Ay! let us end with that most sudden surprising Word of a certain Angel of the Vision and the Voice, who left the Seer lapsed in his solemn Trance with the gay laughing phrase—"But I go dancing!"

The Tables of the Law? Bah! *Solvuntur tabulæ—risu!*

Hymn to Pan

ἔφριξ ἔρωτι περιαρχὴς δ' ἀγεπτόμαγ
ἰὼ ἰὼ Πὰγ Πὰγ
ὦ Πὰν Πυνλιπ ἁλιπλαγχτε, Κυλλανίας Χιουχτύποι
πετραίας ἀπὸ δειράδος φάνηθ', ὦ
θεῶν χοροπόι' ἄναξ

SOPH. AJ.

Thrill with lissome lust of the light,
O man! My man!
Come careering out of the night
Of Pan! Io Pan!
Io Pan! Io Pan! Come over the sea
From Sicily and from Arcady!
Roaming as Bacchus, with fauns and pards
And nymphs and satyrs for thy guards,
On a milk-white ass, come over the sea
To me, to me,
Come with Apollo in bridal dress
(Shepherdess and pythoness)
Come with Artemis, silken shod,
And wash thy white thigh, beautiful God,
In the moon of the woods, on the marble mount,
The dimpled dawn of the amber fount!
Dip the purple of passionate prayer
In the crimson shrine, the scarlet snare,
The soul that startles in eyes of blue
To watch thy wantonness weeping through
The tangled grove, the gnarléd bole
Of the living tree that is spirit and soul
And body and brain—come over the sea,
(Io Pan! Io Pan!)
Devil or god, to me, to me,
My man! my man!
Come with trumpets sounding shrill
Over the hill!

Come with drums low muttering
From the spring!
Come with flute and come with pipe!
Am I not ripe?
I, who wait and writhe and wrestle
With air that hath no boughs to nestle
My body, weary of empty clasp,
Strong as a lion and sharp as an asp—
Come, O come!
I am numb
With the lonely lust of devildom.
Thrust the sword through the galling fetter,
All-devourer, all-begetter;
Give me the sign of the Open Eye,
And the token erect of thorny thigh,
And the word of madness and mystery,
O Pan! Io Pan!
Io Pan! Io Pan Pan! Pan Pan! Pan,
I am a man:
Do as thou wilt, as a great god can,
O Pan! Io Pan!
Io Pan! Io Pan Pan! I am awake
In the grip of the snake.
The eagle slashes with beak and claw;
The gods withdraw:
The great beasts come, Io Pan! I am borne
To death on the horn
Of the Unicorn.
I am Pan! Io Pan! Io Pan Pan! Pan!
I am thy mate, I am thy man,
Goat of thy flock, I am gold, I am god,
Flesh to thy bone, flower to thy rod.
With hoofs of steel I race on the rocks
Through solstice stubborn to equinox.
And I rave; and I rape and I rip and I rend
Everlasting, world without end,
Mannikin, maiden, mænad, man,
In the might of Pan.
Io Pan! Io Pan Pan! Pan! Io Pan!

An Interlude

This detailed Qabalistic analysis of nursery rhymes from *Book 4* is a *Book of Lies* turned on its head. Crowley notes: "Fra. P. said jokingly that everything contained the Truth, if you knew how to find it; and being challenged, proceeded to make good. It is here inserted, not for any value that it may have, but to test the reader. If it is thought to be a joke, the reader is one useless kind of fool; if it is thought that Fra. P. believes that the makers of the rimes had any occult intention, he is another useless kind of fool."

Every nursery rime contains profound magical secrets which are open to every one who has made a study of the correspondences of the Holy Qabalah. To puzzle out an imaginary meaning for this "nonsense" sets one thinking of the Mysteries; one enters into deep contemplation of holy things and God Himself leads the soul to a real illumination. Hence also the necessity of Incarnation: the soul must descend into all falsity in order to attain All-Truth.

For instance:

> Old Mother Hubbard
> Went to her cupboard
> To get her poor dog a bone;
> When she got there,
> The cupboard was bare,
> And so the poor dog had none.

Who is this ancient and venerable mother of whom it is spoken? Verily she is none other than Binah, as is evident in the use of the holy letter H with which her name begins.

Nor is she the sterile Mother Ama—but the fertile Aima; for within her she bears Vau, the son, for the second letter of her name, and R, the penultimate, is the Sun, Tiphareth, the Son.

The other three letters of her name, B, A, and D, are the three paths which join the three supernals.

To what cupboard did she go? Even to the most secret caverns of the Universe. And who is this dog? Is it not the name of God spelt

315

Qabalistically backwards? And what is this bone? This bone is the Wand, the holy Lingam!

The complete interpretation of the rune is now open. This rime is the legend of the murder of Osiris by Typhon.

The limbs of Osiris were scattered in the Nile.

Isis sought them in every corner of the Universe, and she found all except his sacred lingam, which was not found until quite recently (*vide* Fuller, "The Star in the West").

Let us take another example from this rich storehouse of magick lore.

> Little Bo Peep
> She lost her sheep,
> And couldn't tell where to find them.
> Leave them alone!
> And they'll come home,
> Dragging their tails behind them.

"Bo" is the root meaning Light, from which spring such words as Bo-tree, Bodhisattva, and Buddha.

And "Peep" is Apep, the serpent Apophis. This poem therefore contains the same symbol as that in the Egyptian and Hebrew Bibles.

The snake is the serpent of initiation, as the Lamb is the Saviour.

This ancient one, the Wisdom of Eternity, sits in its old anguish awaiting the Redeemer. And this holy verse triumphantly assures us that there is no need for anxiety. The Saviours will come one after the other, at their own good pleasure, and as they may be needed, and drag their tails, that is to say those who follow out their holy commandment, to the ultimate goal.

Again we read:

> Little Miss Muffett
> Sat on a tuffet,
> Eating of curds and whey,
> Up came a big spider,
> And sat down beside her,
> And frightened Miss Muffett away.

Little Miss Muffett unquestionably represents Malkah; for she is unmarried. She is seated upon a "tuffet"; *id est,* she is the unregenerate soul upon Tophet, the pit of hell. And she eats curds and whey, that is, not the pure milk of the mother, but milk which has undergone decomposition.

But who is the spider? Verily herein is a venerable arcanum connoted! Like all insects, the spider represents a demon. But why a spider? Who is this spider "who taketh hold with her hands, and is in King's Palaces"? The name of this spider is Death. It is the fear of death which first makes the soul aware of its forlorn condition.

It would be interesting if tradition had preserved for us Miss Muffett's subsequent adventures.

But we must proceed to consider the interpretation of the following rime:

> Little Jack Horner
> Sat in a corner,
> Eating a Christmas pie.
> He stuck in his thumb,
> And pulled out a plum,
> And said: "What a good boy am I!"

In the interpretation of this remarkable poem there is a difference between two great schools of Adepts.

One holds that Jack is merely a corruption of John, Ion, he who goes—Hermes, the Messenger. The other prefers to take Jack simply and reverently as Iacchus, the spiritual form of Bacchus. But it does not matter very much whether we insist upon the swiftness or the rapture of the Holy Spirit of God; and that it is he of whom it is here spoken is evident, for the name Horner could be applied to none other by even the most casual reader of the Holy Gospels and the works of Congreve. And the context makes this even clearer, for he sits in a corner, that is in the place of Christ, the Corner Stone, eating, that is, enjoying, that which the birth of Christ assures to us. He is the Comforter who replaces the absent Saviour. If there was still any doubt of His identity it would be cleared up by the fact that it is the thumb, which is attributed to the element of Spirit, and not one of the four fingers of the four lesser elements, which he sticks into the pie of the new dispensation. He plucks forth one who is ripe, no doubt to send him forth as a teacher into the world, and rejoices that he is so well carrying out the will of the Father.

Let us pass from this most blessed subject to yet another.

> Tom, Tom, the piper's son,
> Stole a pig and away he run.
> The pig was eat,
> And Tom was beat,
> And Tom went roaring down the street.

This is one of the more exoteric of these rimes. In fact, it is no much better than a sun-myth. Tom is Toum, the God of the Sunset (called the Son of Apollo, the Piper, the maker of music). The only difficulty in the poem concerns the pig; for anyone who has watched an angry sunset in the Tropics upon the sea, will recognize how incomparable a description of that sunset is given in that wonderful last line. Some have thought that the pig refers to the evening sacrifice, others that she is Hathor, the Lady of the West, in her more sensual aspect.

But it is probable that this poem is only the first stanza of an epic. It has all the characteristic marks. Someone said of the Iliad that it did not finish, but merely stopped. This is the same. We may be sure that there is more of this poem. It tells us too much and too little. How came this tragedy of the eating of a merely stolen pig? Unveil this mystery of who "eat" it!

It must be abandoned, then, as at least partially insoluble. Let us consider this poem:

> Hickory, dickory, dock!
> The mouse ran up the clock;
> The clock struck one,
> And the mouse ran down,
> Hickory, dickory, dock!

Here we are on higher ground at once. The clock symbolizes the spinal column, or, if you prefer it, Time, chosen as one of the conditions of normal consciousness. The mouse is the Ego; "*Mus*," a mouse, being only *Sum,* "I am," spelt Qabalistically backwards.

This Ego or Prana or Kundalini force being driven up the spine, the clock strikes one, that is, the duality of consciousness is abolished. And the force again subsides to its original level.

"Hickory, dickory, dock!" is perhaps merely the mantra which was used by the adept who constructed this rime, thereby hoping to fix it in the minds of men; so that they might attain to Samadhi by the same method. Others attribute to it a more profound significance— which it is impossible to go into at this moment, for we must turn to:—

> Humpty Dumpty sat on a wall;
> Humpty Dumpty got a great fall;
> All the king's horses
> And all the king's men
> Couldn't set up Humpty Dumpty again.

This is so simple as hardly to require explanation. Humpty Dumpty is of course the Egg of Spirit, and the wall is the Abyss—his "fall" is therefore the descent of spirit into matter; and it is only too painfully familiar to us that all the king's horses and all his men cannot restore us to the height.

Only The King Himself can do that!

But one hardly dare comment upon a theme which has been so fruitfully treated by Ludovicus Carolus, that most holy illuminated man of God. His masterly treatment of the identity of the three reciprocating paths of Daleth, Teth, and Pe, is one of the most wonderful passages in the Holy Qabalah. His resolution of what we take to be the bond of slavery into very love, the embroidered neckband of honour bestowed upon by the King himself, is one of the most sublime passages in this class of literature.

> Peter, Peter, pumpkin eater,
> Had a wife and couldn't keep her.
> He put her in a peanut shell;
> Then he kept her very well.

This early authentic text of the Hinayana School of Buddhism is much esteemed even to-day by the more cultured and devoted followers of that school.

The pumpkin is of course the symbol of resurrection, as is familiar to all students of the story of Jonah and the gourd.

Peter is therefore the Arahat who has put an end to his series of resurrections. That he is called Peter is a reference to the symbolizing of Arahats as stones in the great wall of the guardians of mankind. His wife is of course (by the usual symbolism) his body, which he could not keep until he put her in a peanut shell, the yellow robe of Bhikkhu.

Buddha said that if any man became an Arahat he must either take the vows of a Bhikkhu that very day, or die, and it is this saying of Buddha's that the unknown poet wished to commemorate.

> Taffy was a Welshman,
> Taffy was a thief;
> Taffy came to my house
> And stole a leg of beef.
> I went to Taffy's house;
> Taffy was in bed.
> I took a carving knife,
> And cut off Taffy's head.

Taffy is merely short for Taphtatharath, the Spirit of Mercury and the God of Welshmen or thieves. "My house" is of course equivalent to "my magick circle." Note that Beth, the letter of Mercury and "The Magus," means "a house."

The beef is a symbol of the Bull, Apis the Redeemer. This is therefore that which is written: "Oh my God, disguise thy glory! Come as a thief, and let us steal away the sacraments!"

In the following verse we find that Taffy is "in bed," owing to the operation of the sacrament. The great task of the Alchemist has been accomplished; the mercury is fixed.

One can then take the Holy Dagger, and separate the Caput Mortuum from the Elixer. Some Alchemists believe that the beef represents that dense physical substance which is imbibed by Mercury for his fixation; but here as always we should prefer the more spiritual interpretation.

> Bye, Baby Bunting!
> Daddy's gone a-hunting.
> He's gone to get a rabbit-skin
> To wrap my Baby Bunting in.

This is a mystical charge to the new-born soul to keep still, to remain steadfast in meditation; for, in *Bye,* Beth is the letter of thought, Yod that of the Hermit. It tells the soul that he Father of All will clothe him about with His own majestical silence. For is not the rabbit he "who lay low and said nuffin' "?

> Pat-a-cake, pat-a-cake, baker's man!
> Bake me a cake as fast as you can!
> Pat it and prick it and mark it with P!
> Bake it in the oven for baby and me!

This rime is usually accompanied (even to-day in the nursery) with a ceremonial clapping of hands—the symbol of Samadhi. Compare what is said on this subject in our comment on the famous "Advent" passage in Thessalonians.

The cake is of course the bread of the sacrament, and it would ill become Frater P. to comment upon the third line—though it may be remarked that even among the Catholics the wafer has always been marked with a phallus or cross.

APPENDIX:
A Magick Chronology

1875	Aleister Crowley born October 12.
1898	Enters the Hermetic Order of the Golden Dawn. Publishes *Aceldama* (his first book of verse) and *White Stains* (his first book of erotica).
1900	Is thrown out of the Golden Dawn London lodge with his spiritual mentor, S. L. MacGregor Mathers. Initiated as a Adeptus Minor in Paris by Mathers.
1901–1903	Travels around the world and studies for an extended time in India with his friend Allan Bennett, a convert to Buddhism.
1903	Breaks ties with Mathers. Travels the Middle East and Far East. Publishes "Berashith" (first essay on magic.)
1904	Receives *The Book of the Law* in Egypt with the aid of his first wife, Rose Kelly (*AL* first published in 1909). Publishes *Snowdrops from a Curate's Garden* (erotica).
1904 – 1907	Publishes his three-volume *Collected Works*.
1907	Founds his magical order, the A ∴ A ∴. Writes his *Holy Books* (published in 1909). Publishes *Konx Om Pax.*
1909	Marches across North Africa with Victor Neuberg, contacting the 30 aethyrs (recorded in *The Vision and the Voice*). Accepts the grade Master of the Temple. Publishes *777.*
1909–1913	Publishes Volume I (ten numbers) of *The Equinox,* the official organ of the A ∴ A ∴ . (Volume II, a "volume of silence," never appeared.)
1910	Performs his "Rites of Eleusis" in public in London. Mathers sues Crowley over publication of Golden Dawn materials in *The Equinox.* Publishes *The Bagh-I-Muattar* (erotica).
1911	Makes magical contact with the spirit Ab-Ul-Diz the Wizard with the mediumistic assistance of Mary d'Este Sturges (Soror Virakam). Ab-Ul-Diz empowers Crowley to write *Book 4* (Part I published in 1911, Part II in 1912).
1912	Meets Theodor Reuss, head of the German O.T.O., and

	founds the British equivalent, the Mysteria Mystica Maxima. Writes the O.T.O. "Gnostic Mass."
	Rewrites the O.T.O. rituals, including "De Arte Magica."
1913	Publishes *The Book of Lies*
1914	Carries out the first of the sex magic workings, the "Paris workings," with his friend Victor Neuberg. Moves to the United States.
1916	Ascends to the grade of Magus.
1918	Meets Leah Hirsig (his first "Scarlet Woman," also known as "the Ape of Thoth"). First magical contact with the wizard Amalantrah. Composes *Liber Aleph* for Frater Achad.
1919	Publishes *The Equinox,* Volume III, Number I in America, and returns to England.
1920	Founds his magical Abbey of Thelema, in Cefalu, Sicily.
1921	Ascends to the highest magical grade possible, Ipsissimus.
1922	Upon Theodor Reuss' resignation, Crowley named Outer Head of the Order O.T.O.
1923	Magical initiate Raoul Loveday dies at the Abbey under mysterious circumstances, and the Italian government expels him. Publishes *The Diary of A Drug Fiend* (novel).
1929	Expelled from France and then Belgium. Again returns to England. Publishes *Magick in Theory and Practice* (Book 4, Part III) and *The Moonchild* (novel).
1930	Banned from presenting a lecture to a poetry group at Oxford. Begins writing his *Confessions,* the first two sections of which were published this year by the Mandrake Press. Exhibits paintings for the first time.
1936	Publishes *The Equinox of the Gods.*
1938	Publishes *Little Essays Toward Truth.*
1939	Publishes *Eight Lectures on Yoga.*
1943	Begins writing the letters that comprise *Magick Without Tears.*
1944	Publishes *The Book of Thoth.*
1947	Dies December 1.

BIBLIOGRAPHY

A complete Aleister Crowley bibliography may always be impossible to compile, particularly in America where so many small presses have taken up the task of publishing and distributing Crowley to occult audiences. Bibliophile Timothy D'Arch Smith has recently published a "Prolegomena" to a British bibliography (in *The Books of the Beast*) in which he throws up his hands at the possibility of cataloguing these "blurred, shoddy, photolithographically etiolated" works. In *The Magical World of Aleister Crowley*, Francis King refers to a guide of "small editions" of Crowley's work, *The Crowley Cross-Index* (published in Britain's *Agape Magazine* in 1976), though Smith says it "has no bibliographical pretensions." For an incomplete but official bibliography of original publication, I refer you to Gerald York's "Bibliography of the Works of Aleister Crowley," at the end of the first edition of John Symonds' *The Great Beast* (later editions, such as the Mayflower paperback, include material from another of Symonds' books, *The Magic of Aleister Crowley*, but omit York's work). The following is a list that includes reprinted editions that I believe are most readily available (some in and some out of print), and in any event are the editions cited. I hope this is a helpful feature of this book. There are many other editions, partial editions, editions with notes, without notes, etc., as well as minor works that I have left uncited.

Recommended Works by Crowley

Atlantis: The Lost Continent. Malton, Canada: Dove Press, approximately 1970.
An entertaining volume on Atlantis, in which Crowley enumerates "the manners and customs, magical rites and opinions of its people, together with a true account of the catastrophe, so called, which ended in its disappearance."

The Banned Lecture: Gilles de Rais. Cincinnati: Black Moon Publishing, 1985.

Pamphlet containing a lecture on Gilles de Rais, suggesting that history's Bluebeard wasn't a figure of horror but a victim of morality. Crowley planned to deliver this lecture to the Oxford University Poetry Society in 1930, but it was "banned" before he gave it.

Book 4. Dallas: Sangreal Foundation, Inc., 1972.

The first two sections of *Magick,* without annotation.

The Book of Changes. Hastings, Great Britain: Metaphysical Research Group, late 1970s (?).

Very unusual verse translation of the *I Ching* which is interesting (as are most of Crowley's translations) for the way it metamorphoses historic materials to conform with Magick.

The Book of Lies. New York: Samuel Weiser, 1978.

My personal favorite of Crowley's works, discussed extensively in the fifth section of this volume. 91 cryptic sermons, reprinted with Crowley's extensive commentary on each.

The Book of Thoth (Egyptian Tarot). New York: U.S. Game Systems, Inc., 1979.

Crowley's last major work contains lengthy explanations of every card in the Tarot and an introductory essay that places his Tarot researches within the body of Qabalah. Originally issued as *The Equinox,* Volume III, Number 5. U.S. Games Systems, Inc. also publishes the Crowley Tarot deck, with original art supervised by Crowley and created by his friend Lady Frieda Harris.

Collected Works of Aleister Crowley, Volumes I., II., III. No place of origin/pub. date: Yogi Publication Society.

Not what the titles say, but rather reprintings of Crowley's earliest volumes of poetry and plays, to 1905. I will leave it to others to decide what verse in these volumes is of interest, but the few essays that appear, including "Berashith: An Essay in Ontology," "Science and Buddhism," "The Initiated Interpretation of Ceremonial Magic" and "Epilogue and Dedication of Volumes I., II., III.—Eleusis" are Crowley's earliest magical and meditational writings.

The Complete Astrological Writings, edited and annotated by John Symonds and Kenneth Grant. London: Tandem Publishing, Ltd., 1976.

"A Treatise on Astrology: Liber 536," written in America in 1917–1918 with the astrologer Evangeline Evans, and not published in his lifetime. This edition includes two additional, brief works.

The Confessions of Aleister Crowley, edited and annotated by John

Symonds and Kenneth Grant. New York: Hill and Wang, 1970 (republished in hardcover by Samuel Weiser, and in paperback by Bantam Books).

Crowley's life story up to the mid 1920s, only the first two of six parts of which were published in his lifetime. Alternately trivial and philosophical, exhausting rather than exhaustive, containing whatever came into his head at the time of its dictation. Extremely idiosyncratic; for example, the first chapters are told in the third person, because, he says, as a child he did not yet have a sense of Self.

Diary of a Drug Fiend. New York: Samuel Weiser, 1970.

Crowley's first published novel, about the addiction problems faced by a young, hedonistic couple.

Eight Lectures on Yoga. Phoenix: Falcon Press, 1985.

A reworking of the ideas in Magick, Section 1, in the form of chatty lectures delivered in the late 1930s. Contains the analysis of his important dream of the SunSponge, and a final lecture on why Crowley would side with Magick over Yoga. Originally issued as *The Equinox,* Volume III, Number 4.

The Equinox, Volume I, Numbers 1–10, and *The Equinox, Volume III, Number I.* New York: Samuel Weiser, 1972.

10 large volumes not readily available, originally issued as journals in England during the years 1909–1913, and (for Volume III, Number I—the "Blue" *Equinox*) in Detroit in 1919. These volumes contain a number of magical texts and non-magical reviews written by Crowley (sometimes in huge "supplements"), as well as the writings of others (for example, a huge, serial survey of Crowley's early life, partially written by Crowley, known as "The Temple of Solomon the King.") Though the volumes now seem terribly padded, some of Crowley's major works first appeared in *The Equinox,* including *The Book of the Law, The Vision and the Voice,* "Energized Enthusiasm," "The Gnostic Mass," "De Lege Libellum," "The Psychology of Hashish," many of the holy books, and a number of other interesting short works. Also the Qabalistic dictionary "Sepher Sephiroth" and his commentary to Madam Blavatsky's *The Voice of the Silence.* Volume II of *The Equinox* never appeared. (It is the silent *Equinox.*) Later Numbers of Volume III have been brought out intermittently by the O.T.O., Numbers 6–9 since Crowley's death. These have all been and have single volumes of unpublished work by Crowley, and most are listed elsewhere in this bibliography.

The Equinox, Volume III, Number 10. New York: Thelema Publications, 1986.

This *Equinox* is, according to the O.T.O., an "ancestor worship" volume, collecting a number of their founding documents (charters, manifestos, etc.) by Crowley and others. The material is of varied quality; the Crowley writings consists of a number of minor "books" as well as *The Book of the Law,* "De Lege Lebellum," a revised "Gnostic Mass," and an excerpt from *The Confessions.* The entire volume characteristically omits any mention of sexual Magick.

The Equinox of the Gods. New York: Gordon Press, 1974.

The story of *The Book of the Law,* told in infinite detail, with unbelievable scrutiny. A fascinating volume. Originally issued as *The Equinox,* Volume III, Number 3.

Gems from the Equinox, edited by Israel Regardie. St. Paul: Llewellyn Publications, 1974.

Despite Dr. Regardie's strange decision to include 250 pages of book reviews in this volume and thus exclude some magical pieces (even though the book claims to collect "All the Magical Writings" from *The Equinox),* this is a solid and generous selection.

The Holy Books of Thelema. York Beach, Maine: Samuel Weiser, 1983.

A well-organized book containing a number of important, often reprinted Crowley texts such as "Liber Liberi vel Lapidis Lazuli," "Liber Cordis Cincti Serpente" and "Liber Trigrammaton." Each of these books, according to Crowley, was divinely inspired. Many of these poetic works rapturously explore aspects of distance and union—the Great Work. Includes an Appendix that lists all Thelemic literature and a manuscript copy of *The Book of the Law.* Issued as *The Equinox,* Volume III, Number 9.

The Holy Books. Dallas: Sangreal Foundation, Inc., 1972.

Because of an error by Israel Regardie, this volume is composed of only three of the holy books, though admittedly they are among the most interesting: "Liber Liberi," "Liber Cordis Cincti Serpente," and "Liber Ararita."

Konx Om Pax. No place of origin/pub. date: Yogi Publication Society.

Four short essays that show off Crowley's great wit, and an introduction. The best two are "The Wake World," a typically "scandalous," fairy tale version of the Great Work, told by a little girl; and "Thein Tao," a fable concerning the Middle Path of Eastern religious masters.

The Law Is for All. Phoenix: Falcon Press, 1982.

The Book of the Law, along with Crowley's original *Equinox* Commentary, and all the Commentaries included by Crowley under the title "Extenuation," assembled by Israel Regardie. A fine book, well presented, deserving a great deal of study (the short *Liber AL* is here subjected to nearly 250 pages of Qabalistic scrutiny). Includes "Liber Trigrammaton" and an almost unreadable replication of *AL*'s original manuscript.

Liber AL: The Book of the Law. Berkeley: O.T.O., 1982.

A widely distributed, 15–cent version of *Liber AL*, though there are many others (with fine shades of difference) before and since. Transmitted to him in 1904 by the alien intelligence Aiwass, Crowley considered it the crucial book of prophecy and instruction for mankind. *AL* is also included in *The Equinox of the Gods, The Holy Books of Thelema* and *The Law is For All.*

Liber Aleph vel CXI: The Book of Wisdom or Folly. Seattle: Aeon Press, 1985.

An often-reprinted "epistle" directed to Crowley's "magical child." Archaic, pretentious and unstructured (the text consists of 120 pages of single paragraphs), *Liber Aleph* nevertheless contains a fair number of important statements on every branch of Magick. Originally published as *The Equinox,* Volume III, Number 6.

Liber XXI: Khing Kang King, The Classic of Purity. Kings Beach, California: Thelema Publications, 1974.

A typically idiosyncratic verse translation of Taoist poetry.

Little Essays Toward Truth. Malton, Canada: Dove Press, approximately 1970.

A short, serious book from the late 1930's, covering familiar territory from new perspectives, including individual essays on the major trance states: "Sorrow," "Wonder," "Beatitude," "Indifference."

The Magical Diaries of . . . Aleister Crowley, edited by Stephen Skinner. York Beach, Maine: Samuel Weiser, Inc, 1979.

Disjointed revelations from a year of heavy heroin use, and the record of his attempt to kick his habit.

The Magical Record of the Beast 666: The Journals of Aleister Crowley, edited and annotated by John Symonds and Kenneth Grant. Quebec: Next Step Publications, 1972.

Another truly interesting, though necessarily rambling account of day-to-day sex activities and philosophical ideas, this volume for the years 1914–1918 and 1919–1920.

Magick, edited and annotated by John Symonds and Kenneth Grant.

New York: Samuel Weiser, Inc., 1974.

Written over many years, *Magick* (parts I, II, and III of *Book 4*) is often considered Crowley's most important (and certainly necessary) work. Section I is on yoga, section II on the workings of ceremonial magic, and section III a sprawling, sometimes only tangentially related series of essays on the many issues, from Qabalah to Pacts with the Devil. At the end of Section III Crowley includes a large number of texts for magical rites. Section IV, Crowley's ultimate commentary on *The Book of the Law,* was never written.

Magick in Theory and Practice. New York: Dover Publications, Inc., 1976.

The third section of *Magick,* with the appendices but without annotation.

Magick Without Tears, edited by Israel Regardie. St. Paul: Llewellyn Publications, 1973 (republished by Falcon Press).

Letters written late in life—in the 1940s—to a prospective student. Extremely wide ranging, lively, funny, and sharp. Though each of the ninety letters is short, his rethinking of key concepts is in most cases more nuanced than in earlier works. A crucial text.

The Moonchild, edited and annotated by John Symonds and Kenneth Grant. London: Sphere Books, 1972.

Also known as *The Butterfly Net,* this is Crowley's second published novel, and is about the conjuration of a magical child.

The Paris Working. St. Albans: Sothis Magazine, 1976.

The published results of Crowley's most famous Sex Magick experiments include a number of lucid magical ideas. *The Paris Working* is very difficult to come by (it is published only in a *very* limited edition). Symonds' *The Magic of Aleister Crowley* and King's *The Magical World of Aleister Crowley* include material on these workings and *The Book of Thoth* excerpts some short texts from it.

Roll Away the Stone, edited by Israel Regardie. St. Paul: Llewellyn Publications, 1968.

This book includes Crowley's "The Psychology of Hashish," his translations of Baudelaire's "Poem of Hashish," and other writings on drugs that appeared in the first few issues of *The Equinox.*

The Scented Garden of Abdullah the Satirist of Shiraz, or *The Bagh-I-Muattar.* No place of origin, listing of publisher, or pub. date.

A tremendously good-humored, robust homosexual parody of the classic heterosexual sex manual *The Perfumed Garden.* The book alternates between poetry and prose, and is one long paean to the beauty of young bottoms.

The Scrutinies of Simon Iff. Chicago: Teitan Press, 1987.

An excellent collection of six occult-detective stories, featuring thinly veiled, fictionalized encounters from Crowley's life. Very clever, very funny, and a beautiful work, which was previously unavailable in book form. Teitan Press is the home of Crowley scholar Martin P. Starr. This book and *Snowdrops from a Curate's Garden* both benefit from knowledgeable historical introductions and carefully annotated texts.

The Secret Rituals of the O.T.O., edited and annotated by Francis King. New York: Samuel Weiser, 1973.

Contains four Sex Magick instructions written for the O.T.O. by Crowley using the title Baphomet, as well as other O.T.O. ritual material for the organization's first six grades. This volume doesn't include the final Sex Magick instruction by Crowley, "De Arte Magica," the essay which tries to "explain" his essential text of Sex Magick, "The Book of the Unveiling of Sangraal."

777 and Other Qabalistic Writings. New York: Samuel Weiser, 1977.

This revision of Crowley's original *777* is an unbelievably large group of tables that lists correspondences between letters, gods, plants, colors, magical weapons, etc. etc., as well as brief essays on the magical alphabet, Qabalah, and numbers and symbols. The edition includes two other long works: "Gematria," Crowley's *Equinox* essay on the Qabalah, and "Sepher Sephiroth," a "dictionary" of word correspondences from *The Equinox,* begun by Crowley's friend Allan Bennett and completed by Crowley. An edition of *777* (Hastings: Metaphysical Research Group, 1977) without "Gematria" and "Sepher Sephiroth" is also available.

Snowdrops from a Curate's Garden. Chicago: Teitan Press, 1986.

The first-class reprinting of a Crowley erotic text more rare and thus more legendary than either *White Stains* or *The Scented Garden.* It lives up to its billing, particularly in "The Nameless Novel," a shamelessly pornographic work written as an "entertainment" for his wife that seemingly seeks to outdo every erotic fiction ever written. Written in 1904, at the time of the transmission of *The Book of the Law.*

The Soul of the Desert. Kings Beach, California: Thelema Publications, 1974.

A very short prose-poem on the place of nomadic wandering in the search for destiny, written in the desert in 1914.

Tao Teh King, edited by Stephen Skinner. New York: Samuel Weiser, 1976.

Translation of and commentary on Lao Tzu's Taoist classic.

The Vision and the Voice, annoted by Israel Regardie. Dallas: Sangreal
Foundation, Inc., 1972.
Originally included in *The Equinox,* Volume I, Supplement to Number
5, this edition includes a number of Crowley's notes and Dr.
Regardie's explanations (often, unfortunately, mixed together). The
book is the extremely complex and arcane record of Crowley's
Enochian magic evocations in Mexico in 1909, using his companion
Victor Neuburg as a scribe. The apocalyptic evocations—30 in
all—sequentially describe the Great Work of Qabalism.
White Stains. No place of origin, listing of publisher, or pub. date.
Unmarked "pirate" editions of *White Stains*—poorly reproducing the
1898 original—are all that are currently available. This "scandalous"
volume of homosexual poetry examines the perverse imagination, à
la Krafft-Ebing's *Psychopathia Sexualis.*
The Works of Aleister Crowley, Volume 1. Keighley, Great Britain:
Kadath Press, 1986.
A misnomer, this short pamphlet contains both "Liber Agape" (or
"The Book of the Unveiling of Sangraal") and "De Arte Magica,"
along with Crowley's annotations and noted by editor Ray Sherwin.
("De Arte Magica" is also included in *Crowley on Christ,* London:
C. W. Daniel, Ltd., 1974.)

Recommended Works by Others

I could make many recommendations, but I have limited myself to
listing only a few works here, not believing that they shed any
necessary light on Aleister Crowley. In the case of magical writings
from before or during his era, the ideas they contain are extended/
subverted by Crowley, their conceptual formations continually under-
mined. In the case of later works on Crowleyan and Golden Dawn
Magick magic, no one, to my mind, has written yet a book that does
justice to the transformative vision of the master. His best known
commentators and student-explicators each suffer from perspective:
pro-Magick or anti-Magick, Humanist or Devil. I have ignored the inept,
such as Louis Culling (*A Manual of Sex Magick*), and the most
hysterical, particularly Daniel Mannix (*The Beast*), which threaten to
drain Crowley of interest completely.

Grant, Kenneth, *Aleister Crowley & The Hidden God.* New York: Samuel Weiser, 1974; and *Cults of the Shadow.* New York: Samuel Weiser, 1976.

Kenneth Grant is in a class by himself. He is an obsessive scholar with a fantastic range of knowledge (the degree of Qabalistic interpretation in which he engages is nothing short of astonishing, sometimes making Crowley seem lazy). He has been a controversial leader within the O.T.O. and over the years has written a series of remarkable works that turn traditional thinking about Crowley and modern occultism on its head, attempting to restore a "left hand path" of magic distinct from black magic. While extremely interesting, he treats Magick as if it's signed, sealed and delivered—not open to the kind of continuing skepticism that was Crowley's stock in trade. The first book listed is a rethinking of the project of Sex Magick, while the second is a broader survey of magic and occultists, with two chapters on Crowley, and one on Crowley's "magical child," Frater Achad. In more recent books Grant more intently develops his own system of magic rather than explicating that of others.

Howe, Ellic, *The Magicians of the Golden Dawn.* New York: Samuel Weiser, 1978.

The "standard," documentary history on the Golden Dawn, good as histories go and containing many references to Crowley. Howe can be supplemented by Francis King's *Ritual Magic in England (1887 to the Present Day)* and the excellent *The Golden Dawn—Twilight of the Magicians* (on the Order's later history, and therefore less directly related to Crowley), by R. A. Gilbert.

Jones, Charles Stanfield (Frater Achad), *Liber 31.* San Francisco: Level Press, 1974.

Crowley considered this work, written in 1918 by his "magical child" in the form of a diary, to be of supreme importance in (not) interpreting *The Book of the Law.* This edition includes two additional short works on *The Book of the Law.* Jones wrote many other works, including a book of *31 Hymns to the Star Goddess* (poetry related to *Liber AL*) and a book that Crowley despised in which Jones turns the Tree of Life upside down in order to interpret it.

King, Francis, *The Magical World of Aleister Crowley.* New York: Coward, McCann & Geoghegan, Inc., 1978.

King doesn't grandstand like Symonds and Regardie, but then he didn't know Crowley. This is a reasonable, concise, well-written work, freshly researched in parts—maybe the best single volume on his life. It mixes biography and Crowleyan theory in equal measure. King's materials on Crowley from his other books—*Ritual Magic in England (1887 to the Present Day)* and *Sexuality, Magic and Perversion*—are included, nearly word for word in the latter case.

Levi, Eliphas, *Transcendental Magic,* translated by A. E. Waite. New York: Samuel Weiser, 1970; and *The Key of the Mysteries,* translated by Aleister Crowley. New York: Samuel Weiser, 1970.

The French magician Eliphas Levi lived in the 19th century, and Crowley claimed to be his reincarnation. These two books tend to overlap, but together they include a number of important ideas about magic, including its relationship to Writing. Crowley considered *The Key of the Mysteries* (which is included as part of *The Equinox*) to be the supreme work written by a magician, in part for its flamboyant and witty style.

Mathers, S. L. MacGregor, and others, edited by Francis King, *Astral Projection, Ritual Magic, and Alchemy.* Rochester, Vermont: Destiny Books, 1987.

Mathers was one of the founders of the Golden Dawn, an early ally and a later enemy to Crowley. This volume attempts to bring together all Golden Dawn papers and materials not included in either Israel Regardie's *The Golden Dawn* or R. G. Torrens' *The Golden Dawn— Its Inner Teachings.* Another volume containing "unknown" writings has recently been edited and published by R. A. Gilbert as *The Sorcerer and His Apprentice.*

Mathers, S. L. MacGregor, translator, *The Book of the Sacred Magic of Abramelin the Mage.* New York: Dover Publications, Inc., 1975.

A 15th century treatise on ceremonial magic, with an introduction by Mathers, closely studied by Crowley. (Mathers also translated the ancient grimoire *The Key of Solomon the King,* which explains the art of the magician).

Mathers, S. L. MacGregor, translator, *The Kaballah Unveiled.* New York: Samuel Weiser, 1968.

This is an English translation of Baron Knorr von Rosenroth's 17th century Latin translation (*Kabbala Denudata*) of three books of the Zohar—the most important treatise on the Qabalah, assembled by various mystics between the 2nd and 13th centuries, A. D. Mather's translation includes his lengthy introduction (partially folded into Crowley's "Gematria" essay) and (particularly in the first book) Rosenroth's copious notes.

Regardie, Dr. Israel, *The Eye in the Triangle.* Phoenix: Falcon Press, 1970.

Dr. Regardie, who knew Crowley late in Crowley's life and who subsequently developed a virtual industry out of Crowley's work, calls this volume "an interpretation of Aleister Crowley." It seems to be a refutation of the work of John Symonds and, as such, is persuasive that Crowley's Great Work was serious and intellectually defensible. Nevertheless, I believe that Dr. Regardie's intense humanism tends to blind him to Crowley's paradoxical ways, and that the theses of the book are rather simplistic. His repetitive style doesn't help.

Regardie, Dr. Israel, *The Golden Dawn, Fourth Edition.* St. Paul: Llewellyn Publications, 1971.

The best work on the Golden Dawn (though they have their limits), these four volumes on its teachings are now issued under one cover. Dr. Regardie's organizing principles in these 1150 pages are mysterious, to say the least. Also mysterious is that this does not purport to be a historic group of documents written by the leaders of the Golden Dawn (there are, according to Francis King, edits and splits in some texts, and no attempt is made to ascribe authorship) nor Regardie's own work. His 100 page introduction is typically unfocused. Regardie is also responsible for a number of other studies of the Golden Dawn and its teachings, all of which are secondary to my interests here. These include, among others, *The Complete Golden Dawn System of Magic* (as large as *The Golden Dawn,* and repeating much, but focused on practical workings), *What You Should Know About the Golden Dawn* (a late, minor work), *The Garden of Pomegranates* (on the Golden Dawn Qabalah), *The Tree of Life* (on Golden Dawn/Crowleyan magic, including a chapter on sexual magic), *My Rosicrucian Adventure* (memoirs on the Order), and an introduction to P. R. Stephenson's *The Legend of Aleister Crowley* (a marginal "biography" told through newspaper clippings).

Suster, Gerald, *The Legacy of the Beast.* York Beach, Maine: Samuel Weiser, 1989.

This recent volume is an attempt to give Aleister Crowley his intellectual due, and is marred only by its relatively simplistic understanding of Yoga, Taoism, Qabalism, and the like. Suster is a sympathetic reader, but not one capable of seeing nuances in Crowley's work.

Symonds, John, *The Great Beast*. London: Rider, 1951; and *The Magic of Aleister Crowley*. London: Muller, 1958.
(Updated and combined to form *The Great Beast*. London: MacDonald & Co., Ltd., 1971. Revised to *The Great Beast*. London: Mayflower, 1973)
Two essential though relatively unflattering works by Crowley's literary executor. The first is Symonds' attempt at full biography, while the second derives its punch from a close examining of Crowley's private records of his Sex Magick workings. The books are valuable for information and quotation of private papers rather than for Symonds' rather limited point of view. His collaborator in the editing of Crowley's works, Kenneth Grant, put it best in his clipped introduction to Crowley's *The Confessions:* "It is reasonably clear ... that John Symonds does not accept the Law of Thelema."

Torrens, R. G., *The Golden Dawn—Its Inner Teachings*. London: Neville Spearman, Ltd., 1969.
A book that seems very orderly—divided into 48 topical chapters—but that often loses its best ideas in a welter of information and, to my mind, relies too much on the less interesting but concurrent teachings of Theosophy. Still, this is a one-of-a-kind book; each chapter ends with a list of sources, 19th and early 20th century treatises, many of which are hard to find.

Westcott, Dr. William Wynn, *An Introduction to the Study of the Kabalah*. Hastings, England: Metaphysical Research Group, 1978.
A brief, easily comprehensible overview of the history and ideas of the Qabalah, presented originally in 1888 by this co-founder of the Golden Dawn as a series of lectures. Crowley recommends it in "Gematria." Includes a translation of the most ancient Qabalistic text, "Sepher Yetzirah."

Wilson, Colin, *Aleister Crowley, The Nature of the Beast*. Wellingborough, Northamptonshire: Aquarian Press, 1987.
Included as a "must avoid," this book is a revision of the famed Wilson's earlier essay on Crowley in his guidebook to *The Occult*. It begins with a chapter that breathlessly relates Wilson's real-life discovery that, yes, "spirits" do exist, and concludes that Crowley wasted most of his life and that he should have been born during the era of Manson and the Sex Pistols. Probably the *laziest* full-length work on Crowley ever—including Mannix's *The Beast,* which at least was stupid fun. Wilson should be embarrassed.

Works Recommended by Crowley

The following is Crowley's recommended list of nonfiction and fiction works for the serious student to read, published originally as an appendix to *Magick in Theory and Practice*.

SECTION 1—Books for Serious Study:

The Equinox. The standard Work of Reference in all occult matters. The Encyclopœdia of Initiation.

Collected Works of A. Crowley. These works contain many mystical and magical secrets, both stated clearly in prose, and woven into the Robe of sublimest poesy.

The Yi King. (S.B.E. Series, Oxford University Press.) The "Classic of Changes"; gives the initiated Chinese system of Magick.

The Tao Teh King. (S.B.E. Series.) Gives the initiated Chinese system of Mysticism.

Tannhäuser, by A. Crowley. An allegorical drama concerning the Progress of the Soul; the Tannhäuser story slightly remodelled.

The Upanishads. (S.B.E. Series.) The Classical Basis of Vedantism, the best-known form of Hindu Mysticism.

The Bhagavad-Gita. A dialogue in which Krishna, the Hindu "Christ", expounds a system of Attainment.

The Voice of the Silence, by H. P. Blavatsky, with an elaborate commentary by Frater O. M.

The Goetia. The most intelligible of the medieval rituals of Evocation. Contains also the favorite Invocation of the Master Therion.

The Shiva Sanhita. A famous Hindu treatise on certain physical practices.

The Hathayoga Pradipika. Similar to The Shiva Sanhita.

Erdmann's "History of Philosophy". A compendious account of philosophy from the earliest times. Most valuable as a general education of the mind.

The Spiritual Guide of Molinos. A simple manual of Christian mysticism.

The Star of the West. (Captain Fuller.) An introduction to the study of the Works of Aleister Crowley.

The Dhammapada. (S.B.E. Series, Oxford University Press.) The best of the Buddhist classics.

The Questions of King Milinda. (S.B.E. Series.) Technical points of Buddhist dogma, illustrated by dialogues.

Varieties of Religious Experience. (James.) Valuable as showing the uniformity of mystical attainment.

Kabbala Denudata, von Rosenroth: also the Kabbalah Unveiled, by S. L. Mathers. The text of the **Kabalah,** with commentary. A good elementary introduction to the subject.

Konx om Pax. Four invaluable treatises and a preface on Mysticism and Magick.

The Pistis Sophia. An admirable introduction to the study of Gnosticism.

The Oracles of Zoroaster. An invaluable collection of precepts mystical and magical.

The Dream of Scipio, by Cicero. Excellent for its Vision and its Philosophy.

The Golden Verses of Pythagoras, by Fabre d'Olivet. An interesting study of the exoteric doctrines of this Master.

The Divine Pymander, by Hermes Trismegistus. Invaluable as bearing on the Gnostic Philosophy.

The Secret Symbols of the Rosicrucians, reprint of Franz Hartmann. An invaluable compendium.

Scrutinium Chymicum, by Michael Maier. One of the best treatises on alchemy.

Science and the Infinite, by Sidney Klein. One of the best essays written in recent years.

Two Essays on the Worship of Priapus, by Richard Payne Knight. Invaluable to all students.

The Golden Bough, by J. G. Frazer. The Text-Book of Folk Lore. Invaluable to all students.

The Age of Reason, by Thomas Paine. Excellent, though elementary, as a corrective to superstition.

Rivers of Life, by General Forlong. An invaluable text-book of old systems of initiation.

Three Dialogues, by Bishop Berkeley. The Classic of subjective idealism.

Essays of David Hume. The Classic of Academic Scepticism.

First Principles, by Herbert Spencer. The Classic of Agnosticism.

Prolegomena, by Emanuel Kant. The best introduction to Metaphysics.

The Canon. The best text-book of Applied Qabalah.

The Fourth Dimension, by H. Hinton. The text-book on this subject.

The Essays of Thomas Henry Huxley. Masterpieces of philosophy, as of prose.

The object of this course of reading is to familiarize the student with all that has been said by the Great Masters in every time and country. He should make a critical examination of them; not so much with the idea of discovering where truth lies, for he cannot do this except by virture of his own spiritual experience, but rather to discover the essential harmony in those varied works. He should be on his guard against partisanship with a favourite author. He should familiarize himself thoroughly with the method of mental equilibrium, endeavouring to contradict any statement soever, although it may be apparently axiomatic.

The general object of this course, besides that already stated, is to assure sound education in occult matters, so that when spiritual illumination comes it may find a well-built temple. Where the mind is strongly biased towards any special theory, the result of an illumination is often to inflame that portion of the mind which is thus overdeveloped, with the result that the aspirant, instead of becoming an Adept, becomes a bigot and fanatic.

The A ∴ A ∴ does not offer examination in this course, but recommends these books as the foundation of a library.

SECTION 2.—Other books, principally fiction, of a generally suggestive and helpful kind:

Zanoni, by Sir Edward Bulwer Lytton. Valuable for its facts and suggestions about Mysticism.

A Strange Story, by Sir Edward Bulwer Lytton. Valuable for its facts and suggestions about Magick.

The Blossom and the Fruit, by Mabel Collins. Valuable for its account of the Path.

Petronius Arbiter. Valuable for those who have wit to understand it.

The Golden Ass, by Apuleius. Valuable for those who have wit to understand it.

Le Comte de Gabalis. Valuable for its hints of those things which it mocks.

The Rape of the Lock, by Alexander Pope. Valuable for its account of elementals.

Undine, by de la Motte Fouqué. Valuable as an account of elementals.

Black Magic, by Marjorie Bowen. An intensely interesting story of sorcery.

La Peau de Chagrin, by Honoré de Balzac. A magnificent magical allegory.

Number Nineteen, by Edgar Jepson. An excellent tale of modern magic.

Dracula, by Bram Stoker. Valuable for its account of legends concerning vampires.

Scientific Romances, by H. Hinton. Valuable as an introduction to the study of the Fourth Dimension.

Alice in Wonderland, by Lewis Carroll. Valuable to those who understand the Qabalah.

Alice Through the Looking Glass, by Lewis Carroll. Valuable to those who understand the Qabalah.

The Hunting of the Snark, by Lewis Carroll. Valuable to those who understand the Qabalah.

The Arabian Nights, translated by either Sir Richard Burton or John Payne. Valuable as a storehouse of oriental magick-lore.

Morte d'Arthur, by Sir Thomas Mallory. Valuable as a storehouse of occidental magick-lore.

The Works of François Rabelais. Invaluable for Wisdom.

The Kasidah, by Sir Richard Burton. Valuable as a summary of philosophy.

The Song Celestial, by Sir Edwin Arnold. "The Bhagavad-Gita" in verse.

The Light of Asia, by Sir Edwin Arnold. An account of the attainment of Gotama Buddha.

The Rosicrucians, by Hargrave Jennings. Valuable to those who can read between the lines.

The Real History of the Rosicrucians, by A. E. Waite. A good vulgar piece of journalism on the subject.

The Works of Arthur Machen. Most of these stories are of great magical interest.

The Writings of William O'Neill (Blake). Invaluable to all students.

The Shaving of Shagpat, by George Meredith. An excellent allegory.

Lilith, by George MacDonald. A good introduction to the Astral.

Là-Bas, by J. K. Huysmans. An account of the extravagances caused by the Sin-complex.

The Lore of Proserpine, by Maurice Hewlett. A suggestive enquiry into the Hermetic Arcanum.

En Route, by J. K. Huysmans. An account of the follies of Christian mysticism.

Sidonia the Sorceress, by Wilhelm Meinhold.

The Amber Witch, by Wilhelm Meinhold. These two tales are highly informative.

Macbeth; Midsummer Night's Dream; The Tempest, by W. Shakespeare. Interesting for traditions treated.

Redgauntlet, by Sir Walter Scott. Also one or two other novels. Interesting for traditions treated.

Rob Roy, by James Grant. Interesting for traditions treated.

The Magicians, by W. Somerset Maugham. An amusing hotch-pot of stolen goods.

The Bible, by various authors unknown. The Hebrew and Greek Originals are of Qabalistic value. It contains also many magical apologues, and recounts many tales of folk-lore and magical rites.

Kim, by Rudyard Kipling. An admirable study of Eastern thought and life. Many other stories by this author are highly suggestive and informative.

For Mythology, as teaching Correspondences:

Books of Fairy Tales generally.

Oriental Classics generally.

Sufi Poetry generally.

Scandinavian and Teutonic Sagas generally.

Celtic Folk-Lore generally.

This course is of general value to the beginner. While it is not to be taken, in all cases, too seriously, it will give him a general familiarity with the mystical and magical tradition, create a deep interest in the subject, and suggest many helpful lines of thought.

It has been impossible to do more, in this list, than to suggest a fairly comprehensive course of reading.